REAL WORLD
MICRO
SEVENTEENTH EDITION

EDITED BY SMRITI RAO, BRYAN SNYDER, CHRIS STURR,

AND THE *DOLLARS & SENSE* COLLECTIVE

REAL WORLD MICRO

ISBN: 978-1-878585-74-5

Published by:
Economic Affairs Bureau, Inc. d/b/a *Dollars & Sense*
29 Winter Street, Boston, MA 02108
617-447-2177; dollars@dollarsandsense.org.
For order information, contact Economic Affairs Bureau or visit: www.dollarsandsense.org.

Real World Micro is edited by the *Dollars & Sense* Collective, which also publishes *Dollars & Sense* magazine and the classroom books *Real World Macro*, *The Economic Crisis Reader*, *Current Economic Issues*, *Real World Globalization*, *Real World Latin America*, *Real World Labor*, *Real World Banking and Finance*, *The Wealth Inequality Reader*, *The Environment in Crisis*, *Introduction to Political Economy*, *Unlevel Playing Fields: Understanding Wage Inequality and Discrimination*, *Striking a Balance: Work, Family, Life*, and *Grassroots Journalism*.

The 2010 *Dollars & Sense* Collective:
Arpita Banerjee, Ben Collins, Amy Gluckman, Ben Greenberg, Mary Jirmanus, James McBride, James Miehls, John Miller, Larry Peterson, Linda Pinkow, Paul Piwko, Smriti Rao, Alejandro Reuss, Dave Ryan, Bryan Snyder, Chris Sturr, Ramaa Vasudevan, and Jeanne Winner.

Co-editors of this volume: Smriti Rao, Bryan Snyder, and Chris Sturr
Editorial assistant: Jill Mazzetta
Production assistant: Katharine Davies
Design and layout: Chris Sturr

Printed in U.S.A.

CONTENTS

CHAPTER 8 • MARKET FAILURE, GOVERNMENT POLICY, AND CORPORATE GOVERNANCE

CHAPTER 9 • POLICY SPOTLIGHT: GLOBALIZATION AND ECONOMIC DEVELOPMENT

INTRODUCTION

It sometimes seems that the United States has not one, but two economies. The first economy exists in economics textbooks and in the minds of many elected officials. It is a free-market economy, a system of promise and plenty, a cornucopia of consumer goods. In this economy, people are free and roughly equal, and each individual carefully looks after him- or herself, making uncoerced choices to advance his or her economic interests. Government is but an afterthought in this world, since almost everything people need can be provided by the free market, itself guided by the reassuring "invisible hand."

The second economy is described in the writings of progressives, environmentalists, union supporters, and consumer advocates—as well as honest business writers who recognize that real-world markets do not always conform to textbook models. This second economy features vast disparities of income, wealth, and power. It is an economy where employers have power over employees, where large firms have the power to shape markets, and where large corporate lobbies have the power to shape public policies. In this second economy, government sometimes adopts policies that ameliorate the abuses of capitalism and other times does just the opposite, but it is always an active and essential participant in economic life.

If you are reading this introduction, you are probably a student in an introductory college course in microeconomics. Your textbook will introduce you to the first economy, the harmonious world of free markets. *Real World Micro* will introduce you to the second.

Why "Real World" Micro?

A standard economics textbook is full of powerful concepts. It is also, by its nature, a limited window on the economy. What is taught in most introductory economics courses today is in fact just one strand of economic thought—neoclassical economics. Fifty years ago, many more strands were part of the introductory economics curriculum, and the contraction of the field has imposed limits on the study of economics that can confuse and frustrate students. This is particularly true in the study of microeconomics, which looks at markets for individual goods or services.

Real World Micro is designed as a supplement to a standard neoclassical textbook. Its articles provide vivid, real-world illustrations of economic concepts. But beyond that, our mission is to address two major sources of confusion in the study of economics at the introductory level.

1

The first source of confusion is the striking simplification of the world found in orthodox microeconomics. Standard textbooks describe stylized economic interactions that bear scant resemblance to the messy realities of buying, selling, producing, and consuming that we see around us. There is nothing wrong with simplifying. In fact, every social science *must* develop simplified models—precisely because reality is so complex, we must look at it a little bit at a time in order to understand it. Still, much mainstream economic analysis calls to mind the story of the tipsy party-goer whose friend finds him on his hands and knees under a streetlight. "What are you doing?" asks the friend. "I dropped my car keys across the street, and I'm looking for them," the man replies. "But if you lost them across the street, how come you're looking over here?" "Well, the light's better here." In the interest of greater clarity, economics often imposes similar limits on its areas of inquiry.

As the title *Real World Micro* implies, one of our goals is to rub mainstream microeconomic theory up against reality—to direct attention to the areas not illuminated by the streetlight, and particularly to examine how inequality, power, and environmental imbalance change the picture. The idea is not to prove the standard theory "wrong," but to challenge you to think about *where* the theory is more and less useful, and *why* markets may not act as expected.

This focus on *real-world* counterpoints to economic theory connects to the second issue we aim to clarify. Most economics texts uncritically present key assumptions and propositions that form the core of standard economic theory. They offer much less exploration of a set of related questions: What are alternative propositions about the economy? Under what circumstances will these alternatives more accurately describe the economy? What difference do such propositions make? Our approach is not to spell out an alternative theory in detail, but to raise questions and present real-life examples that bring these questions to life. For example, textbooks carefully lay out "consumer sovereignty"—the notion that consumers' wishes ultimately determine what the economy will produce. But can we reconcile consumer sovereignty with an economy where one of the main products—in industries such as soft drinks, autos, and music—is consumer desire itself? We think it is valuable to see ideas like consumer sovereignty as debatable propositions—and that requires hearing other views in the debate.

In short, our goal in this book is to use *real-world* examples from today's economy to raise questions, stimulate debate, and dare you to think critically about the models in your textbook.

What's in This Book

Real World Micro is organized to follow the outline of a standard economics text. Each chapter leads off with a brief introduction, including study questions for the entire chapter, and then provides several short articles from *Dollars & Sense* magazine that illustrate the chapter's key concepts—60 articles in all. In many cases, the articles have been updated or otherwise edited to heighten their relevance.

Here is a quick overview of the chapters.

Chapter 1, Markets: Ideology and Reality, starts off the volume by taking a hard look at the strengths and weaknesses of markets, with special attention to weaknesses that standard textbooks tend to underemphasize.

Chapter 2, Supply and Demand, presents real-world examples of supply and demand in action. *Dollars & Sense* authors question the conventional wisdom on topics such as the minimum wage and rising gas prices.

Chapter 3, Consumers, raises provocative questions about utility theory and individual consumer choice. What happens when marketers shape buyers' tastes? What happens when important information is hidden from consumers? Does consumer society threaten environmental sustainability?

Chapter 4, Firms, Production, and Profit Maximization, illustrates how business strategies often squeeze workers to boost profits—and challenges students to think about other ways of organizing work.

Chapter 5, Market Structure and Monopoly, explores monopoly power, just one example of the unequal power relationships that pervade our economic system. The chapter critiques monopoly power in pharmaceutical and agribusiness companies, but also questions whether small business dominance would be an improvement.

Chapter 6, Labor Markets, examines the ways in which labor markets can be affected by discrimination, unionization, and a host of other factors beyond supply and demand.

Chapter 7, The Distribution of Income, discusses the causes and consequences of inequality and counters the mainstream view that inequality is good for growth.

Chapter 8, Market Failure, Government Policy, and Corporate Governance, addresses when and how public policy should address both particular and systemic failures of markets, from environmental issues to tax havens to health care.

Chapter 9, Policy Spotlight: Globalization and Development, covers key issues in the world economy and the current economic crisis. There are also particular articles on the timely issues of Brazilian land reform and the tragic situation of Haiti.

What's New in This Edition

We have updated this seventeenth edition of *Real World Micro* to reflect the global economic crisis and current controversies, and we have added sixteen articles written over the past year.

Chapter 1

MARKETS: IDEOLOGY AND REALITY

INTRODUCTION

Economics is all about tradeoffs. The concept of opportunity cost reminds us that in order to make a purchase, or even to make use of a resource that you control (such as your time), you must give up other possible purchases or other possible uses. Markets broaden the range of possible tradeoffs by facilitating exchange between people who do not know each other, and in many cases never meet at all—think of buying a pair of athletic shoes in Atlanta from a company based in Los Angeles that manufactures shoes in Malaysia and has stockholders all over the world. As the idea of gains from trade suggests, markets allow many exchanges that make both parties better off.

But markets have severe limitations as well. The economic crisis that began in 2008 has made those limitations all too clear. Even life-long free-marketeers such as Alan Greenspan have been forced to question their belief in the "invisible hand." Markets are vulnerable to excessive risk-taking that leads to speculative bubbles like the one that recently "popped" in the U.S. real-estate market.

Even if regulatory oversight prevented excessive risk-taking, markets have other problems. Markets ration goods to those most able to pay, as Ellen Frank points out (Article 1.1). More generally, if we rely on markets to distribute goods that we think of as basic needs or even rights—health care, housing, education, and so on—lower-income people will be "rationed out," receiving fewer or poorer-quality goods.

Dollars & Sense's current "Dr. Dollar," Arthur MacEwan, has contributed a number of exceptional articles for this seventeenth edition of *Real World Micro*. Article 1.2 is a short piece that asks the simple question "Why Are Things Getting Worse?" and concisely explains why the invisible hand (the market mechanism) will often fail to function in times of economic crisis.

MacEwan (Article 1.4) traces the way the lack of regulatory oversight led directly to the financial crisis of September 2008, countering the popular tendency to blame the crisis on an excess of "greed." He argues further that the ideology of free markets has not "come out of nowhere" but instead has been generated and bolstered by financial firms that have a clear interest in avoiding regulation.

MacEwan then gives us a full-scope analysis of the recent, and ongoing, economic crisis in his article "Inequality, Power, and Ideology" (Article 1.5); this article should be read in conjunction with Chapter 7, which focuses on income inequality. MacEwan's powerful narrative gives us the microeconomic foundations of the current macroeconomic crisis.

With this country and the world in general experiencing the worst economic crisis since the Great Depression, one would assume that the economics profession would adapt to their collective "theory malfunction" and, at least, like former Federal Reserve Chairman Alan Greenspan, issue that *mea culpa* for overselling the efficiency and stability of the market mechanism. Yet, as Mark Maier and Julie Nelson show, the testing, and thus teaching, of economics at the basic high-school level reflects this ideological bias in favor of *laissez-faire* while overlooking many of the ways that markets fail and governments succeed in making the economy fairer and more efficient (Article 1.3).

Discussion Questions

1) (General) What things should not be for sale? Beyond everyday goods and services, think about human bodies, votes, small countries, and other things that might be bought and sold. How do you draw the line between what should be for sale and what should not be?

2) (General) Advocates of unregulated markets often argue that deregulating markets doesn't just promote mutually beneficial exchanges, but also fundamentally expands freedom. Explain the logic of their argument and the logic of the opposing view, and evaluate the two points of view.

3) (General) If not markets, then what? What are other ways to organize economic activity? Which ways are most likely to resolve the problems raised in this chapter?

4) (Article 1.1) Ellen Frank claims that markets erode democracy. Explain her perspective. Do you agree? Do all markets undermine democracy?

5) (Article 1.2) Arthur MacEwan presents a number of "short-run" barriers to market equilibrium. Which "Tilly Assumptions" (see the "realities" listed in the box in Article 8.1) are present here undermining the market mechanism?

6) (Article 1.2) This article provides a concise explanation of the Keynesian "short-run." In economics, what is the difference between a "short-run" and a "long-run" analysis?

7) (Article 1.3) What are some of the examples Maier and Nelson provide that reveal the ideological bias in the testing of economics at the high school level?

8) (Article 1.3) What are some characteristics of the students who tend to receive high scores in standardized economic tests? Based on your experience learning

economics, do you see any link between the content of economic courses and these disparities in outcomes across gender, race, and class? Discuss.

9) (Article 1.4) Some commentators blame excessive greed on the part of Wall Street for the 2008 financial crisis. How does this explanation differ from that provided by Arthur MacEwan in "The Greed Fallacy"? How would the lessons learned be different in each case?

10) (Article 1.5) In Arthur MacEwan's essay "Inequality, Power, and Ideology," we find a number of issues that have both a microeconomic and a macroeconomic side to them. According to MacEwan, which issues responsible for the current economic crisis have both a microeconomic and macroeconomic side to them? Can economists truly separate these issues into a purely macro- or microeconomic analysis? Can we truly study one without the other?

Article 1.1

THE IDEOLOGY OF THE FREE MARKET

BY ELLEN FRANK
February 1999

When the County Commissioner for Lake County, Florida, proposed last year that the fire department be turned over to a private, for-profit company, he unleashed a torrent of opposition and the idea was dropped. Throughout the United States, similar proposals to "privatize" public schools, education, and health services face strong resistance from taxpayers and state workers. Yet the overall trend in U.S. public policy for at least 20 years has been toward greater reliance on market forces and the profit motive to provide what used to be considered public goods and services.

In liberal Massachusetts, substantial portions of the public bus system are now run by private businesses; in New York City, private security forces patrol sections of Manhattan. Nationwide, some 15% of hospital beds are now owned and operated by for-profit corporations. Privately run prisons, trash disposal companies, social service providers are growing in importance everywhere.

"The era of big government," President Clinton announced a few years ago, "is over." In its place we have the market. But can the market deliver?

Market Myths

Markets, boosters contend, foster individual freedom. Consumers in market economies are free to express their individuality, assert their unique identity, by buying the precise things they want. For Americans raised on 28 choices of breakfast cereal, one-size-fits-all, big-government fire departments and health-care programs just won't do. Competition, so the story goes, will lead to more and better choices. Why? Because firms can only make money by producing what consumers are willing to pay for.

Governments and non-profit institutions might be less greedy, more humane in their motives, but they are under no particular pressure to cater to consumer demand. The profit motive is the consumer's best friend, forcing firms, as the textbooks say, to allocate resources efficiently, producing only the goods consumers desire.

Market Realities

The problem with this rosy view of things is that all voices are not equal in the market place. Upper-income consumers, with cash to spare, can bid up prices and walk away with the lion's share of society's output. For poorer folks, the vaunted "rationing" function of prices often means being priced out of the market, unable to afford the goods they want and need.

There is no question that market economies deliver goods in abundance. Wherever capitalism has been given free reign, streets are choked with automobiles and shops overflow with goods. When the former Soviet countries embraced capitalist markets several years ago, for example, commentators noted the extraordinary increase in goods available for sale. Formerly barren store shelves suddenly burst with local and imported goods of every manner and description. Unfortunately, though, few people in Russia could afford to buy any of it. The markets operated mainly for the benefit of a small and wealthy elite.

Market Inequities

Evidence abounds that markets, unless tempered by active government interventions, open up vast chasms of social and economic inequality, generating unprecedented affluence but also astounding poverty. The United Nations in its most recent report on human development found that, as markets expanded throughout the world, the richest one fifth of the world's population consumed 86% of the world's output, while the poorest fifth received just over 1%. The richest 225 people in the world today have assets equal to the annual income of the poorest 2.5 billion people.

In the United States, where faith in markets amounts to a state religion, such issues are rarely broached. Staggering levels of inequality are everywhere to be seen, yet rarely discussed. In a country where exclusion on the basis of race or gender is widely regarded as intolerable, Americans routinely accept exclusion on the basis of income. Imagine if every upscale suburb were to post signs at their borders saying, "Minimum Annual Income of $1,000,000 Required for Residence." Americans might be shocked by the candor, but not by the sentiment.

In America, the wealthy are distrusted, but not despised, and Bill Gates, whose personal wealth (now some $40 billion) equals the total wealth of the poorest 106 million Americans, is feted in the press, a kind of cultural icon.

Markets and Freedom

Advocates of free markets don't apologize for these tremendous inequities. The freedom to choose, they contend, isn't only about breakfast cereals and fashion statements. Individuals in market economies must compete for the rewards the market doles out. People can choose to be rich, or not to be; to work hard or to take it easy; to succeed or to fail. In a market economy, people get what they deserve, or so the myth goes.

But this myth ignores the very serious inequities in power that flow, inevitably, from inequities in income. High incomes lead to wealth and wealth to the exercise of power, the ability to control others, to command their labor and constrain their freedom, including their freedom to buy and sell. This is why it is illegal, in most countries, to sell your organs for transplant, though there is no lack of willing buyers and sellers. It is legal to sell your blood for transfusion or (in some places) your body for sex, and studies of the markets for blood and for prostitutes come to the same finding: when human bodies are exchanged for money, the poor lose control of their bodies.

Markets and Democracy

The freedom promised by markets is, for this reason, incompatible with democratic ideals of free, self-governing citizens. In democratic countries, governments provide basic goods and services and restrict market transactions not because doing so is "efficient," but because the freedom from want and exploitation is a precondition for meaningful citizenship. For example, 43 million Americans currently lack even minimal health care coverage; as the health care system shifts into for-profit mode, these people are at risk of falling too ill to compete in the marketplace or even to participate freely in governance.

If education were to become a buy-and-sell proposition, as some conservatives advocate, large numbers of citizens (and prospective citizens) will go uneducated and unable, therefore, to exercise their rights or protect their freedoms.

Economic inequities are not the only injury markets cause to democratic practice. The insatiable quest for gain that propels behavior in the marketplace disrupts the ecology of the earth and uproots communities. All over the world, clear-cutting, deforestation, strip-mining, toxic-dumping, and other environmentally damaging excesses of unrestrained markets have torn apart stable, self-governing towns and villages, turning secure citizens out on the open road; the hobos and homeless of our modern era.

The competitiveness engendered by markets is also at odds with democratic ideals. Psychologist Alfie Kohn has shown, for example, that people in competitive situations are more likely to cheat and to express feelings of distrust. Yet a spirit of trust and cooperation is essential to successful governance.

In opposing the private takeover of their fire department, the citizens of Lake County, Florida, seem to have understood a basic truth about limitations of markets. It may well be that private, for-profit firms can fight fires or patrol the streets more cheaply than the government can, but a trusted government can fight fires and patrol streets more democratically.

Article 1.2

WHY ARE THINGS GETTING WORSE AND WORSE?

BY ARTHUR MacEWAN
March/April 2009

> Dear Dr. Dollar:
> I learned in my economics classes that in a market economy, problems tend to be self-correcting: when a recession starts, demand weakens; then prices drop, people and firms start to buy more and the economy picks up again. So why don't we see this kind of self-correction now? Why does it seem as if things are getting worse and worse? —*Corina Chio, Los Angeles, Calif.*

Life, it turns out, is more complicated than the way it is presented in many economics classes. "More complicated" means different.

One of the key differences between reality and the standard fare of some economics classes is that the standard fare does not take sufficient account of the time lapses between one event and another. These time lapses don't simply mean that adjustments take longer; they mean that the nature of those adjustments can be very different from what one learns in class.

When demand weakens, prices do tend to drop, but they don't drop immediately. So, for example, when demand weakens and people buy fewer cars, candy, cardigans, and computers, the prices of these goods don't fall right away. But, facing the fall-off in purchases, the firms that make these products cut back on production and lay off workers. So demand falls further because the unemployed have less money to buy all these products. In this situation, things can get worse and worse instead of being turned around by the falling prices. Which way things go is not automatic, but depends on the seriousness of the initial fall-off in demand and the speed with which that fall-off occurs.

A further problem with the simplistic analysis presented in some classes is that people's buying decisions are based on expectations about the future as well as on current prices. If auto dealers try to get me to buy a new car by lowering the price, I am not likely to respond positively if I think I may well lose my job soon and be unable to make the monthly payments. And if my main use for a car is to get to and from work, my expectation of lack of work will make me even less likely to buy a new car regardless of the price.

Firms behave similarly. Why should a firm hire more labor or invest in new plants and equipment if the firm expects that people will be cutting back on demand for the firm's products? Even if interest rates and the prices of labor and raw materials are all falling, firms are unlikely to expand operations if they do not think the demand will be there. Indeed, it is precisely the falling prices that signal to firms that a recession is developing—which means that demand will not be there.

Worse: as prices fall, both consumers and firms are likely to delay purchases, expecting that things will be even cheaper if they wait. But by waiting (i.e., by not spending) they create even more downward pressure. So falling prices (deflation) can make things worse, not better.

And even worse still: because consumers and firms act quite rationally in this manner—cutting back expenditures because they expect things to get worse—things do get worse! When each firm and consumer acts rationally in response to negative expectations, as a group they tend to insure that those negative expectations will become reality. Individual rationality and social rationality come in conflict with one another. This phenomenon is often referred to as "the paradox of thrift." People respond to the situation by being thrifty, doing what is good for them individually. But the outcome for society as a whole is bad. Under these circumstances, there is a need for collective action—that is, government action.

This collective action—this government action—will be most effective when it takes the form of deficit spending. And this is exactly what is meant when people talk about a "stimulus package." By engaging in deficit spending the government is increasing demand more by its spending than it is reducing demand through taxes. The difference is made up by borrowing, and the "stimulus" is greatest when the borrowed money would not have been spent—and it would not have been spent precisely because the private firms and individuals who have the money (the money the government is borrowing) also have poor expectations about the future.

Not every economic downturn gets worse and worse. There can be a process of self-correction. But when a serious downturn develops—as is the case right now—self-correction is not going to solve our problems. The collective action that we can take through government is essential to avoid economic disaster.

Article 1.3

TESTING ECONOMICS
Does the National Economics Assessment test high schoolers on economic literacy or economic ideology?

BY MARK MAIER AND JULIE NELSON
March/April 2008

Last August the National Assessment of Educational Progress (NAEP) program—administered by the federal government's National Center for Education Statistics and well-known for measuring low scores for U.S. students in math, science, and reading—released the results of its first-ever economics assessment, introduced in 2006. Of the national sample of twelfth graders who took the new test, 42% performed at or above "proficient" and 79% percent at or above "basic"— arbitrarily defined standards so meaningless that the headlines ranged from "High Schoolers Aren't Good at Economics" (*The Wall Street Journal*) to "High Schoolers Strong in Economics" (the Associated Press).

What do the results really mean? More important, what is the test actually testing? The good news is that the NAEP's assessment is not as ideological as the corporate-driven set of standards for the elementary through high school economics curriculum on which it draws. Nonetheless, it embodies a conceptually narrow understanding of economics—one that limits the scope of what questions about the economy students might be encouraged to ask and what kinds of answers they might be encouraged to explore.

Who Sets the Content Standards?

Development of the new economics test began in 2001, when the NAEP's governing board hired an outside think tank, which in turn subcontracted the work to the National Council on Economic Education (NCEE) and a school administrators' group. The NCEE was already engaged in shaping how economics should be taught in U.S. schools: in the late 1990s the council spearheaded the development of the only widely recognized national economics curriculum framework, the Voluntary National Content Standards in Economics (VNCS). These standards were then incorporated into the NAEP test. The development of the standards, like the NCEE itself, was funded by corporations, either directly or through their charitable arms. Among those that have pledged at least $100,000 to the NCEE are many corporations in the banking/insurance/financial services sector (such as American Express, Merrill Lynch, Wells Fargo, Bank of America, and Allstate); the telecomm sector (AT&T, Verizon); textbook publishing (McGraw-Hill, Worth); along with all-around pro-business outfits like the Business Roundtable and the Kauffman Foundation.

Unlike standards in other disciplines, these economics standards were written from a single viewpoint, that of neoclassical economic theory. This approach defines economics as the study of choice-making and focuses on the workings of markets, leaving out, among other things, the role of power based on race, class, or gender. Their authors would no doubt claim that the standards are simply objective, non-ideological summaries of the economics discipline's core ideas. But let's look at the first standard:

> *Productive resources are limited. Therefore people cannot have all the goods and services they want; as a result, they must choose some things and give up others.*

We would propose a replacement for this standard:

> *Resources are unequally distributed in most economies. As a result, individuals and households face quite different choices depending on their income and wealth.*

Putting the two versions side-by-side highlights how the most basic-sounding learning standard in fact carries all of the hidden assumptions, omissions, and biases that characterize neoclassical economic theory.

Even many mainstream economists, though they take neoclassical theory as forming the core of the discipline, would say that the national standards give an overly simplistic portrait of what they believe their field to be about. In particular, many would be appalled at the one-sided endorsement of conservative policy recommendations prevalent in many of the classroom activities and bench-mark measures that accompany the VNCS. For example, while there is some disagreement among professional economists about the merits of free trade, materials that follow the VNCS tend to teach the extreme conservative position that markets are essentially self-regulating and that government intervention invariably leads to bad results.

The NAEP Test Improves on the Standards...

Fortunately, in three significant ways the NAEP test departs from the VNCS. First, more than 20% of its questions relate to consumer finance, a topic that some groups such as the Jump$tart Coalition for Personal Financial Literacy argue should form the basis of high school economics courses, but a requirement in only a handful of states and not included in the VNCS. For example, an open-response item on the NAEP test asked:

> *Tom has $1,000 that he can either spend now or deposit into a bank account. The account pays a fixed rate of interest per year and does not allow withdrawal for two years. List two economic factors that Tom should consider in making his decision.*

Being encouraged to develop reasoned approaches to such issues would be a worthy goal for high school economics education, since many consumers, in fact, act far less rationally than neoclassical theory predicts. A more complete curriculum would then use these consumer topics to ask critical questions about the role of advertising, the impact of consumerism on human happiness, and the reasons why U.S. consumer protection is so weak, as seen, for instance, in the 2005 passage, with broad bipartisan support, of strongly anti-consumer bankruptcy legislation.

Equally significant is the emphasis in the NAEP test on macroeconomics, the study of national-level topics such as unemployment, inflation, and total spending. Macroeconomics is given short shrift in the national standards; in contrast, 40% of the NAEP test questions focus on the national economy and an additional 15% deal with the international economy. Students were asked, for example:

> *Which of the following fiscal policy combinations would a government most likely follow to stimulate economic activity when the economy is in a severe recession?*
>
> *a) Increasing both taxes and spending*
> *b) Increasing taxes and decreasing spending*
> *c) Decreasing taxes and increasing spending*
> *d) Decreasing both taxes and spending*

(The correct answer is (c).) In contrast with the national standards—which, by largely omitting macroeconomic issues, lean toward a conservative, markets-are-good-and-government-is-bad position—this question at least acknowledges that severe recessions occur and that government can have a role in overcoming them.

Finally, several questions probe student knowledge of U.S. economic institutions, topics deliberately omitted from the VCNS. For example, one question asked:

> *In the United States, which of the following forms of taxation currently represents the largest source of tax revenue for the federal government?*
>
> *a) Property tax*
> *b) Sales tax*
> *c) Corporate income tax*
> *d) Personal income tax*

(The correct answer is (d).) The NAEP test also included a question on unions, requiring that students identify fringe benefits and work rules as two issues other than wages commonly addressed by collective bargaining.

This combination of personal finance, macroeconomics, and institutional detail means that the NAEP test has far less of a right-wing bias than it would have had it rigorously followed the pro-market, theory-heavy VNCS.

... But Still Falls Short

That is not to say that the test has no ideological bias, however. Here is a question the *Wall Street Journal* approved of:

Which has been the most important in reducing poverty over time:

> *a) Taxes*
> *b) Economic growth*
> *c) International trade*
> *d) Government regulation*

A majority of students chose the "correct" answer, (b). The *Journal* commented that this was not likely to "please the Senate Finance Committee." The phrasing of the question, however, reflects a conservative ideology that views taxes and government regulation as inherently opposed to and obstructive of economic growth—and the fair distribution of the fruits of that growth—rather than as facilitating growth. More sophisticated economic analysis would appreciate the crucial role of government regulation and tax-funded infrastructure in creating an environment in which people can prosper.

Another question demonstrating a clear conservative bias concerned trade:

Two countries are currently trading with each other. The countries agree to remove all trade restrictions on products traded between them. Which of the following is most likely to decrease?

> *a) The variety of goods available*
> *b) The prices of imported goods*
> *c) The quality of goods available*
> *d) The amount of imported goods*

According to free market ideology (and the NAEP), the "correct" answer is (b)—the repeal of tariffs and quotas enacted to protect particular industries ("special interests") is viewed as benefiting the nation as a whole. In fact, however, countries also commonly restrict trade for a number of very good reasons. For instance, they may ban imports of cars that do not meet their emission standards or of foods and toys that do not meet their safety standards. Removing trade restrictions such as these would be highly likely to lead to a decrease in "the quality of goods available"! So were the 31% of students who chose (c) wrong—or merely out of step with the dominant ideological framework?

While we could go on in this vein—critiquing the biases in individual questions on economic systems, specialization, measures of the standard of living, marginal comparisons, and capital—it is probably more instructive to stop at this point and consider the many hugely important issues that the test *fails* to address. Predictably, any test that seeks to measure economics understanding as it is envisioned by those in the leadership of the profession today would severely neglect certain issues: human well-being, income distribution, discrimination, corporate power, and environmental degradation, among others. And the NAEP test does. This is a problem that is not limited to the NAEP or the VCNS, but rather affects the economics profession and economics education as a whole. University-level neoclassical economics, with its emphasis on choice-making, has all but driven out other approaches to economics that give greater centrality to such issues. Meanwhile, the influence of corporations such as Bank of America and pro-corporate foundations such as the Scaife Foundation in designing K-12 economics education assures that some topics will not be brought up.

Teaching a Better Economics Course

For teachers who want to approach the subject of economics with less orthodoxy and more connection to the real world, a growing body of alternative curriculum materials is available. Our book *Introducing Economics: A Critical Guide for Teaching* (M.E. Sharpe, 2007) is one recent addition. But much more work remains to be done, both in outlining alternative sets of curriculum standards and in developing and disseminating learning activities and texts for teaching them.

The results of the first NAEP economics assessment showed startling disparities by gender, race, and ethnicity. Girls scored about 3% lower than boys. Blacks and Hispanics averaged more than 15% below the average for whites—yet another indictment of the United States' education and social systems. The influence of class was evident as well: students whose parents completed college scored 16% higher than students whose parents completed only high school, and students at vocational/technical high schools or general high schools scored significantly lower than students at academic/college prep high schools. (Curiously, neither the number of economics courses students had taken nor whether their teachers were trained in economics appeared to have much impact on students' scores.)

The NAEP economics test won't be repeated until 2012, and the published results are not reported at the state level—the level at which high-school economics curriculum is largely determined. As a result, the test likely will have little impact on how economics is taught, beyond the shaping of curriculum materials already accomplished by the VCNS. Meanwhile, we should pay attention to racism, sexism, class, and corporate power; even though they are absent in neoclassical economic theory, the NAEP test results indicate that in learning economics, our students suffer from their impact.

Article 1.4

THE GREED FALLACY
You can't explain a change with a constant

BY ARTHUR MacEWAN
November/December 2008

Various people explain the current financial crisis as a result of "greed." There is, however, no indication of a change in the degree or extent of greed on Wall Street (or anywhere else) in the last several years. Greed is a constant. If greed were the cause of the financial crisis, we would be in financial crisis pretty much all the time.

But the financial markets have not been in perpetual crisis. Nothing close to the current crisis has taken place since 1929. Yes, there was 1987 and the savings-and-loan debacle of that era. But, the current crisis is already more dramatic—and threatens to get a good deal worse. This crisis emerged over the last decade and appeared full-blown only at the beginning of 2008 (though, if you were looking, it was moving up on the horizon a year or two earlier). The current mess, therefore, is a change, a departure from the normal course of financial markets. So something has to have changed to have brought it about. The constant of greed cannot be the explanation.

So what changed? The answer is relatively simple: the extent of regulation changed.

As a formal matter, the change in regulation is most clearly marked by the Gramm-Leach-Bliley Act of 1999, passed by the Republican-dominated Congress and signed into law by Bill Clinton. This act in large part repealed the Glass-Steagall Act of 1933, which had imposed various regulations on the financial industry after the debacle of 1929. Among other things, Glass-Steagall prohibited a firm from being engaged in different sorts of financial services. One firm could not be both an investment bank (organizing the funding of firms' investment activities) and a commercial bank (handling the checking and savings accounts of individuals and firms and making loans); nor could it be one of these types of banks and an insurance firm.

However, the replacement of Glass-Steagall by Gramm-Leach-Bliley was only the formal part of the change that took place in recent decades. Informally, the relation between the government and the financial sector has increasingly become one of reduced regulation. In particular, as the financial sector evolved new forms of operation—hedge funds and private equity funds, for example—there was no attempt on the part of Washington to develop regulations for these activities. Also, even where regulations existed, the regulators became increasingly lax in enforcement.

The movement away from regulation might be seen as a consequence of "free market" ideology, the belief as propounded by its advocates that government should leave the private sector alone. But to see the problem simply as ideology run amok is to ignore the question of where the ideology comes from. Put simply, the ideology is generated by firms themselves because they want to be as free as possible to pursue profit-making activity. So they push the idea of the "free market" and deregulation any way they can. But let me leave aside for now the ways in which ideas come to dominate Washington and the society in general; enough to recognize that deregulation became increasingly the dominant idea from the early 1980s onward. (But, given the current presidential campaign, one cannot refrain from noting that one way the firms get their ideas to dominate is through the money they lavish on candidates.)

When financial firms are not regulated, they tend to take on more and more risky activities. When markets are rising, risk does not seem to be very much of a problem; all—or virtually all—investments seem to be making money. So why not take some chances? Furthermore, if one firm doesn't take a particular risk—put money into a chancy operation—then one of its competitors will. So competition pushes them into more and more risky operations.

The danger of risk is not simply that one investment—one loan, for example—made by a financial firm will turn out badly, or even that a group of loans will turn out badly. The danger arises in the relation between its loans (obligations to the firm), the money it borrows from others (the firm's obligations to its creditors) and its capital (the funds put in by investors, the stockholders). If some of the loans it has made go bad (i.e., if the debtors default), it can still meet its obligations to its creditors with its capital. But if the firm is unregulated, it will tend to make more and more loans and take on more and more debt. The ratio of debt to capital can become very high, and, then, if trouble with the loans develops, the bank cannot meet its obligations with its capital.

In the current crisis, the deflation of the housing bubble was the catalyst to the general crumbling of financial structures. The housing bubble was in large part a product of the Federal Reserve Bank's policies under the guidance of the much-heralded Alan Greenspan, but let's leave that issue aside for now.

When the housing bubble burst, many financial institutions found themselves in trouble. They had taken on too much risk in relation to their capital. The lack of regulation had allowed them to get in this trouble.

But the trouble is much worse than it might have been because of the repeal of the provisions of Glass-Steagall that prevented the merging of investment banks, commercial banks, and insurance companies. Under the current circumstances, when trouble develops in one part of a firm's operations, it is immediately transmitted throughout the other segments of that firm. And from there, the trouble spreads to all the other entities to which it is connected—through credits, insurance deals, deposits, and a myriad set of complicated (unregulated) financial arrangements.

AIG is the example *par excellence*. Ostensibly an insurance company, AIG has morphed into a multi-faceted financial institution, doing everything from selling life insurance in rural India to speculating in various esoteric types of investments on Wall Street. Its huge size, combined with the extent of its intertwining with other financial firms, meant that its failure would have had very large impacts around the world.

The efforts of the U.S. government may or may not be able to contain the current financial crisis. Success would not breathe life back into the Lehman Brothers, Bear Stearns, and who knows how many other major operators that are on their deathbeds. But it would prevent the financial crisis from precipitating a severe general depression; it would prevent a movement from 1929 to 1932.

The real issue, however, is what is learned from the current financial mess. One thing should be evident, namely that greed did not cause the crisis. The cause was a change in the way markets have been allowed to operate, a change brought on by the rise of deregulation. Markets, especially financial markets, are never very stable when left to themselves. It turns out that the "invisible hand" does some very nasty, messy things when there is no visible hand of regulation affecting the process.

The problem is that maintaining some form of regulation is a very difficult business. As I have said, the firms themselves do not want to be regulated. The current moment may allow some re-imposition of financial regulation. But as soon as we turn our backs, the pressure will be on again to let the firms operate according to the "free market." Let's not forget where that leads.

Article 1.5

INEQUALITY, POWER, AND IDEOLOGY
Getting It Right About the Causes of the Current Economic Crisis

BY ARTHUR MacEWAN
March/April 2009

It is hard to solve a problem without an understanding of what caused it. For example, in medicine, until we gained an understanding of the way bacteria and viruses cause various infectious diseases, it was virtually impossible to develop effective cures. Of course, dealing with many diseases is complicated by the fact that germs, genes, diet, and the environment establish a nexus of causes.

The same is true in economics. Without an understanding of the causes of the current crisis, we are unlikely to develop a solution; certainly we are not going to get a solution that has a lasting impact. And determining the causes is complicated because several intertwined factors have been involved.

The current economic crisis was brought about by a nexus of factors that involved: a growing concentration of political and social power in the hands of the wealthy; the ascendance of a perverse leave-it-to-the-market ideology which was an instrument of that power; and rising income inequality, which both resulted from and enhanced that power. These various factors formed a vicious circle, reinforcing one another and together shaping the economic conditions that led us to the present situation. Several other factors were also involved—the growing role of credit, the puffing up of the housing bubble, and the increasing deregulation of financial markets have been very important. However, these are best understood as transmitters of our economic problems, arising from the nexus that formed the vicious circle.

What does this tell us about a solution? Economic stimulus, repair of the housing market, and new regulation are all well and good, but they do not deal with the underlying causes of the crisis. Instead, progressive groups need to work to shift each of the factors I have noted—power, ideology, and income distribution—in the other direction. In doing so, we can create a *virtuous* circle, with each change reinforcing the other changes. If successful, we not only establish a more stable economy, but we lay the foundation for a more democratic, equitable, and sustainable economic order.

A crisis by its very nature creates opportunities for change. One good place to begin change and intervene in this "circle"—and transform it from vicious to virtuous—is through pushing for the expansion and reform of social programs, programs that directly serve social needs of the great majority of the population (for example: single-payer health care, education programs, and environmental protection and repair). By establishing changes in social programs, we will have impacts on income distribution and ideology, and, perhaps most important, we set in motion *a power shift* that improves our position for preserving the changes. While I emphasize social programs as a means to initiate social and economic change, there are other ways to intervene in the circle. Efforts to re-strengthen unions would be especially important; and there are other options as well.

Causes of the Crisis: A Long Time Coming

Sometime around the early 1970s, there were some dramatic changes in the U.S. economy. The twenty-five years following World War II had been an era of relatively stable economic growth; the benefits of growth had been widely shared, with wages rising along with productivity gains, and income distribution became slightly less unequal (a good deal less unequal as compared to the pre-Great Depression era). There were severe economic problems in the United States, not the least of which were the continued exclusion of African Americans, large gender inequalities, and the woeful inadequacy of social welfare programs. Nonetheless, relatively stable growth, rising wages, and then the advent of the civil rights movement and the War on Poverty gave some important, positive social and economic character to the era—especially in hindsight!

In part, this comparatively favorable experience for the United States had depended on the very dominant position that U.S. firms held in the world economy, a position in which they were relatively unchallenged by international competition. The firms and their owners were not the only beneficiaries of this situation. With less competitive pressure on them from foreign companies, many U.S. firms accepted unionization and did not find it worthwhile to focus on keeping wages down and obstructing the implementation of social supports for the low-income population. Also, having had the recent experience of the Great Depression, many wealthy people and business executives were probably not so averse to a substantial role for government in regulating the economy.

A Power Grab

By about 1970, the situation was changing. Firms in Europe and Japan had long recovered from World War II, OPEC was taking shape, and weaknesses were emerging in the U.S. economy. The weaknesses were in part a consequence of heavy spending for the Vietnam War combined with the government's reluctance to tax for the war because of its unpopularity. The pressures on U.S. firms arising from these changes had two sets of consequences: slower growth and greater instability; and concerted efforts—a power grab, if you will—by firms and the wealthy to shift the costs of economic deterioration onto U.S. workers and the low-income population.

These "concerted efforts" took many forms: greater resistance to unions and unionization, battles to reduce taxes, stronger opposition to social welfare programs, and, above all, a push to reduce or eliminate government regulation of economic activity through a powerful political campaign to gain control of the various branches and levels of government. The 1980s, with Reagan and Bush One in the White House, were the years in which all these efforts were solidified. Unions were greatly weakened, a phenomenon both demonstrated and exacerbated by Reagan's firing of the air traffic controllers in response to their strike in 1981. The tax cuts of the period were also important markers of the change. But the change had begun earlier; the 1978 passage of the tax-cutting Proposition 13 in California was perhaps the first major success of the movement. And the changes continued well after the 1980s, with welfare reform and deregulation of finance during the Clinton era, to say nothing of the tax cuts and other actions during Bush Two.

Ideology Shift

The changes that began in the 1970s, however, were not simply these sorts of concrete alterations in the structure of power affecting the economy and, especially, government's role in the economy. There was a major shift in ideology, the dominant set of ideas that organize an understanding of our social relations and both guide and rationalize policy decisions.

Following the Great Depression and World War II, there was a wide acceptance of the idea that government had a major role to play in economic life. Less than in many other countries but nonetheless to a substantial degree, at all levels of society, it was generally believed that there should be a substantial government safety net and that government should both regulate the economy in various ways and, through fiscal as well as monetary policy, should maintain aggregate demand. This large economic role for government came to be called Keynesianism, after the British economist John Maynard Keynes, who had set out the arguments for an active fiscal policy in time of economic weakness. In the early 1970s, as economic troubles developed, even Richard Nixon declared: "We are all Keynesians now."

The election of Ronald Reagan, however, marked a sharp change in ideology, at least at the top. Actions of the government were blamed for all economic ills: government spending, Keynesianism, was alleged to be the cause of the inflation of the 1970s; government regulation was supposedly crippling industry; high taxes

---

Alan Greenspan, Symbol of an Era

One significant symbol of the full rise of the conservative ideology that became so dominant in the latter part of the 20th century was Alan Greenspan, who served from 1974 through 1976 as chairman of the President's Council of Economic Advisers under Gerald Ford and in 1987 became chairman of the Federal Reserve Board, a position he held until 2006. While his predecessors had hardly been critics of U.S. capitalism, Greenspan was a close associate of the philosopher Ayn Rand and an adherent of her extreme ideas supporting individualism and *laissez-faire* (keep-the-government-out) capitalism.

When chairman of the Fed, Greenspan was widely credited with maintaining an era of stable economic growth. As things fell apart in 2008, however, Greenspan was seen as having a large share of responsibility for the non-regulation and excessively easy credit (see article) that led into the crisis.

Called before Congress in October of 2008, Greenspan was chastised by Rep. Henry Waxman (D-Calif.), who asked him: "Do you feel that your ideology pushed you to make decisions that you wish you had not made?" To which Greenspan replied: "Yes, I've found a flaw. I don't know how significant or permanent it is. But I've been very distressed by that fact."

And Greenspan told Congress: "Those of us who have looked to the self-interest of lending institutions to protect shareholders' equity, myself included, are in a state of shocked disbelief."

Greenspan's "shock" was reminiscent of the scene in the film "Casablanca," where Captain Renault (Claude Rains) declares: "I'm shocked, shocked to find that gambling is going on in here!" At which point, a croupier hands Renault a pile of money and says, "Your winnings, sir." Renault replies, *sotto voce*, "Thank you very much."

were, it was argued, undermining incentives for workers to work and for businesses to invest; social welfare spending was blamed for making people dependent on the government and was charged with fraud and corruption (the "welfare queens"); and so on and so on.

On economic matters, Reagan championed supply-side economics, the principal idea of which was that tax cuts yield an increase in government revenue because the cuts lead to more rapid economic growth through encouraging more work and more investment. Thus, so the argument went, tax cuts would reduce the government deficit. Reagan, with the cooperation of Democrats, got the tax cuts—and, as the loss of revenue combined with a large increase in military spending, the federal budget deficit grew by leaps and bounds, almost doubling as a share of GDP over the course of the 1980s. It was all summed up in the idea of keeping the government out of the economy; let the free market work its magic.

Growing Inequality

The shifts of power and ideology were very much bound up with a major redistribution upwards of income and wealth. The weakening of unions, the increasing access of firms to low-wage foreign (and immigrant) labor, the refusal of government to maintain the buying power of the minimum wage, favorable tax treatment of the wealthy and their corporations, deregulation in a wide range of industries and lack of enforcement of existing regulation (e.g., the authorities turning a blind eye to offshore tax shelters) all contributed to these shifts.

Many economists, however, explain the rising income inequality as a result of technological change that favored more highly skilled workers; and changing technology has probably been a factor. Yet the most dramatic aspect of the rising inequality has been the rapidly rising share of income obtained by those at the very top (see figures below), who get their incomes from the ownership and control of business, not from their skilled labor. For these people the role of new technologies was most important through its impact on providing more options (e.g., international options) for the managers of firms, more thorough means to control labor, and more effective ways— in the absence of regulation—to manipulate finance. All of these gains that might be associated with new technology were also gains brought by the way the government handled, or didn't handle (failed to regulate), economic affairs.

Several sets of data demonstrate the sharp changes in the distribution of income that have taken place in the last several decades. Most striking is the changing position of the very highest income segment of the population. In the mid-1920s, the share of all pre-tax income going to the top 1% of households peaked at 23.9%. This elite group's share of income fell dramatically during the Great Depression and World War II to about 12% at the end of the war and then slowly fell further during the next thirty years, reaching a low of 8.9% in the mid-1970s. Since then, the top 1% has regained its exalted position of the earlier era, with 21.8% of income in 2005. Since 1993, more than one-half of all income gains have accrued to this highest 1% of the population.

Figures 1 and 2 show the gains (or losses) of various groups in the 1949 to 1979 period and in the 1979 to 2005 period. The difference is dramatic. For example, in the earlier era, the bottom 20% saw its income in real (inflation-adjusted) terms rise by

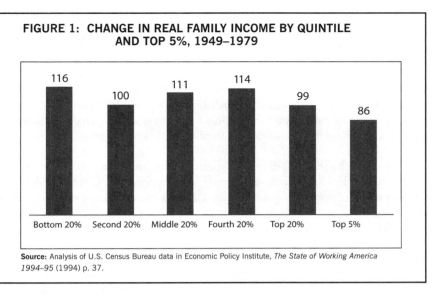

FIGURE 1: CHANGE IN REAL FAMILY INCOME BY QUINTILE AND TOP 5%, 1949–1979

Source: Analysis of U.S. Census Bureau data in Economic Policy Institute, *The State of Working America 1994–95* (1994) p. 37.

116%, and real income of the top 5% grew by only 86%. But in the latter era, the bottom 20% saw a 1% decline in its income, while the top 5% obtained a 81% increase.

The Emergence of Crisis

These changes, especially the dramatic shifts in the distribution of income, set the stage for the increasingly large reliance on credit, especially consumer and mortgage credit, that played a major role in the emergence of the current economic crisis. Other factors were involved, but rising inequality was especially important in effecting the increase in both the demand and supply of credit.

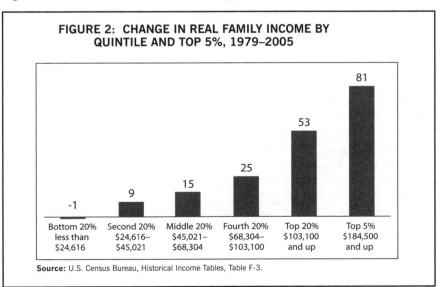

FIGURE 2: CHANGE IN REAL FAMILY INCOME BY QUINTILE AND TOP 5%, 1979–2005

Source: U.S. Census Bureau, Historical Income Tables, Table F-3.

Credit Expansion

On the demand side, rising inequality translated into a growing gap between the incomes of most members of society and their needs. For the 2000 to 2007 period, average weekly earnings in the private sector were 12% below their average for the 1970s (in inflation-adjusted terms). From 1980 to 2005 the share of income going to the bottom 60% of families fell from 35% to 29%. Under these circumstances, more and more people relied more and more heavily on credit to meet their needs—everything from food to fuel, from education to entertainment, and especially housing.

While the increasing reliance of consumers on credit has been going on for a long time, it has been especially marked in recent decades. Consumer debt as a share of after-tax personal income averaged 20% in the 1990s, and then jumped up to an average of 25% in the first seven years of the new millennium. But the debt expansion was most marked in housing, where mortgage debt as a percent of after-tax personal income rose from 89% to 94% over the 1990s, and then ballooned to 140% by 2006 as housing prices skyrocketed.

On the supply side, especially in the last few years, the government seems to have relied on making credit readily available as a means to bolster aggregate demand and maintain at least a modicum of economic growth. During the 1990s, the federal funds interest rate averaged 5.1%, but fell to an average of 3.4% in the 2000 to 2007 period—and averaged only 1.4% in 2002 to 2004 period. (The federal funds interest rate is the rate that banks charge one another for overnight loans and is a rate directly affected by the Federal Reserve.) Corresponding to the low interest rates, the money supply grew twice as fast in the new millennium as it had in the 1990s. (And see the sidebar on the connection of the Fed's actions to the Iraq War.)

The increasing reliance of U.S. consumers on credit has often been presented as a moral weakness, as an infatuation with consumerism, and as a failure to look beyond the present. Whatever moral judgments one may make, however, the expansion of the credit economy has been a response to real economic forces—inequality and government policies, in particular.

The Failure to Regulate

The credit expansion by itself, however, did not precipitate the current crisis. Deregulation—or, more generally, the failure to regulate—is also an important part of the story. The government's role in regulation of financial markets has been a central feature in the development of this crisis, but the situation in financial markets has been part of a more general process—affecting airlines and trucking, telecommunications, food processing, broadcasting, and of course international trade and investment. The process has been driven by a combination of power (of large firms and wealthy individuals) and ideology (leave it to the market, get the government out).

The failure to regulate financial markets that transformed the credit expansion into a financial crisis shows up well in three examples:

The 1999 repeal of the Glass-Steagall Act. Glass-Steagall had been enacted in the midst of the Great Depression, as a response to the financial implosion following the stock market crash of 1929. Among other things, it required that different kinds of financial firms—commercial banks, investment banks, insurance companies—be separate. This separation both limited the spread of financial problems and reduced conflicts of interest that could arise were the different functions of these firms combined into a single firm. As perhaps the most important legislation regulating the financial sector, the repeal of Glass-Steagall was not only a substantive change but was an important symbol of the whole process of deregulation.

The failure to regulate mortgage lending. Existing laws and regulations require lending institutions to follow prudent practices in making loans, assuring that borrowers have the capacity to be able to pay back the loans. And of course fraud—lying about the provisions of loans—is prohibited. Yet in an atmosphere where regulation was "out," regulators were simply not doing their jobs. The consequences are illustrated in a December 28, 2008, *New York Times* story on the failed Washington Mutual

---

Joseph Stiglitz on the War and the Economy

On October 2, 2008, on the Pacifica radio program Democracy Now!, Amy Goodman and Juan Gonzalez interviewed Joseph Stiglitz about the economic situation. Stiglitz was the 2001 winner of the Nobel Prize in Economics, former chief economist at the World Bank, and former chair of President Clinton's Council of Economic Advisers. He is a professor at Columbia University. Following is an excerpt from that interview:

AMY GOODMAN: Joseph Stiglitz, you're co-author of *The Three Trillion Dollar War: The True Cost of the Iraq Conflict.* How does the bailout [of the financial sector] connect to war?

JOSEPH STIGLITZ: Very much. Let me first explain a little bit how the current crisis connects with the war. One of the reasons that we have this crisis is that the Fed flooded the economy with liquidity and had lax regulations. Part of that was this ideology of "regulations are bad," but part of the reason was that the economy was weak. And one of the reasons the economy was weak was oil prices were soaring, and part of the reason oil prices were soaring is the Iraq war. When we went to war in 2003, before we went, prices were $23 a barrel. Futures markets thought they would remain at that level. They anticipated the increase in demand, but they thought there would be a concomitant increase in supply from the low-cost providers, mainly in the Middle East. The war changed that equation, and we know what happened to the oil prices.

Well, why is that important? Well, we were spending—Americans were spending hundreds of millions—billions of dollars to buy—more, to buy imported oil. Normally, that would have had a very negative effect on our economy; we would have had a slowdown. Some people have said, you know, it's a mystery why we aren't having that slowdown; we repealed the laws of economics. Whenever anybody says that, you ought to be suspect.

It was actually very simple. The Fed engineered a bubble, a housing bubble to replace the tech bubble that it had engineered in the '90s. The housing bubble facilitated people taking money out of their . . . houses; in one year, there were more than $900 billion of mortgage equity withdrawals. And so, we had a consumption boom that was so strong that even though we were spending so much money abroad, we could keep the economy going. But it was so shortsighted. And it was so clear that we were living on borrowed money and borrowed time. And it was just a matter of time before, you know, the whole thing would start to unravel.

Bank. The article describes a supervisor at a mortgage processing center as having been "accustomed to seeing babysitters claiming salaries worthy of college presidents, and schoolteachers with incomes rivaling stockbrokers'. He rarely questioned them. A real estate frenzy was under way and WaMu, as his bank was known, was all about saying yes."

One may wonder why banks—or other lending institutions, mortgage firms, in particular—would make loans to people who were unlikely to be able to pay them back. The reason is that the lending institutions quickly combined such loans into packages (i.e., a security made up of several borrowers' obligations to pay) and sold them to other investors in a practice called "securitization."

Credit-default swaps. Perhaps the most egregious failure to regulate in recent years has been the emergence of credit-default swaps, which are connected to securitization. Because they were made up of obligations by a diverse set of borrowers, the packages of loans were supposedly low-risk investments. Yet those who purchased them still sought insurance against default. Insurance sellers, however, are regulated—required, for example, to keep a certain amount of capital on hand to cover possible claims. So the sellers of these insurance policies on packages of loans called the policies "credit-default swaps" and thus were allowed to avoid regulation. Further, these credit-default swaps, these insurance policies, themselves were bought and sold again and again in unregulated markets in a continuing process of speculation.

The credit-default swaps are a form of derivative, a financial asset the value of which is derived from some other asset—in this case the value of packages of mortgages for which they were the insurance policies. When the housing bubble began to collapse and people started to default on their mortgages, the value of credit-default swaps plummeted and their future value was impossible to determine. No one would buy them, and several banks that had speculated in these derivatives were left holding huge amounts of these "toxic assets."

Bubble and Bust

The combination of easy credit and the failure to regulate together fueled the housing bubble. People could buy expensive houses but make relatively low monthly payments. Without effective regulation of mortgage lending, they could get the loans even when they were unlikely to be able to make payments over the long run. Moreover, as these pressures pushed up housing prices, many people bought houses simply to resell them quickly at a higher price, in a process called "flipping." And such speculation pushed the prices up further. Between 2000 and 2006, housing prices rose by 90% (as consumer prices generally rose by only 17%).

While the housing boom was in full swing, both successful housing speculators and lots of people involved in the shenanigans of credit markets made a lot of money. However, as the housing bubble burst—as all bubbles do—things fell apart. The packages of loans lost value, and the insurance policies on them, the credit-default swaps, lost value. These then became "toxic" assets for those who held them, assets not only with reduced value but with unknown value. Not only did large financial firms—for example, Lehman Brothers and AIG—have billions of dollars in losses, but no one knew the worth of their remaining assets. The assets were called "toxic" because they poisoned the operations of the financial system. Under these circumstances, financial institutions stopped lending to one another—that is, the credit markets "froze up." The financial crisis was here.

The financial crisis, not surprisingly, very quickly shifted to a general economic crisis. Firms in the "real" economy rely heavily on a well-functioning financial system to supply them with the funds they need for their regular operations—loans to car buyers, loans to finance inventory, loans for construction of new facilities, loans for new equipment, and, of course, mortgage loans. Without those loans (or with the loans much more difficult to obtain), there has been a general cut-back in economic activity, what is becoming a serious and probably prolonged recession.

What Is to Be Done?

So here we are. The shifts in power, ideology, and income distribution have placed us in a rather nasty situation. There are some steps that will be taken that have a reasonable probability of yielding short-run improvement. In particular, a large increase in government spending—deficit spending—will probably reduce the depth and shorten the length of the recession. And the actions of the Federal Reserve and Treasury to inject funds into the financial system are likely, along with the deficit spending, to "un-freeze" credit markets (the mismanagement and, it seems, outright corruption of the bailout notwithstanding). Also, there is likely to be some re-regulation of the financial industry. These steps, however, at best will restore things to where they were before the crisis. They do not treat the underlying causes of the crisis—the vicious circle of power, ideology, and inequality.

Opportunity for Change

Fortunately, the crisis itself has weakened some aspects of this circle. The cry of "leave it to the market" is still heard, but is now more a basis for derision than a guide to policy. The ideology and, to a degree, the power behind the ideology, have been severely weakened as the role of "keeping the government out" has shown to be a major cause of the financial mess and our current hardships. There is now widespread support among the general populace and some support in Washington for greater regulation of the financial industry.

Whether or not the coming period will see this support translated into effective policy is of course an open question. Also an open question is how much the turn away from "leaving it to the market" can be extended to other sectors of the economy. With regard to the environment, there is already general acceptance of the principle that the government (indeed, many governments) must take an active role in regulating economic activity. Similar principles need to be recognized with regard to health care, education, housing, child care, and other support programs for low-income families.

The discrediting of "keep the government out" ideology provides an opening to develop new programs in these areas and to expand old programs. Furthermore, as the federal government revs up its "stimulus" program in the coming months, opportunities will exist for expanding support for these sorts of programs. This support is important, first of all, because these programs serve real, pressing needs—needs that have long existed and are becoming acute and more extensive in the current crisis.

Breaking the Circle

Support for these social programs, however, may also serve to break into the vicious power-ideology-inequality circle and begin transforming it into a virtuous circle. Social programs are inherently equalizing in two ways: they provide their benefits to low-income people and they provide some options for those people in their efforts to demand better work and higher pay. Also, the further these programs develop, the more they establish the legitimacy of a larger role for public control of—government involvement in—the economy; they tend to bring about an ideological shift. By affecting a positive distributional shift and by shifting ideology, the emergence of stronger social programs can have a wider impact on power. In other words, efforts to promote social programs are one place to start, an entry point to shift the vicious circle to a virtuous circle.

There are other entry points. Perhaps the most obvious ones are actions to strengthen the role of unions. The Employee Free Choice Act may be a useful first step, and it will be helpful to establish a more union-friendly Department of Labor and National Labor Relations Board. Raising the minimum wage—ideally indexing it to inflation—would also be highly desirable. While conditions have changed since the heyday of unions in the middle of the 20th century, and we cannot expect to restore the conditions of that era, a greater role for unions would seem essential in righting the structural conditions at the foundation of the current crisis.

Shifting Class Power

None of this is assured, of course. Simply starting social programs will not necessarily mean that they have the wider impacts that I am suggesting are possible. No one should think that by setting up some new programs and strengthening some existing ones we will be on a smooth road to economic and social change. Likewise, rebuilding the strength of unions will involve extensive struggle and will not be accomplished by a few legislative or executive actions.

Also, all efforts to involve the government in economic activity—whether in finance or environmental affairs, in health care or education, in work support or job training programs—will be met with the worn-out claims that government involvement generates bureaucracy, stifles initiative, and places an excessive burden on private firms and individuals. We are already hearing warnings that in dealing with the financial crisis the government must avoid "over-regulation." Likewise, efforts to strengthen unions will suffer the traditional attacks, as unions are portrayed as corrupt and their members privileged. The unfolding situation with regard to the auto firms' troubles has demonstrated the attack, as conservatives have blamed the United Auto Workers for the industry's woes and have demanded extensive concessions by the union.

Certainly not all regulation is good regulation. Aside from excessive bureaucratic controls, there is the phenomenon by which regulating agencies are often captives of the industries that they are supposed to regulate. And there are corrupt unions. These are real issues, but they should not be allowed to derail change.

The current economic crisis emerged in large part as a shift in the balance of class power in the United States, a shift that began in the early 1970s and continued into the new millennium. Perhaps the present moment offers an opportunity to shift things back in the other direction. Recognition of the complex nexus of causes of the current economic crisis provides some guidance where people might start. Rebuilding and extending social programs, strengthening unions, and other actions that contribute to a more egalitarian power shift will not solve all the problems of U.S. capitalism. They can, however, begin to move us in the right direction.

CHAPTER 2

SUPPLY AND DEMAND

INTRODUCTION

Textbooks tell us that supply and demand work like a well-oiled machine. The Law of Supply tells us that as the price of an item goes up, businesses will supply more of that good or service. The Law of Demand adds that as the price rises, consumers will choose to buy less of the item. Only one equilibrium price can bring businesses' and consumers' intentions into balance. Away from this equilibrium point, surpluses or shortages tend to drive the price back toward the equilibrium. Of course, government actions such as taxation or setting a price ceiling or floor can move the economy away from its market equilibrium, creating what economists call a deadweight loss.

Our authors raise vexing issues about the mechanism of supply and demand. Chris Tilly and Marie Kennedy tell the complex story of the rise in the price of tortillas in Mexico, which turns out to be driven not by a shortage of corn, but by the multiple impacts of a nationwide shift towards free trade. The authors also go beyond an analysis of the causes of the price rise to explore its contribution to rising inequality in Mexico (Article 2.1). Marc Breslow argues that supply and demand do not always produce the best outcomes for society, noting that shortages lead to skyrocketing prices. But he also suggests that government should use the Law of Demand, increasing taxes on fuel to drive down fuel consumption (Article 2.2). Ben Collins discusses the 2008 global market for food, which was characterized by rising commodity prices and financial speculation. The irony of this was that the wealthiest people on the planet were reaping speculative profits by literally taking food out of the mouths of the poorest of people. Collins points out that the rush to bio-fuels is also reducing food production, aggravating the rise in global food prices (Article 2.3). Marc Breslow makes a case for "getting energy prices right" in addressing global warming and the finite nature of the resource. He argues that one can use the market mechanism for addressing environmental and economic goals that are not mutually exclusive (Article 2.4). Ellen Frank questions the textbook idea that rent controls (and other price ceilings) lead to permanent shortages. She maintains that rent control helps to equalize power between landlords and tenants and to assure a supply of affordable housing (Article 2.5). In response to claims by free-market enthusiasts that government-mandated minimum wages (i.e. price floors in the labor market) cause unemployment, Jeanette Wicks-Lim presents data to show both that minimum wage laws "are not job killers," and that the benefits are spread over a wider pool of workers than conventional economic analysis would suggest (Article 2.6).

Taken together, these articles call into question the claims that markets always operate efficiently and lead to the best social allocation of resources. The articles also imply a role for the "visible hand" of government when markets persistently fail.

Discussion Questions

1) (General) Marc Breslow portrays a situation in which suppliers (energy companies) hold disproportionate power over buyers. Can you think of situations in which buyers have disproportionate power over suppliers? (Hint: Large corporations can be buyers as well as suppliers.)

2) (General) The authors of these articles call for a larger government role in regulating supply and demand. What are some possible results of expanded government involvement, positive and negative? On balance, do you agree that government should play a larger role?

3) (Article 2.1) What reasons do Tilly and Kennedy provide for the rise in the price of tortillas in Mexico? Would you classify these reasons as being on the "supply side" or "demand side"? Do you think the authors' analysis deviates in any way from standard economic analyses of changing market prices?

4) (Article 2.1) In Tilly and Kennedy's article, how does the government of Mexico react to the tortilla price rise? What is the reaction of different members of the tortilla industry? What do you think it might take to lower tortilla prices in Mexico?

5) (Article 2.2) One way of summarizing Breslow's article is "The Law of Demand guarantees that there will sometimes be price-gouging." Explain what this means. Do you agree?

6) (Article 2.2) Breslow says that shortages have different effects on prices in the short run and the long run. Explain the difference. How is this difference related to the concepts of elasticity of demand and elasticity of supply?

7) (Article 2.3) Is there a "normative" (ethical/moral) problem with using food for fuels when the world's poor face starvation on a daily basis?

8) (Article 2.3) Is there a "normative" (ethical/moral) problem with speculating on food supplies and prices when the world's poor face starvation on a daily basis? How would a "true believer" in the market mechanism defend speculation of food commodities as leading to "efficient" markets and an optimal social distribution of food?

9) (Article 2.4) Breslow argues that gas prices should be higher than they are, in order to take into account the full cost—including the environmental cost—of gasoline use. If Breslow is right, why are suppliers selling gas for less than its full cost?

10) (Article 2.4) If a gas tax is levied, how should the proceeds of the tax be used? (Breslow offers one suggestion.) What principles of taxation are guiding your answer?

11) (Article 2.4) Why does Breslow suggest that raising the tax on energy will produce a better "social allocation" of energy resources? How can changing the relative price of energy lead to achieving energy, economic, and environmental goals? Is changing the relative price of energy sufficient to achieve these policy goals? If not, why not?

12) (Article 2.5) Frank states that because modern rent control laws are "soft," they do not lead to housing shortages. Explain. Do you agree with her reasoning?

13) (Article 2.6) What is the "ripple effect" of a minimum wage law? According to Wicks-Lim, how large is the impact of the "ripple effect" upon wage costs for employers? What about the impact upon workers?

14) (Article 2.6) Wicks-Lim qualifies her argument about the positive impacts of a higher minimum wage by saying "it depends" on the size of the raise. Congress voted in 2009 to raise the federal minimum wage. Do some research to find out how much the minimum wage was raised. What do you think of this decision?

Article 2.1

SUPPLY, DEMAND, AND TORTILLAS

BY CHRIS TILLY AND MARIE KENNEDY
March/April 2007

The last year has been a fractious one in Mexico. Last May, in San Salvador Atenco in Mexico State, a group of street vendors and a wide range of allies protesting the vendors' expulsion from the central square were brutally repressed, with hundreds arrested, beaten, and sexually abused by police. To the south in Oaxaca, Governor Ulises Ruiz launched a similar police operation against striking teachers in June, sparking the formation of a broad front that occupied the center of the city for months despite constant attacks by police and armed goons, only to be swept out in November by a vicious federal-state police assault. Meanwhile, as the every-six-years presidential campaign heated up, a caravan of Zapatistas headed by *Subcomandante* Marcos toured the country arguing that only grassroots mobilization, not a vote for one of the three major-party candidates, would change Mexican politics. July's presidential election put the right-wing National Action Party (PAN) candidate, Felipe Calderón, ahead of the center-left Party of the Democratic Revolution's (PRD) Andrés Manuel López Obrador by a razor-thin margin, amid evidence of large-scale irregularities. Supporters of López Obrador (popularly known as AMLO) took to the streets, creating a festive tent city stretching miles along Mexico City's main boulevard, La Reforma, and coming together in animated rallies of up to two million. Failing to change the election result, they declared a parallel government.

In early 2007, all of these struggles have been heating up once again. Key Atenco leaders are getting out of jail. Activists are marching in Oaxaca city once again, and a major Triqui indigenous community in that state just declared itself autonomous from the state, federal, and "official" local governments. AMLO and allies across the country are gearing up for what they call the Democratic National Convention, with the aim of building a new politics and writing a new constitution. The Zapatistas held a four day forum—"Encounter with the Peoples of the World"—hosting some 2,000 delegates in their base communities.

And across Mexico, the hot topic of the moment is...the price of tortillas. Prices for this Mexican staple, just a few months ago selling at 5 pesos (about 50 cents) per kilo (2.2 pounds, about 40 tortillas), had by mid-January spiked up to 8, 10, and in some places even 12 or 15 pesos per kilo. It's hard to convey to a U.S. audience how central tortillas are to the Mexican diet, but suffice it to say that *tortillerías* are sprinkled every couple of blocks across urban Mexico, and the great majority of families anchor their main meal with a kilo or two of tortillas. (When we first went to a *tortillería* and asked for ten tortillas, the vendor assumed she had heard us wrong and asked, "Ten kilos?") Perhaps the closest U.S. equivalent in terms of breadth of impact would be if the price of gas doubled and in some places even tripled. Other prices are also climbing—milk, eggs, sugar, meat, and natural gas—but it's the tortilla price surge that has grabbed Mexicans by the throat.

A Peculiar Crisis

A number of things are odd about the tortilla crisis. For one thing, there is no short-age of corn. Mexico had the largest corn harvest ever last year, more than twice as much as in 1980 (the country's population grew 60% over the same period). However, the structure of corn production has changed dramatically. Millions of family farmers in central and southern Mexico once dominated the crop, but free-trade policies have driven many of them off the land. Today, northern Mexican agri-business calls the tune. That plus NAFTA and other free trade agreements and the reduction of government subsidies mean that Mexico's corn price is now driven by the world price. The world price, in turn, increasingly responds to demand for etha-nol as well as for food products. So the price has trended up as oil prices made etha-nol more attractive—prompting *The Economist* to label corn "pure gold." Making matters worse, according to observers including the president of Mexico's central bank, speculation by large Mexican producers and traders is turbocharging the price hikes. Development expert Peter Rosset of the Center for the Study of Rural Change in Mexico points out that Mexican corn prices have spiked up far faster than those in the United States.

While one might expect the remaining small corn farmers in Mexico to ben-efit from rising prices, associations of small producers complain that they have not. Separated from consumers by layers of middlemen, they receive little or no trickle-down. The major beneficiaries are industry giants like Mexico's Maseca and U.S.-based Cargill, along with other large producers and traders. This pat-tern extends beyond Mexico. Guatemala's Institute for Agrarian and Rural Studies reports similar results of the Central American Free Trade Agreement in Guatemala: price increases for consumers, profits for the biggest corporations, and continued marginalization of small farmers.

Then there is the spectacle of a newly elected, pro-free trade president suddenly discovering the virtues of government intervention in the economy, at least to a lim-ited extent. President Calderón speedily negotiated an 8.5 peso cap with major corn meal and tortilla producers and retailers, promising to boost corn supplies so as to underwrite this price and stock the 24,000-odd government-run rural DICONSA stores that sell staples at subsidized prices. Ironically, he's increasing the supply by importing corn from the United States. (Mexico, the birthplace of corn, currently imports almost one-third of its corn consumption!)

Of course, once the price agreement was concluded, the tortilla industry began backing away from it. The corn meal giants clarified that this was a goodwill ges-ture on their part, not an ironclad commitment. Spokespeople for neighborhood *tortillerías* pointed out that they didn't work for the big companies, so the agree-ment wasn't binding on them. A few days after Calderón's tortilla handshake, we spot-checked tortillas in Tlaxcala (central Mexico, where we are living for six months)—the two *tortillerías* we priced were both selling at 9. That same day, the state government of Tlaxcala announced with much fanfare that it had concluded a separate 8.5 peso agreement with *tortillerías*. So the next day we returned to the same two shops: one was closed (we stopped by too late); the other was still charg-ing 9. Around the same time, federal government inspectors found prices over 8.5

at 53% of the *tortillerías* they visited nationwide. Still, two weeks after Calderón's pact, federal authorities had only managed to check prices at just over 3,000 shops out of an estimated 350,000. Even several weeks after the price *convenio*, tortilla sellers in the state of Aguascalientes announced that despite federal and state "agreements," they would not agree to a price ceiling under 10 pesos. On the other hand, the country's giant supermarket chains, including Wal-Mart, made a big show of discounting tortillas to 5 or 6 pesos (as a visit to our local Wal-Mart confirmed). Not a fair comparison, declared the *tortillería* industry: they mix all kinds of non-corn filler into their *nixtamal*, and besides, Mexicans prefer their tortillas fresh, hot, and local off a neighborhood *comal* (griddle).

"No to PAN, Yes to Tortillas!"

Naturally, Calderón's critics were not satisfied with his attempt to pull the tortillas out of the fire. AMLO and the PRD called for a 6-peso ceiling on tortilla prices and a 35% increase in the minimum wage (currently set at a laughably low $US5 a day). Not to be outdone, the Con-federation of Revolutionary Workers and Peasants (CROC —despite its fiery name, a mainstream union federation long affiliated with the Institutional Revolutionary Party [PRI] that ruled Mexico for seventy years until 2000) demanded price ceilings on 30 items in the *canasta básica* (the basket of basic consumer necessities tracked by the government). On January 31, these groups and more organized a peaceful *megamarcha* to protest the growing gap between prices and wages and to demand a "new social contract." Left-leaning daily *La Jornada* described the turnout in Mexico City as "tens of thousands" or "one hundred thousand"—numerically disappointing compared to other recent demonstrations—but what was significant was the presence of activists from the PRI, two smaller parties, and a large number of worker and peasant organizations that had not previously joined PRD-initiated mobilizations. They jointly issued the broadranging "Declaración del Zócalo," named after the central Mexico City square where the demonstration took place, announcing, "We are starting a new stage of struggle for the demands of the majority sectors in Mexico."

Particularly noteworthy is the active participation of peasant groupings such as the Permanent Agrarian Congress, the National Council of Peasant Organizations, and the National Peasant and Fisheries Council in the nationwide mobilizations. Thanks to their involvement, the protest movement has embraced a "food sovereignty" program that goes well beyond wage and price demands. Such a program would include government support for small Mexican producers of staple grains such as corn and beans through government-sponsored research and technology transfer. They also demand a renegotiation of the agricultural section of NAFTA, which is currently scheduled to remove all trade protection from Mexican corn and beans in 2008. A wave of cheaper, subsidized corn and beans from the United States would most likely lead to a temporary drop in Mexican corn prices, but the devastating effect on small Mexican farmers would leave the country far more dependent on imports and more vulnerable to future price fluctuations.

Although we were unable to attend the Tlaxcala branch of the action, we joined a smaller pre-march in Tlaxcala the weekend before. A cheerful crowd of a couple of hundred, including a large contingent from the local chapter of the Social Security Administration union, rallied to slogans like, "No to PAN, yes to tortillas!" (PAN is both the name of the ruling party and the word for bread.) José Roberto Pérez Luna, head of the union, told us, "The system is not meeting the needs of the majority. That's what leads to revolutions. I'd hate to think that our government is fertilizing a revolution."

The "Employment President" Says No

For three weeks after the rally, the government of Calderón, who campaigned as "the employment president" but so far has presided over job losses of 178,000, kept mum about the key demands, apart from some vague promises to help support Mexican corn producers and some noises about prosecuting speculators. Finally on February 21, the government gave its answer: No. No to mandatory price controls. No to an increase in the minimum wage, using the old argument, widely discredited by recent research, that minimum-wage increases destroy jobs. (Around the same time, Calderón announced a 46% increase in wages for the army, a move many see as designed to bolster the harsh repression the government has meted out to protestors in Oaxaca and elsewhere. "In this country, we will no longer confuse illegality with human rights," he remarked recently in a not-very-veiled warning.) And no to reopening NAFTA. Mexico "will not change the rules of the game," the president declared.

In the absence of further government action, Mexican consumers "voted" with their pocketbooks, reducing tortilla consumption by 20% to 30% during January, according to the National Chamber of Tortilla and Corn Flour Producers. Unfortunately, as Marie Antoinette learned to her regret a few centuries ago, for the poorest the alternative to eating unaffordable staples is simply not eating. Nearly one-fifth of Mexicans live in extreme poverty. Poor Mexicans get 40% of their protein from tortillas, and while statistics on short-term changes in nutritional intake are not available, it is safe to assume that more of these people are going hungry. Calderón's secretary of social development, Beatriz Zavala, stirred much outrage when she claimed that tortilla price hikes would not affect food consumption by the rural poor, since so many of them are self-sufficient peasants. The reality is that in rural areas—as in the United States—family farmers are increasingly compelled to reduce planting in order to supplement their income with non-agricultural jobs, or are being forced off their land outright.

The groups that launched the January 31 protests promise further mobilizations. One of the coalition members, the National Peasant and Fisheries Council, also proposes to set up a network of 5,000 small producers who will sell directly to consumers in six states, plus the federal district that includes Mexico City, working with popular organizations wherever possible.

Tlaxcala union leader Pérez Luna is right to warn of "fertilizing a revolution." Whatever happens next with tortilla prices, the issues of the widening gap between most Mexicans' salaries and the cost of living, and the other widening gap between the rich and the rest, are not going away. These are some of the same issues that fueled the Zapatista rebellion, the street vendors' protest in Atenco, the teachers' strike in Oaxaca, and the wave of anger at the elite that has made AMLO's protests much more than the sour grapes of a losing candidate. Calderón's strategy—continued free-market reforms sprinkled with crowd-pleasing tactical concessions like the tortilla pact, and the mailed fist when protests get out of hand—seems more likely to accelerate these trends than halt them. In the coming years, expect Mexican politics to heat up as hot as a *tortillería*'s *comal*.

Resources: *La Jornada* (daily newspaper), www.jornada.unam.mx; "La declaración del Zócalo," www.jornada.unam.mx/2007/02/01/index.php?section=politica&article=006n1pol; Timothy Wise, "Policy space for Mexican maize," Global Development and Environment Institute, www.ase.tufts.edu/gdae/Pubs/wp/07-01MexicanMaize.pdf; Center for the Study of Rural Change in Mexico (CECCAM), "En defensa del maíz," www.ceccam.org.mx/ConclusionesDefensa.htm; Grassroots International, "Fixing the broken food system," grassrootsonline.org/food_is.html.

Article 2.2

PRICE GOUGING: IT'S JUST SUPPLY AND DEMAND

BY MARC BRESLOW
October 2000

- May 2000: Growing demand, along with supply cutbacks by OPEC, lead to soaring gasoline prices around the United States, especially in the upper Midwest, where they reach $2 a gallon, almost twice the levels of a year earlier.
- September 2000: Both presidential candidates, George W. Bush and Al Gore, offer plans to prevent dramatic increases in the price of heating oil during the coming winter, due to expected supply shortages.
- 1999 and 2000: red-hot high-tech economies in the San Francisco Bay and Boston areas draw in more professional workers, and raise the demand for housing. Vacancy rates dwindle to near zero, and prices for both rentals and house purchases rise out of sight. Moderate- and low-income renters are evicted for non-payment and forced to move into smaller quarters or out of these metropolitan areas.

Critics of the oil industry charge that the companies are conspiring to raise prices during shortages, ripping off consumers and gaining huge profits through illegal behavior. The industries respond that there is no conspiracy, prices are rising due to the simple functioning of supply and demand in the market. The media debate the question: can evidence be found of a conspiracy? Or are rising prices simply due to increased costs as supplies are short? Politicians ask whether companies are guilty of illegal activity, and demand that investigations be opened.

What's going on? In reality, critics of the industries are missing the point of how a capitalist "free market" operates during times of shortages. The industry spokespersons are more on target in their explanations—but that doesn't mean what the companies are doing is okay. In fact, they *are* profiting at the expense of everyone who is forced to pay outrageous prices.

Both the media and public officials want to know whether rising costs of operation are causing the high prices, and therefore the companies are justified. Why? Because simple textbook economics says that in a competitive market we should get charged according to costs, with companies only making a "normal" profit. But a careful reading of the texts shows that this is only in the "long run" when new supplies can come into the market. In the short run, when a shortage develops, "supply and demand" can force prices up to unbelievable levels, especially for any product or service that is really a necessity. It doesn't have any relationship to the cost of supplying the item, nor does it take a conspiracy. The industry spokespeople are right that market pressures are the cause.

What confuses consumers is why a relatively small shortage can cause such a huge price jump, as it did for gasoline and electricity. Why, if OPEC reduces world oil supplies by only 1% or 2%, can the price of gasoline rise by perhaps 50%? Why shouldn't prices rise by the 1% or 2%? The answer lies in a common-sense understanding of what happens during a shortage. Everyone who owns a car, and still needs to get to work, drop the kids off at child care, and buy groceries, still needs to drive. In the short run, you can't sell your car for a more energy-efficient one, nor move someplace where public transit is more available, nor find a new day care center closer to home. Even if there are subways or buses available where you live, tight work and family time schedules probably make it difficult for you to leave the car at home.

So, as prices rise, everyone continues trying to buy as much gasoline as they did before (in technical terms, the "short run price elasticity of demand" is very low). But there is 2% less gas available, so not everyone can get as much as they want. Prices will continue rising until some people drop out of the market, cutting back on their purchases because they simply can't afford to pay the higher prices. For something as essential to modern life as gasoline, this can take quite a price jump. If the price goes from $1.20 to $1.30 will you buy less? How about $1.50? Or $1.80? You can see the problem. Prices can easily rise by 50% before demand falls by the 2% needed for supply and demand to equalize.

Note that this situation has nothing to do with the costs of supplying gasoline, nor do oil companies in the United States have to conspire together to raise prices. All they have to do is let consumers bid for the available gasoline. Nothing illegal has taken place—OPEC is acting as a cartel, "conspiring," but the United States has no legal power over other countries. Profits can go up enormously, and they may be shared between OPEC, oil companies such as Exxon/Mobil and Royal Dutch Shell, and firms lower on the supply chain such as wholesalers and retail gas stations.

Housing is perhaps the worst of these situations, as no one should be forced to leave their home. But the "invisible hand" of the market will raise prices, and allocate housing, according to who has the greatest purchasing power, not who needs the housing. A highly-skilled computer programmer, moving into San Francisco from elsewhere, will get an apartment that some lesser-paid worker, maybe a public school teacher or a bus driver, has been living in, perhaps for many years.

In all these cases, the market has done what it does well—allocate sales to those who can afford to buy, without regard to need; and allocate profits to those who have a product in short supply, without regard to costs of production. The human costs to people of moderate- and low-incomes, who are priced out of the market, can be severe. But they can be prevented—by price controls that prevent price-gouging due to shortages. Such controls have been used many times in the United States—for rent in high-demand cities, for oil and gas during the "crises" of the 1970's, and for most products during World War II. Maybe it's time we made them a staple of sensible economic policy.

Resources: "In Gas Prices, Misery and Mystery," Pam Belluck, The *New York Times*, 6/14/2000; "Federal action sought to cut power prices from May," Peter J. Howe, The *Boston Globe*, 8/24/2000; "Industry Blames Chemical Additives for High Gas Prices," Matthew L. Wald, The *New York Times*, 6/26/2000.

Article 2.3

HOT COMMODITIES, STUFFED MARKETS, AND EMPTY BELLIES

What's behind higher food prices?

BY BEN COLLINS
July/August 2008

Since 2003, prices of basic agricultural commodities such as corn, wheat, soybeans, and rice have skyrocketed worldwide, threatening to further impoverish hundreds of millions of the world's poor.

Shifts in fundamental supply and demand factors for food grains have undoubtedly contributed to higher food prices. Prominent among these shifts are the increasing diversion of food crops for biofuel production in the United States and Europe; sustained drought and water scarcity in Australia's wheat-growing regions; flooding in the U.S. grain belt; rising prices for oil and fertilizer worldwide; and the adoption of European and American meat-rich diets by the growing middle classes throughout Asia.

On top of these recent developments, long-term threats to worldwide agricultural output have eroded the world food system's resilience in the face of changing supply and demand. Although decades in the making, a loss of agricultural capacity worldwide caused by soil depletion, climate change, water scarcity, and urbanization has begun to take its toll on food production. Moreover, half a century of import restrictions and cheap agricultural exports by wealthy countries has devastated domestic food production capacity in poorer countries, forcing many countries that were once self-sufficient to rely on imported food from the world market.

At the same time, however, the growing presence of buy-and-hold investors in commodity markets has prompted heated debate among commodity traders, economists, and politicians over other possible causes of higher commodity prices apart from supply and demand shifts.

Since 2001, the declining value of the U.S. dollar, low U.S. interest rates, weak stock market returns, and accelerating inflation have drawn investment dollars away from stocks and into non-traditional investments such as commodities. This flight to perceived safety in commodity markets turned into a stampede in 2007 and early 2008, as a credit-induced financial crisis in the United States compounded these existing stresses on global financial markets.

Rising commodity prices and financial speculation on food are not new phenomena. The 1970s saw a similar rise in commodity prices in the United States, and in the 1920s, U.S. investors formed commodity pools to bet on commodity price movements. But the quantity and liquidity of money flowing through today's global markets is unprecedented in human history. The current commodities boom could be a sign of looming agricultural scarcity, or it may prove to be a short-lived speculative bubble that will deflate over the next few months or years. But regardless of where agricultural commodity prices are headed, the boom has already begun to transform how food is financed, grown, and sold, and may dramatically change how people around the world eat (or don't).

Commodity Investment Goes Retail

Commodity exchanges exist as a mechanism for the producers and consumers of grains, energy, and livestock to transfer risk to financial institutions and other traders. For example, wheat farmers might seek to reduce the risk of price fluctuations by selling a contract for the future delivery of their wheat crop on a commodity exchange. This futures contract will guarantee a price for the farmer selling the contract, enabling them to pay for their planting costs, and avoid the risk that the price of wheat may decrease between the date they sell the contract and the date they agree to deliver the wheat. Food giants such as Kraft and Nabisco, as well as smaller bakers and grain consumers, typically purchase commodity futures contracts to avoid the opposite risk—that the price of their raw materials may increase in the future. (Commodity markets also trade "spot" contracts, which entitle the purchaser to the immediate delivery of a commodity.)

Because producers and consumers seek to reduce risk, they function as so-called hedgers in commodity markets. In contrast, commercial trading firms and other speculators bet on the price of a commodity rising or falling, buying and selling futures contracts frequently in order to profit from short-term changes in their prices.

Since 2001, commodity funds have gained in popularity as a mechanism for institutions and individuals to profit from increases in commodity prices. These funds purchase commodity futures contracts in order to simulate ownership of a commodity. By periodically rolling over commodity futures contracts prior to their maturity date and reinvesting the proceeds in new contracts, the funds allow investors to gain investment returns equivalent to the change in price of a single commodity, or an "index" of several commodities (hence the name "index investor").

Investors in these commodity index funds include public pension funds, university endowments, and even individual investors, through mutual funds, for example. Although these investors are similar to traditional commodity speculators in that both seek to profit from changes in price, traditional speculators zero in on short-term price shifts, while index investors are almost exclusively long-term buyers betting on higher commodity prices in the future.

Some observers have argued that index investors themselves may have pushed already-high prices of commodities even higher. Hedge fund manager Michael Masters testified to the U.S. Senate that the total holdings of commodity index investors on regulated U.S. exchanges have increased from $13 billion in 2003 to nearly $260 billion as of March 2008. And as of April 2008, index investors owned approximately 35% of all corn futures contracts on regulated exchanges in the United States, 42% of all soybean contracts, and 64% of all wheat contracts, compared to minimal holdings in 2001. As Masters emphasized, these are immense commodity holdings. The wheat contracts, for example, are good for the delivery of 1.3 billion bushels of wheat, equivalent to twice the United States' annual wheat consumption.

Index fund managers have defended against charges that commodity index investment contributes to higher prices, arguing that because index funds never take delivery on their futures contracts, they simulate commodity price shifts for their investors without affecting the price of the underlying commodity. Some economists have also expressed skepticism that investment demand has driven commodity prices higher. Paul Krugman of Princeton University has noted that there is no evidence of "the usual telltale signs of a speculative price boom" such as physical hoarding of commodities. Furthermore, Krugman and others have pointed to non-exchange traded commodities such as iron ore that have also experienced rapid price increases during recent years, arguing that fundamental supply and demand factors, not investors, are to blame for higher commodity prices.

Other economists and commodity market observers have argued that despite price increases in non-exchange traded commodities, and an absence of physical hoarding, the recent flood of money into commodity markets has altered the balance between speculators and hedgers, leading to higher prices and greater price volatility. Mack Frankfurter, a commodities trading advisor at Cervino Capital Management, suggests that the influx of commodity index investors has transformed commodity futures from tools for risk management to long-term investments, "causing a self-perpetuating feedback loop of ever higher prices."

One reason the precise impact of index investors on commodity prices is difficult to determine is that the U.S. commodity trading regulator, the Commodity Futures Trading Commission (CFTC), does not collect data on so-called "over-the-counter" commodity trading—that is, trading on unregulated markets—even though the agency estimated that 85% of commodity index investment takes place on these markets. Because Masters's data on the holdings of commodity index investors only include the 15% of index investor contracts that are held on CFTC-regulated exchanges, total commodity index investor holdings may be much higher than his estimates.

In testimony that warned of the influence of these unregulated markets on commodity prices, Michael Greenberger, the former head of the CFTC's Division of Trading and Markets, estimated that if unregulated trading of energy and agricultural commodities were eliminated, the price of oil would drop by 25% to 50% "overnight." If Greenberger is correct, the effect on food commodity prices would likely be similar. However, index investment is just one of many avenues through which money can enter commodity markets, making it difficult to assess the impact of index investors without taking into account the recent deregulation of U.S. commodity markets that has facilitated the current boom in food and energy investments.

Commodity Trading Regulation, Enron-Style

Commodity index investment is deeply intertwined with the growth of unregulated commodity trading authorized by the Commodity Futures Modernization Act of 2000. Before 2000, U.S. commodity futures contracts were traded exclusively on regulated exchanges under the oversight of the CFTC. Traders were required to disclose their holdings of each commodity and adhere to strict position limits, which set a maximum number of futures contracts that an individual institution could hold. These regulations were intended to prevent market manipulation by traders who might otherwise attempt to build up concentrated holdings of futures contracts in order to manipulate the price of a commodity.

The 2000 law effectively deregulated commodity trading in the United States by exempting over-the-counter commodity trading outside of regulated exchanges from CFTC oversight. Soon after the bill was passed, several unregulated commodity exchanges opened for trading, allowing investors, hedge funds, and investment banks to trade commodities futures contracts without any position limits, disclosure requirements, or regulatory oversight. Since then, unregulated over-the-counter commodity trading has grown exponentially. The total value of all over-the-counter commodity contracts was estimated to be $9 trillion at the end of 2007, or nearly twice the value of the $4.78 trillion in commodity contracts traded on regulated U.S. exchanges.

Once these unregulated commodity markets were created, energy traders and hedge funds began to use them to place massive bets on commodity prices. Enron famously exploited deregulated electricity markets in 2001, when the firm managed to generate unheard-of profits by using its trading operations to effectively withhold electricity and charge extortionate rates from power grids in California and other western states.

Although Enron went bankrupt later that year, the hedge fund Amaranth later exploited unregulated natural gas markets prior to its 2006 collapse. The fund had been heavily invested in complicated bets on the price of natural gas, borrowing eight times its assets to trade natural gas futures, and lost $6.5 billion when natural gas prices moved in the wrong direction. One month prior to Amaranth's collapse, the New York Mercantile Exchange (NYMEX), which is regulated by the CFTC, asked Amaranth to reduce its huge natural gas position. Amaranth reduced its position at NYMEX's request, but purchased identical positions on the unregulated InterContinental Exchange, where its transactions were invisible to regulators until the fund finally collapsed.

Amaranth's implosion demonstrated the ineffectiveness of regulating some commodity exchanges but not others. Thanks to the Commodity Futures Modernization Act, traders could flout position limits and disclosure rules with impunity, simply by re-routing trades to unregulated exchanges. Although index investment in commodities does not typically involve white-knuckle, leveraged bets on a single commodity's short-term performance, index investment was made possible by the same deregulated environment exploited by Amaranth and Enron. Like Amaranth, commodity index investors commonly purchase futures contracts on unregulated markets when they exceed CFTC position limits on futures contracts for a particular commodity. And other financial actors such as investment banks, hedge funds, or even the sovereign wealth funds of other countries may also be heavily invested in these over-the-counter commodity contracts, but since this trading is unregulated and unreported, the holders of these $9 trillion worth of contracts remain anonymous.

This year, the CFTC has faced intense scrutiny from investors, politicians, farmers, and agricultural traders over the unprecedented volatility and price increases of several agricultural and energy commodities traded on U.S. exchanges. A lively CFTC roundtable on commodity markets in April appeared to confirm arguments made by Frankfurter, Greenberger, Masters, and other critics of commodity index investment. Representatives for farmers, grain elevator operators, and commercial bankers at the hearing repeatedly stressed that commodity markets were "broken," while the only pleas for calm came from CFTC economists and representatives for index investors and the financial industry. Unlike index investors, farmers have not benefited greatly from higher commodity prices, because extremely high levels of market volatility have made it difficult for some farmers to finance crop planting. National Farmers Union president Tom Buis sounded a particularly dire warning about the consequences of tight commodity supplies and burgeoning index investment demand: "We've got a train wreck coming in agriculture that's bigger than anything else we've seen."

Following these warnings from farmers and food producers about the presence of index investors in commodity markets, the CFTC's acting chair publicly acknowledged the ongoing debate over "whether the massive amount of money coming into the markets is overwhelming the system." Despite this admission, Greenberger, the former CFTC official, remains skeptical of the agency's capacity and willingness to regulate commodity markets effectively. He urged Congress and the Federal Trade Commission to circumvent the CFTC's authority and eliminate unregulated over-the-counter commodity trading. Recently, faced with strong criticism from Congress, the CFTC retreated further from its claim that commodity markets are functioning normally. A CFTC commissioner admitted: "We didn't have the data that we needed to make the statements that we made, and the data we did have didn't support our declarative statements. If we were so right, why the heck are we doing a study now?"

The Consequences of Financializing Food

Facing political pressure by constituents over high oil and food prices, several members of Congress have sponsored legislation that would bar index investors from commodity markets. One bill proposed by Sen. Joseph Lieberman (Ind-Conn.) would prohibit public and private pension funds with more than $500 million in assets from trading in commodity futures, and other bills would limit the maximum number of futures contracts an index investor could hold. These bills may stem the flood of money from index investors into commodities, but comprehensive reform is needed to reverse the Commodity Futures Modernization Act's authorization of over-the-counter commodity trading. Absent an outright repeal of this so-called "Enron loophole," energy and agricultural commodities will continue to be traded outside the reach of government regulation, making future Enron- and Amaranth-style market disruptions inevitable.

Ultimately, eliminating unregulated commodity trading cannot address the fundamental causes of higher agricultural prices. Even if speculative buying is curtailed, supply and demand factors such as falling crop yields, destructive trade policies, and the growing use of biofuels have likely brought the age of cheap food to an end. However, if the critics of commodity index investment are correct, then these investors have amplified recent food price shocks and are needlessly contributing to the impoverishment of the world's poorest citizens. Even though commodity market transparency and regulatory oversight will not solve the global food crisis, eliminating unregulated commodity trading can help resolve the debate over the effects of index investors on commodity prices and restore the accountability of commodity markets to the social interests they were originally established to serve.

Sources: Michael Masters, testimony before the Committee on Homeland Security and Government Affairs, United States Senate, May 20, 2008; Daniel P. Collins, "CFTC to up spec limits," *Futures,* May 1, 2005; Paul Krugman, "Fuels on the Hill," *New York Times,* June 27, 2008; Michael Frankfurter, *The Mysterious Case of the Commodity Conundrum, Securitization of Commodities, and Systemic Concerns,* Parts 1-3, www.marketoracle.co.uk; Michael Frankfurter and Davide Accomazzo, "Is Managed Futures an Asset Class? The Search for the Beta of Commodity Futures," December 31, 2007, *Graziadio Business Report;* "Regulator Admits to Futures Tracking Volatility," Associated Press, June 4, 2008; Commodity Futures Trading Commission, *CFTC Announces Agricultural Market Initiatives.* June 3, 2008; Michael Greenberger, testimony before the Committee on Commerce, Science, and Transportation, United States Senate, June 3, 2008; Sinclair Stewart and Paul Waldie. "Who is responsible for the global food crisis?" *Globe and Mail,* May 30, 2008; Commodity Futures Trading Commission, *Agricultural Markets Roundtable,* April 22, 2008; Ann Davis, "Commodities Regulator Under Fire—CFTC Scrutinized As Congress Looks Into Oil-Price Jump," *Wall Street Journal,* July 7, 2008; Ed Wallace, "ICE, ICE, Baby," *Houston Chronicle,* May 19, 2008; Laura Mandaro, "Lieberman plans would bar funds from commodities," *Marketwatch,* June 18, 2008; "Our Confusing Economy, Explained," *Fresh Air,* April 3, 2008, www.npr.org.

Article 2.4

WANT A COOL PLANET? RAISE GAS PRICES!

BY MARC BRESLOW
May/June 2000, revised June 2006

So gasoline prices have risen above $3.00 a gallon and threaten to go even higher. To hear many commentators and politicians talk, this is a tragedy rivaling the bubonic plague of the Middle Ages. How dare OPEC threaten Americans' god-given right to cheap gas! Why, after all, did we fight two Gulf Wars, if not to keep gas as cheap as bottled water?

No matter that even at $3.00 a gallon, gas is still not much more expensive, adjusted for inflation, than it was in the early 1970s, or that it is half the price that people pay in Britain, France, Germany, and Japan. It's still time to dip into the strategic oil reserve, cut the federal gas tax, and lift restrictions on oil drilling in environmentally-sensitive areas of Alaska.

I beg to differ. It's hard to think of another issue in which U.S. attitudes are more wrong-headed. The rest of the world knows that, because of global warming and because oil is eventually going to run out (unless we allow drilling to destroy every last bit of pristine environment anywhere), we have to reduce our burning of fossil fuels, including oil. Only the United States, under the political domination of the oil and auto companies, refuses to recognize reality.

Higher gas prices are one of the best things that could happen to this country. If we are lucky, they will start a trend toward smaller cars and away from SUVs. In the long run SUVs threaten to destroy the global environment. In the short run, they threaten to kill all of us foolish—or cash poor—enough to continue driving normal cars. Federal regulators have found that in a collision between an SUV and a car, car occupants are three times as likely to be killed as if they were hit by another car.

Just recently automakers have finally acknowledged this fact, and say they will redesign future SUV models with lower frames to make them less of a threat. But wouldn't it make more sense to just get rid of most of them? Doubling gas prices would be the surest way of making that happen.

Won't that hurt the U.S. economy? Well, yes. Unfortunately, once you have built an economy on wasting energy, rebuilding it in an energy-efficient manner will involve substantial costs. And that is a reason to make the transition gradual—perhaps raising gas prices 20 cents a year for the next ten years would be a reasonable schedule. By that time most people would be ready to get rid of their old gas guzzlers anyway. Not only could they downsize, but they could buy one of the new "hybrids," combination gas/electric vehicles (the engine charges the batteries) that Honda and Toyota are releasing this year. Just changing from SUVs (which get 15 or so miles to the gallon) to these hybrids (which get 60 or more), would go a long way toward meeting the United States' commitment to reduce carbon dioxide emissions in response to global warming.

What about the effects of higher fuel prices on moderate- and low-income people, who may be driving regular cars but still can't afford gas at $5 or $6 a gallon?

There is an answer here. Rather than let the Kuwaiti royal family get the benefits of oil scarcity, we should do what Europe and Japan do—tax the hell out of oil (and coal and natural gas, which also create carbon dioxide when burned). Then we should redistribute the tax revenues in a progressive manner, so that low-income people come out even or ahead.

Peter Barnes, creator of the Sky Trust Initiative, has perhaps the best proposal for how to do this. He suggests that rather than letting the federal government use the oil-tax revenue on anything it wants—which could be something horribly regressive like further cuts in income or capital-gains taxes—the money should go into a trust fund. Then it should be handed back to every U.S. resident on an equal per-capita basis. This method would mean low-income households getting back more than they pay for higher fuel costs—so we help the environment and economic equity at the same time. Not to mention sticking it to ExxonMobil.

Resources: The Sky Trust Initiative, *www.skytrust.cfed. org;* the Union of Concerned Scientists, *www. ucsusa.org;* the Sierra Club, including its program on Transportation and Sprawl: *www.sierraclub.org.*

Article 2.5

DOES RENT CONTROL HURT TENANTS?

BY ELLEN FRANK
March/April 2003

Dear Dr. Dollar,

What are the merits of the argument that rent control hurts tenants by limiting the incentives to create and maintain rental housing?

—*Sarah Marxer, San Francisco, Calif.*

The standard story of rent control, laid out in dozens of introductory economics textbooks, goes like this. In the housing market, landlords are willing to supply more rental units when prices are high, and tenants are willing to rent more units when prices are low. In an unregulated market, competition should result in a market-clearing price at which the number of apartments landlords are willing and able to provide just equals the number tenants are willing and able to rent. Thus, when prices are allowed to rise to their correct level, shortages disappear. Rent controls, in this story, disrupt the market mechanism by capping rents at too low a level. Artificially low rents discourage construction and maintenance, resulting in fewer available apartments than would exist without the controls. At the same time, low rents keep tenants in the area, searching for apartments that don't exist. The result: permanent housing shortages in rent-controlled markets.

What's wrong with this story? Just about everything.

First, the story ignores the unequal power that landlords and tenants exercise in an unregulated market. Boston College professor Richard Arnott notes that tenants are, for a number of reasons, averse to moving. This gives landlords inordinate pricing power even in a market where housing is not in short supply—and in areas where vacancy rates are low, land is scarce, and "snob zoning" commonplace, landlords can charge truly exorbitant prices. In Boston, rent controls were eliminated in 1997, and average apartment rents have since climbed nearly 100%. The city's spiraling rents show that without controls, landlords can—and do—gouge tenants.

Second, rent control opponents misrepresent the structure of controls. As practiced in the real world, rent control does not place fixed caps on rent. New York City enacted an actual rent freeze after World War II, and a small number of apartments still fall under this "old-law" rent control. But most rent-controlled apartments in New York and all controlled apartments in other U.S. cities fall under what Arnott calls "second generation" or "soft" controls, which simply restrict annual rent increases. Soft rent controls guarantee landlords a "fair return" on their properties and require that owners maintain their buildings. They allow landlords to pass along maintenance costs, and many allow improvement costs to be recouped on an accelerated schedule, making building upkeep quite lucrative.

Consequently, controlled apartments are not unprofitable. And as Occidental College professor and housing specialist Peter Dreier points out, landlords won't walk away as long as they are making a decent return. Residential landlords are not very mobile: they have a long-term interest in their properties, and only abandon them when *market* rents fall below even controlled levels as a result of poverty, crime, or economic depression. Rent controls themselves do not foster abandonment or poor maintenance.

Third, all second-generation rent control laws—enacted chiefly in the 1970s—exempted newly constructed buildings from controls. Thus, the argument that controls discourage new construction simply makes no sense. As for the oft-heard complaint that developers fear that rent controls, once enacted, will be extended to new buildings, the 1980s and 1990s construction booms in New York, Boston, San Francisco, and Los Angeles—all cities with controls—indicate that developers aren't all that worried. There is plenty of housing and construction in cities with and without rent controls.

Nevertheless, even in many cities with rent controls, there is a shortage of *affordable* apartments. Market housing costs have been rising faster than wages for at least two decades. That some apartments in New York and San Francisco are still affordable to low- and middle-income families is due primarily to rent control.

Indeed, limited as they might be, rent controls deliver real benefits. They prevent price-gouging and ration scarce apartments to existing tenants. The money tenants save in rent can be spent in the neighborhood economy, benefiting local businesses. Meanwhile, more secure tenants create neighborhoods that are stable, safe, and economically diverse. And rent controls are essential if tenants are to have credible legal protection against slumlords: the legal right to complain about lack of heat or faulty plumbing is meaningless if landlords can retaliate by raising rents.

There are many problems with the U.S. housing market. High prices, low incomes, and lack of public housing or subsidies for affordable housing all contribute to homelessness and housing insecurity in major American cities. Rent control is not the cause of these problems, nor is it the whole solution. But along with higher wages and expanded public housing, it is part of the solution. As Dreier puts it, "Until the federal government renews its responsibility to help poor and working-class people fill the gap between what they can afford and what housing costs to build and operate, rent control can at least help to keep a roof over their heads."

Resources: Richard Arnott, "Time for Revisionism on Rent Control?" *Journal of Economic Perspectives*, Winter 1995. Dreier and Pitcoff, "I'm a Tenant and I Vote," *Shelterforce*, July/August 1997. Shelterforce website: <http://www.nhi.org/>.

Article 2.6

MEASURING THE FULL IMPACT OF MINIMUM-WAGE LAWS

Workers who were earning less than the new wage floor are not the only ones who benefit from a higher minimum wage.

BY JEANNETTE WICKS-LIM
May/June 2006

Raising the minimum wage is quickly becoming a key political issue for this fall's midterm elections. In the past, Democratic politicians have shied away from the issue while Republicans have openly opposed a higher minimum wage. But this year is different. Community activists are forcing the issue by campaigning to put state minimum-wage proposals before the voters this fall in Arizona, Colorado, Ohio, and Missouri. No doubt inspired by the 100-plus successful local living-wage campaigns of the past ten years, these activists are also motivated by a federal minimum wage that has stagnated for the past nine years. The $5.15 federal minimum is at its lowest value in purchasing-power terms in more than 50 years; a single parent with two children, working full-time at the current minimum wage, would fall $2,000 below the poverty line.

Given all the political activity on the ground, the Democrats have decided to make the minimum wage a central plank in their party platform. Former presidential candidate John Edwards has teamed up with Sen. Edward Kennedy (D-Mass.) and ACORN, a leading advocacy group for living wage laws, to push for a $7.25 federal minimum. Even some Republicans are supporting minimum-wage increases. In fact, a bipartisan legislative coalition unexpectedly passed a state minimum-wage hike in Michigan this March.

Minimum-wage and living-wage laws have always caused an uproar in the business community. Employers sound the alarm about the dire consequences of a higher minimum wage both for themselves and for the low-wage workers these laws are intended to benefit: Minimum-wage mandates, they claim, will cause small-business owners to close shop and lay off their low-wage workers. A spokesperson for the National Federation of Independent Business (NFIB), commenting on a proposal to raise Pennsylvania's minimum wage in an interview with the *Philadelphia Inquirer*, put it this way: "That employer may as well be handing out pink slips along with the pay raise."

What lies behind these bleak predictions? Mark Shaffer, owner of Shaffer's Park Supper Club in Crivitz, Wisc., provided one explanation to the *Wisconsin State Journal*: "... increasing the minimum wage would create a chain reaction. Every worker would want a raise to keep pace, forcing up prices and driving away customers." In other words, employers will not only be forced to raise the wages of those workers earning below the new minimum wage, but also the wages of their co-workers who earn somewhat more. The legally required wage raises are difficult enough for employers to absorb, they claim; these other raises—referred to as ripple effect raises—aggravate the situation. The result? "That ripple effect is going to lay off people."

Ripple effects represent a double-edged sword for minimum-wage and living-wage proponents. Their extent determines how much low-wage workers will benefit from such laws. If the ripple effects are small, then a higher minimum (or living) wage would benefit only a small class of workers, and boosting the minimum wage might be dismissed as an ineffective antipoverty strategy. If the ripple effects are large, then setting higher wage minimums may be seen as a potent policy tool to improve the lives of the working poor. But at the same time, evidence of large ripple effects provides ammunition to employers who claim they cannot afford the costs of a higher wage floor.

So what is the evidence on ripple effects? Do they bloat wage bills and overwhelm employers? Do they expand the number of workers who get raises a little or a lot? It's difficult to say because the research on ripple effects has been thin. But getting a clear picture of the full impact of minimum and living wage laws on workers' wages is critical to evaluating the impact of these laws. New research provides estimates of the scope and magnitude of the ripple effects of both minimum-wage and living-wage laws. This evidence is crucial for analyzing both the full impact of this increasingly visible policy tool and the political struggles surrounding it.

Why Do Employers Give Ripple-Effect Raises?

Marge Thomas, CEO of Goodwill Industries in Maryland, explains in an interview with *The Gazette* (Md.): "There will be a ripple effect [in response to Maryland's recent minimum-wage increase to $6.15], since it wouldn't be fair to pay people now making above the minimum wage at the same level as those making the new minimum wage." That is, without ripple effects, an increase in the wage floor will worsen the relative wage position of workers just above it. If there are no ripple effects, workers earning $6.15 before Maryland's increase would not only see their wages fall to the bottom of the wage scale, but also to the same level as workers who had previously earned inferior wages (i.e., workers who earned between $5.15 and $6.15).

Employers worry that these workers would view such a relative decline in their wages as unfair, damaging their morale—and their productivity. Without ripple effect raises, employers fear, their disgruntled staff will cut back on hard-to-measure aspects of their work such as responding to others cheerfully and taking initiative in assisting customers.

So employers feel compelled to preserve some consistency in their wage scales. Workers earning $6.15 before the minimum increase, for example, may receive a quarter raise, to $6.40, to keep their wages just above the new $6.15 minimum. That employers feel compelled to give non-mandated raises to some of their lowest-paid workers because it is the "fair" thing to do may appear to be a dubious claim. Perhaps so, but employers commonly express anxiety about the costs of minimum-wage and living-wage laws for this very reason.

The Politics of Ripple Effects

Inevitably, then, ripple effects come into play in the political battles around minimum-wage and living-wage laws—but in contradictory ways for both opponents and supporters. Opponents raise the specter of large ripple effects bankrupting small businesses. At the same time, though, they argue that minimum-wage laws are not effective in fighting poverty because they do not cover many workers—and worse, because those who are covered are largely teens or young-adult students just working for spending money. If ripple effects are small, this shores up opponents' assertions that minimum-wage laws have a limited impact on poverty. Evidence of larger ripple effects, on the other hand, would mean that the benefits of minimum-wage laws are larger than previously understood, and that these laws have an even greater potential to reduce poverty among the working poor.

The political implications are complicated further in the context of living-wage laws, which typically call for much higher wage floors than state and federal minimum-wage laws do. The living-wage movement calls for wage floors to be set at rates that provide a "livable income," such as the federal poverty level for a family of four, rather than at the arbitrary—and very low—level current minimum-wage laws set. The difference is dramatic: the living-wage ordinances that have been passed in a number of municipalities typically set a wage floor twice the level of federal and state minimum wages.

So the mandated raises under living-wage laws are already much higher than under even the highest state minimum-wage laws. If living-wage laws have significant ripple effects, opponents have all the more ammunition for their argument that the costs of these laws are unsustainable for employers.

How Big are Ripple Effects?

My answer is a typical economists' response: it depends. In a nutshell, it depends on how high the wage minimum is set. The reason for this is simple. Evidence from the past 20 years of changes to state and federal minimum wages suggests that while there is a ripple effect, it doesn't extend very far beyond the new minimum. So, if the wage minimum is set high, then a large number of workers are legally due raises and, relatively speaking, the number of workers who get ripple-effect raises is small. Conversely, if the wage minimum is set low, then a small number of workers are legally due raises and, relatively speaking, the number of workers who get ripple-effect raises is large.

In the case of minimum-wage laws, the evidence suggests that ripple effects do dramatically expand their impact. Minimum wages are generally set low relative to the wage distribution. Because so many more workers earn wages just above the minimum wage compared to those earning the minimum, even a small ripple effect increases considerably the number of workers who benefit from a rise in the minimum wage. And even though the size of these raises quickly shrinks the higher the worker's wage rate, the much greater number of affected workers translates into a significantly larger increase in the wage bills of employers.

For example, my research shows that the impact of the most recent federal minimum-wage increase, from $4.75 to $5.15 in 1997, extended to workers earning wages around $5.75. Workers earning between the old and new minimums generally received raises to bring their wages in line with the new minimum— an 8% raise for those who started at the old minimum. Workers earning around $5.20 (right above the new minimum of $5.15) received raises of around 2%, bringing their wages up to about $5.30. Finally, those workers earning wages around $5.75 received raises on the order of 1%, bringing their wages up to about $5.80.

This narrow range of small raises translates into a big overall impact. Roughly 4 million workers (those earning between $4.75 and $5.15) received mandated raises in response to the 1997 federal minimum-wage increase. Taking into account the typical work schedules of these workers, these raises translated into a $741 million increase to employers' annual wage bills. Now add in ripple effects: Approximately 11 million workers received ripple-effect raises, adding another $1.3 billion to employers' wage bills. In other words, ripple-effect raises almost quadrupled the number of workers who benefited from the minimum-wage increase and almost tripled the overall costs associated with it.

Dramatic as these ripple effects are, the real impact on employers can only be gauged in relation to their capacity to absorb the higher wage costs. Here, there is evidence that businesses are not overwhelmed by the costs of a higher minimum wage, even including ripple effects. For example, in a study I co-authored with University of Massachusetts economists Robert Pollin and Mark Brenner on the Florida ballot measure to establish a $6.15 state minimum wage (which passed overwhelmingly in 2004), we accounted for ripple-effect costs of roughly this same magnitude. Despite almost tripling the number of affected workers (from almost 300,000 to over 850,000) and more than doubling the costs associated with the new minimum wage (from $155 million to $410 million), the ripple effects, combined with the mandated wage increases, imposed an average cost increase on employers amounting to less than one-half of 1% of their sales revenue. Even for employers in the hotel and restaurant industry, where low-wage workers tend to be concentrated, the average cost increase was less than 1% of their sales revenue. In other words, a 1% increase in prices for hotel rooms or restaurant meals could cover the increased costs associated with both legally mandated raises and ripple-effect raises.

The small fraction of revenue that these raises represent goes a long way toward explaining why economists generally agree that minimum-wage laws are not "job killers," as opponents claim. According to a 1998 survey of economists, a consensus seems to have been reached that there is minimal job loss, if any, associated with minimum-wage increases in the ranges that we've seen.

Just as important, this new research revises our understanding of who benefits from minimum-wage laws. Including ripple-effect raises expands the circle of minimum-wage beneficiaries to include more adult workers and fewer teenage or student workers. In fact, accounting for ripple effects decreases the prevalence of teenagers and traditional-age students (age 16 to 24) among workers likely to be affected by a federal minimum-wage increase from four out of ten to three out of ten. In other words, adult workers make up an even larger majority of likely minimum-wage beneficiaries when ripple effects are added to the picture.

The Case of Living-Wage Laws

With living-wage laws, the ripple effect story appears to be quite different, however—primarily because living wage laws set much higher wage minimums.

To understand why living-wage laws might generate far less of a ripple effect than minimum-wage hikes, it is instructive to look at the impact of raising the minimum wage on the retail trade industry. About 15% of retail trade workers earn wages at or very close to the minimum wage, compared to 5% of all workers. As a result, a large fraction of the retail trade industry workforce receives legally mandated raises when the minimum wage is raised, which is just what occurs across a broader group of industries and occupations when a living-wage ordinance is passed.

My research shows that the relative impact of the ripple effect that accompanies a minimum-wage hike is much smaller within retail trade than across all industries. Because a much larger share of workers in retail receive legally required raises when the minimum wage is raised, this reduces the relative number of workers receiving ripple effect raises, and, in turn, the relative size of the costs associated with ripple effects. This analysis suggests that the ripple effects of living wage laws will likewise be smaller than those found with minimum-wage laws.

To be sure, the ripple effect in the retail trade sector may underestimate the ripple effect of living-wage laws for a couple of reasons. First, unlike minimum-wage hikes, living-wage laws may have ripple effects that extend across firms as well as up the wage structure within firms. Employers who do not fall under a living-wage law's mandate but who are competing for workers within the same local labor market as those that do may be compelled to raise their own wages in order to retain their workers. Second, workers just above living-wage levels are typically higher on the job ladder and may have more bargaining power than workers with wages just above minimum-wage levels and, as a result, may be able to demand more significant raises when living-wage laws are enacted.

However, case studies of living-wage ordinances in Los Angeles and San Francisco do suggest that the ripple effect plays a smaller role in the case of living-wage laws than in the case of minimum-wage laws. These studies find that ripple effects add less than half again to the costs of mandated raises—dramatically less than the almost tripling of costs by ripple effects associated with the 1997 federal minimum-wage increase. In other words, the much higher wage floors set by living-wage laws appear to reverse the importance of legally required raises versus ripple-effect raises.

Do the costs associated with living-wage laws—with their higher wage floors—overwhelm employers, even if their ripple effects are small? To date, estimates suggest that within the range of existing living-wage laws, businesses are generally able to absorb the cost increases they face. For example, Pollin and Brenner studied a 2000 proposal to raise the wage floor from $5.75 to $10.75 in Santa Monica, Calif. They estimated that the cost increase faced by a typical business would be small, on the order of 2% of sales revenue, even accounting for both mandated and ripple-effect raises. Their estimates also showed that some hotel and restaurant businesses might face cost increases amounting to up to 10% of their sales revenue—not a negligible sum. However, after examining the local economy, Pollin and Brenner concluded that even these cost increases would not be likely to force these businesses to close their doors. Moreover, higher productivity and lower turnover rates among workers paid a living wage would also reduce the impact of these costs.

Ultimately, the impact of ripple-effect raises appears to depend crucially on the level of the new wage floor. The lower the wage floor, as in the case of minimum-wage laws, the more important the role of ripple-effect raises. The higher the wage floor, as in living-wage laws, the less important the role of ripple-effect raises.

Making the Case

The results of this new research are generally good news for proponents of living- and minimum-wage laws. Ripple effects do not portend dire consequences for employers from minimum and living wage laws; at the same time, ripple-effect raises heighten the effectiveness of these laws as antipoverty strategies.

In the case of minimum-wage laws, because the cost of legally mandated raises relative to employer revenues is small, even ripple effects large enough to triple the cost of a minimum-wage increase do not represent a large burden for employers. Moreover, ripple effects enhance the somewhat anemic minimum-wage laws to make them more effective as policy tools for improving the lot of the working poor. Accounting for ripple effects nearly quadruples the number of beneficiaries of a minimum-wage hike and expands the majority of those beneficiaries who are adults—in many instances, family breadwinners.

However, ripple effects do not appear to overwhelm employers in the case of the more ambitious living-wage laws. The strongest impact from living-wage laws appears to come from legally required raises rather than from ripple-effect raises. This reinforces advocates' claims that paying a living wage is a reasonable, as well as potent, way to fight poverty.

Sources: D. Fairris, et al., *Examining the Evidence: The Impact of the Los Angeles Living Wage Ordinance on Workers Businesses,* Los Angeles Alliance for a New Economy, 2005; V. Fuchs, et al., "Economists' Views About Parameters, Values and Policies: Survey Results in Labor and Public Economics," *Journal of Economic Literature,* Sept. 1998; R. Pollin, M. Brenner, and J. Wicks-Lim, "Economic Analysis of the Florida Minimum Wage Proposal, " Center for American Progress, 2004; R. Pollin and M. Brenner, "Economic Analysis of the Santa Monica Living Wage Proposal," Political Economy Research Institute, 2000; M. Reich et al., *Living Wages and Economic Performance,* Institute of Industrial Relations, 2003; J. Wicks-Lim, "Mandated Wage Floors and the Wage Structure: Analyzing the Ripple Effects of Minimum and Prevailing Wage Laws," Ph.D. dissertation, University of Massachusetts-Amherst, 2005.

Chapter 3

CONSUMERS

INTRODUCTION

In the theory of consumer choice, the "two economies" described in the Introduction—the textbook economy and the economy portrayed by critics of the status quo—come into sharp contrast. In the textbook model of consumer choice, rational individuals seek to maximize their well-being by choosing the right mix of goods to consume—a decision that includes how they spend their time. They decide for themselves how much they would enjoy various things, and make their choices based on full information about the options. More of any good is almost always better, but diminishing marginal utility says that each unit of a good brings less enjoyment than the one before. The theory looks at one individual at a time, and tells us that there is no accurate way to compare utilities across individuals.

But critics launch a variety of challenges to this simplified model. The first two articles in this chapter contend that the idea of consumer sovereignty—that consumer wishes determine what gets produced—does not fit the facts. The advertising that saturates our daily lives constantly creates new wants, and increasingly targets children, convincing them to nag their parents into buying products they suddenly "need" (Article 3.2). In many transactions, consumers are also less than fully informed about what they are getting or even the price they are paying. For example, young children targeted by advertisers are unaware of the consequences of many of their consumption decisions. Predatory lending, in which unscrupulous lenders saddle borrowers with hidden fees and high interest rates, is an extreme example of this problem of incomplete information (Article 3.1). Alan Durning puts forward an even more radical critique of standard consumer theory, arguing that more is often worse, not better—that the accumulation of material goods in affluent societies threatens the environment, widens global inequalities, and hollows out our lives (Article 3.3).

Mainstream models of consumption also justify increased consumption by arguing that consumers maximize their happiness (utility) through consumption. Thad Williamson uses survey data for the United States to challenge that connection. The data suggests that beyond a certain level of material comfort—which he argues has already been achieved in the West—more money does little to increase happiness. Instead, the pursuit of money makes it harder for individuals to seek out those things that do indeed make them happier—connections with family and friends and participation in religious and other community organizations. He points out that the structure of the political economy today makes economic stability—another factor that increases a sense of satisfaction with one's life—impossible to attain for most Americans. He argues that it is time to shift the focus from increases in material wealth towards broader moral concerns that would truly result in increased well-being (Article 3.4).

Discussion Questions

1) (General) Standard consumer theory still applies if advertising is simply a way to inform consumers. But many of the authors in this chapter suggest that advertising shapes our tastes and desires. Think of some of the purchases that you have made in the last six months. For which purchases was advertising primarily a source of information, and for which was it more of a taste-shaper?

2) (Article 3.1) Leffall alleges that predatory lenders often target African-American borrowers. Why would they do this? More generally, why would businesses discriminate (by race, gender, or other categories) in which consumers they seek out and are willing to sell to?

3) (Article 3.2) According to Scharber, what are the negative impacts of advertising directed at children? Would you support a law banning advertising to young children? Why or why not?

4) (Articles 3.1 and 3.2) Mainstream economic theory depicts consumers as autonomous individuals making careful choices based on the preferences they themselves have developed. Scharber and Leffall describe consumers as manipulated by crafty advertisers and dishonest businesses. In what areas of consumer choice is each picture more accurate? Which do you think is more accurate overall?

5) (Article 3.3) Durning says that it's wrong for people in rich countries to consume so much when others in the world live in poverty. His viewpoint could be summarized as, "Live simply, so that others may simply live." Do you agree with this outlook?

6) (Article 3.3) One conclusion from Durning's argument is that rather than seeking pleasure by consuming material goods, we should seek enjoyment through family, friends, and community. How could you use standard utility theory to describe this kind of choice? (Hint: can family, friends, and community be "goods"?) What are some possible problems in using the theory in this way?

7) (Article 3.4) According to the survey data Williamson cites, what is the connection between income/consumption and happiness? How does this contradict the standard economic model of consumption?

8) (Article 3.4) Williamson argues that the moral task set out by Adam Smith—of ensuring enough economic growth to allow everyone to live in material comfort—has in fact been attained. Do you agree with him? What is your reaction to Williamson's argument that the focus from here on should not be on economic growth, but rather the fulfillment of other "real goods of human life"?

Article 3.1

A MATTER OF LIFE AND DEBT
The Impact of Predatory Lending on the Black Community

BY JABULANI LEFFALL
March/April 2003

Think of it as a word problem. Problem is the operative word: If "company A" lends $50,000 to "consumer F" at an interest rate 7 points above the prime rate, charging finance fees equal to 10% of the loan and a prepayment penalty, how long would it take for consumer F to pay back the interest, let alone the principal?

Sound complicated? Well it is and that's how the lenders want it to be. The answer to the problem: too long. (As long as possible is also acceptable.) This complex equation is what is known as predatory lending—loans made with abusive terms like hidden or excessive fees and foreclosure defaults. Predatory lending banks use deceptive solicitation and often target borrowers who should qualify for credit on better terms.

While poor people in general are the main quarry in this multi-billion dollar business, it's African Americans who are the biggest losers. "We are targeted more than any other group through aggressive marketing and mail-out campaigns," says Yolanda Clark, a Los Angeles-based black mortgage broker who deals with homebuyers every day.

Although not all subprime (high interest) loans are predatory, almost all predatory loans are subprime. And, according to a November 2002 report by the Association of Community Organizers for Reform Now (ACORN), subprime lenders account for more than half of all housing refinance loans made in predominately black neighborhoods. From 1995 to 2001 the number of subprime purchase loans to African Americans rose 686%.

Large financial concerns and the subprime lending lobby deny that blacks are being targeted. They point out the true fact that whites procure subprime loans in greater number than blacks and that the loans some black consumers get reflect their poor credit.

But even though more whites get subprime loans, the likelihood that these same loans are predatory is higher for blacks, according to another report, "Risk or Race?" issued last year by the Center for Community Change. Its findings dispel the claim that bad credit or poverty explains predatory lending patterns. In fact, the study found that racial inequities increased as homeowners' salaries and creditworthiness went up.

The report, which ranks all 331 metropolitan areas in the nation, finds that:

- African Americans are three times more likely than whites to receive a subprime loan.
- Upper-income African Americans are more likely to receive subprime loans than are lower-income whites.
- Subprime lending and racial disparities are found in all regions and in urban areas of all sizes.

Allen J. Fishbein, general counsel of the Center for Community Change, says the overall racial disparities are due to a lack of mainstream prime lenders in the black community.

Predatory lenders contribute to neighborhood deterioration by stripping homeowners of their equity and overcharging those who can least afford it, adds David Swanson, ACORN's spokesman.

"The circle of debt is killing our community," says Earl Ofari Hutchinson, author and talk show host for KPFK, a Pacifica affiliate in Los Angeles. "It's peonage and indentured servitude to the loans. Black people in greater and greater numbers are subjected to piracy by legalized thieves."

Lena J.

Lena J, a community resource adviser for United Way and a resident of Inglewood, Calif.—a predominately black city on the outskirts of Los Angeles—knows the perils of predatory lending all too well.

Ms. J requested that her last name not be used out of fear of reprisal from her lender. She bought her home three years ago for $149,000, with two loans through a neighborhood bank. She pays interest rates of 7.2% and 7.3%. (The prime rate currently hovers slightly above 4%.)

When Ms. J decided she needed a second mortgage, she went to Household International, Inc. subsidiary Beneficial to apply for a personal line of credit to pay off her car loans and provide some extra cash for home improvement.

Beneficial first told her that the loan was denied. Then, out of the blue, she got a call saying it had been approved and was being processed. The total amount of the loan was $52,904 including $3,903 in points and fees at an interest rate of 11.5%. Money is money, she surmised. So she rushed back over to Beneficial and signed up.

Beneficial neglected to mention that there was a prepayment penalty on her loan for five years costing six months interest minus 20% of the loan amount.

Even worse, Beneficial set up her loan as a home equity loan instead of the regular line of credit that she requested.

Beneficial indicated in fine print that it would pay off her second mortgage. But when Ms. J got the checks from Beneficial, they were for the wrong amounts. Even though the loan went through and $21,000 for her second mortgage is listed on page two of her Truth in Lending Disclosure form, Beneficial never paid that amount.

It has to be true if it's on the "Truth in Lending Disclosure" form right? Wrong. While Beneficial did send her a check, the company paid off far less of her mortgage balance than it led her to believe it would. Meanwhile Ms. J thought her second mortgage had been paid in full by Beneficial and so did not submit her second mortgage payments. Late charges hit her like a ton of bricks falling from a "fixer upper."

Ms. J now makes three payments per month when she should only have two. Her monthly payments (on the original housing loans and the Beneficial loans combined) total $1,150. Her monthly net income is less than $2,000.

She joins a host of others forced to pay 60% or more of their net income toward high-interest mortgages. A domino effect ensues, as there is less money for other essentials such as groceries, phone and utilities and car payments. If Ms. J does not make her payments, she pays in a different way—foreclosure.

False and misleading Beneficial information (in both its written and person-to-person communication with Ms. J) were factors in her victimization. Because Ms. J trusted Beneficial and did not suspect a shady deal was brewing, when she found out the loan was approved, she signed on the dotted line. Ms. J cannot take her fight in earnest to the courts—because a signature, even on a confusing loan form, is binding in most cases.

Definitions

The line between "legal" subprime lending and "predatory lending" is a contested one. Many deny that a clear definition of predatory lending exists. Without a widely understood definition of the term, the enemy remains faceless. People cannot fight what they do not understand.

Although several states and localities have recently passed laws clarifying the scope of illegal lending practices, and recent court settlements may have begun to curb some of the worst fraudulent practices of a few large corporations, a wide scope of deceptive activity remains legal in most of the country.

Further, although predatory lending is a discriminatory practice, most of the media has not defined it as such. It is not treated as a matter of overt racial discrimination the way racial profiling, police brutality, and voter disenfranchisement sometimes are. Instead, too often the Ms. J's of the world are simply labeled "irresponsible" and left to fend for themselves.

Federal Reserve Board Governor Edward M. Gramlich, who has called for additional research to explore the "significance" of predatory lending, gave a vague and unmistakably political take on the definition question.

The Federal Reserve is charged with supervising and regulating banking institutions and protecting the credit rights of consumers. Addressing the Consumer Federation of America, Gramlich said: "Just as with safety and soundness and unfair and deceptive trade practices," there should be no final definition of the term "predatory lending."

Gramlich's remarks are about as clear as what happened to Ms. J. It is evident that he wants to tread lightly until the debate reaches Capitol Hill. When in doubt, commission a study.

The truth of the matter is that a list of predatory lending practices can be named, and the effects of predatory lending can be measured. An independent study on the economic cost of predatory lending in the housing arena by the Durham, N.C.-based Coalition for Responsible Lending identified three clusters of predatory lending practices and analyzed their costs:

- *Equity Stripping:* Charging borrowers exorbitant processing fees, resulting in substantially higher payments that are subtracted from the equity of the home when a borrower refinances or sells his or her house.
- *Rate-Risk Disparities:* Charging borrowers a higher rate of interest than their credit histories would justify.
- *Excessive Foreclosures:* Homeowners struggling to make payments under the combined weight of excessive fees and high interest rates often pay the ultimate price—the loss of their home and all the equity they have accumulated.

The Coalition for Responsible Lending's report goes on to say that the equity of the neighbors of the foreclosed is also reduced as foreclosures start to permeate the neighborhood. "Finally," the study states, "there are significant social costs to the pending wholesale loss of neighborhoods of homeowners, particularly in African-American communities."

And the housing finance arena represents just one branch of the predatory lending industry. Housing finance predatory lenders target consumers of a particular stratum; those with incomes high enough to permit homeownership. More pervasive still are smaller-scale predatory-lending operations geared to personal finance.

High Finance Connections

Predatory lenders have been called "pirates" and "scavengers" by their victims, but while this banking niche is on its face morally reprehensible, these "pirates" are not from some underworld of organized crime. They are among the most respected institutions in the world, companies whose leaders mix with powerful dignitaries as stewards of high finance. Their billboards celebrate the American dream.

But for two groups in particular: Citigroup Inc. and Household International Inc.—better known by their opponents as "Citigrope" and "Chokehold"—the term "high finance" takes on a whole new meaning. Both are mainstream institutions with ties to predatory lending practices.

"Citigrope"

New York-based Citigroup is the world's second largest financial services concern and is America's largest consumer finance firm. Its 2001 revenue was $112 billion with profits of $14 billion.

Citigroup's chief executive, Sanford Weill, is revered on Wall Street as a banking legend and the "best deal-maker on the planet." Weill presided over the historic 1998 merger between Traveler's Group and Citibank (hence Citigroup) and parlayed his company into the top ten of the *Fortune 500*.

In 2001's *Fortune 500* edition, *Fortune* magazine said of Weill: "Weill is a star: His shareholders earned an average annual total return of 40.8% (in 2001) a stunning result that only 15 other companies in the list—all of them smaller—beat."

In the years since the article appeared, both Citigroup and Weill have drawn fire for analyst improprieties at Salomon Smith Barney—its investment banking arm—and more recently for the actions of CitiFinancial, its subprime consumer-lending arm.

CitiFinancial sells bill consolidation, debt refinancing and subprime home equity home improvement and personal loans through more than 2,000 offices in North America. It was CitiFinancial's $31 billion acquisition of notorious predatory lender Associates First Capital in 2000 that tarnished Citigroup's reputation. In 2001, the Federal Trade Commission (FTC) alleged that Associates violated the Federal Trade Commission Act through what it called "deceptive marketing practices that induced consumers to refinance existing debts into home loans with high interest rates, costs, and fees, and to purchase high-cost credit insurance."

The FTC also said the company violated the Truth in Lending Act, the Fair Credit Reporting Act, and Equal Credit Opportunity Act, and used unfair tactics in collecting consumers' payments on its loans.

Jodie Bernstein, then the Director of the FTC's Bureau of Consumer Protection, stated in a press release:

"(Associates) hid essential information from consumers, misrepresented loan terms, flipped loans, and packed optional fees to raise the costs of the loans. What had made the alleged practices more egregious is that they primarily victimized consumers who were the most vulnerable—hard working homeowners who had to borrow to meet emergency needs and often had no other access to capital."

To protect the merger and shield itself from liability and attacks from the press, Citigroup launched a website called "Tell Citibank." The homepage says: "Associates Customer: Are you a customer of Associates First Capital? If so, you already may be a victim of predatory lending."

Despite Citigroup's newly deployed campaign for the little guy, it once again found itself the object of protest late last year. A San Francisco-based advocacy group, the California Reinvestment Committee (CRC), attacked the parent company for discrimination and openly fought the bank's expansion in the western United States.

Said CRC executive director Alan Fisher, "We fear a growing Citigroup presence in California and believe it will be harmful to California communities."

According to the CRC, Citigroup hides behind its subsidiary CitiFinancial, which CRC contends still charges high points and fees on subprime loans, imposes prepayment penalties that trap borrowers into high cost loans, and sets arbitration provisions denying borrowers access to legal recourse.

The CRC further contends that CitiFinancial lends subprime monies to African-American and Latino borrowers, while low-cost lenders are three to four times as likely to deny African Americans as they are white applicants.

"It's the bait and switch," says Donnette Heard, treasurer for the Los Angeles-based Multicultural Real Estate Alliance For Urban Change. "If the big bank denies you, they send you to their subprime lenders who will then contact you. They keep your business and deal with you on their terms."

"Chokehold"

Such is the case with Chicago-based Household International, Inc. whose Beneficial subsidiary played the bait and switch with Ms. J from Inglewood.

According to Internet business portal Hoovers, Household has "made lending to the little people profitable." With a company slogan that says: "Helping everyday people everyday," it is the second largest consumer finance company behind Citigroup.

Yet for the past several years, consumer advocacy groups and Attorneys General from scores of states have dragged Household through the courts for duping the Ms. J's of America into high-interest hell.

In 2001 Household still managed to post $13 billion in revenues with a profit of $1.9 billion. Moreover, Household caught a break in November of 2002 when powerful British Bank HSBC, led by chairman Sir John Bond, snapped it up in a $14 billion dollar deal. At the time of the deal, Bond assured investors that Household's "aggressive" lending practices were a thing of the past. Bond laughed his way to the bank because Household's legal troubles and bad press helped him acquire the company at a bargain-basement price. It was nevertheless one of the largest acquisitions of 2002.

With assets of more than $100 billion and about 50 million customers at 1,400 retail branches, Household will lift the earnings before taxes of HSBC's North American operation to more than 30% of the conglomerate's total profits. It will also boost HSBC's credit card business, adding about 2 million new Household customers.

This deal, much like Citigroup's acquisition of Associates, is not without controversy. The Bronx, N.Y.-based Inner City Press (ICP), which in the past attacked big banks such as Citigroup, opposes the HSBC-Household deal. ICP revealed data showing that HSBC, even before the acquisition was announced, denied African-American loan applications 2.7 times more frequently than whites' applications. Groups like the ICP believe HSBC will willingly participate in the bait and switch, using Household and its units to trap consumers.

What Citigroup and Household have in common, other than being lenders under fire, is that they both were involved in multi-billion dollar mergers in which subprime lenders sought refuge. The danger of the absorption of subprime lending groups into publicly traded mainstream banks is that the holding companies do not have to submit transparent financial records for private subsidiaries to the Securities and Exchange Commission (SEC) or any other regulatory body. The figures can hide in long, tedious financial statements and be signed off on by accounting firms and lawyers retained by these large companies.

For instance, Associates was absorbed into CitiFinancial, a private arm of Citigroup, which is traded on the New York Stock Exchange. Moreover, now that it has acquired Household and is facing public scrutiny, publicly traded HSBC may clean up the house by burying Household financials deep into the number soup that comprises an SEC filing.

Both Citigroup and Household declined to comment for this article. Company spokespeople did, however, point to the large settlements made to predatory lending plaintiffs.

In the fall of 2002, Citigroup put up almost $250 million and Household about $484 million. The combined settlement money represents the largest sum in American history paid to settle a consumer lending complaint.

But considering that since 1995 predatory lending institutions have raked in almost $100 billion, the $734 million is, in layman's terms, chump change.

Citigroup settled with the FTC to shake the shame off its merger with Associates. In the case of Household, regulators and attorneys general from 20 states had accused it of violating state laws by misrepresenting loan terms and failing to disclose material information. "We could have litigated, but the headline and litigation risk over an extended period would have been worse for the company," said Household's Chief Executive William Aldinger in a conference call with analysts last October. "We made a call to get it over with quickly." Household said it would record a $330 million charge in the third quarter as a result of the settlement and that its earnings for 2003 would miss Wall Street expectations.

Since the settlement, Citigroup and Household have issued "best practices guidelines" that they say can further prevent future exploitation of borrowers with low-incomes or weak credit histories.

One promise they have made is to reform up-front points and fees. In the opinion of ACORN's David Swanson, Household should lower its cap on up-front points and fees from 5% of the loan amount to 3%. Citigroup already caps them at 3%.

Yet a cap on points and fees does not help if there is no limit to how high a basic interest rate can go. If a lender still really wants to bilk a borrower, it can lower the points and raise the interest rate. For example, if maximum points are 3% of the loan instead of 5 or 6%, a lender can raise a rate to 12 or 13% and be satisfied with a 3% cap on points.

There are also stipulations in both Household's and Citigroup's guidelines that ban the selling of single-premium credit insurance and establish customer hotlines for complaints (e.g., "Tell Citibank").

Despite Citigroup's and Household's mea culpa, the companies still differ in where they draw the line on abusive practice. And neither will concede that a good number of their predatory loans were issued based on race.

The Fight for Predatory Lending Reform

"The fight needs to be taken to the seats of local, state and national governments," says ACORN spokesman David Swanson.

And it has been. In the past year alone nearly a dozen state and local city government bodies have debated and passed anti-predatory lending legislation. By November of 2002 the New York, Los Angeles, and Oakland city councils had each passed such ordinances.

In New York, the ordinance bans the city from doing business with predatory lenders or companies that purchase predatory loans. ACORN members in Manhattan packed City Hall at each stage in this process and successfully promoted this bill over the fervent opposition of major lenders, including Citigroup. ACORN's New York branch estimates that the ordinance will save homeowners between $75 million and $100 million. The legislation is expected to take effect sometime this year. Los Angeles' proposed ordinance was even more comprehensive.

According to ACORN, there are several state-level bills on the table in New Jersey, Massachusetts, and New Mexico—where in November the group protested at a local branch of Wells Fargo, with victims talking about the damage caused by the predatory loans they received from the lender. Most of the bills would ban prepayment penalties, put caps on points, and establish Annual Percentage Rate (APR) thresholds.

Georgia and North Carolina already have strict predatory lending regulations. In North Carolina it is a violation to make a high-cost home loan if a lender believes the consumer will be unable to make the scheduled payments. North Carolina also makes it a violation to issue any loan that "does not have reasonable tangible net benefit to the borrower." Both states require all homeowners to seek loan counseling, a measure which consumer advocates support.

In the wake of the state bills, Sen. Paul Sarbanes (D-Maryland), the chair of the Senate Banking Committee in the 107th U.S. Congress, proposed a bill with provisions to ban certain practices characteristic in subprime lending, such as prepayment penalties, credit insurance bundling, financing of fees, and balloon payments (large, lump-sum payments scheduled at the end of a series of smaller payments).

But while ACORN's David Swanson praises these recent small victories, as well as the apparent move toward curbing or eradicating most forms of predatory lending, he is concerned about what might happen if a Republican-controlled Congress and White House decide to reverse the progress that has been made.

"I'd hate to think that this will all go for naught. That's why we're urging people to get involved in whatever way they can. We can't let the work be in vain," Swanson adds.

Groups such as the Coalition for Responsible Lending, ACORN, and the Center for Community Change say predatory lenders are likely to push laws banning state and local restrictions on abusive lending.

Late last year, Rep. Bob Ney (R-Ohio) passed around a draft for a bill that ACORN claims bans states from passing laws to protect borrowers. ACORN also alleges that the bill was co-written by Wright Andrews of Butera and Andrews, the firm that represents a coalition of subprime lenders.

Time and filibusters will tell. There is uncertainty about which bills will or will not be passed by session's end. There is also uncertainty as to whether the financial settlements from Citigroup and Household will be enough to placate opponents of predatory lending. So, as the days go by, the lawmakers legislate, corporate mergers and acquisitions commence, and the seats of power shift, the interest accrues and the bills pile up—particularly in the black community.

And one thing *does* remain certain: Ms. J of Inglewood and those like her have bills to pay next month and the month after that.

Article 3.2

THE 800-POUND RONALD McDONALD IN THE ROOM

BY HELEN SCHARBER
January 2007

When your child's doctor gives you advice, you're probably inclined to take it. And if 60,000 doctors gave you advice, ignoring it would be even more difficult to justify. Last month, the American Academy of Pediatrics (AAP) issued a policy statement advising us to limit advertising to children, citing its adverse effects on health. Yes, banning toy commercials might result in fewer headaches for parents ("Please, please, pleeeeeeease, can I have this new video game I just saw 10 commercials for????"), but the AAP is more concerned with other health issues, such as childhood obesity. Advertising in general—and to children specifically—has reached astonishingly high levels, and as a country, we'd be wise to take the doctors' orders.

Advertising to kids is not a new phenomenon, but the intensity of it is. According to Juliet Schor, author of *Born to Buy*, companies spent around $100 million in 1983 on television advertising to kids. A little more than 20 years later, the amount earmarked for child-targeted ads in a variety of media has jumped to at least $12 billion annually. That's over $150 per boy and girl in the U.S. And it's not as though kids only see ads for action figures and sugary cereal; the other $240 billion spent on advertising each year ensures that they see ads for all kinds of products, everywhere they go. According to the AAP report, "the average young person views more than 3,000 ads per day on television, on the Internet, on billboards, and in magazines." Ads are also creeping into schools, where marketers have cleverly placed them in "educational" posters, textbook covers, bathroom stalls, scoreboards, daily news programs, and bus radio programming.

If advertising to children is becoming increasingly ubiquitous, it's probably because it's becoming increasingly profitable. Once upon a time, kids didn't have as much market power as they do today. The AAP report estimates that kids under 12 now spend $25 billion of their own money annually, teenagers spend another $155 billion, and both groups probably influence around $200 billion in parental spending. Not too surprising, considering that 62 percent of parents say their children "actively participate" in car-buying decisions, according to a study by J.D. Power & Associates. Marketers are also becoming more aware of the long-term potential of advertising to children. While they may not be the primary market now, they will be someday. And since researchers have found that kids as young as two can express preferences for specific brands, it's practically never too early to begin instilling brand loyalty.

But while small children have an incredible memory for commercial messages, they may not have developed the cognitive skills necessary to be critical of them. In 2004, the American Psychological Association (APA) also called for setting limits on advertising to kids, citing research that "children under the age of eight are unable to critically comprehend televised advertising messages and are prone to accept advertiser messages as truthful, accurate and unbiased." Many people take offense at the idea that we might be manipulated by marketing. Aren't we, after all, intelligent enough to make up our own minds about what to buy? The research cited by the APA, however, shows that children are uniquely vulnerable to manipulation by advertising. Marketers therefore should not be allowed to prey on them in the name of free speech.

Such invasive advertising to children is not only an ethical problem. The American Academy of Pediatrics cited advertising's effects on health through the promotion of unhealthy eating, drinking and smoking as the main motivation for setting limits. Children's health issues certainly merit attention. The Center for Disease Control, for example, has found that the prevalence of overweight children (ages 6 to 11) increased from 7 percent in 1980 to about 19 percent in 2004, while the rate among adolescents (ages 12 to 19) jumped from 5 percent to 17 percent. In addition to physical health problems, Schor argues that extensive marketing has negative effects on children's emotional well being. In her research for Born to Buy, Schor found links between immersion in consumer culture and depression, anxiety, low self esteem and conflicts with parents. The big push to consume can also lead to financial health problems, as many Americans know all too well, with credit card debt among 18 to 24-year-olds doubling over the past decade.

Not even the staunchest critics of marketing to children would argue that advertisements are completely at fault for these trends. Yet, the commercialization of nearly everything is negatively affecting children's well being in rather profound ways. Why, then, is hardly anyone paying attention to the 800-pound Ronald McDonald in the room? Perhaps it's because advertising appears to be a necessary evil or a fair tradeoff—maybe little Emma's school couldn't afford a soccer team without Coke on the scoreboard, for example. Or perhaps some would argue that parents who don't approve of the commercial culture should limit their kids' exposure to it. Increasingly invasive marketing techniques make it practically impossible to simply opt out of commercial culture, though. Thus, decisions to limit marketing to children must be made by the country as a whole. Sweden, Norway, Greece, Denmark, and Belgium have already passed laws curbing kid-targeted advertising, and according to 60,000 pediatricians, if we care about the health of our kids, we should too.

Sources: American Association of Pediatrics, Policy Statement on Children, Adolescents, and Advertising, December 2006 (pediatrics.aappublications.org/cgi/content/full/118/6/2563); American Psychological Association, "Television Advertising Leads to Unhealthy Habits in Childen" February 2004 (releasees/childrenads.html); Jennifer Saranow, "Car makers direct more ads at kids," *Wall Street Journal*, November 9th, 2006 (www.commercialexploitation.org/news/carmakers.html); David Burke, "Two-year olds branded by TV advertising" (www.whitedot.org/issue/isssory.aps?slug=Valkenburg); Center for a New American Dream, *Kids and Commercialism* (www.newdream.org/kids/);; Juliet Schor, Born to Buy: The Commercialized Child and the New Consumer Culture (New York: Scribner, 2004); Center for Disease Control, "Facts about Childhood Overweight" www.cdc.gov/Healthy Youth/overweight/index.html).

Article 3.3

ENOUGH IS ENOUGH
Why more is not necessarily better than less

BY ALAN DURNING
June 1991, updated May 2009

> "Our enormously productive economy ... demands that we make consumption our way of life, that we convert the buying and use of goods into rituals, that we seek our spiritual satisfaction, our ego satisfaction, in consumption... We need things consumed, burned up, worn out, replaced, and discarded at an ever increasing rate."
>
> —*Victor Lebow, U.S. retailing analyst, 1955*

Across the country, Americans have responded to Victor Lebow's call, and around the globe, those who could afford it have followed. And many can: Worldwide, on average, a person today is four-and-a-half times richer than were his or her great-grandparents at the turn of the last century.

Needless to say, that new global wealth is not evenly spread among the earth's people. One billion live in unprecedented luxury; one billion live in destitution. Overconsumption by the world's fortunate is an environmental problem unmatched in severity by anything except perhaps population growth. Surging exploitation of resources threatens to exhaust or unalterably disfigure forests, soils, water, air, and climate. High consumption may be a mixed blessing in human terms, too. Many in the industrial lands have a sense that, hoodwinked by a consumerist culture, they have been fruitlessly attempting to satisfy social, psychological, and spiritual needs with material things.

Of course, the opposite of overconsumption—poverty—is no solution to either environmental or human problems. It is infinitely worse for people and bad for the natural world. Dispossessed peasants slash and burn their way into Latin American rain forests, and hungry nomads turn their herds out onto fragile African range land, reducing it to desert. If environmental destruction results when people have either too little or too much, we are left to wonder how much is enough. What level of consumption can the earth support? When does having more cease to add appreciably to human satisfaction?

The Consuming Society

Consumption is the hallmark of our era. The headlong advance of technology, rising earnings, and cheaper material goods have lifted consumption to levels never dreamed of a century ago. In the United States, the world's premier consuming society, people today on average own twice as many cars, drive two-and-a-half times as far, and travel 25 times further by air than did their parents in 1950. Air conditioning spread from 15% of households in 1960 to 64% in 1987, and color televisions from 1% to 93%. Microwave ovens and video cassette recorders reached almost two-thirds of American homes during the 1980s alone.

Japan and Western Europe have displayed parallel trends. Per person, the Japanese today consume more than four times as much aluminum, almost five times as much energy, and 25 times as much steel as they did in 1950. They also own four times as many cars and eat nearly twice as much meat. Like the Japanese, Western Europeans' consumption levels are only one notch below Americans'.

The late 1980s saw some poor societies begin the transition to consuming ways. In China, the sudden surge in spending on consumer durables shows up clearly in data from the State Statistical Bureau: Between 1982 and 1987, color televisions spread from 1% to 35% of urban Chinese homes, washing machines quadrupled from 16% to 67%, and refrigerators expanded their reach from 1% to 20%. By 2002 there were 126 color televisions, 93 washing machines, and 87 refridgerators for every 100 urban Chinese households.

Few would begrudge anyone the simple advantages of cold food storage or mechanized clothes washing. The point, rather, is that even the oldest non-Western nations are emulating the high-consumption lifestyle. Long before all the world's people could achieve the American dream, however, we would lay waste the planet.

The industrial world's one billion meat eaters, car drivers, and throwaway consumers are responsible for the lion's share of the damage humans have caused common global resources. Over the past century, the economies of the wealthiest fifth of humanity have pumped out two-thirds of the greenhouse gases threatening the earth's climate, and each year their energy use releases three-fourths of the sulfur and nitrogen oxides causing acid rain. Their industries generate most of the world's hazardous chemical wastes, and their air conditioners, aerosol sprays, and factories release almost 90% of the chlorofluorocarbons destroying the earth's protective ozone layer. Clearly, even one billion profligate consumers is too much for the earth.

Beyond the environmental costs of acquisitiveness, some perplexing findings of social scientists throw doubt on the wisdom of high consumption as a personal and national goal: Rich societies have had little success in turning consumption into fulfillment. Regular surveys by the National Opinion Research Center of the University of Chicago reveal, for example, that no more Americans report they are "very happy" now than in 1957.

Likewise, a landmark study by sociologist Richard Easterlin in 1974 revealed that Nigerians, Filipinos, Panamanians, Yugoslavians, Japanese, Israelis, and West Germans all ranked themselves near the middle of a happiness scale. Confounding any attempt to correlate affluence and happiness, poor Cubans and rich Americans were both found to be considerably happier than the norm.

If the effectiveness of consumption in providing personal fulfillment is questionable, perhaps environmental concerns can help us redefine our goals.

In Search of Sufficiency

By examining current consumption patterns, we receive some guidance on what the earth can sustain. For three of the most ecologically important types of consumption—transportation, diet, and use of raw materials—the world's people are distributed unevenly over a vast range. Those at the bottom clearly fall below the "too little" line, while those at the top, in the cars-meat-and-disposables class, clearly consume too much.

Approximately one billion people do their traveling, aside from the occasional donkey or bus ride, on foot. Unable to get to jobs easily, attend school, or bring their complaints before government offices, they are severely hindered by the lack of transportation options.

Another three billion people travel by bus and bicycle. Kilometer for kilometer, bikes are cheaper than any other vehicle, costing less than $100 new in most of the Third World and requiring no fuel.

The world's automobile class is relatively small: Only 8% of humans, about 400 million people, own cars. The automobile makes itself indispensable: Cities sprawl, public transit atrophies, shopping centers multiply, workplaces scatter.

The global food consumption ladder has three rungs. According to the latest World Bank estimates, the world's 630 million poorest people are unable to provide themselves with a healthy diet. On the next rung, the 3.4 billion grain eaters of the world's middle class get enough calories and plenty of plant-based protein, giving them the world's healthiest basic diet.

The top of the ladder is populated by the meat eaters, those who obtain close to 40% of their calories from fat. These 1.25 billion people eat three times as much fat per person as the remaining four billion, mostly because they eat so much red meat. The meat class pays the price of its diet in high death rates from the so-called diseases of affluence—heart disease, stroke, and certain types of cancer.

The earth also pays for the high-fat diet. Indirectly, the meat-eating quarter of humanity consumes nearly 40% of the world's grain—grain that fattens the livestock they eat. Meat production is behind a substantial share of the environmental strains induced by agriculture, from soil erosion to overpumping of underground water.

In consumption of raw materials, such as steel, cotton, or wood, the same pattern emerges. A large group lacks many of the benefits provided by modest use of nonrenewable resources—particularly durables like radios, refrigerators, water pipes, tools, and carts with lightweight wheels and ball bearings. More than two billion people live in countries where per capita consumption of steel, the most basic modern material, falls below 50 kilograms a year.

Roughly 1.5 billion live in the middle class of materials use. Providing each of them with durable goods every year uses between 50 and 150 kilograms of steel. At the top of the heap is the industrial world or the throwaway class. A typical resident of the industrialized fourth of the world uses 15 times as much paper, 10 times as much steel, and 12 times as much fuel as a Third World resident.

In the throwaway economy, packaging becomes an end in itself, disposables proliferate, and durability suffers. Americans toss away 180 million razors annually, enough paper and plastic plates and cups to feed the world a picnic six times a year, and enough aluminum cans to make 6,000 DC-10 airplanes. Similarly, the Japanese use 30 million "disposable" single-roll cameras each year, and the British dump 2.5 billion diapers.

The Cultivation of Needs

What prompts us to consume so much? "The avarice of mankind is insatiable," wrote Aristotle 23 centuries ago. As each of our desires is satisfied, a new one appears in its place. All of economic theory is based on that observation.

What distinguishes modern consuming habits, some would say, is simply that we are much richer than our ancestors, and consequently have more ruinous effects on nature. While a great deal of truth lies in that view, five distinctly modern factors play a role in cultivating particularly voracious appetites: the influence of social pressures in mass societies, advertising, the shopping culture, various government policies, and the expansion of the mass market into households and local communities.

In advanced industrial nations, daily interactions with the economy lack the face-to-face character prevailing in surviving local communities. Traditional virtues such as integrity, honesty, and skill are too hard to measure to serve as yardsticks of social worth. By default, they are gradually supplanted by a simple, single indicator—money. As one Wall Street banker put it bluntly to the *New York Times*, "Net worth equals self-worth."

Beyond social pressures, the affluent live completely enveloped in pro-consumption advertising messages. The sales pitch is everywhere. One analyst estimates that the typical American is exposed to 50 to 100 advertisements each morning before nine o'clock. Along with their weekly 22-hour diet of television, American teenagers are typically exposed to three to four hours of TV advertisements a week, adding up to at least 100,000 ads between birth and high school graduation.

Advertising has been one of the fastest-growing industries during the past half-century. In the United States, ad expenditures rose from $198 per capita in 1950 to $498 in 1989 to $930 for every man, woman, and child in the country in 2007. Worldwide, over the same period, per person advertising expenditures grew from $15 in 1950 to $46 in 1989 and $71 in 2002. In developing countries, the increases have been astonishing. Advertising billings in India jumped fivefold in the 1980s; newly industrialized South Korea's advertising industry grew 3540% annually in the late 1980s.

Government policies also play a role in promoting consumption and in worsening its ecological impact. The British tax code, for example, encourages businesses to buy thousands of large company cars for employee use. Most governments in North and South America subsidize beef production on a massive scale.

Finally, the sweeping advance of the commercial mass market into realms once dominated by family members and local enterprise has made consumption far more wasteful than in the past. More and more, flush with cash but pressed for time, households opt for the questionable "conveniences" of prepared, packaged foods, miracle cleaning products, and disposable everything—from napkins to shower curtains. All these things cost the earth dearly.

Like the household, the community economy has atrophied—or been dismembered—under the blind force of the money economy. Shopping malls, superhighways, and strips have replaced corner stores, local restaurants, and neighborhood theaters—the very places that help create a sense of common identity and community. Traditional Japanese vegetable stands and fish shops are giving way to supermarkets and convenience stores, and styrofoam and plastic film have replaced yesterday's newspaper as fish wrap.

All these things nurture the acquisitive desires that everyone has. Can we, as individuals and as citizens, act to confront these forces?

The Culture of Permanence

The basic value of a sustainable society, the ecological equivalent of the Golden Rule, is simple: Each generation should meet its own needs without jeopardizing the prospects of future generations to meet theirs.

For individuals, the decision to live a life of sufficiency—to find their own answer to the question "how much is enough?"—is to begin a highly personal process. Social researcher Duane Elgin estimated in 1981—perhaps optimistically—that 10 million adult Americans were experimenting "wholeheartedly" with voluntary simplicity. India, the Netherlands, Norway, Western Germany, and the United Kingdom all have small segments of their populations who adhere to a non-consuming philosophy. Motivated by the desire to live justly in an unjust world, to walk gently on the earth, and to avoid distraction, clutter, and pretense, their goal is not ascetic self-denial but personal fulfillment. They do not think consuming more is likely to provide it.

Realistically, voluntary simplicity is unlikely to gain ground rapidly against the onslaught of consumerist values. And, ultimately, personal restraint will do little if not wedded to bold political and social steps against the forces promoting consumption. Commercial television, for example, will need fundamental reorientation in a culture of permanence. As religious historian Robert Bellah put it, "That happiness is to be attained through limitless material acquisition is denied by every religion and philosophy known to humankind, but is preached incessantly by every American television set."

Direct incentives for overconsumption are also essential targets for reform. If goods' prices reflected something closer to the environmental cost of their production, through revised subsidies and tax systems, the market itself would guide consumers toward less damaging forms of consumption. Disposables and packaging would rise in price relative to durable, less-packaged goods; local unprocessed food would fall in price relative to prepared products trucked from far away.

The net effect might be lower overall consumption as people's effective purchasing power declined. As currently constituted, unfortunately, economies penalize the poor when aggregate consumption contracts: Unemployment skyrockets and inequalities grow. Thus arises one of the greatest challenges for sustainable economics in rich societies—finding ways to ensure basic employment opportunities for all without constantly stoking the fires of economic growth.

Article 3.4

AMERICA BEYOND CONSUMERISM
Has capitalist economic growth outlived its purpose?

BY THAD WILLIAMSON
May/June 2008

O ne of the great benefits of studying the history of economic ideas is coming to the recognition that the founding figures of capitalist economics, and in particular Adam Smith, author of the pivotal *Wealth of Nations*, were often deeply ambivalent about the acquisitive way of life. Consider the famous parable of the poor man's son, presented by Smith in his *Theory of Moral Sentiments*:

> The poor man's son, whom heaven in its anger has visited with ambition, when he begins to look around him, admires the condition of the rich. He finds the cottage of his father too small for his accommodation, and fancies he should be lodged more at his ease in a palace. He is displeased with being obliged to walk a-foot, or to endure the fatigue of riding on horseback. He sees his superiors carried about in machines, and imagines that in one of these he could travel with less inconveniency. ... He thinks if he had attained all these, he would sit still contentedly, and be quiet, enjoying himself in the thought of the happiness and tranquility of his situation. He is enchanted with the distant idea of this felicity. It appears in his fancy like the life of some superior rank of beings, and, in order to arrive at it, he devotes himself forever to the pursuit of wealth and greatness. To obtain the conveniencies which these afford, he submits in the first year, nay in the first month of his application, to more fatigue of body and more uneasiness of mind than he could have suffered through the whole of his life from want of them. He studies to distinguish himself in some laborious profession. With the most unrelenting industry he labours night and day to acquire talents superior to all his competitors. He endeavours next to bring those talents into public view, and with equal assiduity solicits every opportunity of employment. For this purpose he makes his court to all mankind; he serves those whom he hates, and is obsequious to those whom he despises. Through the whole of his life he pursues the idea of a certain artificial and elegant repose which he may never arrive at, for which he sacrifices a real tranquility that is at all times in his power, and which if in the extremity of old age, he should at last attain to it, he will find to be in no respect preferable to that humble security and contentment which he had abandoned for it. It is then ... that he begins at last to find that wealth and greatness are mere trinkets of frivolous utility, no more adapted for procuring ease of body or tranquility of mind than the tweezer-cases of the lover of toys; and like them too, more troublesome to the person who carries them about with him than all the advantages they can afford him...
>
> In his heart he curses ambition, and vainly regrets the ease and the indolence of youth, pleasures which are fled for ever, and which he has foolishly sacrificed for what, when he has got it, can afford him no real satisfaction.

Adam Smith, traditionally regarded as the patron saint of capitalist economics, here avers that the fundamental engines of the market economy—ambition and acquisitiveness—rest on what he terms a "deception," the illusion that all the objects we spend our days striving for will make us happy.

Fast forward over 200 years. Here is how a contemporary economist, Juliet Schor of Boston College, describes "Greg," a sixth grader in a Boston suburb, in her 2004 book *Born to Buy: The Commercialized Child and the New Consumer Culture*:

> Greg is an avid consumer. He loves professional wrestling, Gameboy, Nintendo, television, movies, junk food, and CDs (especially those with parental advisories). Since he came to live with his [father and step-mother], they've had a succession of incidents, most of which resulted in Greg's losing privileges to one or another of these things. He isn't allowed to do wrestling moves on his younger sister, but he does, and he loses the right to watch wrestling. He's supposed to do his homework, but he has lied and said he doesn't have any so he can spend his time playing a new Gameboy. He's supposed to tell the truth, but he stole [his stepmom's] Snickers bar and denied it. He knows he's not allowed to have CDs with parental advisories, but he went behind [his parents]' back and asked his [biological] mother to buy them for him...
>
> Another couple described their son Doug as "the ultimate consumer." He wanted to buy every product he saw advertised on television. Doug was now in sixth grade, and they were fighting constant battles. He would stay on the computer all day if they let him. He has a weakness for fast food. He has a lot of trouble holding on to money. His mother even described trying to sneak out to the store without him to avoid conflicts about buying stuff.

Schor was stunned to find that persistent parent-child conflicts over money and goods were widespread, not confined to a few severe cases like Greg and Doug. In a survey of some 300 Boston-area fifth and sixth graders, Schor found strong evidence of a causal relationship between heavier involvement in consumer culture and strained relationships with parents, greater feelings of boredom and physical pain, higher levels of depression and anxiety, and lower self-esteem.

This finding is troubling precisely because corporate advertisers, as Schor and others have amply documented, have become increasingly brazen in the past 10 to 15 years about marketing directly to children, with the explicit purpose of establishing brand identifications and consumer loyalty as early as possible. By age ten, the average American kid is aware of over 300 specific brand names. A particular goal of this marketing is to persuade children to nag their parents to buy them things. A recent study reveals that the average American child aged three to eight now nags his or her parents nearly five times a day for material goods. Furthermore, research shows that over 80% of parents respond positively to such nagging at least some of the time, and marketers have estimated that up to one-half of sales of popular products for kids are a direct result of children nagging their parents. Probably not coincidentally, since the 1970s, as the impact of commercial culture on childhood has increased, the observed mental and physical health outcomes of American children, including levels of depression, obesity, and attention deficit disorder, have worsened.

So maybe it's not good to be obsessed with consumer goods, or to be, consciously or subconsciously, the slave of some advertising executive who knows how to play on your insecurities, self-image, and aspirations. But isn't money, at some level, necessary to make us happy?

Here the answer is slightly more complicated, but a large body of research—much of it usefully summarized by political scientist Robert Lane in his 2000 book *The Loss of Happiness in Market Democracies*—suggests it is not at all inconsistent with the view Aristotle expressed over 2,000 years ago: we need some material goods to be happy, but not an excess of them. Consider evidence from the Social Capital Community Benchmark Survey, a survey of some 33,050 Americans conducted by the Saguaro Center for Civic Engagement at Harvard in 2000. Among many other topics, this survey asked people how happy they are, allowing researchers to assess the most important predictors of greater happiness. How does income stack up in importance compared to having friends, confidantes, and close family relationships, and to being an active member of the community?

The survey data suggest that holding other demographic factors equal, an individual who earns $30,000 to $50,000 a year, visits with relatives three times a month, has at least ten "close friends" and at least three people he or she can confide in, and belongs to a religious congregation as well as three other organizations has a 47.5% likelihood of self-reporting as "very happy." In contrast, consider someone demographically alike in all other respects who earns over $100,000 a year, but visits with relatives just one time a month, has only one to two "close friends," has only one person to confide in, is not part of a religious congregation, and belongs to only one organization. That person—richer in income but poorer in social connections—is estimated to have just a 28.6% chance of feeling "very happy."

Now, it's true that higher income, while not connected at all to family visits, is somewhat correlated with having more friends and confidantes and even more strongly associated with increased group memberships. Nor can anyone deny that economic circumstances influence well-being: controlling for other factors, moving from $30,000-$50,000 to over $100,000 a year in income is associated with a substantial rise in the likelihood of being "very happy"—from 34.4% to 45.3%. But the projected increase in the likelihood of being "very happy" associated with moving from having just three to five friends and two confidantes to over ten friends and at least three confidantes is even more substantial (from 32.2% to 44.2%). For most people, making five new friends and developing one or two especially close friendships are more realistic goals than doubling their income. The evidence suggests that expanding social ties is also a better strategy for finding happiness—especially if the alternative, chasing after more income, comes at the cost of fewer friends and weaker social connections. Income matters in shaping subjective well-being, but social connections matter more.

It would be misleading to leave the story at that, however. So far we have only been discussing raw income figures. But a closer look reveals that what people value more than their raw income is a sense of being *satisfied* with their economic circumstances. When we include both measures in statistical models predicting individual happiness, economic satisfaction predominates; it's a far more powerful predictor of well-being than absolute income. *Controlling for income level,* individuals who are "very satisfied," "somewhat satisfied," or "not at all satisfied" with their economic circumstances have sharply divergent chances of being very happy: 48.7%, 33.3%, and 20.8% respectively. In contrast, if we control for people's level of economic satisfaction, more income does relatively little to promote happiness: a leap from the $30,000–$50,000 income bracket to the over-$100,000 bracket implies an increase of just four percentage points in the predicted likelihood of being "very happy," from 34.8% to 38.9%. Put another way, a person earning $30,000 to $50,000 who reports being "very satisfied" with her financial condition has, controlling for other factors, a 48.8% likelihood of being "very happy," whereas a person earning over $100,000 who is only "somewhat satisfied" with her financial condition has just a 37.5% likelihood of being "very happy." How much money one earns is, in itself, not an overwhelmingly decisive factor driving individual well-being, but being satisfied with what one has certainly is.

What is it that allows people to be happy with what they have? It could be that people who are psychologically disposed to be happier also tend to look more positively on whatever economic circumstances they find themselves in. But it's equally if not more plausible to think that two other factors drive economic satisfaction: a sense of economic security—in other words, knowing that you will be able to sustain your current lifestyle in the future—and freedom from the compulsion to compare your own versus others' income and consumption. But as scholars like Jacob Hacker and Robert Frank have pointed out, recent political-economic trends in the United States have had precisely the effect of weakening economic security and encouraging social comparisons. In his recent book *Falling Behind*, Frank insightfully discusses how the explosion in consumption by the super-rich in the last 20 years has shaped the behavior of middle- and upper-middle-class households, who feel that they too should have a bigger house or, to take Frank's favorite illustration, a more expensive barbecue grill.

If Consuming More Doesn't Make Us Happier, What's the Point of Capitalism?

This brings us back to Adam Smith, who anticipated much of this body of evidence when he described the poor man's son who forsakes enjoyment of life for a life of industry and self-advancement as suffering from a fundamental delusion. Yet this insight did not lead Smith to reject capitalism. On the contrary, he thought this deception had a socially productive purpose: namely, helping to fuel economic progress, the advancement of industry, and the gradual rise of living standards—not just the living standards of the rich, but the living standards of average working people as well.

Indeed, in the subsequent 200 years, capitalism—or more accurately, capitalism modified by a range of state interventions, public spending, social welfare programs, and labor laws—has been remarkably successful in lifting overall living standards in places like the United Kingdom and the United States (albeit with often enormous social costs borne by millions of nameless workers who labored for capitalist employers under horrific conditions, enforced by the threat of hunger, and in some cases literally at gunpoint). In the 20th century alone, per capita income in the United States increased eightfold and life expectancy rose from 49 to 77 years.

That's the good news. The bad news is, median wage growth has stalled in the United States in the last 30 years, and has gone backwards for the least educated Americans. Total hours worked per household have risen as women work longer hours without a corresponding reduction in men's work hours. The hope of a secure, stable job has all but disappeared—hence today's widespread feelings of economic insecurity and dissatisfaction across income brackets. More to the point, there is good reason to doubt that simply continuing to "grow the economy" is going to address any of these concerns—or make most people any happier.

Consider just how rich a society this is. The U.S. Gross Domestic Product now stands at $13.8 trillion. If it were divided equally, that would come to over $180,000 for a family of four, or about $125,000 in take-home pay assuming an effective tax rate of 30%. In other words, the U.S. economy is large enough to provide a very comfortable life for each and every American.

But it doesn't. Why not?

A skyrocketing degree of economic inequality is one reason. The median income for married couple households in 2006 was $70,000, with of course many families making far, far less. While the income and wealth of the top 1% spike to unimaginable levels, many Americans simply do not have enough money to get by. With inequality comes not just poverty, but also widening disparities in status which themselves help fuel ever-greater levels of consumption as people spend more and more to try to keep up with the (ever-richer) Joneses.

The second reason is the widespread fact of economic insecurity. People whose jobs, health coverage, wage levels, and pensions are fragile naturally feel pressure to accumulate and advance as far as they can, lest they fall behind and lose what they now have. And, every week, we read about workers and communities who do in fact lose what they have as layoffs and plant shutdowns are announced. As we have seen, survey data (as well Adam Smith's intuitions) suggest that what matters most for well-being is the sense that one has enough and can feel comfortable about the future—that is, the very thing that the American economy fails to provide to the vast majority of families.

This insecurity is most potent in blue-collar America, but the middle class does not escape it either. Consider the life pattern of the average white-collar American. To go to college and get ahead, you have to borrow money and incur debt; to pay off the debt, you're under pressure to land a high-paying job; when you start a family, financial responsibilities multiply: you take on a mortgage, begin paying for child care or else accept a drop in household income, and within a few years face the stark realization that unless you make enough to either pay for private education or live in a neighborhood with good public schools, your children's education will suffer; and by the time you are finally done paying your children's college costs, it's already past time to begin building a nest egg for retirement and a cushion against illness. At no point does it seem to most people prudent—or even possible—simply to get off the treadmill.

Little wonder, then, that the Harvard social capital survey found just 26% of Americans to be "very satisfied" with their economic status (including just 54% of those making over $100,000 a year). It is impossible to address the issue of runaway consumerism without also addressing the issue of economic security. Indeed, as Knox College psychologist Tim Kasser, author of *The High Price of Materialism*, notes, a host of studies by psychologists and others demonstrate a strong relationship between numerous kinds of insecurity, especially economic insecurity, and the development of a materialist outlook on life.

This brings us to the third major reason the U.S. economy fails to foster a comfortable life for most Americans: long hours and overwork. Stress, fatigue, and sleep deprivation have become hallmarks of the American way of life. Over three-quarters of Americans report feeling stressed at least "sometimes," with a full one-third saying they experience stress "frequently." (The figures are higher still for persons holding jobs and for parents.) Likewise, roughly one-half of all Americans—including three-fifths of employed workers, parents, and persons aged 18 to 49—say they do not have enough time to do what they would like to in daily life, such as spend time with friends. Harvard political scientist Robert Putnam reports that the percentage of Americans regularly eating dinner together declined by one-third between 1977 and 1999. Research by the Families and Work Institute indicates that almost two-thirds (63%) would like to work fewer hours. On average those questioned said they would reduce their work week by more than ten hours if they could. But what people want and what the political economy provides are two different things: in the past generation, the centuries-long trend towards reducing the length of the work week has come to a screeching halt.

So the U.S. economy, as presently constituted, produces tremendous inequality, insecurity, and overwork. Nor is there reason to think that growing from a $14 trillion to, say, a $20 or $25 trillion economy will change these destructive trends.

It doesn't have to be this way. There is no inherent reason why we could not cease to regard more income as a good in itself, but instead alter our political economy so that it provides what Americans really need and want: greater employment security, stronger protection against the pitfalls of poverty, and more free time. We could choose to have the public guarantee employment opportunities for every willing worker, to put a floor on income, to decommodify health care and education, to reduce the gross inequalities of income and status which themselves help fuel consumerism, and to take future productivity growth in the form of more time, not more stuff.

To be sure, doing so would not be easy, and would require substantial institutional changes, possibly even a shift to a system that, as economist Gar Alperovitz puts it, lies "beyond capitalism." Many careful analysts, including Alperovitz and Schor, have thought long and hard about just how that could happen; indeed, there has been a rich debate in the past 15 years about the long-term possibilities of alternative political-economic frameworks that would reshape the logic of our current system.

It would be very easy to dismiss these ideas as "crazy" or "utopian." But, I submit, the moral task Adam Smith set for capitalism—that of making it economically possible for each and every person to live a materially comfortable life—has been achieved, at least in the advanced industrialized countries. The acquisitive life that goes with capitalism Smith never endorsed as good in itself. Neither should we, especially given the unhealthy consequences of an excessive consumerism that is now warping children's lives from their earliest years, and given the potentially planet-melting consequences of a way of life based on continual increases in consumption and economic activity.

That wasn't what Adam Smith wanted. Nor was it what the most influential and pragmatic of 20th-century economists, John Maynard Keynes, the man many credit with saving capitalism from itself, wanted. In a famous but too often neglected essay called "Economic Possibilities for Our Grandchildren," Keynes looked to a time when at last it would be possible for humanity (at least in the affluent nations) to turn its attention away from acquisition and toward broader moral concerns— such as "how to use his freedom from pressing economic cares, how to occupy the leisure, which science and compound interest will have won for him, to live wisely and agreeably and well."

That time has not yet come. But the remaining barriers to it are political, not economic; and the great task of this century is to assure that our prodigious economic capacities are directed towards supplying the real goods of human life: material security, meaningful work, and plentiful time for the friends and family who are the most lasting source of human happiness.

Sources: Adam Smith, *The Theory of Moral Sentiments* (1759) (Liberty Fund, 1984); Juliet Schor, *Born to Buy: The Commercialized Child and the New Consumer Culture* (Scribner, 2004); Tim Kasser, *The High Price of Materialism* (MIT Press, 2002); "Half of Americans are Pressed for Time; A Third Are Stressed Out," *Gallup News Svc*, May 3, 2004; "No time for R&R," *Gallup News Svc*, May 11, 2004; "Who Dreams, Perchance to Sleep?" *Gallup News Svc*, Jan. 25, 2005; Robert Putnam, *Bowling Alone: The Collapse and Revival of American Community* (Simon & Schuster, 2000); J. Bond, E. Galinsky, and J. Swanberg, *The 1997 National Study of the Changing Workforce*, Families and Work Institute, 1998; Gar Alperovitz, *America Beyond Capitalism: Reclaiming Our Wealth, Our Liberty, and Our Democracy* (Wiley, 2004); Jerome Segal, *Graceful Simplicity: Towards a Philosophy and Politics of Simple Living* (Henry Holt, 1999); Juliet Schor, *A Sustainable Economy for the 21st Century* (Open Media, 1995); John Maynard Keynes, *Essays in Persuasion* (W.W. Norton, 1963); Jacob S. Hacker, *The Great Risk Shift* (Oxford Univ. Press, 2006); Robert H. Frank, *Falling Behind: How Rising Inequality Harms the Middle Class* (Univ. of Calif. Press, 2007); Robert E. Lane, *The Loss of Happiness in Market Democracies* (Yale Univ. Press, 2000); Robert M. Biswas-Diener, "Material Wealth and Subjective Well-Being," in M. Eid and R. J. Larsen, eds., *The Science of Subjective Well-Being* (Guilford Press, 2008).

Chapter 4

FIRMS, PRODUCTION, AND PROFIT MAXIMIZATION

INTRODUCTION

How do producers make decisions? Textbooks describe a process that is rational, benign, and downright sensible. There is one best—that is, least costly and most profitable—way to produce any given amount of goods or services. Given a particular scale of operations, there is one most profitable amount to produce. Businesses adjust their total output and the mix of inputs at the margin until they achieve these most profitable outcomes. They pay the going wage for labor, just as they pay the going price for any input. And when businesses have achieved the lowest possible costs, market competition ensures that they pass on savings to consumers.

This chapter describes a reality that is more complicated, and in some ways uglier than the textbook model. John Miller opens the discussion by suggesting that there may not be just "one best way" for retail businesses, but rather two—a "high road" based on high levels of service, skilled, decently-paid employees and higher prices, as exemplified by the business model at Costco; and a "low road" that offers low prices, no frills, and a low-paid, high-turnover workforce, which is Wal-Mart's business model. Despite Wal-Mart's growth and its position as the world's largest retailer, the author questions whether the business model has in fact proven beneficial for the U.S. economy as a whole (Article 4.1).

Roger Bybee points to a particularly egregious case of "low road" profit making that threatens to undermine the economy's ability to recover from this recession (Article 4.2). Bybee documents how corporations such as ArcelorMittal are closing *profitable* plants and laying off unionized workers. Doing so when there are no other willing buyers for a factory is one thing, but these closures are occurring despite the interest other corporations have shown in buying these plants. In part, this is because companies such as ArcelorMittal strip out the machines and equipment inside these factories and reinstall them abroad; but another reason is that they are unwilling to give up the tax breaks they receive when they close down "loss-making" units. Not only does this "anti-stimulus" strategy cost the U.S. economy precious unionized jobs with benefits, it adds to unemployment, making it harder for all of us to escape the effects of the recession.

Siobhán McGrath and Nina Martin discuss some of the less obvious factors enabling this "low-road" strategy in their article on unregulated work in the United States (Article 4.3). Global competition is certainly one such factor, but the authors find the same trends in businesses insulated from global competition. They point out that U.S. immigration policy is a less explored but equally important factor, as is the state's reluctance to enforce existing labor laws.

Arthur MacEwan then looks *inside* large companies and asks how they set CEO salaries. He concludes that executive pay does not fit with the "one best way" analysis of business decision-making. According to MacEwan, corporate directors set executive pay at high levels not because of profit-maximizing principles, but because they themselves are top executives—peers and in some cases buddies of the CEOs whose compensation they are deciding. But more fundamentally, the much higher CEO pay in the United States than elsewhere reflects the fact that work is organized differently in different countries—again, a departure from the idea of "one best way" (Article 4.4). Thomas Palley offers a very concise and useful metaphor for the effect of globalization and outsourcing on productive industry in the United States (Article 4.5). And in an industry study of the financial sector (Article 4.6), Robert Larson explains how deregulation and the pursuit of economies of scale and scope helped create banks that were deemed "too big to fail" in the recent financial crisis.

All of these articles argue that the purchase and utilization of labor raises social and moral questions different from those involved in other decisions about production. They suggest that businesses' pursuit of profit may have unacceptable costs to workers. What's more, they maintain that production can be organized in a variety of different ways, with very different implications for workers' well-being.

Discussion Questions

1) (General) Do you agree that the use and purchase of labor raises different issues other than inputs for production? Why or why not?

2) (Article 4.1) John Miller implies that there is more than one "best" way to organize production. Do you agree? If other ways of organizing production are equally good, why are certain ways dominant, at least in particular industries?

3) (Article 4.1) Miller suggests that we should change the rules of the competitive game to steer businesses toward better treatment of workers. Current-day capitalism already has some such rules (such as those forbidding slavery), so it makes sense to think through what rules would best meet our goals as a society. What rule changes do each of these articles propose? What do you think of these proposals? Would other rule changes work better? Or do you think we should leave the rules as they are?

4) (Article 4.1) Given the comparatively low wages at Wal-Mart, why do you think there is still strong demand for Wal-Mart jobs? Would you characterize this labor market as being "free"?

5) (Articles 4.1 and 4.5) Both Miller and Palley discuss how the promise of low prices allows Wal-Mart to get away with its labor practices. What is each author's response to this claim of "low prices"? According to Cervantes (sidebar, p. 91), how does Costco keep prices low while following very different labor practices?

6) (Article 4.1) Miller discusses the ways in which Wal-Mart minimizes labor costs. When does aggressive cost-cutting cross the line? Would you draw the line at law-breaking, or are there some legal business practices—in addition to illegal ones—that you consider unacceptable?

7) (Article 4.2) What explains the corporate strategy Bybee calls "counter-stimulus"? Bybee argues that this strategy constitutes an illegitimate and socially costly pursuit of profits. How does he justify his opinion?

8) (Article 4.2) What are some strategies unions are pursuing to counter this "counter-stimulus" corporate strategy? What do you think is the appropriate role of the government here?

9) (Article 4.3) Why do McGrath and Martin believe that global competition alone cannot explain the rise of unregulated work? How does U.S. immigration policy contribute to the situation?

10) (Article 4.4) MacEwan maintains that in the case of CEO compensation, boards of directors pay high salaries rather than minimizing costs because they see it as the "right" thing to do. Do companies do this in areas other than executive pay? Why doesn't competition drive out such practices?

11) (Article 4.5) In the article by Thomas Palley, he argues that the relative benefits and costs of "globalization" are not evenly distributed. Some folks gain from globalization and others lose. What is "Palley's Clock"? Explain in detail the metaphor and mechanism.

12) (Article 4.5) Does Palley's assessment of globalization differ at all from your text-book's? What time is it according to "Palley's Clock"?

13) (Article 4.6) Explain how "economies of scale" and "economies of scope" shaped the U.S. banking industry, according to Robert Larson. What are the arguments for and against greater regulation in that sector?

14) (General) The authors in this chapter present various corporate strategies as a choice, rather than an imperative. How does this compare with the standard microeconomic analysis of business decision-making?

Article 4.1

WHAT'S GOOD FOR WAL-MART . . .

BY JOHN MILLER
January/February 2006

"Is Wal-Mart Good for America?"

It is a testament to the public relations of the anti-Wal-Mart campaign that the question above is even being asked.

By any normal measure, Wal-Mart's business ought to be noncontroversial. It sells at low costs, albeit in mind-boggling quantities. ...

The company's success and size ... do not rest on monopoly profits or price-gouging behavior. It simply sells things people will buy at small markups and, as in the old saw, makes it up on volume. ... You may believe, as do service-workers unions and a clutch of coastal elites—many of whom, we'd wager, have never set foot in Wal-Mart—that Wal-Mart "exploits" workers who can't say no to low wages and poor benefits. You might accept the canard that it drives good local businesses into the ground, although both of these allegations are more myth than reality.

But even if you buy into the myths, there's no getting around the fact that somewhere out there, millions of people are spending billions of dollars on what Wal-Mart puts on its shelves. No one is making them do it. ... Wal-Mart can't make mom and pop shut down the shop anymore than it can make customers walk through the doors or pull out their wallets.

What about the workers? ... Wal-Mart's average starting wage is already nearly double the national minimum of $5.15 an hour. The company has also recently increased its health-care for employees on the bottom rungs of the corporate ladder.

—*Wall Street Journal* editorial, December 3, 2005

"Who's Number One? The Customer! Always!" The last line of Wal-Mart's company cheer just about sums up the *Wall Street Journal* editors' benign view of the behemoth corporation. But a more honest answer would be Wal-Mart itself: not the customer, and surely not the worker.

The first retail corporation to top the Fortune 500, Wal-Mart trailed only Exxon-Mobil in total revenues last year. With 1.6 million workers, 1.3 million in the United States and 300,000 offshore, Wal-Mart is the largest private employer in the nation and the world's largest retailer.

Being number one has paid off handsomely for the family of Wal-Mart founder Sam Walton. The family's combined fortune is now an estimated $90 billion, equal to the net worth of Bill Gates and Warren Buffett combined.

But is what's good for the Walton family good for America? Should we believe the editors that Wal-Mart's unprecedented size and market power have redounded not only to the Walton family's benefit but to ours as well?

Low Wages and Meager Benefits

Working for the world's largest employer sure hasn't paid off for Wal-Mart's employees. True, they have a job, and others without jobs line up to apply for theirs. But that says more about the sad state of today's labor market than the quality of Wal-Mart jobs. After all, less than half of Wal-Mart workers last a year, and turnover at the company is twice that at comparable retailers.

Why? Wal-Mart's oppressive working conditions surely have something to do with it. Wal-Mart has admitted to using minors to operate hazardous machinery, has been sued in six states for forcing employees to work off the books (i.e., unpaid) and without breaks, and is currently facing a suit brought by 1.6 million current and former female employees accusing Wal-Mart of gender discrimination. At the same time, Wal-Mart workers are paid less and receive fewer benefits than other retail workers.

Wal-Mart, according to its own reports, pays an average of $9.68 an hour. That is 12.4% below the average wage for retail workers even after adjusting for geography, according to a recent study by Arindrajit Dube and Steve Wertheim, economists at the University of California's Institute of Industrial Relations and long-time Wal-Mart researchers. Wal-Mart's wages are nearly 15% below the average wage of workers at large retailers and about 30% below the average wage of unionized grocery workers. The average U.S. wage is $17.80 an hour; Costco, a direct competitor of Wal-Mart's Sam's Club warehouse stores, pays an average wage of $16 an hour (see sidebar, p. 91).

Wal-Mart may be improving its benefits, as the *Journal's* editors report, but it needs to. Other retailers provide health care coverage to over 53% of their workers, while Wal-Mart covers just 48% of its workers. Costco, once again, does far better, covering 82% of its employees. Moreover, Wal-Mart's coverage is far less comprehensive than the plans offered by other large retailers. Dube reports that according to 2003 IRS data, Wal-Mart paid 59% of the health care costs of its workers and dependents, compared to the 77% of health care costs for individuals and 68% for families the average retailer picks up.

A recent internal Wal-Mart memo leaked to the *New York Times* confirmed the large gaps in Wal-Mart's health care coverage and exposed the high costs those gaps impose on government programs. According to the memo, "Five percent of our Associates are on Medicaid compared to an average for national employees of 4 percent. Twenty-seven percent of Associates' children are on such programs, compared to a national average of 22 percent. In total, 46 percent of Associates' children are either on Medicaid or are uninsured."

A considerably lower 29% of children of all large-retail workers are on Medicaid or are uninsured. Some 7% of the children of employees of large retailers go uninsured, compared to the 19% reported by Wal-Mart.

Wal-Mart's low wages drag down the wages of other retail workers and shutter downtown retail businesses. A 2005 study by David Neumark, Junfu Zhang, and Stephen Ciccarella, economists at the University of California at Irvine, found that Wal-Mart adversely affects employment and wages. Retail workers in a community with a Wal-Mart earned 3.5% less because Wal-Mart's low prices force other businesses to lower prices, and hence their wages, according to the Neumark study. The same study also found that Wal-Mart's presence reduces retail employment by 2% to 4%. While other studies have not found this negative employment effect, Dube's research also reports fewer retail jobs and lower wages for retail workers in metropolitan counties with a Wal-Mart. (Fully 85% of Wal-Mart stores are in metropolitan counties.) Dube figures that Wal-Mart's presence costs retail workers, at Wal-Mart and elsewhere, $4.7 billion a year in lost earnings.

In short, Wal-Mart's "everyday low prices" come at the expense of the compensation of Wal-Mart's own employees and lower wages and fewer jobs for retail workers in the surrounding area. That much remains true no matter what weight we assign to each of the measures that Wal-Mart uses to keep its costs down: a just-in-time inventory strategy, its ability to use its size to pressure suppliers for large discounts, a routinized work environment that requires minimal training, and meager wages and benefits.

How Low are Wal-Mart's Everyday Low Prices?

Even if one doesn't subscribe to the editors' position that it is consumers, not Wal-Mart, who cause job losses at downtown retailers, it is possible to argue that the benefit of Wal-Mart's low prices to consumers, especially low-income consumers, outweighs the cost endured by workers at Wal-Mart and other retailers. Jason Furman, New York University economist and director of economic policy for the 2004 Kerry-Edwards campaign, makes just such an argument. Wal-Mart's "staggering" low prices are 8% to 40% lower than people would pay elsewhere, according to Furman. He calculates that those low prices on average boost low-income families' buying power by 3% and more than offset the loss of earnings to retail workers. For Furman, that makes Wal-Mart "a progressive success story."

But exactly how much savings Wal-Mart affords consumers is far from clear. Estimates vary widely. At one extreme is a study Wal-Mart itself commissioned by Global Insight, an economic forecasting firm. Global Insight estimates Wal-Mart created a stunning savings of $263 billion, or $2,329 per household, in 2004 alone.

At the other extreme, statisticians at the U.S. Bureau of Labor Statistics found no price savings at Wal-Mart. Relying on Consumer Price Index data, the BLS found that Wal-Mart's prices largely matched those of its rivals, and that instances of lower prices at Wal-Mart could be attributed to lower quality products.

Both studies, which rely on the Consumer Price Index and aggregate data, have their critics. Furman himself allows that the Global Insight study is "overly simplistic" and says he "doesn't place as much weight on that one." Jerry Hausman, the M.I.T. economist who has looked closely at Wal-Mart's grocery stores, maintains that the CPI data that the Bureau of Labor Statistics relies on systematically miss the savings offered by "supercenters" such as Wal-Mart. To show the difference between prices at Wal-Mart and at other grocers, Hausman, along with Ephraim Leibtag, USDA Economic Research Service economist, used supermarket scanner data to examine the purchasing patterns of a national sample of 61,500 consumers from 1988 to 2001. Hausman and Leibtag found that Wal-Mart offers many identical food items at an average price about 15%-25% lower than traditional supermarkets.

The Costco Alternative?

Wall Street Prefers Wal-Mart

In an April 2004 online commentary, *BusinessWeek* praised Costco's business model but pointed out that Costco's wages cause Wall Street to worry that the company's "operating expenses could get out of hand." How does Costco compare to low-wage Wal-Mart on overhead expenses? At Costco, overhead is 9.8% of revenue; at Wal-Mart, it is 17%. Part of Costco's secret is that its better paid workers are also more efficient: Costco's operating profit per hourly employee is $13,647; each Wal-Mart employee only nets the company $11,039. Wal-Mart also spends more than Costco on hiring and training new employees: each one, according to Rutgers economist Eileen Appelbaum, costs the company $2,500 to $3,500. Appelbaum estimates that Wal-Mart's relatively high turnover costs the company $1.5 to $2 million per year.

Despite Costco's higher efficiency, Wall Street analysts like Deutsche Bank's Bill Dreher complain that "Costco's corporate philosophy is to put its customers first, then its employees, then its vendors, and finally its shareholders. Shareholders get the short end of the stick." Wall Street prefers Wal-Mart's philosopy: executives first, then shareholders, then customers, then vendors, and finally employees.

Average Hourly Wage		Percentage of U.S. Workforce in Unions		Employees Covered by Company Health Insurance		Employees Who Leave After One Year	
Wal-Mart	Costco	Wal-Mart	Costco	Wal-Mart	Costco	Sam's Club*	Costco
$9.68	$16.00	0.0%	17.9%	48%	82%	21%	6%

* Sam's Club is the Wal-Mart unit that competes directly with Costco.

In 2004, Wal-Mart paid CEO Lee Scott $5.3 million, while a full-time employee making the average wage would have received $20,134. Costco's CEO Jim Senegal received $350,000, while a full-time average employee got $33,280. And *BusinessWeek* intimates that the top job at Costco may be tougher than at Wal-Mart. "Management has to hustle to make the high-wage strategy work. It's constantly looking for ways to repackage goods into bulk items, which reduces labor, speeds up Costco's just-in-time inventory, and boosts sales per square foot. Costco is also savvier ... about catering to small shop owners and more affluent customers, who are more likely to buy in bulk and purchase higher-margin goods."

Costco's allegedly more affluent clientele may be another reason that its profit per employee is higher than Wal-Mart's and its overhead costs a lower percentage of revenue. However, Costco pays its employees enough that they could afford to shop there. As the *BusinessWeek* commentary noted, "the low-wage approach cuts into consumer spending and, potentially, economic growth."

—Esther Cervantes

While Hausman and Leibtag report substantial savings from shopping at Wal-Mart, they fall far short of the savings alleged in the Global Insight study. The Hausman and Leibtag study suggests a savings of around $550 per household per year, or about $56 billion in 2004, not $263 billion. Still, that is considerably more than the $4.7 billion a year in lost earnings to retail workers that Dube attributes to Wal-Mart.

But if "Wal-Mart hurts wages, not so much in retail, but across the whole country," as economist Neumark told *BusinessWeek*, then the savings to consumers from Wal-Mart's everyday low prices might not outweigh the lost wages to all workers. (Retail workers make up just 11.6% of U.S. employment.)

Nor do these findings say anything about the sweatshop conditions and wages in Wal-Mart's overseas subcontractors. One example: A recent Canadian Broadcasting Corporation investigative report found that workers in Bangladesh were being paid less than $50 a month (below even the United Nation's $2 a day measure of poverty) to make clothes for the Wal-Mart private label, Simply Basic. Those workers included ten- to thirteen-year-old children forced to work long hours in dimly lit and dirty conditions sewing "I Love My Wal-Mart" t-shirts.

Making Wal-Mart Do Better

Nonetheless, as Arindrajit Dube points out, the relevant question is not whether Wal-Mart creates more savings for consumers than losses for workers, but whether the corporation can afford to pay better wages and benefits.

Dube reasons that if the true price gap between Wal-Mart and its retail competitors is small, then Wal-Mart might not be in a position to do better—to make up its wage and benefit gap and still maintain its price advantage. But if Wal-Mart offers consumers only minor price savings, then its lower wages and benefits hardly constitute a progressive success story that's good for the nation.

If Wal-Mart's true price gap is large (say, the 25% price advantage estimated by Hausman), then Wal-Mart surely is in a position to do better. For instance, Dube calculates that closing Wal-Mart's 16% overall compensation gap with other large retailers would cost the company less than 2% of sales. Raising prices by two cents on the dollar to cover those increased compensation costs would be "eminently absorbable," according to Dube, without eating away much of the company's mind-boggling $10 billion profit (2004).

Measures that set standards to force Wal-Mart and all big-box retailers to pay decent wages and provide benefits are beginning to catch on. Chicago, New York City, and the state of Maryland have considered or passed laws that would require big-box retailers to pay a "living wage" or to spend a minimum amount per worker-hour for health benefits. The Republican board of Nassau County on Long Island passed an ordinance requiring that all big-box retailers pay $3 per hour toward health care. Wal-Mart's stake in making sure that such proposals don't become law or spread nationwide goes a long way toward explaining why 80% of Wal-Mart's $2 million in political contributions in 2004 went to Republicans.

Henry Ford sought to pay his workers enough so they could buy the cars they produced. Sam Walton sought to pay his workers so little that they could afford to shop nowhere else. And while what was good for the big automakers was probably never good for the nation, what is good for Wal-Mart, today's largest employer, is undoubtedly bad for economic justice.

Sources: "Is Wal-Mart Good for America?" *Wall Street Journal*, 12/3/05; "Gauging the Wal-Mart Effect," *WSJ*, 12/03/05; Arindrajit Dube & Steve Wertheim, "Wal-Mart and Job Quality—What Do We Know, and Should We Care?" 10/05; Jason Furman, "Wal-Mart: A Progressive Success Story," 10/05; Leo Hindery Jr., "Wal-Mart's Giant Sucking Sound," 10/05; A. Bernstein, "Some Uncomfortable Findings for Wal-Mart," *Business Week* online, 10/26/05, and "Wal-Mart: A Case for the Defense, Sort of," *Business Week* online, 11/7/05; Dube, Jacobs, and Wertheim, "The Impact of Wal-Mart Growth on Earnings Throughout the Retail Sector in Urban and Rural Counties," *Institute of Industrial Relations Working Paper*, UC Berkeley, 10/05; Dube, Jacobs, and Wertheim, "Internal Wal-Mart Memo Validates Findings of UC Berkeley Study," 11/26/05; Jerry Hausman and Ephraim Leibtag, "Consumer Benefits from Increased Competition in Shopping Outlets: Measuring the Effect of Wal-Mart," 10/05; Hausman and Leibtag, "CPI Bias from Supercenters: Does the BLS Know that Wal-Mart Exists?" *NBER Working Paper No. 10712*, 8/04; David Neumark, Junfu Zhang, and Stephen Ciccarella, "The Effects of Wal-Mart on Local Labor Markets," *NBER Working Paper No. 11782*, 11/05; Erin Johansson, "Wal-Mart: Rolling Back Workers' Wages, Rights, and the American Dream," American Rights at Work, 11/05; Wal-Mart Watch, "Spin Cycle"; CBC News, "Wal-Mart to cut ties with Bangladesh factories using child labour," 11/30/05; National Labor Committee, "10 to 13-year-olds Sewing 'I Love My Wal-Mart' Shirts," 12/05; Global Insight, "The Economic Impact of Wal-Mart," 2005.

Article 4.2

CORPORATE AMERICA'S COUNTER-STIMULUS STRATEGY
Firms decide to shut profitable plants while spurning buyers.

BY ROGER BYBEE
May/June 2009

"Is it too late? I hope not," said an exasperated Anthony Fortunato, president of the 260-worker United Steelworkers (USW) Local 2604 at an ArcelorMittal steel mill in Lackawanna, N.Y., as he and his members watched the mill being systematically taken apart.

An eager buyer has been pressing the company—the world's largest steel firm—for at least two months to sell the mill and thus keep the profitable operation open and the jobs alive. Fortunato is hoping the buyer will remain interested despite ArcelorMittal's aggressive drive to gut the mill. ArcelorMittal is rushing to dismantle complex, custom-built ovens and other equipment that will take months to replace.

Day by day, the dismantling continues relentlessly, with each step reducing the value of the mill. "Our members are getting sick watching this happen," said Fortunato.

Arcelor's plans to close the Lackawanna mill are occurring against the backdrop of a widely supported effort by President Barack Obama to stimulate the nation's flat-lining economy with the $787 billion American Recovery and Reinvestment Act. But even as Obama is moving to counter the nation's economic free-fall, major corporations are moving in the opposite direction when it comes to maintaining employment and consumer demand. A recent survey showed 71% of CEOs expecting more layoffs in the coming six months.

Not only are they accelerating the pace of outsourcing to low-wage nations like China, but there have been several recent instances of corporations closing profitable plants in the United States and then refusing to sell them to other companies interested in keeping the plants open and retaining the current workforce.

"These Jobs Aren't Coming Back"

The Lackawanna mill isn't ArcelorMittal's only closure. ArcelorMittal is also shutting down its Hennepin, Ill., steel mill, even though other firms have expressed strong interest in buying that mill, reports USW Local 7367 president David York.

At a moment when unemployment around Hennepin—about 100 miles west of Chicago—has hit 10%, ArcelorMittal is preparing to discard the 285 USW members who have performed the hard work of steel production.

The plant has been consistently profitable, earning $48.4 million even in a recessionary year like 2008. Yet ArcelorMittal is intent on shipping one product line to low-wage Brazil and another to France. Moreover, ArcelorMittal has rebuffed a proposal by another major steel company to buy the Hennepin mill and keep it running.

The Hennepin workers have little prospect of finding jobs paying anywhere close to the $70,000 their old jobs averaged, including overtime and productivity bonuses, says York. Few family-supporting jobs are available nearby.

And ArcelorMittal's strategy is not unique. Last fall, the Cerberus private equity group, through its NewPage subsidiary, shut down a highly profitable, technologically advanced paper mill in Kimberly, Wisc. Cerberus is headed by John Snow, former Treasury secretary under George W. Bush; Dan Quayle, former vice president under George H.W. Bush; and Richard Feinberg, who personally raked in $330 million in compensation from Cerberus in 2007. USW Local 2-9 President Andy Nirschl speculates that Cerberus (the name is derived from the mythological dogs who guard the gates of Hades) essentially wanted to raise paper prices by reducing capacity, regardless of the human cost to 600 workers and their families.

"This wasn't like the usual scenario we've seen again and again," says Nirschl, "where a corporation moves jobs to Mexico or China to increase their profits by paying less than a dollar an hour. This was a case of a corporation taking a productive, profitable plant and closing it, refusing to sell it to anyone." The paper mill turned a profit of $66 million in 2007, says Nirschl. Four firms showed interest in buying the plant, but Cerberus and NewPage remained uninterested, frankly admitting that it had no plan at all to market the plant to another buyer.

Meanwhile, many major firms are adopting what can best be described as a "counter-stimulus" economic program, precisely following what Nirschl called "the usual scenario." The *New York Times* reported on a massive wave of job offshoring and wholesale divesting of product lines.

"These jobs aren't coming back," John E. Silvia, chief economist at Wachovia in Charlotte, N.C., told the *Times*. "A lot of production either isn't going to happen at all, or it's going to happen somewhere other than the United States. There are going to be fewer stores, fewer factories, and fewer financial services operations. Firms are making strategic decisions that they don't want to be in their businesses."

"The decimation of employment in legacy American brands such as General Motors is a trend that's likely to continue," said Robert E. Hall, an economist at Stanford University's Hoover Institution.

Productive Base Goes Out the Window

Mark Meinster, a representative of the United Electrical Workers (UE) international, said that this latest round of job destruction is simply an intensification of trends visible in recent decades, but made all the more galling because of the wanton closing of profitable plants at a time when good jobs are increasingly scarce. "We see this every day," said Meinster. For the past 20 years, you have everything from out-and-out trickery to private equity firms transferring debt from a money-losing operation to a profitable plant, and then shutting down the plant and stripping its assets. "Meanwhile, our productive capacity completely goes out the window."

Meinster helped to coordinate the December sit-down strike at Chicago's Republic Windows and Doors. Workers there faced both an employer secretly moving equipment to a new non-union plant in Iowa and the Bank of America—which received $20 billion in grants and $118 billion in loan guarantees from the bank bailout—cutting off the firm's line of credit, which, in turn, deprived workers of vacation and severance pay.

With the plant already closed, the workers decided to take over the plant, thereby taking control of Republic's valuable inventory and holding it hostage. The result: Bank of America re-opened the financial spigot, the workers were paid, an environmentally oriented firm bought the plant and will be rehiring the workers, and the sit-down achieved worldwide fame.

The Republic sit-down also inspired non-union workers, faced with a plant closing at the Colibri Group jewelry factory in East Providence, R.I., to stage a sit-in. The action resulted in 15 arrests while intensifying pressure on the firm's owner, the Founders' Group private-equity firm.

UE Western Regional President Carl Rosen, who played a leading role in backing the sit-down strike, noted that the action—both illegal and highly unusual in the United States—ignited enormous support, including from President Obama. "We made our message everybody's message," explained Rosen. "This economy is failing because workers cannot buy back what they are making. Corporations are being bailed out and workers are being sold out."

"We're Willing to Sell"

As a Luxembourg-based firm owned by an Indian-born billionaire living in London, ArcelorMittal is clearly following the "take the money and run" model of Anglo-American capitalism. This system is far harsher than the Western European model in which employers' incentives have been more influenced by social-democratic traditions and the ongoing strength of the labor movement.

In Lackawanna, ArcelorMittal's foot-dragging on a potential sale could soon mean the loss of 260 jobs. "Until yesterday [March 26], the company was not admitting that they even had heard of any interested buyers," said USW Local 2604 president Fortunato. But the forceful intervention of Sen. Chuck Schumer (D-NY) finally produced a meeting between ArcelorMittal's U.S. CEO James Ripley and one interested buyer.

"At this point, we don't know the results of the negotiations," Fortunato told *Dollars & Sense*, the frustration and anxiety evident in his voice. The outcome of the negotiations may depend on whether ArcelorMittal's decision to aggressively dismantle the steel operation has made purchasing the existing, hollowed-out plant and re-starting production far more difficult and costly than simply beginning production from scratch.

The involvement of members of the U.S. Congress at Lackawanna—as at Hennepin and Kimberly—has forced the corporations to claim that they were willing to sell the plants and retain jobs. But once the meetings were concluded, corporate interest in selling and saving the jobs of local workers rapidly melted away. For example, a Cerberus/NewPage official was asked recently whether the company had any plans in place to market the Kimberly plant. The response: "No."

Cooperation: A One-Way Street

Particularly frustrating for Local 2604 is the fact that the union made such extensive efforts to assist the corporation. It lobbied successfully for a two-thirds reduction in their electricity costs, lined up training grants, and supported reductions in sales- and property-tax rates for the corporation. "We as a union have done a lot to help the company. They've tried to tell us we're not competitive as a plant. If that's the case, why not sell us?"

Rather than being grateful for the union's efforts to lower its costs, ArcelorMittal instead changed its internal accounting procedures so that the Lackawanna plant actually booked a loss, by charging that plant more for shipping and supplies from other ArcelorMittal plants around the United States. In that way, ArcelorMittal aimed to evade New York's higher corporate taxes, Fortunato suspects. Until ArcelorMittal made that shift in accounting, the plant had been consistently showing a profit of about $6 million a month.

With annual wages typically running in the $40,000-to-$50,000 range, his members will have a hard time finding comparable-paying work. Fortunato believes the real unemployment rate in Lackawanna, near the similarly hard-hit industrial city of Buffalo, is about 25% to 30%. "Our guys will have to work two or three jobs to make what they earn here," he said.

The process of watching the Lackawanna mill being slowly dismantled, with custom-made parts being wrecked by being disassembled or simply scrapped, is difficult for the workers who invested their lives in the plant, says Fortunato. "Our guys are getting sick at what they're scrapping."

The steelworkers in Illinois also complain of the corporation's indifference to commitments by the public to subsidize ArcelorMittal. ArcelorMittal's decision to locate its U.S. headquarters in Chicago unleashed a flow of incentives, including $2 million in assistance for furnishing corporate offices.

At the Hennepin plant, the union's current contract commits ArcelorMittal to keeping the plant open through the agreement and maintaining its viability through adequate investment. The union has taken the case to arbitration.

What Benefits? What Retraining?

As major corporations continue to undermine the impact of Obama's stimulus efforts by slashing jobs, the conventional wisdom among leading economists and elected officials in both parties is that worker retraining is the best public-policy response. As the *New York Times* put it recently, "For decades, the government has reacted to downturns by handing out temporary unemployment insurance checks, relying upon the resumption of economic growth to restore the jobs lost. This time, the government needs to place a greater emphasis on retraining workers for other careers."

But this approach, while conveniently allowing elected officials to sidestep an uncomfortable confrontation with corporations' unilateral control over the fate of workers and communities, has little empirical support as a successful strategy for "adapting" to deindustrialization and the offshoring of jobs. As the supply of family-supporting jobs is reduced, workers are essentially losing at a game of musical chairs in which good jobs are disappearing and not being replaced. When displaced workers successfully complete retraining programs, they are generally unable to find jobs comparable in pay and benefits to the ones they lost.

"Out of a hundred laid-off workers," says *New York Times* economics writer Louis Uchitelle in his book *The Disposable American: Layoffs and Their Consequences*, "27 are making their old salary again, or more, and 73 are making less, or not working at all." But even if retraining were an effective strategy, the very politicians who tout it as a solution have been unwilling to fund training in a serious way. Funding for training has plummeted from $20 billion in 1979 to just $6 billion last year (in constant dollars), according to one expert cited by the *Times*. These cutbacks in funding would seem to indicate that leading politicians, especially in the Bush era, were never quite sincere in their willingness to match their proclaimed faith in the power of retraining with an equivalent level of funding.

Further, the traditional unemployment-compensation safety net has been shredded over the past four decades, reaching a much smaller percentage of workers than in past, less severe recessions. During the 1975 recession, unemployment compensation reached 75% of the jobless and thus was a significant factor in restoring consumer demand. But thanks to radical cuts in unemployment compensation eligibility rammed through by the Reagan administration, only 45% of the unemployed received any benefits during the much more severe recession of 1982-83. The National Association of Manufacturers was delighted with the cutbacks in eligibility, crowing that under the old rules, "there was no incentive to go back to work under that program."

By 2003, the number of unemployed workers eligible for benefits had fallen further from the 1982 level of 45% down to just 41%, according to the Ohio-based

---

Corporate Royalty Ignores Workers' Years of Loyalty

Corporations are often accused of having an imperious, Marie Antoinette-style attitude toward their workers, unaware and uncaring about their daily struggles to provide for their families.

Marie Antoinette, wife of Louis XVI, was informed that the poor of Paris were too poor to afford bread. Her infamous response: "Let them eat cake." She was later beheaded in 1793 during the French Revolution.

But in the case of ArcelorMittal, which is preparing to shut down steel mills in Hennepin, Ill. and Lackawanna, N.Y., the comparison to Marie Antoinette may not be much of an exaggeration. The workers and local communities have been bewildered by the corporation's commitment to closing the profitable mills despite offers from other firms that wanted to keep them open.

Meanwhile, corporate CEO Lakshmi Mittal lives in near-royal grandeur in London in a $125 million home right next to the posh Kensington Palace. Mittal's home was constructed by combining the former Russian and Egyptian embassies. The swimming pool is inlaid with jewels, and the estate includes a 20-car garage. Lakshmi Mittal has a personal fortune estimated at $25 billion.

For the wedding of his daughter Vanisha, who is also a member of the corporation's board of directors, Mittal shelled out $55 million. If you're wondering how even the super-rich could manage to spend such a sum on a wedding, it might help to know that the five-day celebration was capped by a party—at Versailles.

That's right—Versailles, the magnificent and legendary palace that King Louis XVI gave to his 19-year-old bride, Marie Antoinette, as a wedding present. *Plus ça change...*

group Public Policy Matters. While Obama's American Recovery and Reinvestment Act may begin to reverse some cutbacks in eligibility, it remains to be seen how widely these changes will positively affect the fates of the jobless.

Needless Job Losses

The toll of unemployment extends far beyond a drop in family income, access to health care, and a loss of self-esteem for the displaced worker. Peter Dreier, a political scientist at Occidental College, recently released a study showing that each 1% increase in the national U.S. unemployment rate produces an additional 47,000 deaths, with 26,000 of the fatalities cardiac-related, 1,200 due to suicides, and 831 due to homicides.

Given these grim realities about passively accepting the consequences of deindustrialization, coupled with growing resentment about the greed and malfeasance of Wall Street, the egregious damage to workers and communities imposed by firms like Cerberus and ArcelorMittal may raise corporate investment decisions to a high-profile political issue. Corporations are closing profitable, productive plants in the midst of a severe economic crisis, and then capriciously refusing to seriously consider selling the plants to keep them open.

This would be unthinkable in a number of Western European democracies like Germany and Sweden that have long required that corporations provide a compelling rationale for shutdowns to regional government labor-market bodies. Most other Western European nations offer workers and communities some degree of protection from the effects of shutdowns, although not as extensively as in Germany or Sweden, nor with the same degree of worker and community participation in decisions about the company's plans.

In the United States, the increasingly destructive impact of arbitrary corporate decisions to close plants amidst a severe economic crisis may finally unleash public demands to place corporations' conduct under democratic constraints.

Sources: Roger Bybee, "Pulp Friction: A private equity firm's decision to shut down a profitable paper mill devastates a Wisconsin community," *In These Times*, Jan. 2009; Peter S. Goodman and Jack Healy, "Job Losses Hint at Vast Remaking of Economy," *New York Times*, Mar. 7, 2009; Matt Glynn, "ArcelorMittal says it's willing to sell Lackawanna plant," *Buffalo News*, Mar. 26, 2009; Stanley Reed, "Mittal & Son: An inside look at the dynasty that dominates steel," *Business Week*, Apr. 16, 2007; New release, Northwestern University Medill News Service, Oct. 7, 2005; Making Steel.com, Feb. 21, 2007; Peter Dreier: "This Economy is a Real Killer," Huffington Post, Mar. 10, 2009, Barry Bluestone and Bennett Harrison, *The Deindustrialization of America: Plant Closings, Community Abandonment, and the Dismantling of Basic Industry* (NY: Basic Books, 1982); Lawrence Rothstein, *The Fight Against Plant Closings* (Auburn Books: Dover Mass. and London, 1986); Mark Richtel, "A Sea of Unwanted Imports, *New York Times*, Nov. 18, 2008; William K. Tabb, "Financialization Appropriation," *Z Magazine*, June 2008; William K. Tabb, "Four Crises of the Contemporary World Capitalist System," *Monthly Review*, October 2008; Vinaya Saksena, "15 arrested at EP rally," *Pawtucket Times*, Mar. 20, 2009.

Article 4.3

UNREGULATED WORK
Is enforcement the next battle in the fight for workers' rights?

BY SIOBHÁN McGRATH AND NINA MARTIN
September/October 2005

Guillermo* regularly puts in 70-hour weeks as a prep cook in a New York City restaurant. He came to the United States from Ecuador six years ago because he heard that "you can earn something for your family." But these aspirations soured after he wasn't paid for three weeks. Small sums of money and continued promises from the boss keep Guillermo returning to work each day for his 12-hour shifts.

Non-payment of wages plagues Guillermo and his co-workers, but their employer uses other tactics to reduce labor costs as well. Guillermo explains, "Workers have to punch out as if they had worked eight hours. So after eight hours, they punch out and then work four more hours. It is almost like a threat that if you don't punch the card, you're fired." With an average wage of about $300 per week, these long hours translate into just over $4 per hour. Some of Guillermo's co-workers have left the restaurant for other jobs, usually at food establishments, but often the working conditions they face are frustratingly similar.

Brenda, an African-American grandmother, is a child care worker in Brooklyn. Formerly a home health care worker, Brenda's own health no longer permits her to make the long commute to her patients' homes. Caring for children in her home seemed like a good way to replace this lost income. The parents of the children she cares for receive subsidized child care as they move from welfare to work. Brenda has no sick days or vacation days, and she only has health insurance through her husband's job.

Worse, her pay often dips below minimum wage. But the city's Human Resources Administration, which cuts her check, maintains that this does not break the law. Even though the city effectively sets her pay, it classifies her as an "independent contractor," rather than an employee. So Brenda doesn't have the same rights as a regular employee, such as the minimum wage, overtime, or paid leave.

Unfortunately, the experiences of Guillermo and Brenda are far from unique. Violations of employment and labor laws are a growing problem in U.S. workplaces. Employers in many sectors of the economy are breaking the law in order to cut costs, gain a competitive edge, and boost profits, and workers are suffering the consequences. In some industries, the abuses have become so common that they are now routine practice. And enforcement by the government has steadily declined, so that more and more workers are facing abusive and unsafe conditions at work. Anyone who pays attention knows that U.S. workers in certain industries and occupations have long been vulnerable to employer abuses. But today, illegal and abusive practices are becoming common in a far larger swath of the economy, and the will and resources to enforce worker-protection laws are shrinking.

We are part of a large research team working out of three universities that is studying this phenomenon—what we call "unregulated work"—in New

---

* The names of the workers have been changed.

York City and Chicago. Over the past two years we have conducted in-depth interviews with over 400 workers, employers, government officials, community groups, union staff, and policy advocates. The next phase of our project will be a survey of workers in unregulated jobs, in order to estimate the size of this hidden zone of the economy. To date, we have found unregulated work in 14 industries. While many people are familiar with the conditions faced by garment workers and construction day laborers, the tentacles of unregulated work stretch into many other sectors of the economy, including workplaces as diverse as restaurants, grocery stores, security companies, nail salons, laundries, warehouses, manufacturers, building services firms, and home health care agencies.

We have documented considerable variety in how employers violate laws. They pay their workers less than minimum wage, fail to pay them overtime, refuse to pay them for all hours worked, or simply don't pay them at all. They disregard health and safety regulations by imposing unsafe conditions, forcing employees to work without providing necessary safety equipment, and failing to give training and information. The list of ways employers break the law goes on: they refuse to pay Unemployment Insurance or Workers' Compensation; they discriminate against workers on the basis of race, gender and immigration status; they retaliate against attempts to organize; they refuse medical leaves.

Such stories of substandard working conditions may sound familiar—they carry strong echoes of the experiences of workers at the beginning of the last century. At that time, the solution was to pass laws to create wage minimum standards, protect workers who speak up for their rights, and eventually, guarantee workplace safety and outlaw discrimination. That these very laws are now being so widely violated poses new challenges. While efforts to pass new laws raising workplace standards are still critical, a new battle has emerged to ensure that existing laws are enforced.

What Explains Unregulated Work?

The rise of unregulated work is closely tied to many of the same factors that are thought to be responsible for declining wages and job security in key sectors of the economy. Over the last 30 years, for example, global economic competition has been extinguishing the prospects of workers in manufacturing. Local manufacturers struggle to drive down their costs in order to compete against firms located in Asian or Latin American countries where wages and safety standards are lower.

Yet unregulated work cannot be explained simply as a byproduct of globalization. It's true that the competitive pressure felt in manufacturing may ripple through other parts of the economy, as wage floors are lowered and the power of labor against capital is diminished. But we found businesses that serve distinctly local markets—such as home cleaning companies, grocery stores, and nail salons— engaging in a range of illegal work practices, even though they are insulated from global competition.

Declining unionization rates since the 1970s also contribute to the spread of unregulated labor. One effect has been a general rise in inequality accompanied by lower wages and workplace standards: a weaker labor movement has less influence on the labor market as a whole, and offers less protection for both unionized and non-union workers. More directly, union members are more likely to report workplace violations to the relevant government authority than non-union workers, as a number of studies have shown. So it makes sense that employers are increasingly committing such violations in the wake of a long-term decline in the percentage of workers in unions.

But even the powerful one-two punch of globalization and de-unionization provides only a partial explanation. Government policy is also instrumental in shaping unregulated work—not only employment policies per se, but also immigration, criminal justice, and welfare "reform" policies that create pools of vulnerable workers. In this environment employers can use a variety of illegal and abusive cost-cutting strategies. Perhaps most significantly, they are deciding whether or not to break the law in an era of declining enforcement, when they are likely to face mild penalties or no penalties at all.

Immigration Policy

The deeply flawed immigration policy in the United States creates a labor supply that is vulnerable at work. For example, employers often convince undocumented workers that they have no rights at the workplace. If undocumented workers demand to be paid the minimum wage, their employers threaten not just to fire them, but also to "call immigration." Armed with such threats, employers break the law with little fear of being held accountable. Yet this strategy is only possible because U.S. immigration policy currently denies an estimated 10 million undocumented immigrants legal recognition, thereby ensuring a steady stream of vulnerable workers. In spite of the protections they have on paper, undocumented workers consistently report feeling that government assistance is off-limits because of their immigration status.

The victims of unregulated work are not, however, limited to undocumented immigrants. Immigrants who are authorized to work are also a significant part of this workforce. Employers sometimes simply assume that people from certain countries are undocumented. Some workers are hampered by a lack of proficiency in English. Many new arrivals also lack knowledge of U.S. labor and employment laws and employers can, and do, exploit this ignorance.

For example, the newly arrived Polish women we interviewed who work at A-1 Cleaning in Chicago are usually very pleased to have quickly found work that does not require a full command of English. A Polish immigrant founded the home cleaning company, using his ties in the community to find new workers. But this is not a story of ethnic solidarity. This employer often fails in his duty to inform these workers that their rights under U.S. law include such novel concepts as a minimum wage and overtime pay, and routinely violates these rights. If employees don't fully understand workplace regulations and their rights under the law, an unscrupulous employer can get them to work for less than minimum wage.

Prison, Welfare, and Discrimination

Immigrants are not the only workers made more vulnerable to workplace exploitation by government policies. Many workers, like Brenda, were born and raised in the United States but face barriers to employment in the more regulated part of the labor market. Predictably, race, ethnicity, and gender play a role in determining who ends up in the unregulated workforce. In addition, people leaving the welfare rolls or coming out of prison are especially vulnerable: they are pushed to find work as soon as possible, yet the stigma attached to having been on welfare or in prison limits the options available to them. For "ex-offenders," this is compounded by the fact that they are legally barred from certain jobs. Similarly, some features of welfare reform policies, such as abrupt or arbitrary benefit cutoffs, or "work first" policies that force people to take the first job offered, only make it more difficult to find a satisfactory job. Ironically, the only stable employment history some workers are able to build is in unregulated work, but because they are "off the books" this does not translate into better prospects in formal jobs, so they stay mired in exploitative jobs.

Employers also keep workers trapped in unregulated jobs through illegal discrimination. In New York City's restaurant industry, for example, a white college student applying for a job will be given a front-of-the-house job such as waiting tables, seating people, or operating the cash register. A Mexican worker, regardless of language skills or immigration status, will instead be funneled into a back-of-the-house job such as dishwashing, cooking, or janitorial work. These behind-the-scenes workers are then more vulnerable to violations and extremely unlikely to be promoted to better positions.

Externalization and Exclusion from Legal Protection

New business strategies in recent decades have produced a clear shift towards the "externalization" of work. Various forms of subcontracting and outsourcing are now widespread, and allow employers to evade responsibility for mistreating workers. When workers complain about abusive or illegal practices, the firm and its subcontractor can always point fingers at each other. Overall, the growth of outsourcing has driven many jobs into spaces where the reach of regulation is weak or nonexistent.

Employers also insulate themselves from workers' demands for improved working conditions by hiring temporary workers or using subcontractors. Some use placement agencies to do their dirty work, routinely asking them to screen workers on the basis of gender, race, age and other characteristics. In one of the most egregious examples we discovered, some employment agencies in New York demand sensitive health information from job seekers. A group of workers explained to us that these agencies also post signs refusing job applications from western Africans or South Africans. In this way, they seem to believe that they are screening out potentially HIV-positive candidates for their clients. One of the main services these agencies provide, then, is to discriminate simultaneously on the basis of national origin and disability.

Tapping into a contingent workforce of day laborers allows many employers to keep their costs to an absolute minimum. The emergence of day labor corners in many cities is one of the most visible examples of unregulated work. Day laborers are hired for a variety of jobs, including construction, cleaning, and moving. Besides the often dangerous and difficult working conditions they face, day laborers may work for employers who scrimp on promised wages or fail to pay them at all.

Chicago's largest day labor corner is on the city's northwest side, in the parking lot of a gas station. Known colloquially as the "slave station," the corner is the morning destination for large numbers of men who hope to find a day's work. Many of the men are Polish; others are Mexican, Ecuadorian, Guatemalan, and Ukrainian. They have often just arrived in the city and have large debts incurred while traveling to the United States. Contractors actively try to bid down wages of workers by playing them off against one another. While the going wage in the area for these jobs is between $8 and $10 per hour, day laborers are sometimes forced to accept as little as $4 per hour rather than go without work.

Some workers are especially vulnerable to employers' abuses because they are located outside the reach of some, or even all, legal protections. For example, although domestic workers are covered by minimum-wage laws and other protections, they are not covered by the National Labor Relations Act, and so they don't have the right to organize. This means that their employers are effectively given free reign to fire them for complaining about their jobs or demanding better treatment. Farm workers are similarly vulnerable, since they are exempt from protection of many labor laws.

Employers are increasingly misclassifying their workers as "independent contractors" in order to evade workplace regulations. The problem, as Cathy Ruckelshaus of the National Employment Law Project points out, is that this classification is only supposed to be applied to independent businesspersons. "You have to ask yourself, especially in the case of some of the low-wage workers," she says, "whether these people are actually running their own businesses or not." Child care workers, construction day laborers, janitors, street vendors, delivery people and bathroom attendants have been placed into this category, when in fact they were dependent upon their employer for scheduling, job assignments, equipment and training—signaling their status as traditional employees.

The Enforcement Problem

Our fieldwork indicates that unregulated work is a growing feature of business strategies at the bottom of the labor market. Very few attempts have been made to estimate the prevalence of workplace violations, but our preliminary findings are in line with evidence gathered by other researchers. For example, in the late 1990s the U.S. Department of Labor (DOL) carried out several surveys to assess compliance with the Fair Labor Standards Act (FLSA)—the law that regulates the minimum wage, overtime, and the use of child labor. Among their results: in 1999, only 42% of restaurants in Chicago and only 35% of garment shops in New York City were in compliance with FLSA.

Unfortunately, just as employer violations appear to be increasing, the resources allocated to enforcement are waning. Data we recently received from the Department of Labor shows that while the number of workplaces in the United States more than doubled between 1975 and 2004, the number of compliance actions by the DOL's Wage and Hour Division (WHD) declined by more than a third. As Howard Wial, a senior researcher at the Brookings Institution, writes, "The general picture that emerges … is that there has been a long-term decline in the adequacy of enforcement resources, which has probably resulted in a long-term decline in the amount of attention that the WHD pays to low-wage workers."

So employers are unlikely to be the target of WHD inspections, and if they are, penalties are unlikely to be high enough to provide a deterrent. An unprincipled employer may find that it is cheaper to break the law—and run the slight risk of getting caught—than it is to comply. David Weil, an economist at Boston University, conducted a cost-benefit analysis of compliance in the garment industry, including data on the annual likelihood of inspection, the average underpayment per worker, and the median civil penalty. He found that for an apparel contractor with 35 workers, "the potential cost of not complying [with minimum-wage requirements] is $121 versus a benefit of $12,205, implying that an apparel employer should clearly choose not to comply."

The problem of unregulated work is not just a "race to the bottom." It is a race that is taking place below the bottom. The legal floors on wages and working conditions are increasingly irrelevant to American employers. For the workers who populate this segment of the labor market, there is no guarantee that workplace laws will protect them.

Workers Push Back

The good news is that on the ground, community groups and other advocates are taking action. Workers are protesting for the wages owed them even as they are filing complaints with the Department of Labor or filing suits in court. In New York, workers have also collaborated with the state Attorney General's office, which has undertaken a number of initiatives to bring law-breaking employers into compliance. Immigrant workers in particular are organizing, either with unions or through Worker Centers, on the basis of industry and occupation. Day-labor groups across the country are creating "job centers," where wage rates and rules for hiring are collectively set and enforced by workers.

Advocates are also using legislation to pressure the relevant government agencies to enforce the law to protect workers. Campaigns are also underway to pass state legislation that would tie businesses' operating licenses to their compliance with labor and employment laws. In 2003, a new law in California increased employers' responsibility for violations carried out by their subcontractors. And a local law passed the same year in New York City increased the responsibility of employment agencies for the actions of their clients who hire domestic workers.

Clearly, a greater commitment to workplace enforcement, backed up by sufficient resources, will be necessary to combat the increasing number of violations of workers' rights. Yet more enforcement alone will not be enough. A deeply flawed immigration policy also needs to be fundamentally changed, so that all workers enjoy the minimum standards under the law, regardless of their citizenship status. In practice, our current immigration system accepts people into the country but then effectively denies them rights in the workplace. This creates a steady stream of vulnerable workers. Comprehensive immigration reform, with a sound path to legalization, is an essential component of efforts to guarantee workers' rights. Similarly, comprehensive changes to welfare and penal policies would make people returning to the workforce less vulnerable to exploitation in the unregulated workforce.

The growth of unregulated jobs has created a new terrain in the battle for workers' rights. While continuing efforts to raise the minimum wage and improve workplace standards are critical, in practice employers are routinely violating the standards that already exist. A greater commitment to enforcement, comprehensive reform in a range of areas of government policy (including immigration, penal, and welfare policy), and efforts to close the loopholes employers are currently taking advantage of, will all be necessary to fulfill the promise of protective labor legislation.

Article 4.4

WHY CEO SALARIES SKYROCKET

BY ARTHUR MacEWAN
November/December 1998

Dear Dr. Dollar,

Why do companies compensate CEOs with such high salaries and bonuses? Do the CEOs themselves decide on their pay? Isn't it always said that no one is indispensable?

— *Gwen Nottingham, Laurel, Montana*

CEOs and other top executives of large corporations do not *formally* decide on their own salaries—that's the job of the board of directors. The board members, however, are generally high level executives of other corporations, who by supporting the big pay packages of others, win support for big pay packages for themselves.

For example, top executives of industrial companies with over $250 million in sales were compensated an average of $870,000 in 1997, according to *Forbes*. Consider Frank Newman, who runs Bankers Trust, one of the banks that fueled the current crisis in Asia with ill-conceived loans. His 1997 salary and bonuses added up to $10.9 million. Or Harvey Golub, who oversaw the layoffs of 3,300 workers from American Express in 1997, and was compensated $33.4 million—that's about $10,000 for each layoff.

Yet the huge salaries are not only a result of executives taking good care of each other. Other countries also have "interlocking directorates" of top executives serving on other companies' boards, yet CEO salaries are not nearly so high as in the United States. Top executives in Canada, Japan, the United Kingdom, and Germany are paid only half as much as their U.S. peers (with pay including salaries, bonuses, perks, and long-term incentives). You can find individual executives in those countries who take home millions, but nowhere do top executives as a group come close to the U.S. corporate elite.

So what's the difference? Are U.S. executives more valuable than European or Japanese executives in producing profits? The answer lies not in their productivity, but in their power.

Over many decades, U.S. companies have created a highly unequal corporate structure that relies heavily on management control while limiting workers' authority. Large numbers of bureaucrats work to maintain the U.S. system. While in the United States about 13% of nonfarm employees are managers and administrators, that figure is about 4% in Japan and Germany. So U.S. companies rely on lots of well-paid managers to keep poorly paid workers in line, and the huge salaries of the top executives are simply the tip of an iceberg.

This highly unequal corporate system is buttressed by an unequal political and social structure. Without a powerful union movement, for example, there is little pressure on Washington to adopt a tax code that limits corporate-generated inequality. Several other high-income countries have a wealth tax, but not the United States. In addition, U.S. laws governing the operation of unions and their role in corporate decision making are relatively weak (and often poorly enforced). Without powerful workers' organizations, direct challenges to high CEO pay levels are very limited (as is the power to raise workers' wages). So income distribution in the United States is among the most unequal within the industrialized world, and high executive salaries and low wages can be seen as two sides of the same coin.

Article 4.5

THE GLOBALIZATION CLOCK
Why corporations are winning and workers are losing.

BY THOMAS PALLEY
May/June 2006

Political economy has historically been constructed around the divide between capital and labor, with firms and workers at odds over the division of the economic pie. Within this construct, labor is usually represented as a monolithic interest, yet the reality is that labor has always suffered from internal divisions—by race, by occupational status, and along many other fault lines. Neoliberal globalization has in many ways sharpened these divisions, which helps to explain why corporations have been winning and workers losing.

One of these fault lines divides workers from themselves: since workers are also consumers, they face a divide between the desire for higher wages and the desire for lower prices. Historically, this identity split has been exploited to divide union from nonunion workers, with anti-labor advocates accusing union workers of causing higher prices. Today, globalization is amplifying the divide between people's interests as workers and their interests as consumers through its promise of ever-lower prices.

Consider the debate over Wal-Mart's low-road labor policies. While Wal-Mart's low wages and skimpy benefits have recently faced scrutiny, even some liberal commentators argue that Wal-Mart is actually good for low-wage workers because they gain more as consumers from its "low, low prices" than they lose as workers from its low wages. But this static, snapshot analysis fails to capture the full impact of globalization, past and future.

Globalization affects the economy unevenly, hitting some sectors first and others later. The process can be understood in terms of the hands of a clock. At one o'clock is the apparel sector; at two o'clock the textile sector; at three the steel sector; at six the auto sector. Workers in the apparel sector are the first to have their jobs shifted to lower-wage venues; at the same time, though, all other workers get price reductions. Next, the process picks off textile sector workers at two o'clock. Meanwhile, workers from three o'clock onward get price cuts, as do the apparel workers at one o'clock. Each time the hands of the clock move, the workers taking the hit are isolated. In this fashion globalization moves around the clock, with labor perennially divided.

Manufacturing was first to experience this process, but technological innovations associated with the Internet are putting service and knowledge workers in the firing line as well. Online business models are making even retail workers vulnerable—consider Amazon.com, for example, which has opened a customer support center and two technology development centers in India. Public sector wages are also in play, at least indirectly, since falling wages mean falling tax revenues. The problem is that each time the hands on the globalization clock move forward, workers are divided: the majority is made slightly better off while the few are made much worse off.

Globalization also alters the historical divisions within capital, creating a new split between bigger internationalized firms and smaller firms that remain nationally centered. This division has been brought into sharp focus with the debate over the trade deficit and the overvalued dollar. In previous decades, manufacturing as a whole opposed running trade deficits and maintaining an overvalued dollar because of the adverse impact of increased imports. The one major business sector with a different view was retailing, which benefited from cheap imports.

However, the spread of multinational production and outsourcing has divided manufacturing in wealthy countries into two camps. In one camp are larger multinational corporations that have gone global and benefit from cheap imports; in the other are smaller businesses that remain nationally centered in terms of sales, production and input sourcing. Multinational corporations tend to support an overvalued dollar since this makes imports produced in their foreign factories cheaper. Conversely, domestic manufacturers are hurt by an overvalued dollar, which advantages import competition.

This division opens the possibility of a new alliance between labor and those manufacturers and businesses that remain nationally based—potentially a potent one, since there are approximately seven million enterprises with sales of less than $10 million in the United States, versus only 200,000 with sales greater than $10 million. However, such an alliance will always be unstable as the inherent labor-capital conflict over income distribution can always reassert itself. Indeed, this pattern is already evident in the internal politics of the National Association of Manufacturers, whose members have been significantly divided regarding the overvalued dollar. As one way to address this division, the group is promoting a domestic "competitiveness" agenda aimed at weakening regulation, reducing corporate legal liability, and lowering employee benefit costs—an agenda designed to appeal to both camps, but at the expense of workers.

Solidarity has always been key to political and economic advance by working families, and it is key to mastering the politics of globalization. Developing a coherent story about the economics of neoliberal globalization around which working families can coalesce is a key ingredient for solidarity. So too is understanding how globalization divides labor. These narratives and analyses can help counter deep cultural proclivities to individualism, as well as other historic divides such as racism. However, as if this were not difficult enough, globalization creates additional challenges. National political solutions that worked in the past are not adequate to the task of controlling international competition. That means the solidarity bar is further raised, calling for international solidarity that supports new forms of international economic regulation.

Article 4.6

NOT TOO BIG ENOUGH
Where the big banks come from.

BY ROB LARSON
April 2010

The government bailout of America's biggest banks set off a tornado of public anger and confusion. When the House of Representatives initially rejected the bailout bill, the *Wall Street Journal* attributed it to "populist fury," and since then the public has remained stubbornly resentful over the bailout of those banks considered "too big to fail." Now, the heads of economic policy are trying to gracefully distance themselves from bailouts, claiming that future large-scale bank failures will be avoided by stronger regulation and higher insurance premiums.

Dealing with the collapse of these "systemically important banks" is a difficult policy issue, but the less-discussed issue is how the banking industry came to this point. If the collapse of just one of our $100 billion megabanks, Lehman Brothers, was enough to touch off an intense contraction in the supply of essential credit, we must know how some banks became "too big to fail" in the first place. The answer lies in certain incentives for bank growth, which after the loosening of crucial industry regulations drove the enormous waves of bank mergers in the last thirty years.

Geographical Growth

Prior to the 1980s, American commercial banking was a small-scale affair. State-chartered banks were prohibited by state laws from running branches outside their home state, or sometimes even outside their home county. Nationally chartered banks were likewise limited, and federal law allowed interstate acquisitions only if a state legislature specifically decided to permit out-of-state banks to purchase local branches. No states allowed such acquisition until 1975, when Maine and other states began passing legislation allowing at least some interstate banking. The trend was capped in 1994 by the Riegle-Neal Act, which removed the remaining restrictions on interstate branching and allowed direct cross-state banking mergers.

This geographic deregulation allowed commercial banks to make extensive acquisitions, in state and out. When Wells Fargo acquired another large California bank, Crocker National, in 1986 it was the largest bank merger in U.S. history. Since "the regulatory light was green," a single banking company could now operate across the uniquely large U.S. market, opening up enormous new opportunities for economies of scale in the banking industry.

Economies of scale are savings that companies enjoy when they grow larger and produce more output. The situation is similar to a cook preparing a batch of cookies for a Christmas party, and then preparing a batch for New Year's while all the ingredients and materials are already out. Producing more output (cookies) in one afternoon is more efficient than taking everything out again later to make the New Year's batch separately. In enterprise, this corresponds to spreading the large costs of startup investment over more and more output, and is often thought of as lower per-unit costs as the level of production increases. In other words, there's less effort per cookie if you make them all at once. Economies of scale, when present in an industry, create a strong incentive for firms to grow larger, since profitability will improve. But they also give larger, established firms a valuable cost advantage over new competitors, which can put the brakes on competition.

Once unleashed by the policy changes, these economies of scale played a major role in the industry's seemingly endless merger activity. "In order to compete, you need scale," said a VP for Chemical Bank when buying a smaller bank in 1994. Of course, in 1996 Chemical would itself merge with Chase Manhattan Bank.

Economies of Scale in Banking and Finance

Economies of scale are savings that companies benefit from as they grow larger and produce more output. While common in many industries, in banking and finance, these economies drove bank growth after industry deregulation in the 1980s and 90s. Some of the major scale economies in banking are:

- **Spreading investment over more output.** With the growth in importance of large-scale computing power and sophisticated systems management, the costs of setting up a modern banking system are very large. However, as a firm grows it can "spread out" the cost of that initial investment over more product, so that its cost per unit decreases as more output is produced.

- **Consolidation of functions.** The modern workforce is no stranger to the mass firings of "redundant" staff after mergers and acquisitions. If one firm's payroll staff and computer systems can handle twice the employees with little additional expense, an acquired bank may see its payroll department harvest pink slips while the firm's profitability improves. When Citicorp merged with the insurance giant Travelers Group in 1998, the resulting corporation laid off over 10,000 workers—representing 6% of the combined company's total workforce and over $500 million in reduced costs for Citigroup. This practice can be especially lucrative in a country like the United States, with a fairly unregulated labor market where firms are quite free to fire. Despite the economic peril inflicted on workers and their families, this consolidation is key to increasing company efficiency post-merger. Beyond back-office functions, core profit operations may also benefit from consolidation. When Bank of America combined its managed mutual funds into a single fund, it experienced lower total costs, thanks to trimming overhead from audit and prospectus mailing expenses. Consolidating office departments in this fashion can yield savings of 40% of the cost base of the acquired bank.

- **Funding mix.** The "funding mix" used by banks refers to where banks get the capital they then package into loans. Smaller institutions, having only limited deposits from savers, must "purchase funds" by borrowing from other institutions. This increases the funding cost of loans for banks, but larger banks will naturally have access to larger pools of deposits from which to arrange loans. This funding cost advantage for larger banks relative to smaller ones represents another economy of scale.

- **Advertising.** The nature of advertising requires a certain scale of operation to be viable. Advertising can reach large numbers of potential customers, but if a firm is small or local, many of those customers will be too far afield to act on the marketing. Large firm size, and especially geographic reach, can make the returns on ad time worth the investment.

Spreading big investment costs over more output is the main source of generic economies of scale, and in banking, the large initial investments are in sophisticated computer systems. The cost of investing in new computer hardware and systems development is now recognized as a major investment obstacle for new banks, although once installed by banks large enough to afford them, they are highly profitable. The *Financial Times* describes how "the development of bulk computer processing and of electronic data transmission…has allowed banks to move their back office operations away from individual branches to large remote centers. This had helped to bring real economies of scale to banking, an industry which traditionally has seen diseconomies set in at a very modest scale."

Economies of scale are common in manufacturing, and in the wake of deregulation the banking industry was also able to exploit a number of them. Besides spreading out the cost of computer systems, economies of scale may be present in office consolidation, in the funding mix used by banks, and in advertising. (See sidebar.)

Industry-to-Industry Growth

BusinessWeek's analysis is that the banking industry "has produced large competitors that can take advantage of economies of scale…as regulatory barriers to interstate banking fell," although not until the banks could "digest their purchases." The 1990s saw hundreds of bank purchases annually and hundreds of billions in acquired assets.

But an additional major turn for the industry came with the Gramm-Leach-Bliley Act of 1999 (GLB), which further loosened restrictions on bank growth, this time not geographically but industry-to-industry. After earlier moves in this direction by the Federal Reserve, GLB allowed for the free combination of commercial banking, insurance, and the riskier field of investment banking. These had been separated by law for decades, on the grounds that the availability of commercial credit was too important to the overall economy to be tied to the volatile world of investment banking.

GLB allowed firms to grow further, through banks merging with insurers or investment banks. The world of commercial credit was widened, and financial mergers this time exploited economies of scope—where production of multiple products jointly is cheaper than producing them individually. As commercial banks, investment banks, and insurers have expanded into each others' fields in the wake of GLB, their different lines of business can benefit from single expenses—for example, banks perform research on loan recipients that can also be used to underwrite bond issues. Scope economies such as these allow the larger banks to both run a greater profit on a per-service basis and attract more business. Thanks to the convenience of "one stop shopping," Citigroup now does more business with big corporations, like IT giant Unisys, than its component firms did pre-merger.

Exploiting economies of scope to diversify product lines in this fashion can also help a firm by reducing its dependence on any one line of business. Bank of America weathered the stock market downturn of 2001 in part because its corporate debt underwriting business was booming. Smaller, more specialized banks can become "one-trick ponies" as the *Wall Street Journal* put it—outdone by larger competitors with low-cost diversification thanks to scope economies.

These economies of scope are parallel to the scale economies, since both required deregulatory policy changes to be unleashed. Traditionally, banking wasn't seen as an industry with the strong economies of scale seen in, say, manufacturing. But the deregulation and computerization of the industry have allowed these firms to realize returns to greater scale and wider scope, and this has been a main driver of the endless acquisitions in the industry in recent decades.

Market Power

The enormous proportions that the banking institutions have taken on following deregulation have meant serious consequences for market performance. A number of banks have reached sufficient size to exercise market power—the ability of firms to influence prices and to engage in anticompetitive behavior. The market power of our enormous banks allows them to take positions as price leaders in local markets, where large firms use their dominance to elevate prices (i.e., increase fees and rates on loans, and decrease interest rates on deposits). Large firms can do this because smaller firms may perceive that lowering their prices to take market share could be met by very drastic reductions in prices from the larger firm in retaliation. Large firms, having deeper pockets, may be able to withstand longer periods of operating at a loss than the smaller firms.

Small banks are likely to perceive that the colossal size and resources of the megabanks make them unprofitable to cross—better to follow along and charge roughly what the dominant, price-leading firm does. Empirical research by Federal Reserve Board senior economist Steven Pilloff supported this analysis, finding that the arrival of very large banks in local markets tended to increase bank profitability for reasons of price leadership, due to the larger banks' economies of scale and scope, financial muscle, and diversification.

Examples of the use of banking industry market power are easy to find. Several bills now circulating in Congress deal with the fees retail businesses pay to the banks and the credit card companies. When consumers make purchases with their Visas or MasterCards, an average of two cents of each dollar goes not to the retailer but to the credit card companies that run the payment network and the banks that supply the credit. These "interchange fees" bring in over $35 billion in profit in the United States alone, and they reflect the strong market power of the banks and credit card companies over the various big and small retailers. The 2% charge comes to about $31,000 for a typical convenience store, just below the average per-store yearly profit of $36,000, and this has driven a coalition of retailers to press for congressional action.

Visa has about 50% of the credit card market (including debit cards), and MasterCard has 25%, which grants them profound market power and strong bargaining positions. Federal Reserve Bank of Kansas City economists found the United States "maintains the highest interchange fees in the world, yet its costs should be among the lowest, given economies of scale and declining cost trends." The *Wall Street Journal*'s description was that "these fees...have also been paradoxically tending upward in recent years when the industry's costs due to technology and economies of scale have been falling." Of course, there's only a paradox if market power is omitted from the picture. The dominant size and scale economies of the banks and the credit card oligopoly allow for high prices to be sustained—bank muscle in action against a less powerful sector of the economy. The political action favored by the retailers includes proposals for committees to enact price ceilings or (interestingly) collective bargaining by the retailers. As is often the case, the political process is the reflection of the different levels and positions of power of various corporate institutions, and the maneuvering of their organizations.

Market power brings with it a number of other advantages. A powerful company is likely to have a widespread presence, make frequent use of advertising, and be able to raise its profile by contributing to community organizations like sports leagues. This allows the larger banks to benefit from stronger brand identity—their scale and resources make customers more likely to trust their services. This grants a further advantage in the form of customer tolerance of higher prices due to brand loyalty.

Political Clout

Crucially, large firms with market power are free to participate meaningfully in politics—using their deep pockets to invest in electoral campaigns and congressional lobbying. The financial sector is among the highest-contributing industries in the United States, with total 2008 campaign contributions approaching half a billion dollars, according to the Center For Public Integrity. So it's unsurprising that they receive so many favors from the government, since they fund the careers of the decision-making government personnel. This underlying reality is why influential Senator Dick Durbin said of Congress, "The banks own the place."

Finally, banks may grow so large by exploiting scale economies and market power that they become "systemically important" to the nation's financial system. In other words, the scale and interconnectedness of the largest banks is considered to have reached a point where an abrupt failure of one or more of them may have "systemic" effects—meaning the broader economic system will be seriously impaired. These "too big to fail" banks are the ones that were bailed out by act of Congress in the fall 2008. Once a firm becomes so enormous that the government must prevent its collapse for the good of the economy, it has the ultimate advantage of being free to take far greater risks. Riskier investments come with higher returns and profits, but the greater risk of collapse that accompanies them will be less intimidating to huge banks that have an implied government insurance policy.

Some analysts have expressed doubt that such firms truly are too large to let fail, and that the banks have pulled a fast one. It might be pointed out in this connection that in the past the banks themselves have put their money where their mouths are—they have paid out of pocket to rescue financial institutions they saw as too large and connected to fail. An especially impressive episode took place in 1998, when several of Wall Street's biggest banks and financiers agreed to billions in emergency loans to rescue Long Term Capital Management. LTCM was a high-profile hedge fund that borrowed enormous sums of capital to make billion-dollar gambles on financial markets.

America's biggest banks aren't in the habit of forking over $3.5 billion of good earnings, but they had loaned heavily to LTCM and feared losing their money if the fund went under. The Federal Reserve brought the bankers together, and in the end, they paid up to bail out their colleagues, and the *Wall Street Journal* reported that it was the Fed's "clout, together with the self-interest of several big firms that already had lent billions of dollars to Long-Term Capital, that helped fashion the rescue." Interestingly, the banks insisted on real equity in the firm they were pulling out of the fire, and they gained a 90% stake in the hedge fund. Comparing this to the less-valuable "preferred stock" the government settled for in its 2008 bailout package of the large banks is instructive. The banks also got a share of control in the firm they rescued, again in stark contrast to the public bailout of some of the same banks.

Even Bigger?

In fact, the financial crisis and bailout led only to further concentration of the industry. The crisis gave stronger firms an opportunity to pick up sicker ones in another "wave of consolidation," as *BusinessWeek* put it. And a large part of the government intervention itself involved arranging hasty purchases of failing giants by other giants, orchestrated by the Federal Reserve. For example, the Fed helped organize the purchase of Bear Stearns by Chase in March 2008 and the purchase of Wachovia by Wells Fargo in December 2008. Even the bailout's "capital infusions" were used for further mergers and acquisitions by several recipients. The Treasury Department was "using the bailout bill to turn the banking system into the oligopoly of giant national institutions," as the *New York Times* reported.

The monumental growth of the largest banks owes a lot to the industry's economies of scale and scope, once regulations were relaxed so firms could exploit them. While certainly not unique to finance, these dynamics have brought the banks to such enormous size that their bad bets can put the entire economy in peril. Banking therefore offers an especially powerful case for the importance of these economies and the role of market power, since it's left the megabanks holding all the cards.

In fact, many arguments between defenders of the market economy and its critics center on the issue of competition vs. power—market boosters reliably insist that markets mean efficient competition, where giants have no inherent advantage over small, scrappy firms. However, the record in banking clearly shows that banks have enjoyed a variety of real benefits from growth. The existence of companies of great size and power is a quite natural development in many industries, due to the appeal of returns to scale and power. This is why firms end up with enough power to influence government policy, or such absurd size that they can blackmail us for life support.

And leave us crying all the way to the bank.

Sources: Judith Samuelson and Lynn Stout, "Are Executives Paid Too Much?" *Wall Street Journal*, February 26, 2009; Tom Braithwaite, "Geithner Presses Congress for Action on Reform," *Financial Times*, September 23, 2009; Phillip Zweig, "Intrastate Mergers Between Banking Giants Might Not Be Out of the Question Anymore," *Wall Street Journal*, March 25, 1986; Bruce Knecht, "Chemical Banking plans acquisition of Margaretten," *Wall Street Journal*, May 13, 1994;

Eric Weiner, "Banks Will Post Good Quarterly Results," *Wall Street Journal*, January 10, 1997; Gabriella Stern, "Four Big Regionals To Consolidate Bank Operations," *Wall Street Journal*, July 22, 1992; "Pressure for change grows," *Financial Times*, September 27, 1996; Tracy Corrigan and John Authers, "Citigroup To Take $900 million charge: Cost-cutting Program to Result in Loss of 10,400 Jobs," *Financial Times*, December 16, 1998; Eleanor Laise, "Mutual-Fund Mergers Jump Sharply," *Wall Street Journal*, March 9, 2006; Steven Pilloff, "Banking, commerce and competition under the Gramm-Leach-Bliley Act," *The Antitrust Bulletin*, Spring 2002; David Humphrey, "Why Do Estimates of Bank Scale Economies Differ?" *Economic Review* of Federal Reserve Bank of Richmond, September/October 1990, note four; Michael Mandel and Rich Miller, "Productivity: The Real Story," *BusinessWeek*, November 5, 2001; John Yang, "Fed Votes to Give 7 Bank Holding Firms Additional Power in Securities Sector," *Wall Street Journal*, July 16, 1987; "Banking Behemoths—What Happens Next: Many companies Like to Shop Around For Their Providers of Financial Services," *Wall Street Journal*, September 14, 2000; Carrick Mollenkamp and Paul Beckett, "Diverse Business Portfolios Boost Banks' Bottom Lines," *Wall Street Journal*, July 17, 2001; *Journal of Financial Services Research*, "Does the Presence of Big Banks Influence Competition in Local Markets?" May 1999; "Credit-Card Wars," *Wall Street Journal*, March 29, 2008; *Economic Review* of the Federal Reserve Bank of Kansas City, "Interchange Fees in Credit and Debit Card Markets: What Role for Public Authorities," January-March 2006; "Credit Where It's Due," *Wall Street Journal*, January 12, 2006; Keith Bradsher, "In One Pocket, Out the Other," *New York Times*, November 25, 2009; Center For Public Integrity, Finance/Insurance/Real Estate: Long-Term Contribution Trends, opensecrests.org; Dean Baker, "Banks own the U.S. government," *Guardian*, June 30, 2009; Anita Raghavan and Mitchell Pacelle, "To the Rescue? A Hedge Fun Falters, So the Fed Persuades Big Banks to Ante Up," *Wall Street Journal*, September 24, 1998; Theo Francis, "Will Bank Rescues Mean Fewer Banks?" *BusinessWeek*, November 25, 2008; Joe Nocera, "So When Will Banks Give Loans?" *New York Times*, October 25, 2008.

Chapter 5

MARKET STRUCTURE AND MONOPOLY

INTRODUCTION

With monopoly, we finally encounter a situation in which most economists, orthodox and otherwise, agree that unfettered markets lead to an undesirable outcome. If a firm is able to create a monopoly, it faces a downward-sloping demand
curve—that is to say, if it reduces output, it can charge a higher price. The monopolist
has a profit incentive to restrict output in order to charge consumers that higher price.
The result is a dead-weight loss—a loss to consumers that is not fully offset by the gains
to the monopolist. Economists argue that competitive forces tend to undermine any
monopoly, but failing this, they support antitrust policy as a backstop. The concept
of monopoly not only points to an important failing of markets, but it opens the door
to thinking about many possible market structures other than perfect competition—
including oligopoly, in which a small group of producers dominate the market.

In this chapter, our authors are in the unaccustomed position of agreeing with
much of what standard economics textbooks have to say. Still, they manage to stir
up some controversy. In the first article, Chris Tilly summarizes the pluses and
minuses of large and small businesses, and finds *both* wanting (Article 5.1).

Paul Cummings tackles a market often used to illustrate the role of monopolies—the global oil market (Article 5.2). However, rather than focusing on the
monopoly power of OPEC—the standard example of how monopolies affect the
price of oil—he instead asks what lay behind the rising demand for oil from 2006
to mid-2008. He argues that the explanation cannot stop with the desires/needs
of individual consumers, who are in fact "captive" to the mix of technologies that
determine the extent to which their economies are dependent on oil. And this mix
of technologies, as Cummings shows, has been carefully and consciously shaped
by lobbying on the part of car and oil companies to stop government efforts to
improve fuel efficiency. Cummings' analysis of the multiple market failures in this
market emphasizes just how far the economy is from any ideal of perfect competition and just how inadequate standard models based upon perfect competition are
in explaining shifts in supply and demand.

Dean Baker describes how large pharmaceutical concerns use monopoly power
to wring extra profits from buyers, creating a variety of problems along the way. But

there's a twist: The source of these monopolies is intellectual property rights—patents—which standard economic analysis sees as necessary to provide the incentive to innovate (Article 5.3).

The recent financial crisis has provided us with a particularly egregious example of what happens when we allow the growth of companies that are "too big to fail." Heterodox economists have long pointed to the contradiction between the belief in perfect competition and the advocacy of deregulation that can lead to the growth of monster corporations. Edward S. Herman provides historical context for this discussion by reviewing the history of U.S. antitrust law and criticizing economists for justifying a hands-off policy toward big business mergers over the last few decades (Article 5.4).

Completing this chapter is Marty Wolfson's piece "The Bailouts Revisited" (Article 5.5). This particularly timely piece explores the "*too big to fail*" phenomenon stemming from the current economic crisis as a necessary expression of "*market power*."

The authors in this chapter agree with mainstream economics textbook authors that monopoly typically has harmful effects. They disagree about how often and how dramatically the U.S. economy differs from perfect competition. They also (at least in the case of Tilly) question whether an economy made up of small, perfectly competitive firms would be an improvement.

Discussion Questions

1) (Article 5.1) List the pros and cons that Tilly comes up with for large and small businesses. How does this compare with the problems your textbook mentions? Be sure to compare Tilly's list of small business flaws with what your textbook has to say about small business.

2) (Article 5.2) What are some of the ways in which consumers in the oil market are "captive" to the power of oil companies? If you noticed that oil prices were falling rather than rising (e.g. in the last half of 2008), would Cummings' argument still hold? Explain.

3) (Article 5.2) What are the different kinds of "market failures" that result from oil companies' ability to influence the structure of demand for oil?

4) (Articles 5.1 and 5.3) Baker says that a company with a monopoly on a drug has "an enormous incentive to overstate the benefits and understate the risks." Tilly says that in the case of oligopoly, the incentive is for a business to pour huge amounts of money into advertising and other ways to make its brand stand out. Explain why even though both companies have an incentive to spin the truth about its product, the incentives are somewhat different in the two cases, monopoly and oligopoly.

5) (Article 5.3) Baker sharply criticizes the monopoly effects of the patent system. But others argue that patents are necessary for innovation—they give companies

a monopoly for a limited time so that they can recoup their research investment. How should this clash be resolved? Should patents be granted in some industries but not others? If so, how should we encourage research in areas with no patent protection?

6) (Articles 5.1, 5.3, and 5.4) Tilly describes how corporations fund "citizens'" groups to push policies that the corporations want. Baker says that giant drug companies fund scientists to prove that the companies' drugs work. Herman states that large businesses hired economists to come up with theories that showed why huge businesses and mega-mergers can be beneficial (or at least not harmful). What are some likely results if corporations control "the marketplace of ideas?" What, if anything, should be done about it?

7) (Article 5.5) What does it mean to say a company is "too big to fail?" Does the sheer size of a company "change the rules" as to how that company operates in the economy? Assessing the definition of "Market Power" from Article 8.1 (box) of this reader, might that definition have to be expanded? If so, how?

8) (General) Looking back at the readings in Chapter 4 as well as Chapter 5, the authors worry a lot about how business power can harm both workers and consumers. But in orthodox economics texts, almost all the attention is on how consumers alone get hurt by business power. Why do you think the emphasis is so different in this book compared to a standard text?

IS SMALL BEAUTIFUL? IS BIG BETTER?
Small and big businesses both have their drawbacks.

BY CHRIS TILLY
July/August 1989, revised April 2002

Beginning in the late 1980s, the United States has experienced a small, but significant boom in small business. While big businesses have downsized, small enterprises have proliferated. Should we be glad? Absolutely, declare the advocates of small business. Competition makes small businesses entrepreneurial, innovative, and responsive to customers.

Not so fast, reply big business's boosters. Big corporations grew big because they were efficient, and tend to stay efficient because they are big—and thus able to invest in research and upgrading of technology and workforce skills.

But each side in this debate omits crucial drawbacks. Small may be beautiful for consumers, but it's often oppressive for workers. And while big businesses wield the power to advance technology, they also often wield the market power to bash competitors and soak consumers. In the end, the choices are quite limited.

Big and Small

Is the United States a nation of big businesses, or of small ones? There are two conventional ways to measure business size. One is simply to count the number of employees per firm. By this measure, small businesses (say, business establishments with less than 20 employees) make up the vast majority of businesses (Table 1). But they provide only a small fraction of the total number of jobs.

The other approach gauges market share—each firm's share of total sales in a given industry. Industries range between two extremes: what economists call "perfect competition" (many firms selling a standardized product, each too tiny to affect the market price) and monopoly (one business controls all sales in an industry). Economy-wide, as with employment, small businesses are most numerous, but control only a small slice of total sales. Sole proprietorships account for 73% of established businesses, far outnumbering corporations, which are 20% of the total (the remainder are partnerships). But corporations ring up a hefty 90% of all sales, leaving sole proprietors with only 6%. It takes a lot of mom and pop stores to equal General Motors' 1999 total of $177 billion in sales.

Industry by industry, the degree of competition varies widely. Economists consider an industry concentrated when its top four companies account for more than 40% of total sales in the industry (Table 2). At the high end of the spectrum are the cigarette, beer, and aircraft industries, where four firms account for the bulk of U.S. production.

No market comes close to meeting the textbook specifications for perfect competition, but one can still find industries in which a large number of producers compete for sales. The clothing and restaurant industries, for example, remain relatively competitive. Overall, about one-third of U.S. goods are manufactured in concentrated industries, about one fifth are made in competitive industries, and the rest fall somewhere in between.

Beating the Competition

Those who tout the benefits of small, competitive business make a broad range of claims on its behalf. In addition to keeping prices low, they say the quality of the product is constantly improving, as companies seek a competitive edge. The same desire, they claim, drives firms toward technological innovations, leading to productivity increases.

The real story is not so simple. Competition does indeed keep prices low. Believe it or not, clothing costs us less—in real terms—than it cost our parents. Between 1960 and 1999, while the overall price level and hourly wages both increased nearly sixfold, apparel prices didn't even triple. And small businesses excel at offering variety, whether it is the ethnic restaurants that dot cities or the custom machine-tool work offered by small shops. Furthermore, however powerful small business lobbies may be in Washington, they do not influence the legislative process as blatantly as do corporate giants.

TABLE 1
SMALL BUSINESS NATION?

Most businesses are small, but most employees work for big businesses

Company size (number of employees)	Percent of all firms	Percent of all workers
1–4	54%	6%
5–9	20%	8%
10–19	13%	11%
20–49	8%	16%
50–99	3%	13%
100–249	2%	16%
250–499	0.4%	10%
500–999	0.2%	7%
1,000 or more	0.1%	13%

Note: "Businesses" refers to establishments, meaning business locations.

Source: County Business Patterns, 1998.

TABLE 2
WHO COMPETES, WHO DOESN'T

Industry	Percent of sales by top four firms
Light truck and utility vehicle manufacturing	96%
Breweries	91%
Home center stores	91%
Breakfast cereal manufacturing	78%
General book stores	77%
Credit card issuing	77%
Lawn equipment manufacturing	62%
Cable providers	63%
Computer and software stores	51%
Sock manufacturing	30%
Hotels and motels (excl. casinos)	22%
Gas stations	9%
Real estate	4%
Bars	2%

Source: 2002 Economic Census.

But those low prices often have an ugly underside. Our sportswear is cheap in part because the garment industry increasingly subcontracts work to sweatshops—whether they be export assembly plants in Haiti paying dollar-a-day wages, or the "underground" Los Angeles stitcheries that employ immigrant women in virtual slavery. Struggling to maintain razor-thin profit margins, small businesses cut costs any way they can—which usually translates into low wages and onerous working conditions.

"There is a rule of survival for small business," Bill Ryan, president of Ryan Transfer Corporation, commented some years ago. "There are certain things you want to have [in paying workers] and certain things you can afford. You had better go with what you can afford." Bottom line, workers in companies employing 500 or more people enjoy average wages 30% higher than their counterparts in small businesses.

Part of this wage gap results from differences other than size—unionization, the education of the workforce, the particular jobs and industries involved. But University of Michigan economist Charles Brown and his colleagues controlled for all these differences and more, and still found a 10% premium for big business's employees. A note of caution, however: Other recent research indicates that this wage bonus is linked to long-term employment and job ladders. To the extent that corporations dissolve these long-term ties—as they seem to be rapidly doing—the pay advantage may dissolve as well.

Small business gurus make extravagant claims about small businesses' job-generation capacity. An oft-quoted 1987 report by consultant David Birch claimed that businesses with fewer than 20 employees create 88% of new jobs. The reality is more mundane: over the long run, businesses with 19 or fewer workers account for about one quarter of net new jobs. One reason why Birch's statistics are misleading is that new small businesses are created in great numbers, but they also fail at a high rate. The result is that the *net* gain in jobs is much smaller than the number created in business start-ups.

For companies in very competitive markets, the same "whip of competition" that keeps prices down undermines many of competition's other supposed benefits. The flurry of competition in the airline industry following deregulation, for example, hardly resulted in a higher quality product. Flying became temporarily cheaper, but also less comfortable, reliable, and safe.

Technological innovation from competition is also more myth than reality. Small firms in competitive industries do very little research and development. They lack both the cash needed to make long-term investments and the market power to guarantee a return on that investment. In fact, many of them can't even count on surviving to reap the rewards: only one-third to one-half of small business startups survive for five years, and only about one in five makes it to ten years. A 1988 Census Bureau survey concluded that in manufacturing, "technology use is positively correlated with plant size." Agriculture may be the exception that proves the rule. That highly competitive industry has made marked productivity gains, but its research is supported by the taxpayer, and its risks are reduced by government price supports.

Of course, the biggest myth about competition is that it is in any way a "natural state" for capitalism. In fact, in most markets the very process of competing for high profits or a bigger market share tends to create a concentrated, rather than a competitive, market structure. This process occurs in several ways. Big firms sometimes drive their smaller competitors out of business by selectively cutting prices to the bone. The smaller firms may lack the financial resources to last out the low prices. In the 1960s, several of IBM's smaller competitors sued it for cutting prices in a pattern that was designed to drive the smaller firms out of the market. Large corporations can also gain a lock on scarce resources: for example, large airlines like United and American operate the comprehensive, computerized information and reservation systems that travel agents tap into—and you can bet that each airline's system lists their own flights first. Or businesses may exploit an advantage in one market to dominate another, as Microsoft used its control of the computer operating system market to seize market share for its Internet browser.

Other firms eliminate competitors by buying them out—either in a hostile takeover or a friendly merger. Either way, a former competitor is neutralized. This strategy used to be severely limited by strict antitrust guidelines that prohibited most horizontal mergers—those between two firms that formerly competed in the same market. The Reagan administration's team at the Justice Department, however, loosened the merger guidelines significantly in the early 1980s. Since that time, many large mergers between former competitors have been allowed to go through, most notably in the airline industry.

The Power of Concentration

Concentration, then, is as natural to market economies as competition. And bigness, like smallness, is a mixed bag for us as consumers and workers. For workers, bigness is on the whole a plus. Whereas competition forces small businesses to be stingy, big firms are on average more generous, offering employees higher wages, greater job security, and more extensive fringe benefits. In 1993, 97% of businesses with 500 or more workers provided health insurance; only 43% of businesses with 25 or fewer employees did so. Large firms also provide much more employee training. The strongest unions, as well, have historically been in industries where a few firms control large shares of their markets, and can pass along increased costs to consumers—auto, steel, and tires, for example. When profits are threatened, though, firms in concentrated markets also have more resources with which to fight labor. They are better able to weather a strike, oppose unionization, and make agreements with rivals not to take advantage of each other's labor troubles. In addition, large companies, not surprisingly, score low on workplace autonomy.

What about consumers? Corporations in industries where there are few competitors may compete, but the competitive clash is seldom channeled into prolonged price wars. The soft drink industry is a classic example. David McFarland, a University of North Carolina economist, likens soft drink competition to professional wrestling. "They make a lot of sounds and groans and bounce on the mat, but they know who is going to win," he remarked.

Coke and Pepsi introduce new drinks and mount massive ad campaigns to win market share, but the net result is not lower prices. In fact, because competition between industry giants relies more on product differentiation than price, companies pass on their inflated advertising expenses to consumers. In the highly concentrated breakfast cereal market, the package frequently costs more than the contents. And of every dollar you pay for a box, nearly 20 cents goes for advertising.

It takes resources to develop and market a new idea, which gives large corporations distinct advantages in innovation. The original idea for the photocopier may have come from a patent lawyer who worked nights in his basement, but Xerox spent $16 million before it had a product it could sell. RCA invested $65 million developing the color television. RCA could take this gamble because its dominance in the television market ensured that it would not be immediately undercut by some other firm.

But market dominance can also translate into complacency. The steel industry illustrates the point. A few major producers earned steady profits through the 1950s and 1960s but were caught off-guard when new technologies vaulted foreign steel-makers to the top of the industry in the 1970s. Similarly, when IBM dominated the computer industry in the 1960s and early 1970s, innovation proceeded quite slowly, particularly compared to the frantic scramble in that industry today. With no competitors to worry about, it was more profitable for IBM to sit tight, since innovation would only have made its own machines obsolete.

And large corporations can also put their deep pockets and technical expertise to work to short-circuit public policy. In the 1980s, when Congress changed corporate liability laws to make corporate executives criminally liable for some kinds of offenses, General Electric's lobbyists and legal staff volunteered to help draft the final regulations, in order to minimize the damage.

Big businesses sometimes hide their lobbying behind a "citizen" smokescreen. The largest-spending lobby in Washington in 1986 was Citizens for the Control of Acid Rain. These good citizens had been organized by coal and electric utility companies to oppose tighter pollution controls. Along the same lines, the Coalition for Vehicle Choice (now, who could be against that?) was set up by Ford and General Motors in 1990 to fight higher fuel efficiency standards.

Concentration or Conglomeration

Over the last couple of decades, the mix of big and small businesses has changed, but the changes are small and—at first glance—contradictory. Over time, employment has shifted toward smaller firms, though the shift has been subtle, not revolutionary. Meanwhile, the overall level of industry-by-industry sales concentration in the economy has increased, but only slightly. As older industries become more concentrated, newer, more competitive ones crop up, leaving overall concentration relatively steady. In his book *Lean and Mean*, economist Bennett Harrison points out that there is actually no contradiction between the small business employment boomlet and big firms' continued grip on markets. Big businesses, it turns out, are orchestrating much of the flowering of small business, through a variety of outsourcing and subcontracting arrangements.

But if industry-by-industry concentration has changed little over the decades, conglomeration is a different matter. Corporate ownership of assets has become much more concentrated over time, reflecting the rise in conglomerates—corporations doing business in a variety of industries. Five decades ago, the top 200 manufacturing firms accounted for 48% of all sales in the U.S. economy. By 1993, the 200 biggest industrial businesses controlled 65% of sales.

Most mainstream economists see these groupings as irrelevant for the competitive structure of the economy. Antitrust laws place no restrictions on firms from different industries banding together under one corporate roof. But sheer size can easily affect competition in the markets of the individual firms involved. A parent company can use one especially profitable subsidiary to subsidize start-up costs for a new venture, giving it a competitive edge. And if one board of directors controls major interests in related industries, it can obviously influence any of those markets more forcefully.

A case in point is the mega-merger of Time Inc. and Warner, which will soon be joining with America Online. The resulting conglomerate will control massive sections of the home entertainment business, bringing together Time's journalists, film and television producers, and authors, Warner's entertainment machine, which includes Home Box Office, the nation's largest pay television channel, and AOL's huge share of the Internet access market. The conglomerate can influence the entertainment business from the initial point—the actors, writers, and directors—up to the point where the finished products appear on people's televisions or computers. Conglomeration also multiplies the political clout of large corportions. No wonder Disney and other entertainment giants have also hopped on the conglomeration bandwagon.

Choose your Poison

Competition, concentration, or conglomeration: The choice is an unsavory one indeed. Opting for lots of tiny, competing firms leaves labor squeezed and sacrifices the potential technological advantages that come with concentrated resources. Yet the big monopolies tend to dominate their markets, charge high prices, and waste countless resources on glitzy ad campaigns and trivial product differentiation. And the big conglomerate firms, while not necessarily dominant in any single market, wield a frightening amount of political and economic power, with budgets larger than those of most countries.

Of course, we don't have much to say about the choice, no matter how much "shopping for a better world" we engage in. Market competition rolls on—sometimes cutthroat, other times genteel. Industries often start out as monopolies (based on new inventions), go through a competitive phase, but end up concentrating as they mature. As long as bigness remains profitable and the government maintains a hands-off attitude, companies in both competitive and concentrated industries will tend to merge with firms in other industries. This will feed a continuing trend toward conglomeration. Since bigness and smallness both have their drawbacks, the best we can do is to use public policies to minimize the disadvantages of each.

Resources: Lean and Mean: The Changing Landscape of Corporate Power in the Age of Flexibility, Bennett Harrison, 1994; *Employers Large and Small,* Charles Brown, James Hamilton, and James Medoff, 1990.

Article 5.2

THE GLOBAL OIL MARKET
How it operates, why it doesn't work, and who wants to keep it that way.

PAUL CUMMINGS
July/August 2008

Since the United States-led coalition invaded Iraq in March 2003, the price of a barrel of oil has just about quadrupled to around $135. With U.S. oil imports currently totaling 4.5 billion barrels a year, this translates into a staggering $600 billion annual oil bill. Many energy economists predict that oil prices could top $200 a barrel in the near future, particularly if U.S. opposition to Iran's nuclear enrichment program leads to a confrontation, either directly or through surrogate states.

Why are oil prices skyrocketing? Many economists and business analysts like to talk about "the fundamentals": supply (constrained) and demand (strong). They point to rapid economic growth in China and India driving demand. On the supply side, it's the OPEC cartel limiting production while tree-huggers in the United States block the development of new offshore and Alaskan oil supplies.

But other analysts claim the so-called fundamentals tell us little about why oil prices are rising rapidly. Recently the London *Times*'s economy and finance commentator, Anatole Kaletsky, noted that over the past nine months, as the price of oil has doubled, none of the basic determinants of supply or demand has changed much. China's demand growth is in fact slowing, as is the world's demand growth overall. Iraqi oil production is back up to prewar levels. Kaletsky views the current price spikes as symptoms of a classic financial bubble during which, typically, "prices end up bearing almost no relation to the balance of underlying supply and demand."

For now, the experts are displaying a remarkable lack of consensus on whether it's the actions of commodities traders and other financial-market movements or real supply and demand factors that explain the current oil price spike. In any case, the terms "supply" and "demand" are supposed to conjure up images of a free market. But the global oil market is anything but. Even leaving aside the role of financial markets in setting the price of oil, the supply of and demand for oil are heavily shaped by the actions of mammoth multinational oil companies and of governments in both the consuming and producing countries. And while the price of oil is rising fast, causing real pain to consumers, those extra dollars are going straight to the governments of the oil-rich countries and to the major oil companies—*not* to offset the tremendous costs that oil imposes, chiefly on the environment but in multiple other arenas as well.

Supply Management

From the very beginning of the modern oil industry, the supply of oil has been managed by powerful oil companies and the magnates who run them. The first was none other than John D. Rockefeller, who founded Standard Oil in 1870. By 1878 he had gained control of 90% of U.S. oil refining. In the 1880s Rockefeller used his strategic control of refining to build the first vertically integrated oil company, with oil fields, tankers, pipelines, refineries, and retail sales facilities under one corporate roof. By mercilessly undercutting competitors until they were near bankruptcy, and then buying them on the cheap, Standard Oil gained control of over half of the world's then-known oil supply. By the turn of the century Rockefeller had become the richest man in the world, with a fortune valued at around a billion dollars. Then, in 1911, the Supreme Court ruled that Standard Oil was a monopoly and, to create competition, split it into 34 companies, including Esso and Socony, which eventually became Exxon and Mobil, respectively.

Instead of competing, over the next 50 years Exxon, Mobil, and five other giant oil companies (the "majors") essentially formed a cartel. Leveraging their superior technology, production experience, and control of the retail market, the majors engaged in oil colonialism: they pumped and sold oil from a number of developing countries under highly favorable terms, earning vast profits.

In the 1950s, oil-rich countries began nationalizing their oil and training domestic oil technocracies to run the business. The advantages of collusion were no secret to them. In the 1960s Venezuela and Saudi Arabia organized OPEC (the Organization of Petroleum Exporting Countries), a cartel whose explicit purpose was to control the price of oil by regulating supply. By acting together, the oil-rich nations leveled the playing field with the majors and gained a larger share of oil profits.

With this context in mind, let's consider how oil gets to market today. Currently, around 75% of the world's oil is nationalized, managed by state-run oil companies that are monopolies in their own country. These state companies are often their country's largest employer, largest exporter, largest source of hard currency, and largest contributor to state revenue. State oil executives report to political authorities instead of a corporate board, and local political considerations can trump economic factors in their business decisions. For example, state oil companies may site new facilities in poorer communities to spur local economic development. More importantly, nationalized oil earns the money to pay for hospitals, schools, sanitation systems, and roads, projects rarely funded by Western oil corporations. The downside is that oil money all too frequently has been stolen by corrupt rulers or siphoned away to buy expensive weapons— Zaire's Mobutu Sese Seko and Iraq's Saddam Hussein were just two in a long line of oil-funded despots.

State oil ministers set oil production targets taking into consideration both economic and political factors, including current global economic performance, OPEC member production quotas, long-term contracts with oil corporations, International Monetary Fund debt repayment schedules, domestic revenue requirements, the desires of greedy and corrupt rulers, and the cost of oil extraction compared to oil's market price.

Of course, most of the state-owned oil across the globe lies within OPEC, whose policies fundamentally shape supply. The eleven member states of OPEC control over 50% of the world's oil. After both the 1973 Israeli-Arab war and the 1979 Islamic revolution in Iran, OPEC cut oil production, oil prices skyrocketed, cartel members earned hundreds of billions of dollars in windfall profits, and the world economy slid into recession.

Then, in the 1980s, a weak economy and more efficient cars cut oil demand, while newly discovered non-OPEC oil increased supply. OPEC tried to prop up plunging prices by cutting production. In particular, Saudi Arabia cut its output by nearly 8 million barrels per day. When other OPEC members began to cheat on their lower production quotas, the Saudis enforced market discipline by flooding the market with cheap oil, driving many suppliers out of business. With oil supply back under control, prices rose to around $20 a barrel, OPEC's market share was restored, and OPEC production quotas were honored. John D. Rockefeller would have applauded.

In 1990, the first "oil war" was launched when Iraq invaded Kuwait and seized its oil fields. With Iraqi troops poised to attack Saudi Arabia, a U.S.-led coalition drove the Iraqi army out of Kuwait. The Saudis once again demonstrated their market power by pumping enough additional oil to offset the loss of Kuwaiti and Iraqi oil production.

The cartel aims to keep the price of oil high, but it also seeks reasonable stability in the oil market. After all, the lion's share of the petrodollars that OPEC members earn are plowed back into the United States and the other wealthy consuming countries in the form of investments. If oil price volatility begins to damage the U.S. and other industrialized economies, those investments will likely suffer as well. But OPEC's ability to manage supply for the twin goals of profitability and stability is limited. In recent years conflicts in the Middle East, rapidly growing oil demand in China and India, and OPEC's own tendency to overshoot or undershoot planned production levels have all contributed to a more volatile oil market than OPEC perhaps intended.

The remaining 25% of global oil supply comes from fields owned by the majors or by Russia's ostensibly private energy giant Gazprom. This production is more responsive to market signals, but is still influenced by non-price factors such as government tax and environmental policies and Wall Street pressure to report high quarterly earnings.

Perhaps the clearest indicator that the supply of oil is managed and not a simple response to market signals is the curious fact that much of the oil that is brought to market is relatively expensive to produce because of high extraction costs (for instance, deep sea oil), transport costs (Alaskan oil), or refining costs (some of Africa's oil). At the same time, oil that could be brought to market far more cheaply—much of the oil in the Arabian Peninsula, for example—is left in the ground. Saudi oil costs just $1.50 per barrel to produce, while the average production cost of oil outside of the Middle East is $22 per barrel. In a free market, competition would cause the lowest-cost oil to be sold first, since cheap oil can undercut expensive oil. However, in the case of managed supply, producers of cheap oil can hold back their oil, allowing the market price to rise until it exceeds the production price of expensive oil. This means very high profits for the producers of cheap oil, while many energy analysts stimate that consumers are paying twice as much as they would if oil markets were free, Paul Roberts writes in *The End of Oil*.

Retail supplies are influenced by vertically integrated global oil delivery systems—pipelines, supertankers, refineries, delivery tanker trucks, assorted retail sales facilities—which are controlled by the Saudis, Venezuela, and the super-majors (the six largest private oil companies: ExxonMobil, Shell, BP, Chevron, ConocoPhillips, and Total S.A.). Every day 85 million barrels of oil flow to consumers around the world. The massive oil delivery systems are worth a combined $5 trillion dollars and create a large barrier to entry for alternative energy suppliers. Supply can be constrained for other reasons as well, for instance, environmental or other regulations that block expansion or construction of oil pipelines or refineries.

Occasionally a geopolitical or extreme weather event breaks the oil supply system and retail oil prices go through the roof, creating outrageous profits. For example, in the aftermath of Hurricane Katrina, U.S. gasoline prices doubled overnight. The oil industry denied using Katrina to fleece customers, but a 2006 investigation by the Federal Trade Commission found multiple examples of price gouging at the refining, wholesale, and retail levels. Coincidentally, in the last quarter of 2005, the accounting quarter following Katrina, ExxonMobil earned $9.9 billion, the largest quarterly profits ever reported by a U.S. company.

In 2007 oil prices were exploding along with much of Iraq. That year ExxonMobil earned $40.6 billion in profits on $400 billion in revenue, the highest yearly profit ever earned by a public corporation. Amazingly, even this record profit pales in comparison to the 2007 Saudi net oil revenue of $194 billion.

Captive Consumers

The demand for oil is no more a simple result of free-market forces than is the supply. To begin with, energy demand is not created directly by consumers: we do not desire gasoline the way we might desire a new house or a new pair of shoes. Instead, demand is "pulled" by the economy, whose mix of technologies and rate of growth determine how much energy, from oil and other sources, is required to power it. Oil heats tens of millions of homes, offices, and factories and powers 30% of the world's electric generation. Oil is also used as an input in the manufacture of petrochemicals such as plastics.

And, of course, oil moves mountains of raw materials, tons of finished goods, and billions of people every day. The world's armada of oil-fueled vehicles consists of nearly a billion cars, trucks, buses, tractors, bulldozers, ships and airplanes. The troubling reality is that this armada runs only on oil; there is no viable alternative fuel today, and oil companies intend to keep it that way.

Every year the armada grows, moving more people and more stuff over greater distances. Globalization has spread out the production and sales processes over ever-longer international supply chains. U.S. and Canadian commuters drive more and more miles as suburbanization moves home and work farther apart. And the average fuel efficiency of U.S. passenger vehicles *fell* by 5% during the past 20 years, due to aggressive marketing of SUVs and trucks.

Oil companies use their political clout to stop government efforts to increase fuel efficiency. Over the last 20 years, the oil industry has given $200 million to U.S. politicians, mostly Republicans, who believe in free markets but regularly give an invisible helping hand to the oil companies. During those same 20 years, oil lobbyists have rolled back gas mileage standards and created tax subsidies for buying eight-ton Hummers that inhale gas. Oil lobbyists have redirected funding from alternative energy technology to road and bridge repair.

Oil companies have also used their wealth and political power to crush electric powered transportation systems. In the 1920s city-dwellers commuted on electric trolleys, but oil and auto companies wanted to sell them buses and cars. Standard Oil, General Motors, Mack Truck, and Firestone Tire funded a dummy corporation, National City Lines (NCL), to replace trolleys with buses. It didn't matter if NCL lost money; its goal was to create demand for buses, cars, tires, and oil. If it could do so, its parent companies would make a fortune. By 1929 NCL had established its business model and when the Great Depression deepened, over 100 electric utility companies, located in most major cities, were forced to sell their trolley lines at a sharply discounted price to NCL, the only buyer with cash. Once NCL had control, the trolley systems were sold for scrap and within days a new fleet of buses arrived, followed by a tidal wave of cars. In the late 1940s, NCL had served its purpose and was failing. Government lawyers had been investigating NCL, and in 1949 they successfully prosecuted its parent companies for collusion to destroy the nation's trolley system. Each parent company paid a $5,000 fine, which wasn't too bad considering they had made on the order of $100 million in profits from NCL's illegal actions.

By 1990 the Los Angeles basin faced a serious public health problem due to smog from car exhaust. The state of California issued a mandate requiring car companies to develop a zero emission vehicle, or ZEV. Oil and automobile companies launched a full-fledged political campaign to overturn the ZEV mandate, including TV and magazine ads, direct mail, and thousands of calls from phone banks. The ZEV mandate was never enforced and, in 2003, was replaced with a minimal requirement that car companies sell a few gas-electric hybrid cars by 2008. That same year, in a remarkable episode chronicled in the 2006 documentary "Who Killed the Electric Car?," GM was taking back the hundreds of EV1 electric vehicles it had leased to U.S. drivers beginning in 1996. The carmaker assembled most of the EV1s at a site in Arizona where it proceeded to crush them—despite very positive feedback from EV1 lessees, many of whom wanted to purchase and keep the cars. Explanations for GM's decision to halt the EV1 program and destroy the cars vary. GM says it determined the venture could never be profitable, in part because hoped-for breakthroughs in battery technology did not occur. One thing is certain: the car did become less marketable once California gave in to pressure from the oil and auto industries (including GM) and lifted the ZEV mandate.

In 1994 oil companies attacked Ballard Power Systems for developing a hydrogen fuel cell to power cars. With a game plan similar to the one they'd used to undermine the ZEV mandate, they took out ads decrying the fuel cell, challenged the company's veracity at trade conferences, and questioned its ability to actually bring a viable product to market. Oil companies pointed out that useable hydrogen was in short supply and an entirely new hydrogen refining, delivery, and fueling infrastructure would need to be built at the cost of many billions of dollars. As a result of these attacks Ballard backed off, and further development of its fuel cell was hidden in an internal R&D program for over a decade.

So the demand for oil is driven by economic and social trends far beyond the control of individual consumers, who are stuck, at least in the short term, paying whatever price the oil companies set if they want to fill their tanks and heat their homes.

Finally, it's impossible to get the whole picture of demand for oil without recognizing one very special oil consumer: the U.S. military. Every tank, armored vehicles, truck, humvee, jet, and missile runs on refined oil, as do most ships. In 2007, the U.S. military consumed about 250 million barrels of oil and 2.6 billion gallons of jet fuel, making it the world's single largest fuel-burning entity. Without oil the Army and Marines could not maneuver, the Air Force could not fly, and most of the Navy could not sail. The United States would be a paralyzed superpower, unable to project power throughout the world. Since all the other military forces in the world also run on oil, the ability to cut their oil lifelines is a tremendous strategic advantage in any conflict. These factors make oil more than just another commodity. Oil is a weapon, a strategic commodity, a national security resource; it is not just like wheat or widgets. By the same token, any shift in U.S. foreign policy that reduces the country's military engagements can also represent a sizeable drop in U.S. oil demand.

Multiple Market Failures

Today's global oil market is working well for the major oil companies, their managers, and their shareholders. It is also working well for the oil-producing countries, at least to the extent that they are garnering vast revenues. (Of course, the extent to which these revenues are benefiting ordinary people in the oil-rich countries varies dramatically.)

But the oil market is characterized by many kinds of market failure: the workings of the market are producing less-than-optimal results on multiple levels. For instance, oil price spikes can lead to "demand shocks" that suck money rapidly out of the economies of the oil-importing nations. If the global financial system cannot get this money re-invested and generating demand quickly, the result can be a drop in global demand followed by an economic downturn. According to energy economist Philip Verleger, over the last 50 years there have been six major oil price spikes, each causing economic losses that have totaled more than $1 trillion. Verleger posits that a 20% increase in the price of a barrel of oil results in a 0.5% decline in global economic growth. Based on that formula, the current $100 spike in the price of oil, if sustained, could wind up causing a reversal in the global economy from a baseline of 2% growth to a 1% contraction.

By and large, Americans have benefited from the fact that the price of oil worldwide is denominated in dollars rather than another currency. Right now, though, the falling value of the dollar against other major currencies is one factor pushing up the price of oil in the United States. Moreover, not only can fluctuations in the value of the dollar affect oil prices; oil market shifts can affect the value of the dollar. Hence, a second type of market failure in the global oil market is the increased "risk premium" that attaches to a whole range of financial transactions when a build-up of petrodollars makes the financial markets worry about an increased risk of either a devaluation of the dollar or a run on the dollar. In both cases the U.S. Federal Reserve may not be able to successfully intervene because trillions of petrodollars are outside of the Fed's control. In general, increased risk is bad for the economy and leads to higher interest rates and slower economic growth.

A third group of oil market failures are environmental. Oil is a dirty business that pollutes the air, water, and earth, often in health-threatening ways. Take oil spills for example. In Ecuador a pipeline runs over the Andes, connecting Ecuador's eastern jungle oil fields to its Pacific coast refinery. When earthquakes or landslides break the pipeline, all the oil between the break and the shut-off valve simply pours out, contaminating a broad swath of the mountain below.

Six thousand miles to the north, Exxon's supertanker, the Valdez, struck Bligh Reef on March 24, 1989, spilling 11 million gallons of oil into Prince William Sound. The oil contaminated 1,500 miles of Alaskan shoreline; nearly 20 years later, local economies dependent on fishing and tourism have still not entirely recovered. There are thousands of similar cases all over the planet.

The mother of all oil market failures is climate change. When oil is converted to energy, it gives off CO_2 which traps heat in the atmosphere and, in large quantity, can alter the climate. The result is a global, cumulative, and intergenerational problem that an increasing number of climate scientists fear may become a crisis of biblical proportions: higher sea levels flooding coastal cities around the globe; droughts, heat waves, pests, and more frequent extreme weather events affecting food supplies and human health.

No matter where CO_2 originates, it spreads quickly throughout the entire atmosphere, and so makes the problem a global one. The longevity of atmospheric CO_2 creates a cumulative problem. Since 1850, our species has dumped so much carbon into the sky that atmospheric CO_2 levels are at their highest point in a million years. That is 500,000,000,000,000 pounds of carbon stuck in the sky, as if the atmosphere were an open sewer! And that longevity makes the problem intergenerational: it will take the earth 16 generations (400 years) to reabsorb 80% of the CO_2 we emit today, and the remaining 20% will stay in the sky for thousands of years.

Solving climate change begins by realizing that the oil market doesn't have to be managed for the benefit of a small number of extremely rich people. We must also put to rest the canard that oil resources are best allocated by the free market's "invisible hand." Columbia University economist Joseph Stiglitz points out, "the reason that the hand may be invisible is that it is simply not there— or at least that if is there, it is palsied." The public needs to fight to remove the control of oil pricing from the oil corporations and establish an oil market that is more fair and sustainable.

In a sustainable energy market, the price of gasoline and other fossil fuel products should reflect the real costs these energy sources impose—above all, on the environment. That means prices that are higher than what Americans are accustomed to. But a progressive oil agenda would include recapturing that additional revenue and using it to compensate low-income consumers and, especially, to move the economy toward one based on renewable energy. Paying that extra dollar or more a gallon at the pump would feel very different if U.S. consumers knew the money was being spent not to line the pockets of dictators and oil executives, but instead to offset the extra cost for low-income families and, especially, to generously fund myriad projects to put the economy on a green-energy path.

Sources: Sohbet Karbuz, "US military energy consumption: facts and figures," *Energy Bulletin*, May 20, 2007; Chalmers Johnson, "The Arithmetic of America's Military Bases Abroad: What Does It All Add Up To?" www.tomdispatch.com, 2004; OPEC, "World Oil Outlook 2007"; Paul Roberts, *The End of Oil* (Houghton Mifflin, 2005); U.S. Federal Trade Comm., "Investigation of Gasoline Price Manipulation and Post-Katrina Gasoline Price Increases: Report to Congress" (Spring 2006); Eric Noe, "For Oil Giants, Pricey Gas Means Big Profits," ABC News, Jan. 25, 2006; Steven Mufson, "ExxonMobil's Profit in 2007 Tops $40 Billion," *Washington Post*, Feb. 2, 2008; U.S. Energy Information Admin., "OPEC Oil Export Revenues 2007"; Michael Renner, "Five Hundred Million Cars, One Planet—Who's Going to Give?" (Worldwatch Institute, August 2003); Daniel Engber, "How Gasoline Becomes CO2: A gallon turns into 19 pounds?" Slate.com, Nov. 1, 2006; Matthew Kahn, "The Environmental Impact of Suburbanization," *Jrnl of Policy Analysis and Mgmt* 19:4 (Fall 2000); Philip Verleger, "A Collaborative Policy to Neutralize the Economic Impact of Energy Price Fluctuations," Policy paper, June 10, 2003; "The Real Price of Gasoline: An Analysis of the Hidden External Costs Consumers Pay to Fuel Their Automobiles," Int'l Ctr for Technology Assessment, 1998; Joseph Stiglitz, *Making Globalization Work* (W.W. Norton, 2006); Laura Peterson, "Big Oil Wields Ultra Deep Influence," Ctr for Public Integrity, Dec. 2004.

Article 5.3

DRUG PRICES IN CRISIS
The Case Against Protectionism

BY DEAN BAKER
May/June 2001

In recent years, drug prices have risen to astronomical levels. In the United States, senior citizens are increasingly unable to afford prescription medication, while in developing nations, life-saving drugs are being priced out of reach for tens of millions of people with AIDS. In both cases, there is a single explanation for soaring drug prices: patent protection. If the pharmaceutical industry's patent monopolies were eliminated, most drugs would sell for only a fraction of their current cost.

Remarkably, however, the issue of drug patent monopolies rarely arises in public debate. Patent protection is a form of protectionism, but that's problematic terminology in a political climate where support for "free trade" is considered the only respectable opinion. So the pharmaceutical industry has managed to frame patent protection as a matter of "intellectual property rights" instead. Rarely has an industry been so successful in controlling the language of debate.

The industry has had a lot of help from the economics profession. Mainstream economists have developed an extensive body of research on the expected consequences of protection or monopoly pricing. If they were really as committed to efficiency and free trade as they pretend to be, they would be screaming about drug patents at the top of their lungs. The reason they don't is that they hold the drug industry in much higher esteem than manufacturing workers who might benefit from other forms of protectionism.

Of course, patent protection for prescription drugs, like all forms of protectionism, does serve a purpose—to provide industry with an incentive to research new drugs. If any firm could produce and sell every new drug that was developed, then no company would ever have a reason to spend money on research. However, the fact that drug patents *can* provide an incentive for research does not mean that they are the only or best way to support research. In fact, most biomedical research is currently supported by the federal government or private foundations, charities, and universities—not undertaken by private companies in anticipation of future sales.

We can only assess the full costs of patent protection if we recognize it as a form of protectionism, and look for all of the distortions that economists would expect protectionism to create. Once we do that, we'll see that the benefits derived from state-sanctioned monopoly protection are not justified by the quality and quantity of research that the pharmaceutical industry undertakes.

The Economics of Protectionism

Patent monopolies are a windfall for the pharmaceutical industry. Under the present system, a single firm gets to control the sale of a drug for the duration of its patent. Evidence from countries without effective protection for patents, or for drug prices after patents expire, indicates that most drugs would only sell for 25% of their patent protected price. In some cases, the difference is much greater. For example, the current state-of-the-art combination of anti-viral AIDS drugs sells in the United States for approximately $10,000 a year, according to the pharmaceutical industry. By contrast, a leading Indian manufacturer of generic drugs believes that it can sell the same combination profitably for $350 per year.

Why the huge gap between the monopoly patent protected price and the competitive market price? Because most drugs are relatively cheap to produce. Drugs are expensive because the government gives the industry a monopoly, not because they cost a lot to manufacture.

The costs of patent protection to consumers are enormous. The industry, which includes such giants as GlaxoSmithKline, Pfizer, and Bristol-Myers Squibb, estimates that it sold $106 billion worth of drugs in 2000. If eliminating patent protection had reduced the price of these drugs by 75%, then consumers would have saved $79 billion. This figure, to put it in perspective, is 30% more than what the federal government spends on education each year. It's more than ten times the amount that the federal government spends on Head Start. And it roughly equals the nation's annual bill for foreign oil.

What do we get for this money? Last year, the pharmaceutical industry, according to its own figures, spent $22.5 billion on domestic drug research (and another $4 billion on research elsewhere). For tax purposes, the industry claimed research expenditures of just $16 billion. Since these expenditures qualify for a 20% tax credit, the federal government directly covered $3.2 billion of the industry's research spending (20% of the $16 billion reported on tax returns). Even if we accept the $22.5 billion figure as accurate, this still means that the industry, after deducting the government contribution, spent just over $19 billion of its own money on drug research.

In other words, consumers (and the government, through Medicaid and other programs) spent an extra $79 billion on drugs because of patent protection, in order to get the industry to spend $19 billion of its own money on research. This comes out to more than four dollars in additional spending on drugs for every dollar that the industry spent on research. The rest of the money went mainly to:

- *Marketing*: The industry spends tens of billions each year to convince us (or our doctors) that its new drugs are absolutely essential and completely harmless.
- *Protecting patent monopolies*: Pharmaceutical companies regularly stand near the top in contributing to political campaigns. It's no accident that so many politicians are willing to push their cause.
- *Profits*: The pharmaceutical industry consistently ranks at the top in return on investment. It pulled in more than $20 billion in profits for 1999.

If spending an extra four dollars on drugs in order to persuade the industry to spend one dollar on research doesn't sound like a good deal, don't worry. It gets worse.

The Inefficiencies of Protectionism

Mainstream economists, who usually love to recite the evils of government protection, have been mostly silent on the issue of patent protection for drugs. But the evils are visible for all to see.

One major source of waste is research spending on imitation or "copycat" drugs. When a company gets a big hit with a new drug like Viagra or Claritin, its competitors will try to patent comparable drugs in order to get a slice of the market. In a world with patent protection, this can be quite beneficial to consumers, since a second drug creates some market competition. However, in the absence of patent protection, the incentive for copycat research would be unnecessary, since anyone who wanted to produce Viagra or Claritin would be free to do so, thereby pushing prices down.

How much do drug companies spend on copycat research? The industry won't say. But the Food and Drug Administration (FDA), in evaluating "new" drugs, considers only one third of them to be qualitatively new or better than existing drugs, while classifying the other two thirds as comparable to existing drugs. This doesn't mean that two thirds of research spending goes to copycat drugs; after all, the breakthrough drugs probably require more research spending, on average, than copycats. But suppose the industry wasted just 20% of its $19 billion in research spending on copycat drugs. This would bring the value of that spending down to $15 billion. That means consumers and the government are paying more than five dollars on drugs for each dollar of useful research.

The evils of protectionism don't end there. Prescription drugs present a classic case of asymmetric information: The drug companies know more about their drugs than the doctors who prescribe them, and far more than the patients who take them. The lure of monopoly profits gives the industry an enormous incentive to overstate the benefits and understate the risks of the newest wonder drugs. A June 2000 *New England Journal of Medicine* study found that the media consistently offered glowing accounts of drug breakthroughs. According to the study, the main villains in distorting the news were the public-relations departments of the drug manufacturers.

Still more serious is evidence that published research findings may be influenced by the drug industry's support. Last summer, the *New York Times* cited data showing that drugs, when tested by researchers who were supported by the drug's manufacturer, were found to be significantly more effective than existing drugs 89% of the time. By contrast, drugs tested by neutral researchers were found to be significantly more effective only 61% of the time.

Even if the industry's research could be completely trusted, there is still another problem created by the patent system—secrecy. The industry generally maintains the right to control the dissemination of findings from the research it supports. In some cases, this can mean a delay of months or even years before a researcher can disclose her findings at a conference or in a journal. In April 1996, for example, the *Wall Street Journal* reported on a British drug company's efforts to suppress a study showing that Synthroid, a drug to control thyroid problems, was no more effective than much cheaper alternatives.

In other cases, the secrecy is even more extreme. When the industry funds studies designed to prove that drugs are safe and effective enough to win FDA approval, it routinely keeps the results secret as proprietary information. This research may contain important clues about how best to use the new drug, or even about other factors affecting patients' health. Generally, however, the scientific community will not have access to it.

By creating incentives to misrepresent, falsify, or conceal research findings, patent monopolies are harmful to our pocketbooks as well as our health. At the very least, consumers may waste money on new, patent-protected drugs that are no more effective than existing drugs whose patents have expired. For example, a recent study estimated that consumers were spending $6 billion a year on a patented medication for patients with heart disease, which was no more effective than generic alternatives in preventing heart problems. As a result of industry propaganda, consumers might also spend money on drugs that could be less effective than cheaper alternatives—or on drugs that could even be hazardous to their health.

Another byproduct of monopoly drug pricing—the underground market—also has detrimental effects. When drugs can be sold profitably at prices that are much lower than their patent protected prices, consumers may seek underground sources for drugs. The most obvious way to do this is to purchase drugs in countries that either impose price controls or don't have the same patent protection as the United States. In recent years, there has been a much-publicized flow of senior citizens to Canada and Mexico in search of lower cost drugs. In the case of people traveling to Canada, the major cost to consumers is the waste of their time. However, when people buy drugs in countries with less stringent safety regulations, the health consequences may be severe.

The Proven Alternative

Listing the problems associated with drug patents would be an empty intellectual exercise—unless there were alternative ways to support research. Fortunately, there are. The federal government currently supports $18 billion a year in biomedical research through the National Institutes of Health (NIH) and the Centers for Disease Control (CDC). (The vast majority of NIH-funded research is carried out at universities and research centers across the country; less than 20% is conducted on the campus of the Institutes themselves.) In addition, universities, private foundations, and charities fund a combined total of approximately $10 billion worth of research annually. Added together, these institutions spend 25% more on research than the pharmaceutical industry claims to spend, and nearly twice as much as the industry reports on tax returns.

Over the years, the research supported by government and non-profit institutions has led to numerous medical breakthroughs, including the discovery and development of penicillin and the polio vaccine. More recently, NIH-supported research has played a central role in developing AZT as an AIDS drug, and in developing Taxol, a leading cancer drug. The NIH's impressive list of accomplishments over the last five decades proves that the government can support effective research.

Traditionally, the NIH has focused on basic research and early phases of drug testing, while the pharmaceutical industry has engaged primarily in the later phases of drug testing—which include conducting clinical trials and carrying drugs through the FDA approval process. However, there is not a sharp division between the type of research done by the NIH and that undertaken by the pharmaceutical industry; the NIH has conducted research in all areas of drug development. There is no reason to believe that, given enough funding, the NIH could not effectively carry out all phases of drug research.

While the idea of a panel of government-supported scientists (most of whom would probably be affiliated with universities and other research institutions) deciding which drugs should be researched may seem scary, consider the current situation. Drug-company executives make their research decisions based on their assessment of a drug's profitability. In turn, that assessment depends on whether the company can get insurance companies to pay for the drug, whether it can effectively lobby legislators to have Medicaid and other government programs pay for it, and whether it can count on the courts to fully enforce its patents against competitors. It is these factors—not consideration of what will benefit the public's health—that dominate the industry's decisions about research. It is hard to believe that publicly accountable bodies that are charged with directing research for the general good would not produce better results.

The arithmetic behind a proposed switch is straightforward. If the federal government spent an additional $20 billion a year to support research at the NIH and various non-profit and educational institutions, it would more than fully replace the useful research conducted by the pharmaceutical industry. The cost to the federal government would be less than the cost of the prescription drug plan that Al Gore advocated in last year's presidential campaign. If patent protection for drugs were eliminated, consumers would save more than $79 billion a year. These savings would increase with each passing year, since spending on drugs is currently rising at more than twice the rate of inflation.

Even assuming that the United States continues to rely on patent protection to support drug research for the immediate future, interim steps can be taken. First, it will be important to sharply restrict the worst abuses of the patent system. At the top of the list, the U.S. government should not be working with the pharmaceutical

THE USES OF DRUG MONEY

Drug Company Revenues, Profits, and Spending, 1999

Company	($ millions) Revenues	Profits (as % of revenue)	Mrktg Costs (as % of revenue)	R&D (as % of revenue)
Merck	$32,714	18.0%	15.9%	6.3%
Pfizer	$16,204	19.6%	39.2%	17.1%
Eli Lilly	$10,003	27.2%	27.6%	17.8%
Schering-Plough	$9,176	23.0%	37.4%	13.0%
Pharmacia & Upjohn	$7,253	11.1%	38.6%	19.8%

Source: Families USA

industry to impose its patents on developing countries. This is especially important in the case of AIDS drugs, since patent protection in sub-Saharan Africa may effectively be sentencing tens of million of people to death. There should also be pressure to allow the importation of drugs from nations where they are sold at lower prices, or even better, the imposition of domestic price controls.

A second priority is to create a greater opening for alternative sources of research. There should be more support for the NIH to carry some of its research through to the actual testing and approval of new drugs. The patents for these drugs should then be placed in the public domain, so that the industry can compete to supply the drugs at the lowest cost. In addition to bringing immediate benefits to consumers, this would allow for a clear test of the patent system's value as a means of supporting research, as compared with direct public support.

Back in the Middle Ages, the guild system was established to protect the secrets of masters from their apprentices. If you tried to make and sell hats but didn't belong to the hatmakers' guild, you'd be subject to arrest. Patents (and their cousin, copyrights) come out of this tradition. While most medieval restrictions have long since been discarded, patents have managed to survive and are now deeply enmeshed in our economic system. Not all forms of patent protection cause the problems associated with drug patents; in some areas, such as industrial processes, it may be reasonable to keep patent protection intact. But the case of drug patents cries out for the free market that economics say they favor, to wipe this feudal relic away.

Sources: *Annals of Thoracic Surgery* (September 2000): 883-888; *Wall Street Journal*, 25 April 1996, p. A1; Pharmaceutical Research and Manufacturers of America <www.phrma.org>; Families USA (familiesusa.org).

Article 5.4

A BRIEF HISTORY OF MERGERS AND ANTITRUST POLICY

BY EDWARD HERMAN
May/June 1998

Government efforts to prevent or break up monopolies are called antitrust policy. They assume that when a few companies dominate an industry, this weakens competition and hurts the public by reducing production, raising prices, and slowing technical advance. Antitrust has gone through cycles during this century. In some years, strongly pro-business presidencies (usually Republican) have allowed businesses to merge at will. These have often been followed by "reform" administrations, which tend to restrain, but not to reverse, concentrations of corporate power.

The federal government first took on a strong antitrust role with the Sherman Act of 1890, which outlawed monopoly and efforts to obtain it. In 1914 the Clayton Act also put restrictions on stock purchases and interlocking directorates that would reduce competition. This legislation responded to public anger and fears about "trusts," which brought separate firms under common control. Most notorious were Rockefeller's Standard Oil Trust and James Duke's American Tobacco Company, which employed ruthless tactics to drive their competitors out of business.

Early on the antitrust laws also treated organized labor as a "monopoly," and were used in breaking the Pullman strike in 1892. In 1908, the Supreme Court awarded damages to an employer against whom unions had organized a secondary boycott. This led to the Clayton Act exempting unions from its restrictions.

Otherwise, the federal government only minimally enforced the Sherman Act until Theodore Roosevelt was elected in 1900. Then in 1911 the Supreme Court decided that both the Standard Oil and American Tobacco trusts were "bad trusts," and ordered their dismantling. But in 1920 the Court refused to condemn the U.S. Steel consolidation, because it was a "good trust" that didn't attack its smaller rivals. This began a long period when the Antitrust Division and the courts approved mergers that produced industries with a few dominant firms, but which were "well-behaved." And in the 1920s, Republicans virtually ended antitrust enforcement.

The Golden Age

Franklin Roosevelt revived antitrust during 1938 to 1941, and antitrust law had its golden age from 1945 to 1974, fueled by a liberal Supreme Court, anti-merger legislation passed in 1950, and mildly progressive enforcement (though less so in the Republican years). During this period Alcoa's monopoly over aluminum production was broken (1945), and the Court found the tobacco industry guilty of "group monopoly" (1946), although the companies were only assessed a modest fine.

During the 1960s, when antitrust law blocked mergers among companies in the same industry, businesses adapted by acquiring firms in unrelated industries. Many such "conglomerate" mergers took place during 1964-68, when Lyndon Johnson was president. Companies like International Telephone and Telegraph, Ling-Temco-Vought, Gulf & Western, Tenneco, and Litton Industries grew rapidly.

The Reagan-Bush Collapse

Antitrust policy went into recession around 1974, then plunged during the presidencies of Ronald Reagan and George Bush. They aggressively dismantled antitrust, imposing drastic cuts in budgets and manpower, installing officials hostile to the antitrust mission, and failing to enforce the laws. During 1981-89, the Antitrust Division of the Justice Dept. challenged only 16 of over 16,000 pre-merger notices filed with them.

Despite his high-profile contest with Microsoft, Bill Clinton has largely accepted the conservative view that most mergers are harmless. In recent years, federal authorities have approved or ignored many giant mergers. These include Westinghouse's buyout of CBS, the joining of "Baby Bells" Bell Atlantic and Nynex, and the combination of Chemical Bank and Manufacturers Hanover. During 1997 alone, 156 mergers of $1 billion or more, and merger transactions totalling more than *$1 trillion*, passed antitrust muster.

Clinton's failure to attack giant mergers rests nominally on the alleged efficiency of large firms and the belief that globalized markets make for competition. FTC head Robert Pitofsky said, "this is an astonishing merger wave," but not to worry because these deals "should be judged on a global market scale, not just on national and local markets."

But the efficiency of large size—as opposed to the profit-making advantages that corporations gain from market power and cross-selling (pushing products through other divisions of the same company)—is eminently debatable. And many markets are not global—hospitals, for example, operate in local markets, yet only some 20 of 3,000 hospital mergers have been subjected to antitrust challenge. Even in global markets a few firms are often dominant, and a vast array of linkages such as joint ventures and licensing agreements increasingly mute global competition.

The Clinton administration's failure to contest many giant mergers does not rest only on intellectual arguments. It also reflects political weakness and an unwillingness to oppose powerful people who fund elections and own or dominate the media. This was conspicuously true of the great media combinations—Disney and Cap-Cities/ABC, and TimeWarner and Turner—and the merger of Boeing and McDonnell-Douglas, which involved institutions of enormous power, whose mergers the stock market greeted enthusiastically.

The Economists Sell Out

Since the early 1970s, powerful people and corporations have funded not only elections but conservative economists, who are frequently housed in think-tanks such as the American Enterprise, Hoover, and Cato Institutes, and serve as corporate consultants in regulatory and anti-trust cases. Most notable in hiring economic consultants have been AT&T and IBM, which together spent hundreds of millions of dollars on their antitrust defenses. AT&T hired some 30 economists from five leading economics departments during the 1970s and early 1980s.

Out of these investments came models and theories downgrading the "populist" idea that numerous sellers and decentralization were important for effective competition (and essential to a democratic society). They claimed instead that the market can do it all, and that regulation and antitrust actions are misconceived. First, theorists showed that efficiency gains from mergers might reduce prices even more than monopoly power would cause them to rise. Economists also stressed "entry," claiming that if mergers did not improve efficiency any price increases would be wiped out eventually by new companies entering the industry. Entry is also the heart of the theory of "contestable markets," developed by economic consultants to AT&T, who argued that the ease of entry in cases where resources (trucks, aircraft) can be shifted quickly at low cost, makes for effective competition.

Then there is the theory of a "market for corporate control," in which mergers allow better managers to displace the less efficient. In this view, poorly-managed firms have low stock prices, making them easy to buy. Finally, many economists justified conglomerate mergers on three grounds: that they function as "mini capital markets," with top managers allocating capital between divisions of a single firm so as to maximize efficiency; that they reduce transaction costs; and that they are a means of diversifying risk.

These theories, many coming out of the "Chicago School" (the economics department at the University of Chicago), suffer from over-simplification, a strong infusion of ideology, and lack of empirical support. Mergers often are motivated by factors other than enhancing efficiency—such as the desire for monopoly power, empire building, cutting taxes, improving stock values, and even as a cover for poor management (such as when the badly-run U.S. Steel bought control of Marathon Oil).

Several researchers have questioned the supposed benefits of mergers. In theory, a merger that improves efficiency should increase profits. But one study by Dennis Mueller, and another by F. W. Scherer and David Ravenscraft, showed that mergers more often than not have reduced returns to stockholders. A study by Michael Porter of Harvard University demonstrated that a staggering 74% of the conglomerate acquisitions of the 1960s were eventually sold off (divested)—a good indication that they were never based on improving efficiency. William Shepherd of the University of Massachusetts investigated the "contestable markets" model, finding that it is a hypothetical case with minimal applicability to the real world.

Despite their inadequacies, the new apologetic theories have profoundly affected policy, because they provide an intellectual rationale for the agenda of the powerful.

Sources: "Competition Policy in America: The Anti-Antitrust Paradox," James Brock, *Antitrust Bulletin*, Summer 1997; "The Promotional-Financial Dynamic of Merger Movements: A Historical Perspective," Richard DuBoff and Edward Herman, *Journal of Economic Issues*, March 1989; "Antimerger Policy in the United States: History and Lessons," Dennis C. Mueller, *Empirica*, 1996; "Dim Prospects: effective competition in telecommunications, railroads and electricity," William Shepherd, *Antitrust Bulletin*, 1997.

Article 5.5

THE BAILOUTS REVISITED
Who gets bailed out and why? Is there any alternative to "Too Big to Fail"?

BY MARTY WOLFSON
September/October 2009

Bank of America got bailed out, but Lehman Brothers was allowed to fail. The insurance company American International Group (AIG) was rescued, but in July federal authorities refused to bail out a significant lender to small and medium-sized businesses, the CIT Group (not to be confused with Citigroup, which did get bailed out).

What is the logic behind these decisions? Who is being bailed out—and who should be? The AIG story offers an instructive case study, one that sheds light on these and other questions.

Last September, the Federal Reserve Board announced that it was lending AIG up to $85 billion to prevent the firm's collapse. Unless it bailed out AIG, the Fed warned, financial markets could panic, loans could become more difficult to get, and many more businesses, jobs, and homes could be lost. To counter public anger over the bailout, the Fed argued that the ultimate beneficiaries would be the American people.

Citing proprietary information, AIG initially released few details about how it paid out the money it received. But this March, AIG's plan to pay $165 million in bonuses to employees at its Financial Products unit hit the headlines. An angry firestorm erupted: why should public bailout money be used to pay excessive bonuses to the very people who had caused the problem? U.S. officials and AIG CEO Edward Liddy denounced the payments as outrageous, but claimed they could not rescind the bonuses because they were bound by legal contracts. As it turned out, many AIG employees returned the bonuses voluntarily. And in a rare display of bipartisanship, the House of Representatives voted 328 to 93 to enact a 90% tax on bonuses paid to executives at companies that had received at least $5 billion in bailout money.

But the AIG bailout involved billions of dollars. The Financial Products employees only got millions. Who got the rest of the money? Under mounting public pressure, and after consulting with the Federal Reserve, AIG finally revealed who the beneficiaries were.

It's the Banks!

Yes, the money went primarily to large banks, those same banks that took their own large risks in the mortgage and derivatives markets and that are already receiving billions of dollars in federal bailout money. The banks are using AIG's bailout money to avoid taking losses on their contracts with the company.

Why did AIG, an insurance company, have such extensive dealings with the large banks, and why did those transactions cause so much trouble for AIG?

The story begins with AIG's London-based Financial Products unit, which issued a large volume of derivatives contracts known as credit default swaps (CDSs).

These were essentially insurance contracts that provided for payments to their purchasers (known as "counterparties") in the event of losses on collateralized debt obligations (CDOs), another kind of derivative. Many of the CDOs were based in complicated ways on payments on home mortgages. When the speculative housing bubble popped, mortgages could not be repaid, the CDOs lost value, and AIG was liable for payment on its CDSs.

By September 2008, AIG's situation had deteriorated to the point where its credit ratings were downgraded; this meant the company was required to post collateral on its CDS contracts, i.e., to make billions of dollars in cash payments to its counterparties to provide some protection for them against possible future losses. Despite its more than $1 trillion in assets, AIG did not have the cash. Without assistance it would have had to declare bankruptcy. After attempts to get the funding from private parties, including Goldman Sachs and JPMorgan Chase, failed, the Federal Reserve stepped in. The initial $85 billion credit line was followed by an additional $52.5 billion in credit two months later. By March 2009 the Treasury had invested $70 billion directly in the company, after which the Fed cut back its initial credit line to $25 billion.

AIG paid out those billions in several categories. Between September and December of 2008, $22.4 billion went to holders of CDSs as cash collateral. This cash was paid not only to those who sought insurance for CDOs they actually held, but also to speculators who purchased CDSs without owning the underlying securities. (Data to evaluate the extent of speculation involved have not been published.)

The largest beneficiaries of these payments were Société Générale, Deutsche Bank, Goldman Sachs, and Merrill Lynch.

Second, in an effort to stop the collateral calls on these CDSs, AIG spent $27.1 billion to purchase insured CDOs from its counterparties in return for their agreement to terminate the CDSs. Again, the largest beneficiaries of this program were Société Générale, Goldman Sachs, Merrill Lynch, and Deutsche Bank.

Third, it turned out that a significant cash drain on AIG was its securities lending program. Counterparties borrowed securities from AIG and in turn posted cash collateral with AIG. When AIG got into trouble, though, the counterparties decided that they wanted their cash back and sought to return the securities they had borrowed. However, AIG had used the cash to buy mortgage-backed securities, the same securities that were falling in value as the housing market crashed. So $43.7 billion of AIG's bailout money went to those counterparties—chiefly Barclays, Deutsche Bank, BNP Paribas, Goldman Sachs, and Bank of America, with Citigroup and Merrill Lynch not too far behind.

Necessary Bailouts?

Without all that bailout money going to the banks via AIG, wouldn't the financial system have crashed, the banks have stopped lending, and the recession have gotten worse? Well, no.

At least, the banks did not need to receive all the money they did. If a regulatory agency such as the Federal Reserve or the Federal Deposit Insurance Corporation had taken over AIG, it could have used the appropriate tools to, as Fed chair Ben Bernanke told a House committee this March, "put AIG into conservatorship or receivership, unwind it slowly, protect policyholders, and impose haircuts on creditors and counterparties as appropriate. That outcome would have been far preferable to the situation we find ourselves in now." (A haircut in this context is a reduction in the amount a claimant will receive.)

A sudden and disruptive bankruptcy of AIG could indeed have caused a crash of the financial system, especially as it would have come just one day after the sudden fall of Lehman Brothers on September 15. It is the element of surprise and uncertainty that leads to panic in financial markets. On the other hand, an orderly takeover of AIG such as Bernanke described, with clear information on how much counterparties would be paid, likely could have avoided such a panic.

So why didn't the Federal Reserve take over AIG? It said it did not have the legal authority to take over a nonbank financial institution like AIG. Indeed, to his credit, Bernanke frequently asks for such authority when he testifies to Congress. So why didn't the Fed demand it last September? Wasn't such authority important enough to make it a condition of the bailout? And couldn't Congress have passed the necessary legislation as quickly as it passed the bank bailout bill last fall and the tax on AIG bonuses? Even if that took a few weeks, the Fed could have lent money to AIG to keep it from failing until it had the authority to take the company over.

Of course, the Fed already has the authority to take over large troubled banks—but refuses to use it. Now, Fed and Treasury officials claim that since all the major banks passed the recently administered "stress test," such takeovers are unnecessary. However, even some of the banks that passed the test were judged to be in need of more capital. If they can't get it from private markets then, according to Treasury Secretary Timothy Geithner, the government is prepared to supply them with the capital they need.

In other words, the federal government's strategy of transferring extraordinary amounts of public money to large banks that lose money on risky deals will continue. In fact, the same strategy is evident in the Treasury's proposed Public Private Investment Program, which uses public money to subsidize hedge funds and other private investors to buy toxic assets from the banks. The subsidy allows the private investors to pay a higher price to the banks for their toxic assets than the banks could have received otherwise.

Bail Out the People

The consistent principle behind this strategy is that no large bank can fail. This is why the relatively small CIT Group wasn't rescued from potential bankruptcy but Bank of America was. The decision not to bail out Lehman Brothers, which led to panic in financial markets, is now considered a mistake. However, policymakers drew the wrong lesson from the Lehman episode: that all large bank failures must be prevented. They failed to recognize the important distinction between disruptive and controlled failures.

Yes, there are banks that are too big to fail suddenly and disruptively. However, any insolvent bank, no matter what its size, should be taken over in a careful and deliberative way. If this means nationalization, then so be it. Continental Illinois National Bank, at the time the 11th largest bank in the United States, was essentially nationalized in 1984, ending the turmoil in financial markets that Continental's difficulties had created.

This "too big to fail" strategy equates stabilizing the financial system and promoting the people's welfare with saving the corporate existence of individual large banks. Likewise the auto companies: while GM and Chrysler have been treated much more harshly than the banks, the auto bailout was similarly designed to keep these two corporate entities alive above all else, even at the expense of thousands of autoworker jobs.

The federal government's current bank-bailout strategy may be well-meaning, but there are four problems with it. It uses public money unnecessarily and is unfair to taxpayers. It may not work: it risks keeping alive "zombie banks" that are really insolvent and unwilling to lend, a recipe for repeating Japan's "lost decade" experience. It makes financial reform going forward much more difficult. Protecting the markets for derivative products like CDOs and CDSs allows for a repeat of the risky practices that got us into the current crisis. And finally, by guaranteeing the corporate existence of large banks, we are maintaining their power and priorities and thus are not likely to see gains on predatory lending, foreclosure abuse, and other areas where reform is sorely needed.

If we want to help the people who are suffering in this crisis and recession, then we should make financial policies with them directly in mind. Just throwing money at the banks will not get the job done.

Chapter 6

LABOR MARKETS

INTRODUCTION

Mainstream economics textbooks emphasize the ways that labor markets are similar to other markets. In the standard model, labor suppliers (workers) decide how much to work in the same way that producers decide how much to supply, by weighing the revenues against the costs—in this case, the opportunity costs of foregone leisure, and other potential costs of having a job, like physical injury. Labor demand is derived demand: Consumer demands for goods and services drive firms' production decisions, which in turn dictate the amount of labor to use. Workers are paid based on their marginal products—the amount that they contribute, per hour, to output. Thus workers earn different wages because they contribute different marginal products to output. Of course, economists of every stripe acknowledge that in reality, many non-market factors, such as government assistance programs, unionization, and discrimination, affect labor markets. But in most economics textbooks, these produce only limited deviations from the basic laws of supply and demand.

The authors in this chapter focus on these "deviations." In the first article, Amy Gluckman points out the persistent wage gap between men and women, and outlines "comparable worth" policies that compensate female-dominated jobs equally with male-dominated ones (Article 6.1). As her article suggests, the analyses in this chapter demand ambitious public policy—not simply ensuring the smooth operation of markets for labor and other inputs, but creating a better set of rules. Anna Sussman points to one of the more horrific consequences of the lack of "decent" jobs in the Democratic Republic of Congo, where children are driven by poverty to become child soldiers, thus participating in a vicious cycle whereby armed conflicts in turn make economic development even more unlikely (Article 6.2). The next article takes us from child soldiers to another kind of "Guard Labor" closer to home. Michael Perelman lists the ways in which the managers and supervisors who account for a growing share of the U.S. workforce divert society's resources from more productive functions to "guarding" property and disciplining workers. Perelman's discussion of the causes and consequences of this rising share of guard labor suggest a society with seriously misplaced priorities (Article 6.3).

The final set of articles addresses the impact of the "Great Repression" upon labor markets in the United States. Heather Boushey writes on how women workers are faring during the current economic "troubles." As men are losing jobs at an astonishing rate, women are increasingly the sole family breadwinners, although they play this role in lower-paid and precarious job sectors (Article 6.4). Meanwhile, older workers are returning to the labor force in an effort to rebuild retirement funds devastated by the 2008 financial collapse (Article 6.5).

When the invisible hand fails the labor market and we find crushing levels of unemployment, the short-run Keynesian solution is for the government to directly purchase labor. The American precedent was during the Great Depression, when Franklin Delano Roosevelt set up the Works Projects Administration (WPA) and the Civilian Conservation Corps (CCC) as part of the National Recovery Act. Unfortunately, no one in Washington seems willing to contemplate bold solutions of this nature. Instead, the only safety net available to the unemployed is an unemployment insurance system that Marianne Hill describes as "broken" (Article 6.6). As Hill points out, the system today covers both shrinking numbers of those in need, as well as a shrinking percentage of the incomes workers earn when employed.

Workers are thus beginning to take matters into their own hands as the recession deals a final blow to the tottering labor-management collective bargaining system. Immanuel Ness and Stacy Maddern report on the growing incidence of worker direct action (often without the support of unions) in the global north (Article 6.7). They point out that these actions have had some success and present us with cause for optimism about workers' abilities to regain some measure of economic "voice."

Discussion Questions

1) (Article 6.1) "Equal pay for equal work" has not proven sufficient to equalize women's and men's pay. Why not? Contrast the explanations of mainstream economic commentators with those of comparable worth advocates. Where do you come down in this debate?

2) (Article 6.1) Gender discrimination means that women workers (like workers from other marginalized groups) are "underpriced" relative to their true marginal products. If this is so, why don't rational, cost-minimizing businesses snap up these low-cost workers, bidding their wages back up to their marginal product?

3) (Article 6.1) At the close of her article, Amy Gluckman contrasts comparable worth with a "far more radical" revaluation of different types of work. Explain the difference between the two. How do each of these programs of reform relate to the idea that wages are set to equal marginal product?

4) (Article 6.2) Do you view the market for child soldiers in the Congo as a labor market like any another? Why or why not?

5) (Article 6.3) What are some examples of "guard labor"?

6) (Article 6.4) What would account for the recent labor market decline of American men? What challenges does this place on the increasing share of women who are

now the sole breadwinners for their families? Do you see these trends continuing no matter what the economic future brings?

7) (Article 6.5) What do you know about the current U.S. system of Social Security? What are some ways in which the greater workforce participation of senior citizens could affect the current system? What do you see as the pros and cons of "privatizing" Social Security?

8) (Article 6.6) The current system of unemployment insurance is based upon a combination of tax and subsidy. How would your textbook analyze the pros and cons of such a system? Does Marianne Hill's analysis differ from that?

9) (Article 6.6) What are some reasons why Hill describes the unemployment insurance system as "broken"?

10) (Article 6.7) What was the traditional "collective bargaining" arrangement between unions and managements? Why have the workers described in Ness and Maddern turned to "direct action" instead?

11) (General) A number of *Real World Micro* authors, including Amy Gluckman in this chapter, claim that labor unions are much-needed equalizers that help low-wage workers. Orthodox economists tend to be much more negative about unions, arguing that they interfere with the smooth functioning of labor markets and pit the interests of a small group of workers against the broader interests of all workers and consumers. Explain how these differing assessments of unions are connected to differing views of *how the labor market works*. Where do you come down in this debate?

Article 6.1

COMPARABLE WORTH

BY AMY GLUCKMAN
September/October 2002

There must be something to an idea that the business press has recently labeled "crackpot," "more government humor," an attempt "to Sovietize U.S. wage scales," and one of ten "dumbest ideas of the century." The idea is comparable worth (or "pay equity"), a broad term for a range of policies aimed at reducing the pay gap between occupations traditionally filled by women and those traditionally filled by men.

Comparable worth proposals first appeared in the 1970s, when women's rights campaigners began to recognize that much of the pay gap between men and women occurred not because women were paid less for doing the exact same work, but because women workers were concentrated in occupations that paid less than male-dominated occupations.

Consider a nurse who earns less than a maintenance worker working for the same employer. (This is typical of the pay gaps researchers uncovered in studies of municipal pay scales in several U.S. cities in the 1970s.) The nurse is responsible for the well-being and even the lives of her patients, and the job typically requires at least two years of postsecondary education. The maintenance worker may have far less serious responsibilities and probably did not even need a high-school diploma to get the job. Why might he earn more? His job may be physically demanding and may entail unpleasant or risky working conditions (although so may hers!). But in many cases, any reasonable evaluation of the two jobs supports the nurse's claim that she should earn the higher salary.

Comparable worth advocates argue that this kind of pay gap is the result of gender bias. Historically, they claim, employers set wages in various occupations based on mistaken stereotypes about women—that women had little to contribute, that they were just working for "pin money." These wage differences have stuck over time, leaving the 60% of women who work in female-dominated occupations (as well as the small number of men who do) at a disadvantage. Studies show that even after other factors affecting wages are accounted for, the percentage of women in an occupation has a net downward effect on that occupation's average wage.

Mainstream economists take issue with this view. How do they explain the persisting wage gap between male-dominated and female-dominated occupations? The market, of course. Wages are not set by evaluating the requirements of each job, they claim, but rather by shifts in the supply of and demand for labor. In this view, the nurse-janitor pay gap represents the outcome of past employment discrimination against women. Discrimination in hiring kept women out of many occupations, resulting in an oversupply of women entering the traditionally-female jobs such as nursing. This oversupply kept wages in those fields low. Not to worry: as gender bias against women wanes and women are able to enter the full range of occupations, some economists argue, this situation will resolve itself and the pay gap between female- and male-dominated occupations will disappear.

As it turns out, the majority of women workers continue to labor within the confines of the "pink-collar" ghetto. Women have indeed entered certain professions in significant numbers over the past thirty years. Physicians were 10% female in 1972, but 27.9% female in 2000. Lawyers and judges were 3.8% female in 1972, but 29.7% female in 2000. But the extent of sex segregation in a wide range of occupations has barely budged during this time. Teachers (K-12) were 70% female in 1972; 75.4% female in 2000. Secretaries were 99.1% female in 1972; 98.9% female in 2000. Hairdressers were an identical 91.2% female in 1972 and in 2000! Retail sales clerks were 68.9% female in 1972; 63.5% female in 2000. On the other side, automobile mechanics were 0.5% female in 1972; 1.2% female in 2000. Plumbers were 0.3% female in 1972; 1.9% female in 2000. (Women moved into a few blue-collar jobs in greater—but still relatively low—numbers. For example, telephone installers were 0.5% female in 1972, but 13.1% female in 2000.) So either employers are still discriminating directly against women to a significant degree, or else the mainstream economists' predictions about the effects of waning job discrimination are wrong—or both.

Another analysis points to the lower wages women earn as the price they pay for choosing jobs that give them the flexibility to fulfill parenting responsibilities. For example, many women (and a few men) choose to become teachers so that they can be home with their children in the late afternoon and during school vacations. But leaving gender aside, do employees typically trade off lower wages for greater flexibility? Higher-paid jobs tend to have more flexibility, not less. If this argument has some relevance for women in female-dominated professions such as teaching, it ignores entirely the vast number of women in low-wage, female-dominated occupations: retail clerk, direct care worker, waitress, beautician. These jobs certainly don't offer their occupants flexibility in return for their low wages.

Conservative commentators also stress that the overall wage gap between men and women—women employed full time, year round earn about 74% as much as men—is reasonable because women on average have fewer years of work experience and less seniority. That's true, but accounts for only about 40% of the gap. That leaves about 15 to 16 cents on every dollar unaccounted for. (Ironically, it is deindustrialization and the resulting decline in men's wages—not growth in women's wages—that has been primarily responsible for the shrinking of the gender wage gap, down from 59% in 1970.)

So the work force continues to be segregated by sex, and women's wages continue to lag behind men's, if not as much as in the past. What can be done? Comparable worth advocates have used a variety of strategies: legislation, lawsuits, collective bargaining agreements. Typically, advocates call for employers to use job evaluation instruments that rate different jobs according to several criteria such as skill, responsibility, and working conditions. Job evaluation instruments like these are not new; many large corporations already use them in their ordinary personnel procedures.

Of course, a job rating scale does not automatically indicate how to weight different factors in determining compensation, and so does not in itself determine how much a job should pay. Usually, this piece of the puzzle comes from information about what employers actually do pay. In other words, these instruments don't exclude the market from consideration. Instead, they usually take market wages for various occupations as baseline data to determine how much value to assign to different job characteristics. Then, however, employees and employers can recognize jobs that fall off the curve—jobs that pay much more or much less than the broad average of jobs with the same rating. On this basis, workers can then push employers to raise the wages of "underpaid" jobs.

The comparable worth movement made a lot of headway in the 1970s and early 1980s, primarily in unionized, public-sector workplaces. However, comparable worth barely made a dent in the private sector. Even in the public sector, the movement's momentum slowed by the late 1980s. Today, Congress is again considering legislation authorizing workers to sue their employers in order to correct pay inequities between male- and female-dominated job titles and also between race-segregated job titles.

Comparable worth legislation, if enacted, could potentially give an enormous boost to low-wage women workers. One study estimates that "among those currently earning less than the federal poverty threshold for a family of three, nearly 50% of women of color and 40% of white women would be lifted out of poverty" by a national comparable worth policy that addressed both race-segregated and sex-segregated occupations.

However, comparable worth is not a cure-all. Since comparable worth typically addresses wage gaps within a single workplace, it does not help workers whose employers pay everyone the minimum wage. Without strong unions, comparable worth won't get very far even if new legislation were enacted; for one thing, it is unions that are most likely to be able to fund the expensive litigation necessary to force companies to revise their pay scales. At a deeper level, existing comparable worth policies largely accept how the U.S. economic system has typically rewarded different job factors. It is one thing to even out pay inequities between jobs that rate the same on existing job-evaluation instruments. It would be far more radical to rebuild our notions of fair compensation in a way that values the skills of caring, communication, and responsibility for people's emotional well-being that are critical to many female-dominated occupations.

Sources: Deborah M. Figart and Heidi I. Hartmann, "Broadening the Concept of Pay Equity: Lessons for a Changing Economy" in Ron Baiman, Heather Boushey, Dawn Saunders, eds., *Political Economy and Contemporary Capitalism: Radical Perspectives on Economic Theory and Policy* (M. E. Sharpe, 2000); "In Pursuit of Pay Equity" in *Women at Work: Gender and Inequality in the '80s*, Economic Affairs Bureau, 1985; Paula England, "The case for comparable worth," *Quarterly Review of Economics and Finance* 39:3, Fall 1999; *Forbes*, December 27, 1999; *Statistical Abstract of the United States.*

Article 6.2

CONSCRIPTED BY POVERTY

BY ANNA SUSSMAN
November/December 2007

Providing economic alternatives has been key to the successful demobilization of nearly 30,000 child soldiers in eastern Congo.

Ronaldo is covered with a thin layer of sawdust. As the sun sets over a hilltop woodshop in eastern Congo, the 16-year-old takes a moment to rest, wiping his brow with a cloth. He's been sawing all day, cutting wood for chairs, tables and shelves. The work is hard and physically demanding, but it's better than his last job: child soldier.

Two years ago, at the age of 14, Ronaldo, whose name has been changed to protect his identity, joined a local armed rebel group.

"I thought it would give me a better life," he said.

He says he joined voluntarily. But advocates here say that Ronaldo's recruitment was not exactly voluntary: while he was not forced with a gun or knife, Ronaldo, like thousands of other child soldiers in the Congo, was compelled to join an armed group by extreme poverty. "My family didn't have enough food or money," he says. "That's why I decided to join."

In the Democratic Republic of the Congo, more than 33,000 young people have been associated with armed groups in recent years, mostly in the troubled eastern Congo region. UNICEF officials and international aid agencies operating here say the child soldier epidemic in eastern Congo can be traced largely to economics. Across the globe there are many reasons children join armed groups—some are forcibly abducted, for example, while others are looking for revenge or prestige. But advocates here are finding that poverty is the driving force: many children enlist for the minimal food and shelter it will provide them.

"In such a poor country as the Democratic Republic of the Congo, there are economic factors that drive children towards joining armed groups or forces," says Pernile Ironside, a protection specialist with UNICEF in eastern Congo. "Families tend to be very large, so there is a certain allure for children to join up with a military group, where they are able to get enough food to eat," she said. "Occasionally parents, as well, drive children to join [an armed group], recognizing that they can't meet the needs of their child and that the child may be better off in their view by leaving the family and joining up with a group."

That's why UNICEF, along with other international agencies, is focusing its demobilization efforts on economic solutions.

"Fundamentally the reason is economic," says Murhabazi Namegabe, who directs a child soldier demobilization center in Bukavu. "Ninety-nine percent of these children come from poor families. The main problem we are dealing with is how to provide assistance for their families."

In Congo, where civil war has raged since President Mobutu Sese Seko was overthrown in 1997, young people have grown up in a climate of brutal warfare in which families are regularly slaughtered, homes burned, and villages destroyed.

Although the war is officially over and the country held democratic elections last year, the fighting continues today as ethnic, political, and government factions battle along Congo's mineral-rich border with Rwanda.

The eastern Congo region is controlled by more than a dozen armed groups, many battling over the valuable mineral resources abundant in this region of the country: gold, diamonds, and coltan (short for columbite-tantalite), a mineral widely used in the manufacture of electronic gadgets like mobile phones, computer chips, and VCRs. But the billions of dollars extracted from the ground here are enjoyed by an elite few, while hundreds of warlords and soldiers on the ground vie for control over civilian territories with brutal force.

Many children, including Ronaldo, have joined local "Mai-Mai" militias, decentralized armed groups operating across the region who claim they are engaging in self-defense against the government and ethnic rebel groups. Others are conscripted by the national army, says Ironside.

But amid the fighting, UNICEF is successfully negotiating for the removal of children from armed groups. Today, nearly 6,000 former child soldiers are learning income-generating activities like sewing, woodworking, and bicycle repair. This way, children like Ronaldo will be able to survive without the patronage of an armed group, says Ironside.

Restricting Re-recruitment

The "skill-building" demobilization programs championed by UNICEF and others, like Save the Children, began several years ago and have been hugely successful. In all, 29,000 child soldiers have been demobilized in the Congo since 2002. But at the same time the financial security promised by armed groups continues to draw in poor children.

"Re-recruitment is something that is best prevented by giving real opportunities to children once they've left an armed group," says Ironside. "Opportunities could entail going back to school, learning a trade, or having a small income-generating project or business because children really need to regain their hope for the future and visualize what else they may be able to become, aside from being part of an armed group."

In a small cement building in the city of Bukavu, 300 former child soldiers have just completed a six-month training course in sewing and tailoring with the Dutch-based nongovernmental organization War Child. At the graduation ceremony, students and parents sing songs, bang drums, and dance. Then, they stand up and give testimony to their newly learned skills.

"With this experience I will never go back to armed forces," says 19-year-old Papi Bijeri. "My weapon now is what I learned; that is how I will survive." Bijeri, who was orphaned at a young age, says he joined a rebel group "to earn some money and survive."

While fighting, Bijeri participated in gang-rape and killing, and eventually earned the position of bodyguard to a high-ranking commander, a job that earned him about $9 a month plus a bar of soap and food.

The War Child program takes children directly from drop-off centers, where they are left by armed rebel groups taking the steps required to integrate into the national army. During their six-month training, most of the children live with relatives or friends in the town. When the course is completed, they receive a small tool kit, including a prized sewing machine. It's a model that is repeated, with some variation, in programs across the region.

When Basic Needs Go Unmet

There are between 200,000 and 300,000 child soldiers worldwide. Many are abducted and forced into armed groups. Others "volunteer." Stating that young people require special protection because of their physical and mental immaturity, however, the U.N. Convention on the Rights of the Child prohibits military recruitment—voluntary or not—of children under 18.

Most child soldiers come from nations that have dissolved into civil war. Child soldiers are a symptom that states which lack the capacity to meet their citizens' most basic needs. "Poverty and its link to the crisis of child soldiers around the globe is inextricably linked to other antecedent factors," says Eddie Mandhry of the New York-based group Global Kids. "These factors include the deterioration of social infrastructures prior to or during times of war and the economic and political marginalization and disaffection of youth."

Just as poverty can motivate the struggle over resources that is often at the root of war, war itself amplifies poverty and the problems that often accompany it—problems like corruption, lawlessness, and limited education. Families collapse, schools stop running, work opportunities disappear, and food becomes scarce. Looking to bolster their ranks, warlords lure physically vulnerable and economically desperate children, many without families, into armed groups. Most end up being forced to do terrible things. Many former child soldiers in Congo report being forced to rape and kill villagers. Ronaldo says he was forced to work on the frontlines, walking for days on end without food.

"Children are quite easily manipulated," Ironside says. "And it doesn't take a whole lot for them to perhaps become motivated to do something, given their extreme poverty and the fact that they might not consider the consequences of a particular action."

As violent instability and war have ravaged Congo, per-capita annual income (adjusted for inflation) fell from $380 in 1960 to $100 in 2004, according to the IMF. The vast majority of households in eastern Congo have no running water or electricity, and few of the children attend school. Women report that armed groups regularly steal crops from their fields, leaving their families hungry.

Across the African great lakes region, where violent unrest spills across borders between Uganda, Burundi, Rwanda, and Congo, the vast majority of households live on less than a dollar a day. Not surprisingly, potential child soldiers are in large supply.

A Generation of Soldiers

But demobilization programs are taking hold in eastern Congo. Most of the income-generating and skill-building programs run by UNICEF and its partners here are coupled with counseling and group play-therapy, where children learn to cope with the atrocities they have seen or carried out.

In towns like Bukavu in the South Kivu province of eastern Congo where UNICEF programs work one-on-one with children to teach them job skills, most children are able to resist re-recruitment.

But farther north in the villages of North Kivu, where ethnic fighting between Hutu militants and the Congolese army continues to play out, the situation is worse. UNICEF officials estimate that hundreds of former child soldiers have been re-recruited in North Kivu in recent months. "About three-quarters of children who were demobilized have been re-recruited because of a lack of jobs," says Namegabe.

The head of U.N. humanitarian efforts in North Kivu, Patrick Lavand'Homme, says he fears the United Nations will be unable to meet the huge demand for basic supplies like food and water if the fighting continues. And the Congolese government has shown little interest in providing humanitarian help. As needs become more desperate, Ironside says, more than 5,000 more children in North Kivu are at risk of being re-recruited.

There are many reasons for the child soldier crisis, but until real economic needs are met here, children will continue to be attracted to the promises of food, money, and shelter offered by armed groups.

The conflict in this region has been called Africa's World War. Asked why his homeland has seen so much war, 16-year-old Ronaldo does not pause to think. As he picks up his saw and resumes his woodwork, he gives a simple answer.

"There are no jobs here. People want to work but there is no work to do. If everyone had a job that had a decent salary, there would be peace in the country."

Resources: UNICEF, "Displaced children especially vulnerable to illness and military re-recruitment in North Kivu," 2007; Child Rights Information Network, crin.org; Human Rights Watch Child Soldiers Campaign, hrw.org/campaigns/crp; Amnesty International, "Democratic Republic of Congo: Children at War," 2003.

Article 6.3

THE RISE OF GUARD LABOR

How the capitalists' need to control access to goods and services—and to control workers—deforms the productive process and stifles creativity.

BY MICHAEL PERELMAN
January/February 2010

Guards are everywhere in a capitalist economy. A few are dressed up in uniforms, so they are easy to spot. But most do not look like guards at all. Some sit in comfortable offices; others work on assembly lines in factories. James O'Connor, a prolific sociologist from UC Santa Cruz, describes one familiar set of guards whom we do not usually think of as guards:

> Consider the labor of the ticket seller at a movie house. The seller's task is merely to transfer the right to sit in the theater to the moviegoer in exchange for the price of a ticket. But it may not be immediately obvious that it is not the lack of a ticket that keeps you out of the theater...The ticket is actually torn up and discarded by a husky young man who stands between the box office and the seat that I want.

These guards are a central feature of capitalism. Capitalists depend upon guard labor to protect their commodities, including the goods and premises they own, but especially the labor-power in their employ. Capitalism's reliance on guard labor deforms the entire productive process, not only wasting labor, but also snuffing out badly needed creativity.

Counterproductive Capitalist Control

Capitalists are only able to market their goods to the extent that they can deny people access to goods without payment. Therefore, business must devote considerable effort just to protect its ownership.

Theaters have layers of guards: one sells the tickets; another tears them up. With the advent of modern technology, a new generation of guards works to prevent people from accessing the show outside of the theater: hordes of lawyers and technicians work to create laws or develop new technologies to prevent the digital leakage of these commodities.

Unlike the movie theater operator, some providers of goods and services allow the consumer access to the product before payment. The guardians still must make sure that consumers complete the transaction by paying their bills. This activity employs many people—cashiers, bill collectors, etc. Then, to ensure that all this guard labor works effectively, another layer of guardians must oversee the accounts.

Millions of auxiliary workers labor to provide the resources necessary to support guard labor. These workers build and maintain the offices, produce the telecommunications infrastructure, and supply other goods and services required by the guards to do their work. These workers have their own complement of guards to oversee their work.

Guard labor is everywhere. Look at the shelves of a store. Layers of packaging encase commodities. The purpose of some packaging is to entice consumers to find the product more appealing or to protect it from damage. The function of much more of the packaging is to deter theft. Small items are wrapped in plastic and packed in boxes, which themselves are wrapped in plastic. This means that consumers have to assist in guarding the commodity by putting up with the nuisance of tediously extracting the commodity and disposing of the wasted materials. A long chain of guard labor associated with the packaging extends from the production of the raw materials to those who finally haul away the extra garbage.

Much white-collar work consists of nothing more than guard labor. Even some blue-collar work that appears to be directly providing services is actually guard labor. Years ago, gas station attendants pumped gas. In exceptional cases, some people needed assistance in filling their tanks, but most people did not. The attendant, who was supposed to be a service worker, was actually performing guard labor to make sure that the customers paid.

Eventually, this deception fell apart. Once modern technology allowed one person to lock and unlock the pumps at a distance, one guard could supervise several pumps. People began to pump the gas on their own, revealing the previous attendants' chief function as guards. This is one exceptional case in which the total amount of guard labor has declined. Across the U.S. economy as a whole, however, it has increased dramatically over the last century.

The rise in guard labor represents a significant drain on economic potential. The U. S. Department of Labor predicts that by 2012, the nation will have more private security guards than high school teachers. Although such comparisons do not constitute proof of inefficiency, they do indicate a distorted set of priorities.

Guard Labor in the Workplace

Where the commodity in question is the employees' working time, the direct supervision of labor represents an obvious form of guard labor. Rather than empower workers to take on more responsibility, employers restrict workers' autonomy by relying instead on guard labor (supervisors).

In 1890, supervisors made up a mere 0.8% of the U.S. labor force. By 1979, just before the time when corporations began their efforts to flatten their hierarchical bureaucratic structures, the share of supervisors in the labor force had risen to 11.7%. By 2002, that number had risen by more than a third, to 15.7%. If we add in guards in the narrowest sense (security personnel) and military personnel, that number swells to nearly 20%. If we add in prisoners and the unemployed, whose fate serves to warn existing providers of labor-power to keep their noses to the grindstone, the 2002 figure tops 26%. These numbers do not even include the millions of workers who supply the material resources necessary for the guards to carry out their work, including the modern technology used to spy on workers.

The rising share of guard labor is not a uniform consequence of modernization. Significant differences exist among modern societies. In particular, the United States uses a far higher share of supervisory workers than any other advanced capitalist economy, employing 15.7% of its labor force in some sort of supervisory position. England, with 13.4%, is not far behind. In comparison, Sweden, with its more egalitarian society, has only 4.4% of its labor force working as supervisors. The share of supervisory labor in the United States is closely related to increasing inequality over the last 35 years, now approaching levels found in impoverished Third World countries.

The maintenance of the authority of guard labor requires additional resources, perhaps most transparently in the military, where soldiers must march around in formation, something that does nothing whatsoever to improve their ability to fight. Nothing would make soldiers more vulnerable than to march in formation on the battlefield. This activity merely habituates the troops to mindlessly take orders. Presumably, once responding to command becomes instinctual, soldiers in the heat of battle will instantaneously follow orders regardless of the consequences for their own well-being.

Some capitalist firms seem to engage in a similar strategy. In his memoir, *Notes From Toyota-Land: An American Engineer in Japan*, Darius Mehri describes this scene at a Toyota plant:

> A huge group of company employees was lined up, military-style, all dressed in Toyota company uniforms of one-piece jumpers and soft brimmed hats. The hat was the same style used by Japanese soldiers during World War II, and it was standard issue for all employees at the company. One employee stood at the front directing the drill. He would shout out a slogan and the group would shout back in unison. This display of group obedience reminded me of old films of the Japanese military.

The point of this memoir was that the system dissipated enormous energy in enforcing dysfunctional hierarchies.

This sort of discipline-enforcing practice is certainly not limited to any particular company or country. Business meetings offer an interesting analogue to military

TABLE 1: GUARD LABOR AND ITS COMPONENTS AS A PERCENTAGE OF THE LABOR FORCE IN THE UNITED STATES: 1890–2002

	1890	1929	1948	1966	1979	1989	2002
Supervisors	0.8	1.4	9.8	9.9	11.7	13.2	15.7
Guards	0.3	0.7	0.8	0.9	1.7	1.8	2.2
Military	0.3	0.8	3.3	5.4	3	3.1	1.8
Prisoners	0.4	0.2	0.2	0.3	0.3	0.5	1.5
Unemployed	4.2	3.8	4.7	4.5	6.7	6.3	4.8
Total	6	6.9	18.9	20.9	23.4	24.9	26.1

Source: Arjun Jayadev, "Estimating Guard Labor.," U. Mass-Boston working paper series, 2006.

marches. The ostensible purpose of meetings is to improve efficiency, but anybody who attends a few soon realizes that they are mostly pointless.

Simon Ramo, co-founder of the defense company TRW Inc., estimated that of the more than 40,000 meetings he attended, about 30,000 could have been shorter or eliminated altogether without any loss to the company—even ignoring the extra productivity that the company could enjoy allowing people to work rather than attend meetings. Since he probably called many of these meetings himself, he may even be giving these meetings too much credit. Yet the frequency of meetings continues to rise. The average executive participated in twice as many meetings in the 1980s as in the 1960s.

Anybody familiar with managerial procedures realizes that much of the meeting time spent is more ceremonial than functional. People come face to face with their superiors. The underlings watch others fall in line and realize that any dissent can jeopardize a career. In short, meetings function as a means to impose discipline on white-collar workers, much like the soldiers' marches.

Although managers might justify meetings as a morale booster, survey data indicate that more frequent meetings *reduce* participants' sense of well-being. Even more important, authoritarian relations themselves snuff out valuable creativity. A system more devoted to meeting the needs of people and less intent on solidifying hierarchy would encourage more autonomy and voluntary collaboration without the formalities of meetings.

The metaphor of guard labor becomes more literal for workers employed in the U.S. criminal justice system. In 2001, the system employed 2.3 million. Its clientele has also multiplied. By 2003, the number of prisoners had reached more than six times the 1972 level. As of year-end 2006, more than 2.2 million people in the United States were in federal or state prisons or in local jails, representing a population larger than 17 individual states of the union. An additional 5 million adults were on probation or parole.

	Supervisors	Unemployed	Military	Prisoners	Total
Switzerland	5.8	2.7	1	0.1	9.7
Iceland	7.9	2.6	0	0.1	10.6
Sweden	4.4	5.3	1.1	0.1	10.9
Denmark	6.9	3.6	0.9	0.1	11.5
Norway	7.3	3.6	1.4	0.1	12.4
Austria	6.8	4.3	1.3	0.2	12.6
Portugal	6.7	4.4	1.4	0.3	12.7
Italy	2.9	9.7	1.5	0.2	14.3
Netherlands	11.6	3	0.8	0.2	15.7
Ireland	10.6	4.1	0.9	0.2	15.8
Canada	8.5	7.2	0.4	0.2	16.3
Belgium	10.3	6.6	1	0.2	18.1
Australia	11.1	6.3	0.5	0.2	18.2
New Zealand	11.9	5.5	0.5	0.3	18.3
Spain	6.7	11.9	0.9	0.3	19.8
United Kingdom	13.4	5.5	0.7	0.2	19.9
United States	15.7	4.8	1	1.4	22.9
Greece	9.1	10.3	4.5	0.2	24

TABLE 2: GUARD LABOR AND ITS COMPONENTS AS A PERCENTAGE OF THE LABOR FORCE IN EIGHTEEN ADVANCED ECONOMIES, 2002:

Notes: Unemployment data are average of 2001–2003. Military data do not include civilian employees of the military. Prisoner data are for the latest year available,1998 to 2001.

Sources: Arjun Jayadev, "Estimating Guard Labor." U. Mass-Boston working paper series, 2006; Roy Walmsley, "A world prison population list," Research, Development and Statistics Directorate, Home Office, UK, 2003.

Prisons represent an important tool of control. Besides serving as a vital component of guard labor in protecting private property, the criminal justice system threatens members of the working class who might resist the discipline of the market. What might pass for an immature prank for a wealthy college student will be punished as a serious offense for a member of the working class. Perhaps nothing symbolizes this disparity as much as the differential penalties for powder cocaine and crack cocaine. More often than not, the courts require only that privileged people caught with powder cocaine enter some sort of clinic while severely punishing a similar offense by a poor, often black man found with crack.

The intended lesson of the prison-industrial complex is that working-class people are expected to work hard and toe the line. No deviations will be tolerated. Maybe if they get rich enough, then society will permit them to do more or less what they choose.

Less Obvious Forms of Guard Labor

By any rational standards, guard labor should be in decline. As the example of gas station attendants suggests, rapid progress in information technologies should have the effect of reducing the number of people keeping track of others; instead, business has largely taken advantage of information technologies to refine its control.

Businesses use computers to record the keystrokes of data-entry workers or the movements of truck drivers. The potential scope of such tracking expands almost daily. For example, Radio Frequency Identification chips now offer the potential to keep track of every employee's physical location.

Such applications of modern technology serve as a reminder of how extensive the ranks of guard labor are. At least some of the efforts of scientists and engineers who develop such technologies should count as guard labor. The same logic holds for the workers who build the computers and maintain the buildings that support this technology.

Some forms of guard labor become so familiar that people might not recognize them for what they really are. For example, consider the ubiquitous cash register. Toy makers even produce models of cash registers for children. The original purpose of the cash register was intended to help storeowners prevent employee theft. Since the register kept a record of each transaction that the employee rang up, clerks were more likely to deposit customers' payments. Warren Buffett's partner, Charles Munger, once proposed: "The cash register did more for human morality than the Congregational Church."

The registers were not foolproof, however, since employees still had the option of not ringing up the sale and then pocketing the money for themselves. To make the clerk more likely to record the sale, employers turned to ninety-nine-cent pricing, making customers less likely to pay the exact price. The clerk, in turn, would need to ring up the sale to get the proper change. Today, fast food restaurants offer a variant of this strategy. Customers can receive free meals if the clerk fails to give them a receipt, which serves the same function as the penny.

New technology also allows specialized businesses to track the behavior of private citizens outside of the workplace. These companies aggregate information from banks, credit card companies, government agencies, credit reports, magazine subscriptions, mailing lists, and every other imaginable source. This industry provides important services that make certain kinds of guard labor far more effective—for example, in tracking down past-due bills.

In effect then, the efforts to track and monitor workers and commodities spill over into everyday life where the justification of guarding one's property is no longer relevant. This amalgamation of detailed personal information, which makes a mockery of the right to privacy, gives business enormous power in the marketplace. Business even makes the claim that its detailed knowledge of personal information, such as an individual's financial situation and consumption patterns, allows it to serve the public better—as if profit were the farthest thing from the mind of corporate executives.

How Rigid Control Paralyzes Creativity

Although authoritarian measures might be a convenient means of ensuring that people carry out orders with a minimum of hassle for those in authority, they also destroy individual initiative, especially for lower-ranking workers. Over the long run, the stifling of creativity causes significant cumulative losses, making authoritarian measures of control self-defeating.

For example, in the open-source software movement, thousands of programmers voluntarily contribute to the ever-growing mass of software. Some people have the responsibility of coordinating these inputs but nobody commands the programmers. Even so, the open-source software movement manages to produce software that is superior to the products of the mammoth Microsoft empire.

One might argue that open-source software is not a very convincing example. After all, the process of creating software does not require split-second coordination, even though the programs themselves have to be tightly drawn. As a result, the process itself has considerable leeway. The same conclusions about the value of greater latitude for workers' creativity, however, carry over even to the factory assembly line.

Shoshana Zuboff, a professor at Harvard Business School, reported on her experience as a consultant for a number of paper factories during the 1980s when computer controls were first being introduced throughout the industry. In one factory, the computer system was initially accessible by everybody, including the workers on the production line. Workers could see the same information on costs and prices as management. At first, the workers used their newfound information to make very profitable modifications of the production process. Management, horrified by the possibility that workers were going to make managerial control at least partially irrelevant, quickly cut off the workers' access to the system.

The behavior of the managers of the paper factory illustrate the conflict between desire to control subordinates and the opportunity to take advantage of their otherwise hidden capacities. Therefore, in the end, crude techniques of control might be able to force outward compliance, but ultimately they are unable to harness people's full potential. Nobody can make another person work very effectively at the point of a bayonet—especially if that work requires any skill or discretion.

The sharing of information should be a high priority in any organization in which information is supposed to be a central input. Besides, sharing can stimulate productivity in other ways. Jeffrey Pfeffer, professor of organizational behavior at Stanford University, observed:

> Sharing information with another party signifies trust. That trust is likely to be reciprocated. Conversely, when a company keeps secrets from its employees it signals it does not trust its employees to keep secrets or to use the withheld information effectively. Those feelings of distrust and disdain are also likely to be reciprocated ... Decentralizing decision-making also signals trust and a belief in employees' competence, again engaging the norm of reciprocity.

Unfortunately, control has more allure than profits. After all, the exercise of power and control becomes a major source of enjoyment in itself, over and above providing a defense of existing privileges. Much more than personal psychology is involved here. Hardened managerial traditions resist change. Besides, the corporate structure with is many layers prevents information from filtering up.

Resistance from Below

Because most people do not enjoy taking orders and have a natural tendency to assert some independence, workers can become downright rebellious when workplace authorities do not treat them with respect, especially when they feel confident that comparable jobs are readily available.

For that reason, when unemployment was unusually low in the late 1960s, workplace authority was far less effective. For example, in 1968, sociologist Bill Watson spent a year working in a Detroit automobile factory, where he witnessed several dramatic examples of the lengths to which workers went to challenge management. In one instance, workers revolted against the production of a poorly designed car. After management rejected workers' suggestions for improvements in the production and design, the workers initiated a "counterplan," beginning with acts of deliberately misassembling or omitting parts. Later, workers in inspection made alliances with workers in several assembly areas to ensure a high rate of defective motors. Eventually, even more complicated measures were taken.

In the process, workers and foremen argued over particular motors. Tension escalated. Workers went ahead and installed defective motors in cars, thereby requiring that management would have to go to the trouble and expense of removing them later. The conflict only ended when management suddenly moved the entire assembly and inspection operation to another end of the plant, presumably at great cost.

In a second instance, the company, intending to save money by shutting down its foundry early, attempted to build engines using already-rejected parts. Workers in the motor-test area protested, but management hounded inspectors to accept the defective motors. After the motor-test men communicated their grievances to other workers, they began to collaborate in intentional sabotage. Inspectors agreed to reject three of every four motors. Stacks of motors piled up at an accelerating pace until the entire plant shut down, losing more than 10 hours of production time to deal with the problem. When management summoned inspectors to the head supervisor's office, the inspectors slyly protested that they were only acting in the interest of management.

Watson's third example is the most telling of all. During a model changeover period, management had scheduled a six-week inventory buildup, keeping fifty people on the job. These workers would have earned 90% of their pay if they had been laid off. Workers reacted to the opportunity, attempting to finish the inventory buildup in three or four days instead of the six weeks. They trained each other in particular skills, circumventing the established ranking and job classification system to slice through the required time.

Management responded harshly, forcing workers to halt, claiming that they had violated the legitimate channels of authority, training, and communication. If workers had been given the opportunity to organize their own work, Watson claims, they could have completed the task in one-tenth the scheduled time. Management, however, was determined to stop workers from organizing their own work, even when it would have been finished more quickly and management would have saved money because of the speed up. So much for the idea that market forces lead to efficient choices!

These incidents illustrate the enormous costs associated with a conflictive system of labor relations. One might argue that the particular managers that Watson described were unusually shortsighted, but I suspect that something else was at stake. To admit that workers have something to contribute—besides blindly carrying out the demands of management—undermines, at least in part, the ultimate rationale for management's domination. As a result, managers often instinctually resist all encroachments on their authority.

Indeed, Watson's experience may not have been particularly unique. In the 1980s, the United States automobile industry had to dedicate 20% of its plant area and 25% of its workers' hours to fixing mistakes. The industry could intensify its supervision over workers or it could actively engage them by surrendering some control. The first option is not only expensive; it further alienates the workers, perhaps encouraging other forms of sabotage.

One could also argue that the behavior that Watson described was evidence of the need for a firm hand to control rebellious workers. That rebellion, however, may be less a product of some deficiency in the behavior of these workers than a natural response to the conflict inherent in the relationship between labor and capital.

Just imagine how much the company lost because management stubbornly refused to take advantage of the workers' on-the-spot knowledge of the business. To do so, however, would have weakened the dysfunctional hierarchy that allows managers the privilege of seeing themselves as superior to their underlings.

Perhaps the most interesting insight from Watson's experience is the degree to which the workers were able to organize themselves. Had their objective been to earn profits, their efforts would have qualified as entrepreneurial—and far more so than is usually expected from the mostly uneducated workers that made up the work force at the plant.

Unfortunately, the human and economic costs of guard labor usually pass unnoticed. Authority trumps efficiency, despite the outpouring of economic rhetoric praising the productive merits of markets. In contrast, a more rational system would both nurture and draw upon the expertise of the entire workforce rather than relying on a system of command and control.

Guarding What?

Guard labor is symptomatic of contradictions of capitalism. Guards often make sense from the perspective of an individual employer, but they entail serious waste that imposes enormous costs on society.

In the wake of deindustrialization, the fate of the U.S. economy was supposed to rest upon the transition to an information economy, which would take advantage of workers' creativity. Instead, the actual practices snuff out horrendous amounts of creativity.

The failure to nurture productivity set off a chain of events. Productivity faltered, helping to cause the profitability as well as the extent of productive industry to shrink. Capital shifted from production to finance—so much so that finance represented a minimum 40% of corporate profits. This tactic only worked so long as the bubble was inflating.

In this sense, the current economic crisis is, at least in part, due to the excesses of guard labor and the corresponding gap between the vision and practice of capitalist economics. Corrective action requires a new form of society that guards people's welfare rather than commodities.

Sources: Lynn Bauer and Steven D. Owens. 2004. Justice Expenditure and Employment Statistics, U.S. Department of Justice, Bureau of Justice Statistics (www.ojp.usdoj.gov/bjs/), 2004; Samuel Bowles and Arjun Jayadev, "Guard Labor," *Journal of Development Economics*, April 2006; Samuel Bowles and Arjun Jayadev, "Garrison America," *The Economists' Voice*, Vol. 4, Issue 2, 2007 (bepress.com/ev); Robert H. Frank, *The Economic Naturalist: In Search of Explanations for Everyday Enigmas*, Basic Books, 2007; Samuel Gompers, "Testimony Taken by the Senate Committee Upon the Relations Between Labor and Capital" (1883), in John A. Garraty, ed., *Labor and Capital in the Gilded Age*, Little, Brown, 1968; Samuel Gompers, *Seventy Years of Life and Labor: An Autobiography*, B. P. Button & Company, 1925; John Huston and Nipoli Kamdar, "$9.99: Can 'Just-Below' Pricing Be Reconciled with Rationality?" *Eastern Economic Journal*, Spring 1996; Raymond E. Lombra, "Eliminating the Penny from the U.S. Coinage System: An Economic Analysis," *Eastern Economic Journal*, Fall 2001; Alexandra Luong, and Steven G. Rogelberg "Meetings and More Meetings: The Relationship Between Meeting Load and the Daily Well-Being of Employees," *Group Dynamics: Theory, Research, and Practice*, Vol. 9, No. 1 (2005); Marc Mauer, "Comparative International Rates of Incarceration: An Examination of Causes and Trends Presented to the U.S. Commission on Civil Rights," The Sentencing Project (sentencingproject. org), 2003; Darius Mehri, *Notes From Toyota-Land: An American Engineer in Japan*, Cornell University/ILR Press, 2005; Charles T. Munger, "Academic Economics: Strengths and Faults After Considering Interdisciplinary Needs," Herb Kay Undergraduate Lecture, University of California, Santa Barbara Economics Department, October 3, 2003 (tilsonfunds.com/MungerUCSBspeech. pdf); James O'Connor, "Productive and Unproductive Labor," *Politics and Society*, Vol. 5, No. 3 (1975); Robert O'Harrow, Jr., *No Place to Hide*, Free Press, 2005; Peter Pae, "Aerospace Legend Looks Back at the Time He Wasted—in Meetings," *Los Angeles Times*, November 6, 2005; Michael

Perelman, *The Confiscation of American Prosperity: From Right-Wing Extremism and Economic Ideology to the Next Great Depression*, Palgrave, 2007; Jeffrey Pfeffer, "Human Resources from an Organizational Behavior Perspective: Some Paradoxes Explained," *Journal of Economic Perspectives*, Fall 2007; Bill Watson, "Counter-Planning on the Shop Floor," *Radical America*, May-June 1971; James P. Womack, Daniel T. Jones, and Daniel Roos, *The Machine that Changed the World: The Story of Lean Production*, Harper Perennial, 1990; Shoshana Zuboff, *In the Age of the Smart Machines: The Future of Work and Power* Basic Books, 1988.

Article 6.4

GENDER AND THE RECESSION
The recession is hitting traditionally male jobs hardest.

BY HEATHER BOUSHEY
May 2009

Awoman is now the primary breadwinner in millions of families across the United States because her husband has lost his job. Three out of four jobs lost during our Great Recession, which began in December 2007, have been men's jobs. This has left women to support their families nationwide—a task made more challenging since women typically earn only 78 cents compared to the male dollar.

Men have lost more jobs than women because the industries with the largest job losses so far during the recession have been ones dominated by men. New data from the Bureau of Labor Statistics' Current Establishment Survey for March 2009 shows that since the recession began men have lost 75.0% of all nonfarm jobs and 72.7% of all private-sector jobs.

Women have become a larger share of payroll employees. As of March 2009, the latest data available, women made up nearly half the labor force: 49.7% of all workers employed in the United States are women, up from 48.7% when the recession began in December 2007.

The recession is playing out differently by gender because men and women tend to work in very different industries and occupations. Women especially predominate in financial activities—mostly because they are the majority of real estate agents, not because they are the majority of bankers—as well as in government, education, and health. (See Figure 1.) Men predominate in transportation, construction, and manufacturing, as well as in certain retail professions, such as the sale of automobiles and electronic appliances.

Larger job losses among men have occurred because the recession is hitting traditionally male working-class jobs. Half of the job losses during this recession so far have occurred in either construction or manufacturing. Another quarter of the total job losses have occurred in professional and business services, mostly among temporary workers. Even though it is the financial sector which is driving the economic crisis, the financial activities industry only accounts for 7.4% of the jobs lost so far in this recession.

Yet, it is not just that men work in industries hardest hit by the recession. Within a number of hard-hit industries, men are also losing a disproportionate share of the jobs. For example, within retail, although men accounted for half (49.8%) of all workers at the beginning of the recession, they held two-thirds (64.5%) of the jobs lost. In finance and insurance, men accounted for over a third (36.7%) of the jobs at the beginning of the recession, but have lost half (50.6%) of the jobs.

It is not unique for blue-collar workers to bear the brunt of job losses in a recession. What is notable in this recession is that while manufacturing and construction accounted for a larger share of total job losses than in prior recessions, the industries that are seeing jobs gains—education, health, and government—are seeing smaller

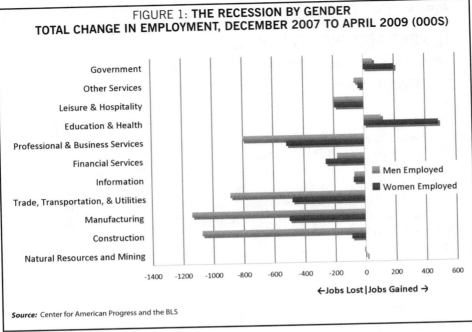

FIGURE 1: **THE RECESSION BY GENDER**
TOTAL CHANGE IN EMPLOYMENT, DECEMBER 2007 TO APRIL 2009 (000S)

Source: Center for American Progress and the BLS

gains than during prior recessions. This does not bode well for women's jobs moving forward, since women are concentrated in these industries.

Notably, during the 1980s recession—when the unemployment rate went above 10%—women actually gained jobs on net because of continued hiring in women-dominated industries. Clearly, that is not the case during the current recession. Women's employment is already 98.5% of its level from December 2007.

As of April 2009 the unemployment rate for adult men was 9.4%—more than double what it was in December 2007. The unemployment rate for adult women was 7.1% in April. The male unemployment rate is now 2.3 percentage points higher than women's—larger than at any other time since 1949.

Women are also less likely than men to be unemployed in married families. The unemployment rate for married men is 6.3%—higher than at any time since 1983. The unemployment rate for married women is 5.5%—the highest since 1986.

That means more and more women in millions of families across the United States will be supporting their families.

Ensuring that those women, and every woman, earn a fair day's pay could not be a more pressing issue for families. A good—and fast—place to start would be for the Obama administration to devote its efforts to simply enforcing the laws already on the books and implementing better monitoring of equal pay. That would be a down payment to help families make ends meet while the labor market is getting back on track.

This article combines two "infographics" written by Heather Boushey, "Gender and The Recession," May 8, 2009, and "The Importance of Women Breadwinners," April 30, 2009. Both are available at the Center for American Progress (americanprogress.org).

Article 6.5

MINING THE GOLDEN YEARS
The Return of Seniors to the Workforce

BY ROBERT LARSON
September/October 2009

With their retirement accounts seriously diminished, the surge of seniors back to work has recently become a focus of media attention. But the departure of older workers from the labor force first reversed itself in 1994. After falling for almost 50 years, seniors' labor force participation has been on the rise for over a decade, and as of the last business cycle peak 37% of seniors were employed, according to the Bureau of Labor Statistics. This striking development reflects changes in both public policy and corporate behavior, and has a variety of implications for labor strategizing.

Retirement timing is strongly influenced by changes in Social Security benefit requirements. The Republican "Contract with America" in 1994 mandated the removal of the Social Security earnings test, allowing workers 65 to 70 to work on the side without jeopardizing their benefits. Additionally, the retirement age for full Social Security benefits has been raised from 65 to 66 or 67 for workers born after 1937; this prolongs the time seniors stay on the clock.

Fundamental changes to corporate retirement plans also play an important role. Defined-benefit pensions put more burden and investment risk on the employer, whereas a defined-contribution plan, such as a 401(k), shifts the responsibility for building retirement assets onto the employee, who also bears the risk of outliving his or her savings. Twenty years ago, defined-benefit pensions and defined-contribution pensions each covered about one third of U.S. private-sector workers. Now defined-contribution plans cover twice as many workers as defined-benefit plans—42% to 21%.

The practical impact of this postponed retirement on younger workers is a subject of debate. The most prominent study of the subject, conducted in July 2008 by Jonathan Gruber and Kevin Milligan of the National Bureau of Economic Research, concluded that there was no strong evidence of older workers crowding out the young that was consistent across data sets, although they considered their conclusion to be "relatively weak." However, this was somewhat before the full gravity of the current recession was felt. Anecdotal evidence of intergenerational crowding has since grown rich, with the *Wall Street Journal* describing old and young workers competing in a "desperate scramble for work."

The rising labor market participation of workers over 55 has political implications as well. For one thing, it is red meat to advocates of raising the eligibility age for Social Security further and ultimately privatizing or abolishing it. Republican columnist William Saletan wrote in the *Washington Post* in 2006 that since people now live longer, Social Security should not pay out by age but by inability to work. This would mean working until you're physically incapable of an active retirement, a tough sell.

At the same time, the growth of older workers as a proportion of the workforce could represent a surprising opportunity for labor organizing. This is because unions are known to have a record of providing fringe benefits of special importance for older workers, including health insurance—a principle lure keeping seniors in the workforce—and pensions. For instance, unionized employees are 22.5% more likely to have a pension, and a far better one than their non-union counterparts, according to analyses by the Economic Policy Institute. Organizers working with mature adult workers could get a lot of mileage out of such advantages.

While people's visions of retirement vary from leisurely to productive, what's universal is the wish to be able to retire on your own terms. Punching in every day just to stretch health insurance coverage could force America's silver foxes and golden girls to make a winter of their autumn years.

Sources: "Trends in Labor Force Participation in the United States," *Monthly Labor Review*, October 2006; Jonathan Gruber and Kevin Milligan, "Do Elderly Workers Substitute for Younger Workers in the U.S.?" National Bureau of Economic Research, July 2008; "Elderly Emerge as a New Class of Workers—and the Jobless," *Wall Street Journal*, Feb. 23, 2009; "Curse of the Young Old," *Washington Post*, March 19, 2006; *State of Working America 2008/2009*, Economic Policy Institute, 2009.

Article 6.6

UNEMPLOYMENT INSURANCE: A BROKEN SYSTEM

BY MARIANNE HILL

September/October 2009

Millions of workers have lost their jobs in the current recession. Employment is down 12% in manufacturing, 7% in professional and business services, and more than 5% overall in the private sector compared to last year. Over 5.6 million people have lost their jobs since last June. The ranks of the unemployed are continuing to grow; the unemployment rate in June hit 9.5%. Good thing that unemployment insurance provides income to help tide these workers over this rough patch, right? Not so fast.

The share of unemployed workers receiving benefits has gradually shrunk since the 1970s. In 1975, over half of unemployed workers received regular benefits. But in 2008, only 37% of the unemployed did; in some states the figure was less than 25%. And so-called "discouraged workers," those who want but are not actively seeking employment, are not considered part of the labor force and so are not even included in these figures.

Unemployment insurance, in short, is not a benefit that everyone who loses a job can count on. Several groups are working to change this. The American Recovery and Reinvestment Act (ARRA), better know as the Obama stimulus package, provides temporary funding for states that expand their unemployment coverage, and so far this year 25 states have done so. Others, however, are resisting even a temporary expansion of coverage that would be fully federally funded.

Why Unemployment Compensation?

When unemployment insurance was established as a nationwide program in 1935, it was hailed as a means of enabling workers to protect their standard of living between jobs. With it, workers are better able to keep their homes and their health. It helps to stabilize family well-being and maintain the labor force in a region. By enabling workers to engage in longer job searches, unemployment compensation also improves workers' job choices. It even enhances employers' flexibility in hiring by making lay-offs less painful.

Unemployment insurance is also an important countercyclical tool: it bolsters consumer spending during economic downturns and then automatically drops off as the economy recovers and unemployment falls. Because it reduces the need for other forms of government intervention to raise demand in a downturn, the program has supporters across the ideological spectrum.

Coverage and benefits vary by state. The average weekly benefit in 2008 was $300—about 35% of the average weekly wage. Benefits are paid from state funds that are financed by a payroll tax on employers. This tax is levied on anywhere from the first $7,000 to the first $35,300 of each worker's annual earnings depending on the state; the national average is $11,482. The tax rate ranges from 0.83% to 5% of the taxable portion of wages, with a national average of 2.42%. (Who bears the cost of this tax is debated: economists have shown that whether or not a company is able to pass the cost of payroll taxes forward to customers or back to employees depends on conditions in its particular product and labor markets.)

Shifts in employment patterns and a tightening of eligibility requirements are behind the nationwide reduction in effective unemployment insurance coverage. Today almost 30% of the U.S. work force is employed in nonstandard work arrangements, including part-time, temporary, contract or on-call work, and self-employment. Most of these jobs are subject to the payroll tax that funds unemployment benefits—yet these workers often find they are ineligible. For instance, persons who are seeking only part-time employment do not qualify for unemployment benefits in many states. This affects women in particular, including heads of households, who often work part time due to dependent care responsibilities. People who work full time but only for part of the year may also find it difficult to qualify for unemployment benefits.

Many workers who are not eligible for benefits provide income that is critical to their families. In 2007, 41% of workers worked only part-time or part-year. Among heads of households, this figure, though lower, is still sizeable: in 2007, it was 32% overall and 42% for female family heads. Besides child care, elder care can also mean part-time or part-year work for many. Nearly one-third of working adults with older parents report missing some work to care for them.

Who Are the Unemployed?

Certain industries, regions, and workers are being hit harder than others this recession. In June, 15 states and the District of Columbia had unemployment rates of over 10%, but only one, North Dakota, had an unemployment rate below 5%. Michigan, Oregon, South Carolina and Rhode Island all had seasonally adjusted jobless rates of 12% or more.

Unemployment hits some population groups much harder than others—young people, people of color, and anyone with relatively few years of education. Among workers over 20 years of age, black men had the highest jobless rate in June at 16.4%. The rate for Hispanic women was 11.5%, for black women 11.3%, and for Hispanic men 10.7%. In contrast, the jobless rate was under 10% for both white men (9.2%) and white women (6.8%).

A combination of factors including occupational segregation, lower educational levels, and discrimination result in lower incomes for women and for black and Latino men, exacerbating the impact of higher unemployment. Data from 2005-2007 show that black women working year-round, full-time earned $15,900 a year less than white men; for Hispanic women the wage gap was $21,400. Lower-income families have fewer assets to see them through rough economic times, and their extended families are also hard-pressed as demands upon them increase. Nonprofits, another part of the social safety net, suffer from increased demand for services and decreased donations during recession. As a result, families of blacks, women and Hispanics suffer severe setbacks during a period of recession, and unemployment insurance can be especially critical to them.

Families in which one or more wage earners lose their jobs bear costs greater than just the lost wages. Savings are exhausted; rates of illness, both mental and physical, increase; debt levels often rise (inadequate medical insurance coverage is a major factor—in 2008, 60% of the unemployed lacked health insurance); and the pursuit of a college education or other training may be postponed. Studies have documented a rise in suicide rates, mental and physical illnesses, and domestic and other violence among the unemployed. These problems become widespread during recessions and become a burden on society, not just on individual families.

Promising Initiatives

Under the Obama stimulus package, states that elect to expand their programs in certain ways receive federal funds to finance these changes for at least two to three years. States can make unemployment benefits more available in a number of ways:

• Changing the base period used to determine whether a worker qualifies for benefits and if so, the amount he or she will receive.

• Making unemployment insurance available to certain individuals who are seeking only part-time work and/or to those who lost or left their jobs due to certain compelling family reasons (for example, domestic violence or a spouse relocating).

• Providing an additional 26 weeks of compensation to workers who have exhausted regular unemployment benefits and are enrolled in and making satisfactory progress in certain training programs.

• Paying an additional dependents' allowance of at least $15 per dependent per week to eligible beneficiaries.

Another potential reform relates to the extension of benefits beyond the regular 13- to 26-week period. States are required to offer extended benefits during periods of especially high unemployment (with half the cost covered by the federal government) only if certain trigger requirements are met—and that does not happen often. The ARRA offers states the option of adopting a new, less stringent trigger requirement. As of mid-July, 29 of the 30 states adopting the new trigger requirements have had extended benefits go into effect, compared with only six of the 20 states that have kept earlier triggers. Last year Congress authorized a separate program, Emergency Unemployment Compensation, to provide federally funded benefits after regular benefits are exhausted. The National Employment Law Project estimated that about 1.2 million workers would exhaust their benefits under *this* program before July 2009 and so become eligible for extended benefits.

A permanent expansion of coverage to a larger share of the unemployed, with or without an increase in benefit levels, would cost more than the average $23 per month in unemployment insurance taxes currently paid per worker. This could be achieved by expanding the portion of wages on which the tax is levied. To reduce the negative impact on low-income workers, this could be accompanied by adjust-ments to the earned income tax credit.

Even if the reforms contained in the Obama administration's stimulus pack-age were fully enacted, benefits and coverage would be low in the United States in comparison to Europe. Much remains to be done to ensure minimal income security here. As the unemployment rate approaches 10%, it is time to revamp our broken system.

Sources: U.S. Department of Labor, especially www.ows.doleta.gov/unemploy/finance.asp; U.S. Bureau of Labor Statistics; National Employment Law Project, www.nelp.org; William Conerly, "European Unemployment: Lessons for the United States," National Center for Policy Analysis, May 26, 2004; National Institutes of Health, www.pubmedcentral.nih.gov; Marcus Walker and Roger Thurow, "U.S., Europe Are an Ocean Apart on Human Toll of Joblessness," *Wall Street Journal,* May 7, 2009.

Article 6.7

WORKER DIRECT ACTION GROWS IN GLOBAL NORTH IN WAKE OF FINANCIAL MELTDOWN

BY IMMANUEL NESS AND STACY WARNER MADDERN
September/October 2009

The traditional path of labor-management collective bargaining has taken a dramatic turn in an era in which unions are too weak or timid to take action even as joblessness grows and companies losing financing are forced into bankruptcy by their creditors. As plants close and layoffs grow—and as workers recognize they can no longer interrupt the workflow with a strike when there is no flow to be interrupted—they are engaging in militant action to save their jobs and livelihoods.

Over the last decade, sit-down strikes were largely confined to Latin America and elsewhere in the global South, where workers occupied factories in response to economic collapse. But the tide of direct action by workers and some unions seems to be moving north. Workers in the global North are now engaging in a wave of factory occupations and other militant actions. Many of these actions are in the syndicalist tradition of workers directly taking power; in some cases workers are acting on their own, in others they are leading lackadaisical unions to support their efforts. The current crisis in manufacturing has rendered a growing number of officially-recognized unions with government-sanctioned collective bargaining agreements nearly helpless and could lay the basis for escalating direct actions by workers, possibly ushering in a more militant union movement.

In the United States and much of Europe, worker radicalism was in check for decades even as unions repeatedly offered up concessions to managers, ostensibly to save their factories. While workers have been viewed by corporate managers as docile and weak-willed, "when workers are threatened by management they seriously consider breaking the rules and fighting back," according to auto worker and activist Gregg Shotwell.

Shotwell, who worked at the Delphi auto parts plant in Flint, Mich., is a founder of Soldiers of Solidarity (SOS), a rank-and-file association that continues to resist United Auto Workers (UAW) policies of concessionary bargaining that have all but destroyed a way of life for unionized manufacturing workers in the United States. SOS formed as a worker insurgency in November 2005 following Delphi's bankruptcy filing and the union leadership's lackluster response. Workers at Delphi plants throughout the Midwest feared the worst—plant closures and abrogation of health and pension benefit agreements that were guaranteed after the auto parts unit was spun off by GM in 1999. Independent of the UAW, they waged a mass "work to rule" campaign as a means of sabotaging the company's plans for mass layoffs.

The 2005-2006 insurgency at Delphi was not a replay of the storied 1936-1937 Flint sit-down strike. Still, through deftly organized slow-downs and direct action on the shop floor (for instance, simply not fixing machines, thereby slowing the production process—known as "putting machines down"), and without the support of the UAW, the Delphi workers saved their health benefits and pensions. Says Shotwell, "A sit-down strike will not come out of a political philosophy, but will occur when workers feel they will lose everything if they stay complacent and take no action."

The global capitalist economic crisis that began in 2007 is unquestionably creating the kinds of conditions Shotwell describes for an increasing number of workers. This crisis has led to the devaluation of labor-management contracts that purportedly exchanged labor peace for decent wage and benefit standards and a modicum of job security. The closure of manufacturing plants in North America and Europe has swelled the ranks of distressed, frequently older, workers seeking to preserve the economic security they once took for granted. As welfare-state-based guaranteed benefits and unemployment insurance have been eroded since the 1980s thanks to the rise of neoliberalism, workers have been forced to rely on employer- or union-based benefits. However, in the last year, the economic collapse has exposed the failure of neoliberal capitalism to ensure economic security through either public or private avenues.

While we have yet to witness the recurrence of factory takeovers on a scale akin to the Italian Bienno-Rosso ("Red Year") of 1919-1920, when some 500,000 factory workers seized and operated factories, mostly without official union sanction, today a resurgence of rank-and-file militancy is palpable. Just in the last year, a growing number of workers who had until recently been viewed as conservative and quiescent have begun to take matters into their own hands, engaging in the most militant of activities.

In the United States, the Republic Window and Door sit-down strike in Chicago in December 2008 and the threatened factory occupation of Hartmarx, the men's suit manufacturer based in Des Plaines, Ill., in May 2009, have received considerable attention. At Republic the occupation got the workers the back pay and other benefits they were owed; at Hartmarx, where workers had the support of their union, the new SEIU affiliate Workers United, a threatened sit-down helped save some 3,000 jobs.

Notably, in both of these cases, workers took on the banks and creditors who sought to liquidate the firms in order to enhance their own balance sheets. Their move to demand accountability not only from their direct employers but also from financial firms, including some that had received government bailouts, strengthened their case and brought added attention to their struggle. If creditors and manufacturers continue a pattern of arbitrarily shutting down profitable firms to improve their financial ratings, it is likely that a wave of worker factory occupations could occur in the United States.

But it is in Europe that the new militancy is already most pronounced. Varied repertoires of direct action are emerging in different countries, from factory occupations in Britain and Ireland to "bossnappings" in France.

During the first six months of 2009, Unite, the UK's largest trade union, representing nearly 2 million members, reported that employers laid off over 94,000 members. Formed in 2007 through a merger of the Transport and General Workers

Union and Amicus, Unite represents workers across many industries, from finance to manufacturing.

As the global economic crisis has erupted, Unite has fought mass layoffs while publicly resisting corporate efforts to abuse the so-called redundancy system when going into bankruptcy. According to the 1965 Redundancy Payments Act, UK workers with at least two years of service are entitled to a severance payment from their employer. The formula for these payments is based on a number of factors such as age and length of service. The law's provision for financial compensation for laid-off workers, combined with the fact that many employers agreed to provide larger severance packages than the law required, resulted in a drop in worker resistance to mass layoffs. In the ensuing years, the average number of days lost through strikes against mass layoffs in all industries dropped—from 161,744 a year from 1960 to 1965, to 74,473 a year from 1966 to 1969.

TABLE 1: 2008-2009 SIT-DOWN STRIKES IN EUROPE AND NORTH AMERICA				
Location	Plant	Industry	Duration	Union
Nantes, France	Goss International	Printing Press Manufacturing	36 Days	CFDT
Chicago, Illinois	Republic Windows	Energy Conservation	6 Days	UEWU
Derry, Ireland	Calcast Auto Manufacturing	Auto Parts Manufacturing	72 Hours	Unite UK
Kilbarry, Ireland	Waterford Crystal	Glass Manufacturing	51 Days	Unite UK
French Alps	Caterpillar "Boss-nappings"	Tractor Manufacturing	24 Hours	None
Dundee, Scotland	Prisme Meatpacking Plant	Packing Supplies	51 Days	None
Great Britain and Northern Ireland	Visteon Car Plants	Auto Manufacturing	6 Weeks	Unite UK
Mantes-la-Jolie, France	FCI Microconnections	Electronics	34 Days	CGT-CFDT
Winsor, Ontario	Catalina Precision Products	Auto Parts Manufacturing	4 Weeks	Canadian Auto Workers

			TABLE 2: EUROPEAN AND AUSTRALIAN SIT-DOWN STRIKES: 1971-2007		
Location	Occupation	Year	Industry	Duration	Union
Glasgow, Scotland	Upper Clyde Shipbuilders	1971	Shipbuilding	11 Months	CSEU
Cambelltown, New South Wales, Australia	Harco Steel Work-In	1971	Steel Manufacturing	4 Weeks	FIA
Kirkby, England	Fisher-Bendix	1972	Washer/Dryer Manufacturing	9 Weeks	AUEW
Besançon, France	LIP Clock Factory	1973	Clock and Watch Manufacturing	5 Months	CGT-CFDT
Greenock, Scotland	Lee Jeans Factory	1981	Clothing	7 Months	NUTG
Dublin, Ireland	Chondalkin Paper Mill	1982	Paper Products	2 Years	Federated Workers Union of Ireland
Uddingston, Scotland	Caterpillar Plant	1987	Tractor/Heavy Machinery	3 Months	Scottish Trade Unions Congress
Saint-Cyr en Val, France	Kimberly-Clark Plant	1998	Paper Products	2 Weeks	FCE-CFDT
Givet, France	Cellatex Chemical Plant	2000	Chemical Technology	13 Days	CGT
Brighton, England	SITA Bin Collectors	2001	Waste Management	5 Days	Unite UK
Grenoble, France	Schneider Electrics	2004	Electronics	15 Days	CGT-CFDT
Viry-Chatillion, France	Buffalo Grill	2007	Hospitality	1 Month	None

However, more recently companies have instead been offering the legal minimum or else going into bankruptcy, in which case plants land in state receivership ("administration"); the state then assumes responsibility for the severance payments. When companies follow this latter strategy, it presents a number of problems for both workers and the economy. The state severance payments come out of a Redundancy Fund financed by a surcharge on the National Insurance Tax, with limits on how much an individual can be paid from that fund. In addition, workers who are forced into a state-funded severance plan lose any pension or other entitlements earned from their term of service.

These were the issues in play this spring, when workers represented by Unite occupied three Visteon auto parts plants in Britain and Ireland—by far the most significant among the recent sit-downs in Europe due to the extensive public support they received and their potential to erupt into a broader movement among workers.

Visteon makes parts for Ford, which spun the parts division off in 2000, one year after GM spun off Delphi. At the time, Ford promised that its wage, pension, and other benefits obligations would be honored by Visteon. Still, many workers viewed these moves as attempts by the auto companies to rid themselves of pension obligations to a segment of their workforce.

On March 31, 2009, workers at Visteon's Belfast plant were given six minutes notice that their services were no longer needed. Stunned by Visteon's arrogance in closing the plant without notice and management's failure to consult workers in any manner, the workers seized control of the plant. Roger Madison, automotive spokesperson for Unite, commented, "Once again we see how cheap and easy it is to sack UK workers. One minute they were working, but six minutes later they were jobless, pensionless, and looking at the state basic in redundancy pay as their company was placed into [bankruptcy receivership]."

Following the Belfast sit-down, workers also occupied Visteon's Basildon and Enfield plants. The arbitrary and abrupt nature of Visteon's mass layoffs traumatized veteran workers. Paul Walker, who had worked at the parts plant in Enfield for 24 years, said the workers wanted to stand firm against global corporations that seek profits at the expense of employees. "This demonstration is to protest how these international companies have treated us. ... We were given six minutes to leave the building, immediate redundancy and that's it. So, we're here for justice for ourselves."

Walker was also struck by how Visteon's abusive treatment developed his working-class consciousness. "It's funny, I was just a worker before. I came to work, I went home. I really didn't pay much attention to anything, but my eyes have been opened up. I think that right now is the right time for this [sit-down strike]."

Visteon had set out to rid itself of nearly 600 workers from the three plants. However, the workers' action forced Visteon and Ford back to the negotiating table. "If we would have walked out, we would have never have gotten [this] far," observed Charlie Maxwell, a Unite representative. The occupations continued for seven weeks when finally members of Unite voted to accept a settlement involving Ford which, according to Madison, was "ten times what people were being offered originally." Visteon agreed to a severance of between six and eighteen months' salary.

The Visteon actions were coordinated and supported by the union to a signifi-cantly greater extent than in most other recent cases of militant worker action. They also garnered significant community support, with supporters holding rallies and picketing Ford dealerships throughout Britain and Northern Ireland. Worker and community solidarity was considered the most crucial factor in reaching a settle-ment at Visteon. At Enfield, the sit-down strike was supported by mass labor and community demonstrations which, according to Ron Clarke, a worker at Enfield, were crucial for the success of the strike: "It took a lot of organizing, but the soli-darity of the membership and the people that work [at Enfield] was incredible. It gathered momentum. There was so much support from outside."

The Visteon sit-downs and protests sent shudders through corporate and gov-ernment leaders in the United States and Europe, who feared they might lead to a militant workers' movement, forcing corporations to take into account the eco-nomic and social rights of laid-off employees. On April 28, 2009, the corporate human resources journal Personneltoday.com posted a warning that "employers should beware—if successful today, Visteon workers stand to set a very public and very dangerous precedent. ... [T]he sheer determination of the workers surely stands as a testament to the lengths employees are now willing to go to secure what they believe is a 'fair deal' when they have nothing left to lose."

Among the other companies in Great Britain and Ireland that have been the tar-gets of militant worker action are auto parts maker Calcast, Waterford Crystal, and Prisme Packaging.

With its skilled labor force and relatively lower wages, Ireland was considered Europe's economic dynamo over the last decade. Now Irish workers facing plant closures have carried out a number of sit-down strikes. In November 2008, Calcast, a subsidiary of the French auto parts manufacturer Montupet SA which produces parts for Audi, Ford, Peugeot, and Renault, announced it was shutting down its plant in Derry and laying off 90 of 102 workers employed there, with the remaining twelve redeployed in jobs elsewhere. Montrupet's plans to close the plant were evi-dent even before the financial meltdown. In August 2008 the company announced plans to move its manufacturing to Ruse, Bulgaria, which was slated to become the firm's primary European factory for auto parts.

Sit-Down in Canada

This March worker resistance resulted in the occupation of the Aradco auto parts plant owned by Catalina Precision Products Ltd. in Windsor, Ontario. Aradco is a privately-owned company that provides parts for Chrysler. After a dispute with Chrysler, which threatened to withdraw from its Canadian operations unless unionized workers made substantial con-cessions and lowered overall parts costs, the plant shut down. In response, twelve workers welded the doors shut from the inside promising not to leave until they were paid. According to the Canadian UAW, the Aradco workers are owed money for severance pay, vacation pay, and termination pay totaling $1.7 million. After an offer by the plant's owner of four weeks severance pay or about $200,000 in total for all 80 workers was rejected, Chrysler stepped in and doubled it.

After management offered severance packages below what it had previously agreed to, the workers occupied the plant, vowing not to leave until better terms were offered. The sit-in had lasted 72 hours when management made a new offer, which the union membership accepted.

In January 2009 another sit-down strike broke out at the Waterford Crystal Factory in Kilbarry, which employed some 700 workers, including nearly 500 factory workers. Waterford workers were not told directly of the plans for a closure, but only found out after it was leaked that a creditor was imminently planning to close the plant. When workers learned of the creditor's plans, they forced their way into Waterford's Visitors Centre and occupied the building, setting up a rotating shift system in which some 50 to 60 workers controlled the factory at any given time. The following week, thousands of workers, trade unionists, and community allies massed in rallies in the city of Waterford demanding that the plant remain open.

Two major U.S. corporations contended for ownership of the company. One was Clarion Capital, which sought a concessionary pact to reemploy workers at much lower wages and inferior conditions. KPS, the second bidder, had no interest in operating the facility; it was only interested in maintaining Waterford's brand names, product designs, and manufacturing processes. With ongoing financial problems in the company, a significant number of workers were prepared to accept a lay-off. But the closure threatened not only 700 jobs but also the workers' severance payments. The Waterford occupation ended on March 23, when KPS gained control over the company and promised to keep 176 workers. The victory was only partial—while workers gained an additional redundancy payment, the agreement did not prevent Waterford from laying off most of the workers at the plant.

Since the company was in bankruptcy, those workers who lost their jobs would have received the basic national statutory payment for loss of work, rather than the company-promised severance package. KPS offered a 10 million Euro severance package to some 800 workers, including those who had lost their jobs even before the plant closure. This package replaces the company pensions, since Ireland has no pension protection plan for laid-off workers. One worker said: "On the pensions, everyone has been talking hard but little has really been done. It'll end up in the European courts—which is fine except that people need their pensions today."

Unite, which represented Waterford's laid-off workers, did not press the Irish government to nationalize the plant, but assisted in the process of identifying a private buyer. Even after the buyout, rank-and-file workers maintained the necessity of resisting the layoffs, with or without the union. The Waterford strike helped lay the basis for the Irish Congress of Trade Unions (ICTU) and Unite to call a one day solidarity strike and demonstration on March 30. Strikers and protesters demanded that private and public employers honor the Irish National Wage Agreement, which requires firms to adjust wages to the inflation rate, and protested mass layoffs and Ireland's lack of protection for worker pension plans. The ICTU contends that the Irish government is in "non-compliance with European legislation on pension protection."

Dundee, Scotland was the site of a sit-down strike in March 2009. A small group of 12 workers occupied the Prisme Packaging factory near the city center to force their employer to pay legally required severance payments, following the company's decision to lay off its entire workforce. The workers had been given one hour's notice that the firm was closing. But after receiving notification that the company was planning to withhold severance pay, holiday pay, and back wages, the seven women and five men decided to take control of the factory to prevent the company from removing potentially valuable materials and equipment.

After a 51-day occupation and significant support from the surrounding community in southeastern Scotland, the managing director of Prisme resigned and plans for an independent worker-managed cooperative went into effect. On May 1, Discovery Packaging and Design, Ltd., opened for business with the support of the community and private donations.

In France, worker demands are even more militant than in Britain and Ireland, as workers are demanding that employers keep factories open and challenging owner claims as to the financial viability of firms. Worker direct action has extended beyond occupying factories to blocking roads and to holding factory owners hostage in what have become known as "bossnappings."

Beginning on February 24, 2009, workers at FCI Microconnections, an electronics manufacturer in Mantes-la-Jolie, demanded that management guarantee the future of the plant. Workers believed the company was formulating a plan for mass layoffs. After FCI denied having any layoff plan, over half of the plant's 400 workers went on strike and occupied the factory, preventing any removal of equipment. The occupation continued for the next seven weeks, even after the French government issued a legal order on March 26 for to the workers to end the sit-down strike. Workers intensified the pressure on management to keep the plant open by traveling to the company headquarters in Versailles where they set up a barricade preventing the chief executive and corporate staff from leaving for four hours.

While management continued to insist no closure was planned, CGT, the union representing the workers, produced an internal document showing that FCI had developed a detailed plant-closure plan for November 2009. After the company's plans were revealed and management finally agreed to negotiate the facility's future, striking workers gained greater support from the non-striking workers. A week later negotiations between the CGT and CFDT unions and management culminated in an agreement guaranteeing that the factory will remain open until 2014 with no job cuts before 2011. FCI workers also won payment for 27 of their 34 strike days.

On Friday, March 6, 300 workers at a Goss International plant in Nantes were informed that the newspaper printing machine plant was to be closed and operations transferred to its factory in Montataire, north of Paris. Goss told workers that due to the "financial crisis," downsizing measures were necessary. However, since the plant had experienced rapid growth in production capacity in the preceding 14 years, the workers, in disbelief, insisted that it remain open and that the plant manager, who had refused to order the closure, be reinstated by the company. The occupation lasted for five days, until Goss offered assurances that certain operations at the plant could be maintained and that they would fight to save "as many jobs as possible."

Jean Luc Bonneau, a delegate of the French trade union CFDT, claims that the site is "viable" due to its earnings of "€50 million in dividends to shareholders" in the last five years. According to Bonneau, the "closure has no justification." In fact, the decision to close the factory at Nantes was made by its ownership MatlinPatterson Global Opportunities Partners, which intends to sell off the entire company to raise cash for new investments in "distressed" businesses. MatlinPatterson is one of the leading "vulture funds" that specialize in buying financially weak businesses and selling them off at a high margin after restructuring. The fate of the Goss workers had little to do with the "financial crisis" and everything to do with higher profitability in other markets.

In late March 2009, workers at a Caterpillar plant in the French Alps briefly held five managers captive in a dispute over severance packages. The incident was the third time in three weeks that French Caterpillar workers had detained their bosses to protest job losses. After announcing 22,000 job cuts worldwide in January and February, Caterpillar sought to lay off 733 workers—about a quarter of the work force—at its factories in the towns of Grenoble and Échirolles. Combined with those already laid off and those whose short-term contracts would not be renewed, a total of about 1,000 workers at the French factories were losing their jobs.

Pierre Piccarreta, a CGT union representative, called the actions an effort to apply "pressure" so as to "restart negotiations." He also added, "At a time when the company is making a profit and distributing dividends to shareholders, we want to find a favorable outcome for all the workers and know as quickly as possible where we are going."

The Caterpillar "bossnappings" seemed to inspire other frustrated workers. In the following weeks workers held a 3M executive overnight, forcing management to discuss job cuts. Workers at Sony's French division held a chief executive and director of human relations for a day. Two managers from a Kleber-Michelin machine-parts factory in Toul were also locked up and held by workers demanding negotiations over lay-offs.

These acts of worker resistance are on the rise globally as millions of workers feel anger at corporations that are seemingly using the current financial crisis as a cover for laying off long-term workers and restructuring labor markets through plant relocations and wage cuts. Unite, which itself is under financial stress, has held events to call attention to the need to reform Britain's redundancy laws to prevent employers from using bankruptcy as a means of circumventing severance pay.

The worker actions in Europe represent working-class resistance to employers who arbitrarily shut down plants without the participation of employees. In South America, factory workers have taken the next step by demanding workers' right to control plants that have been shut down by their owners. In Argentina and Venezuela, workers, who have operated some factories without corporate managers for nearly a decade, are demanding that their governments pass legislation legitimizing the expropriation of factories under worker control.

Under the pretext of the financial crisis, finance capitalists are determined to unload the debt burden off their books, and multinational corporations are closing factories to take advantage of lower-wage workers on a global basis. In response, a growing number of workers vulnerable to layoffs across Europe and North America both within and outside of unions are now resisting closures through sit-down strikes and other forms of direct action. Where unions are unwilling to resist the corporate assault on labor, militant workers are engaging in direct action through factory occupations and mass insurrections demanding that plants be reopened or lay-off benefits improved. The wave of factory occupations continuing through 2009 may represent only the beginning of a broader sit-down movement throughout the world, and, following examples in Latin America, demands for worker control over factories.

Sources: K. Baker, "Visteon Dispute: A Dangerous Precedent to be Set?" April 16, 2009, www.personneltoday.com blog; *Oh Sit Down! Accounts of Sitdown Strikes and Workplace Occupations in the UK and around the World*, compilation by libcom.org, www.libcom.org; R. Rosewell, "Work-ins, Sit-ins and Redundancy," *International Socialism*, No. 50, Jan.-March 1972; L. Root, "Britain's Redundancy Payments for Displaced Workers," *Monthly Labor Review*, June 1987; H. Kahn, *Repercussions of Redundancy*, Allen and Unwin, 1964; "Recession Update May 2009," Unite the Union, June 10, 2009, www.unitetheunion.com; "Factory Occupied for a Second Night," BBC News, June 11, 2009; D. Scheherazade, "French Bossnapper Release Hostage Pair," *Financial Times*, April 22, 2009; B. Groom, "Why Sit-Ins Are So 1970s," *Financial Times*, April 7, 2009; J. Reed and J.M. Brown, "Visteon Protestors Face Deadline to Leave," *Financial Times*, April 9, 2009.

Chapter 7

THE DISTRIBUTION OF INCOME

INTRODUCTION

For many mainstream economists, inequality in the distribution of income is a natural outcome of the functioning of markets. If workers get paid based on productivity, wage differences simply reflect underlying differences in productivity.

People who supply other inputs—investors or lenders supplying capital, land-owners supplying land—are similarly rewarded according to the marginal products of those inputs. Even poverty is largely seen as a result of low productivity—which can be interpreted more compassionately as the consequence of a lack of education and training, or, at an extreme, as a result of shirking. President Reagan's deliberate use of the term "welfare queen" to cast poor, black women as undeserving of society's support is perhaps the most famous example of the latter. Indeed the absence of inequality (or measures to reduce it), in this view, would mean a reduction in incentives for increasing productivity, slowing overall growth. Such economists also argue that because the rich tend to save more (thus increasing the resources for investment and growth) the larger the share of the economic pie that goes to them, the better the entire economy does.

The authors in this section, however, see increasing inequality as neither natural, nor inevitable, nor beneficial for growth. We begin this chapter with an important primer on the lower parameter of income. Ellen Frank provides some context for the discussion of poverty and inequality by explaining how poverty is measured in the United States (Article 7.1).

Chris Tilly, in his remarkable essay "Geese, Golden Eggs, and Traps," provides the arguments for and against income equality. Tilly takes on the rosy view of the economic benefits of inequality, arguing instead that economies such as the United States can end up in an "inequality trap" where high inequality leads to low growth, which in turn can lead to even higher inequality (Article 7.2).

Gar Alperovitz and Lew Daly (Article 7.3) provide some fascinating grist for the mill of assessing property rights in showing the social nature of "collectively pro-duced" and "inherited" knowledge.

Alejandro Reuss adds that increased inequality can even more directly under-mine the quality of life by reducing life expectancy (Article 7.4).

Given that the United States has the most unequal distribution of income and wealth of any advanced industrialized nation, it begs the question as to how we got this way. James Cypher, in his exceptional essay, traces the rise in income inequality in the United States and points to some of the causes for this trend (Article 7.5).

As concern over the level of inequality in the United States spreads to such establishment figures as the chairman of the Federal Reserve, opponents of redistribution have attempted to argue that additional progressive taxation would not only be harmful to growth, but also unfair to those paying the higher taxes. Ramaa Vasudevan's article dismisses this claim in the context of corporate taxation (Article 7.6), while Sam Pizzigati explores the resurgence of "the maximum wage" as a means to redress the recent upward transfer of wealth and check the current excesses of corporate compensation (Article 7.7).

Discussion Questions

1) (Article 7.1) Consult the Census Bureau website (www.census.gov) to find the current federal poverty line for an individual. Did you expect it to be higher or lower? In your opinion, what are the "basic necessities" that should be included in the estimation of the poverty line?

2) (Article 7.1) Why might the federal poverty rate understate poverty in the United States? In what way might it overstate poverty in the United States? Has there recently been any attempt to change the assessment of the poverty line? If so, in which ways have they changed how poverty is measured?

3) (Article 7.2) According to Tilly, many of the mechanisms linking equality and growth are *political*. Should economic models incorporate political behavior as well as economic behavior? What are some ideas about how they could do that?

4) (Article 7.3) Consider the following quotation:

> "I think we've been through a period where too many people have been given to understand that if they have a problem, it's the government's job to cope with it. 'I have a problem, I'll get a grant.' 'I'm homeless, the government must house me.' They're casting their problem on society. And, you know, *there is no such thing as society*. There are individual men and women, and there are families. And no government can do anything except through people, and people must look to themselves first. It's our duty to look after ourselves and then, also to look after our neighbour. People have got the entitlements too much in mind, without the obligations. There's no such thing as entitlement, unless someone has first met an obligation."
>
> —British Prime Minister Margaret Thatcher, talking to *Women's Own* magazine, October 31, 1987

After reading Gar Alperovitz and Lew Daly's article "The Undeserving Rich," how do you think they would respond to Thatcher?

5) (Article 7.4) Death rates are higher where inequality is higher. These mortality differences apply at all income levels, even after taking into account differences in poverty. How can this be explained?

6) (Article 7.5) According to James Cypher, how has globalization increased economic inequality in the United States?

7) (Article 7.5) Explain why mainstream economists believe that increases in "millionairism" can stimulate economic growth. How does Cypher respond to this argument?

8) (Article 7.5) Cypher argues that "we all do better when we all do better." What does he mean? What economic policies would you propose to reduce inequality in the United States?

9) (Article 7.6) While the argument against taxation is often couched in terms of the inefficiency of taxes, Vasudevan is responding to anti-tax arguments based upon the supposed unfairness of taxation. What definition of fairness do you think these opponents of taxation are employing? What definition of fairness do you think Vasudevan is employing?

10) (Article 7.6) In what way have tax policies contributed to growing inequality in the United States? Do you think there is a case for remaking tax policy to be more progressive?

11) (Article 7.7) What is the nature and logic of a "Maximum Wage"? Explore the relative costs and benefits of such a policy using Pizzigati's article and any other sources you can muster. Why do we seem to have new calls for maximum wage legislation in fifteen to twenty year cycles?

Article 7.1

MEASURES OF POVERTY

BY ELLEN FRANK
January/February 2006, updated May 2009

Dear Dr. Dollar:
Can you explain how poverty is defined in government statistics? Is this a realistic definition?
— *Susan Balok, Savannah, Ga.*

Each February, the Census Bureau publishes the federal poverty thresholds—the income levels for different sized households below which a household is defined as living "in poverty." Each August, the bureau reports how many families, children, adults, and senior citizens fell below the poverty threshold in the prior year. As of 2008, the federal poverty thresholds were as follows:

HOUSEHOLD SIZE	FEDERAL POVERTY THRESHOLD
1 person	$11,201
2 people	14,417
3 people	17,330
4 people	21,834
5 people	25,694

Using these income levels, the Census Bureau reported that 12.5% percent of U.S. residents and 18.0% of U.S. children lived in poverty in 2007. Black Americans experience poverty at nearly double these rates: 24.5% of all Blacks and 34.5% of Black children live in households with incomes below the poverty line.

The poverty threshold concept was originally devised by Social Security analyst Mollie Orshansky in 1963. Orshansky estimated the cost of an "economy food plan" designed by the Department of Agriculture for "emergency use when funds are low." Working from 1955 data showing that families of three or more spent one-third of their income on food, Orshansky multiplied the food budget by three to calculate the poverty line. Since the early 1960s, the Census Bureau has simply recalculated Orshansky's original figures to account for inflation.

The poverty line is widely regarded as far too low for a household to survive on in most parts of the United States. For one thing, as antipoverty advocates point out, since 1955 the proportion of family budgets devoted to food has fallen from one-third to one-fifth. Families expend far more on nonfood necessities such as child care, health care, transportation, and utilities today than they did 50 years ago, for obvious reasons: mothers entering the work force, suburbanization and greater dependence on the auto, and soaring health care costs, for example. Were

Orshansky formulating a poverty threshold more recently, then, she would like have multiplied a basic food budget by five rather than by three.

Furthermore, costs—particularly for housing and energy—vary widely across the country, so that an income that might be barely adequate in Mississippi is wholly inadequate in Massachusetts. Yet federal poverty figures make no adjustment for regional differences in costs.

A number of state-level organizations now publish their own estimates of what it takes to support a family in their area, in conjunction with the national training and advocacy group Wider Opportunities for Women. Using local data on housing costs, health care premiums, taxes, and child care costs as well as food, transportation and other necessities, these "self-sufficiency standards" estimate that a two-parent two-child family needs between $40,000 and $70,000 a year, depending on the region, to cover basic needs.

State and federal officials often implicitly recognize that official poverty thresholds are unrealistically low by setting income eligibility criteria for antipoverty programs higher than the poverty level. Households with incomes of 125%, 150%, or even 185% of the federal poverty line are eligible for a number of federal and state programs. In addition, the Census Bureau publishes figures on the number of households with incomes below 200% of the federal poverty line—a level many social scientists call "near poor" or "working poor."

Poverty calculations also have critics on the right. Conservative critics contend that the official poverty rate overstates poverty in the United States. While the Census Bureau's poverty-rate calculations include Social Security benefits, public assistance, unemployment and workers' compensation, SSI (disability) payments, and other forms of cash income, they exclude noncash benefits from state and federal antipoverty programs like Food Stamps, Medicaid, and housing subsidies. If the market value of these benefits were counted in family income, fewer families would count as "poor." On the other hand, by not counting such benefits, policy makers have a better grasp of the numbers of Americans in need of such transfer programs.

Resources: For background information on poverty thresholds and poverty rate calculations, see aspe.hhs.gov/poverty/papers/hptgssiv.htm. Self-sufficiency standards for different states can be found at www.sixstrategies.org/states/states.cfm. In addition, the Economic Policy Institute has calculated family budgets for the 435 metropolitan areas: www.epi.org/content/budget_calculator.

Whenever progressives propose ways to redistribute wealth from the rich to those with low and moderate incomes, conservative politicians and economists accuse them of trying to kill the goose that lays the golden egg. The advocates of unfettered capitalism proclaim that inequality is good for the economy because it promotes economic growth. Unequal incomes, they say, provide the incentives necessary to guide productive economic decisions by businesses and individuals. Try to reduce inequality, and you'll sap growth. Furthermore, the conservatives argue, growth actually promotes equality by boosting the have-nots more than the haves. So instead of fiddling with who gets how much, the best way to help those at the bottom is to pump up growth.

But these conservative prescriptions are absolutely, dangerously wrong. Instead of the goose-killer, equality turns out to be the goose. Inequality stifles growth; equality gooses it up. Moreover, economic expansion does not necessarily promote equality—instead, it is the types of jobs and the rules of the economic game that matter most.

Inequality: Goose or Goose-Killer?

The conservative argument may be wrong, but it's straightforward. Inequality is good for the economy, conservatives say, because it provides the right incentives for innovation and economic growth. First of all, people will only have the motivation to work hard, innovate, and invest wisely if the economic system rewards them for good economic choices and penalizes bad ones. Robin Hood-style policies that collect from the wealthy and help those who are worse off violate this principle. They reduce the payoff to smart decisions and lessen the sting of dumb ones. The result: people and companies are bound to make less efficient decisions. "We must allow [individuals] to fail, as well as succeed, and we must replace the nanny state with a regime of self-reliance and self-respect," writes conservative lawyer Stephen Kinsella in *The Freeman: Ideas on Liberty* (not clear how the free woman fits in). To prove their point, conservatives point to the former state socialist countries, whose economies had become stagnant and inefficient by the time they fell at the end of the 1980s.

If you don't buy this incentive story, there's always the well-worn trickle-down theory. To grow, the economy needs productive investments: new offices, factories, computers, and machines. To finance such investments takes a pool of savings. The rich save a larger fraction of their incomes than those less well-off. So to spur growth, give more to the well-heeled (or at least take less away from them in the form of taxes), and give less to the down-and-out. The rich will save their money and then invest it, promoting growth that's good for everyone.

Unfortunately for trickle-down, the brilliant economist John Maynard Keynes debunked the theory in his *General Theory of Employment, Interest, and Money* in 1936. Keynes, whose precepts guided liberal U.S. economic policy from the 1940s through the 1970s, agreed that investments must be financed out of savings. But he showed that most often it's changes in investment that drive savings, rather than the other way around. When businesses are optimistic about the future and invest in building and retooling, the economy booms, all of us make more money, and we put some of it in banks, 401(k)s, stocks, and so on. That is, saving grows to match investment. When companies are glum, the process runs in reverse, and savings shrink to equal investment. This leads to the "paradox of thrift": if people try to save too much, businesses will see less consumer spending, will invest less, and total savings will end up diminishing rather than growing as the economy spirals downward. A number of Keynes's followers added the next logical step: shifting money from the high-saving rich to the high-spending rest of us, and not the other way around, will spur investment and growth.

Of the two conservative arguments in favor of inequality, the incentive argument is a little weightier. Keynes himself agreed that people needed financial consequences to steer their actions, but questioned whether the differences in pay-offs needed to be so huge. Certainly state socialist countries' attempts to replace material incentives with moral exhortation have often fallen short. In 1970, the Cuban government launched the Gran Zafra (Great Harvest), an attempt to reap 10 million tons of sugar cane with (strongly encouraged) volunteer labor. Originally inspired by Che Guevara's ideal of the New Socialist Man (not clear how the New Socialist Woman fit in), the effort ended with Fidel Castro tearfully apologizing to the Cuban people in a nationally broadcast speech for letting wishful thinking guide economic policy.

But before conceding this point to the conservatives, let's look at the evidence about the connection between equality and growth. Economists William Easterly of New York University and Gary Fields of Cornell University have recently summarized this evidence:

- Countries, and regions within countries, with more equal incomes grow faster. (These growth figures do not include environmental destruction or improvement. If they knocked off points for environmental destruction and added points for environmental improvement, the correlation between equality and growth would be even stronger, since desperation drives poor people to adopt environmentally destructive practices such as rapid deforestation.)

- Countries with more equally distributed land grow faster.

- Somewhat disturbingly, more ethnically homogeneous countries and regions grow faster—presumably because there are fewer ethnically based inequalities.

- In addition, more worker rights are associated with higher rates of economic growth, according to Josh Bivens and Christian Weller, economists at two Washington think tanks, the Economic Policy Institute and the Center for American Progress.

These patterns recommend a second look at the incentive question. In fact, more equality can actually strengthen incentives and opportunities to produce.

Equality as the Goose

Equality can boost growth in several ways. Perhaps the simplest is that study after study has shown that farmland is more productive when cultivated in small plots. So organizations promoting more equal distribution of land, like Brazil's Landless Workers' Movement, are not just helping the landless poor—they're contributing to agricultural productivity!

Another reason for the link between equality and growth is what Easterly calls "match effects," which have been highlighted in research by Stanford's Paul Roemer and others in recent years. One example of a match effect is the fact that well-educated people are most productive when working with others who have lots of schooling. Likewise, people working with computers are more productive when many others have computers (so that, for example, email communication is widespread, and know-how about computer repair and software is easy to come by). In very unequal societies, highly educated, computer-using elites are surrounded by majorities with little education and no computer access, dragging down their productivity. This decreases young people's incentive to get more education and businesses' incentive to invest in computers, since the payoff will be smaller.

Match effects can even matter at the level of a metropolitan area. Urban economist Larry Ledebur looked at income and employment growth in 85 U.S. cities and their neighboring suburbs. He found that where the income gap between those in the suburbs and those in the city was largest, income and job growth was slower for everyone.

"Pressure effects" also help explain why equality sparks growth. Policies that close off the low-road strategy of exploiting poor and working people create pressure effects, driving economic elites to search for investment opportunities that pay off by boosting productivity rather than squeezing the have-nots harder. For example, where workers have more rights, they will place greater demands on businesses. Business owners will respond by trying to increase productivity, both to remain profitable even after paying higher wages, and to find ways to produce with fewer workers. The CIO union drives in U.S. mass production industries in the 1930s and 1940s provide much of the explanation for the superb productivity growth of the 1950s and 1960s. (The absence of pressure effects may help explain why many past and present state socialist countries have seen slow growth, since they tend to offer numerous protections for workers but no right to organize independent unions.) Similarly, if a government buys out large land-holdings in order to break them up, wealthy families who simply kept their fortunes tied up in land for generations will look for new, productive investments. Industrialization in Asian "tigers" South Korea and Taiwan took off in the 1950s on the wings of funds freed up in exactly this way.

Inequality, Conflict, and Growth

Inequality hinders growth in another important way: it fuels social conflict. Stark inequality in countries such as Bolivia and Haiti has led to chronic conflict that hobbles economic growth. Moreover, inequality ties up resources in unproductive uses such as paying for large numbers of police and security guards—attempts to prevent individuals from redistributing resources through theft.

Ethnic variety is connected to slower growth because, on the average, more ethnically diverse countries are also more likely to be ethnically divided. In other words, the problem isn't ethnic variety itself, but racism and ethnic conflict that can exist among diverse populations. In nations like Guatemala, Congo, and Nigeria, ethnic strife has crippled growth—a problem alien to ethnically uniform Japan and South Korea. The reasons are similar to some of the reasons that large class divides hurt growth. Where ethnic divisions (which can take tribal, language, religious, racial, or regional forms) loom large, dominant ethnic groups seek to use government power to better themselves at the expense of other groups, rather than making broad-based investments in education and infrastructure. This can involve keeping down the underdogs—slower growth in the U.S. South for much of the country's history was linked to the Southern system of white supremacy. Or it can involve seizing the surplus of ethnic groups perceived as better off—in the extreme, Nazi Germany's expropriation and genocide of the Jews, who often held professional and commercial jobs.

Of course, the solution to such divisions is not "ethnic cleansing" so that each country has only one ethnic group—in addition to being morally abhorrent, this is simply impossible in a world with 191 countries and 5,000 ethnic groups. Rather, the solution is to diminish ethnic inequalities. Once the 1964 Civil Rights Act forced the South to drop racist laws, the New South's economic growth spurt began. Easterly reports that in countries with strong rule of law, professional bureaucracies, protection of contracts, and freedom from expropriation—all rules that make it harder for one ethnic group to economically oppress another—ethnic diversity has no negative impact on growth.

If more equality leads to faster growth so everybody benefits, why do the rich typically resist redistribution? Looking at the ways that equity seeds growth helps us understand why. The importance of pressure effects tells us that the wealthy often don't think about more productive ways to invest or reorganize their businesses until they are forced to. But also, if a country becomes very unequal, it can get stuck in an "inequality trap." Any redistribution involves a tradeoff for the rich. They lose by giving up part of their wealth, but they gain a share in increased economic growth. The bigger the disparity between the rich and the rest, the more the rich have to lose, and the less likely that the equal share of boosted growth they'll get will make up for their loss. Once the gap goes beyond a certain point, the wealthy have a strong incentive to restrict democracy, and to block spending on education which might lead the poor to challenge economic injustice—making reform that much harder.

Does Economic Growth Reduce Inequality?

If inequality isn't actually good for the economy, what about the second part of the conservatives' argument—that growth itself promotes equality? According to the conservatives, those who care about equality should simply pursue growth and wait for equality to follow.

"A rising tide lifts all boats," President John F. Kennedy famously declared. But he said nothing about which boats will rise fastest when the economic tide comes in. Growth does typically reduce poverty, according to studies reviewed by economist Gary Fields, though some "boats"—especially families with strong barriers to participating in the labor force—stay "stuck in the mud." But inequality can increase at the same time that poverty falls, if the rich gain even faster than the poor do. True, sustained periods of low unemployment, like that in the late 1990s United States, do tend to raise wages at the bottom even faster than salaries at the top. But growth after the recessions of 1991 and 2001 began with years of "jobless recoveries"—growth with inequality.

For decades the prevailing view about growth and inequality within countries was that expressed by Simon Kuznets in his 1955 presidential address to the American Economic Association. Kuznets argued that as countries grew, inequality would first increase, then decrease. The reason is that people will gradually move from the low-income agricultural sector to higher-income industrial jobs—with inequality peaking when the workforce is equally divided between low- and high-income sectors. For mature industrial economies, Kuznets's proposition counsels focusing on growth, assuming that it will bring equity. In developing countries, it calls for enduring current inequality for the sake of future equity and prosperity.

But economic growth doesn't automatically fuel equality. In 1998, economists Klaus Deininger and Lyn Squire traced inequality and growth over time in 48 countries. Five followed the Kuznets pattern, four followed the reverse pattern (decreasing inequality followed by an increase), and the rest showed no systematic pattern. In the United States, for example:

- incomes became more equal during the 1930s through 1940s New Deal period (a time that included economic decline followed by growth);

- from the 1950s through the 1970s, income gaps lessened during booms and expanded during slumps;

- from the late 1970s forward, income inequality worsened fairly consistently, whether the economy was stagnating or growing.

The reasons are not hard to guess. The New Deal introduced widespread unionization, a minimum wage, social security, unemployment insurance, and welfare. Since the late 1970s, unions have declined, the inflation-adjusted value of the minimum wage has fallen, and the social safety net has been shredded. In the United States, as elsewhere, growth only promotes equality if policies and institutions to support equity are in place.

Trapped?

Let's revisit the idea of an inequality trap. The notion is that as the gap between the rich and everybody else grows wider, the wealthy become more willing to give up overall growth in return for the larger share they're getting for themselves. The "haves" back policies to control the "have-nots," instead of devoting social resources to educating the poor so they'll be more productive.

Sound familiar? It should. After two decades of widening inequality, the last few years have brought us massive tax cuts that primarily benefit the wealthiest, at the expense of investment in infrastructure and the education, child care, and income supports that would help raise less well-off kids to be productive adults. Federal and state governments have cranked up expenditures on prisons, police, and "homeland security," and Republican campaign organizations have devoted major resources to keeping blacks and the poor away from the polls. If the economic patterns of the past are any indication, we're going to pay for these policies in slower growth and stagnation unless we can find our way out of this inequality trap.

Article 7.3

THE UNDESERVING RICH

Collectively produced and inherited knowledge and the (re)distribution of income and wealth.

BY GAR ALPEROVITZ AND LEW DALY
March/April 2010

Warren Buffett, one of the wealthiest men in the nation, is worth nearly $50 billion. Does he "deserve" all this money? Why? Did he work so much harder than everyone else? Did he create something so extraordinary that no one else could have created it? Ask Buffett himself and he will tell you that he thinks "society is responsible for a very significant percentage of what I've earned." But if that's true, doesn't society deserve a very significant share of what he has earned?

When asked why he is so successful, Buffett commonly replies that this is the wrong question. The more important question, he stresses, is why he has *so much to work with* compared to other people in the world, or compared to previous generations of Americans. How much money would I have "if I were born in Bangladesh," or "if I was born here in 1700," he asks.

Buffett may or may not deserve something more than another person working with what a given historical or collective context provides. As he observes, however, it is simply not possible to argue in any serious way that he deserves *all* of the benefits that are clearly attributable to living in a highly developed society.

Buffett has put his finger on one of the most explosive issues developing just beneath the surface of public awareness. Over the last several decades, economic research has done a great deal of solid work pinpointing much more precisely than in the past what share of what we call "wealth" society creates versus what share any individual can be said to have earned and thus deserved. This research raises profound moral—and ultimately political—questions.

Recent estimates suggest that U.S. economic output per capita has increased more than twenty-fold since 1800. Output per hour worked has increased an estimated fifteen-fold since 1870 alone. Yet the average modern person likely works with no greater commitment, risk, or intelligence than his or her counterpart from the past. What is the primary cause of such vast gains if individuals do not really "improve"? Clearly, it is largely that the scientific, technical, and cultural knowledge available to us, and the efficiency of our means of storing and retrieving this knowledge, have grown at a scale and pace that far outstrip any other factor in the nation's economic development.

A half century ago, in 1957, economist Robert Solow calculated that nearly 90% of productivity growth in the first half of the 20th century (from 1909 to 1949) could only be attributed to "technical change in the broadest sense." The supply of labor and capital—what workers and employers contribute—appeared almost incidental to this massive technological "residual." Subsequent research inspired by

Solow and others continued to point to "advances in knowledge" as the main source of growth. Economist William Baumol calculates that "nearly 90 percent . . . of current GDP was contributed by innovation carried out since 1870." Baumol judges that his estimate, in fact, understates the cumulative influence of past advances: Even "the steam engine, the railroad, and many other inventions of an earlier era, still add to today's GDP."

Related research on the sources of invention bolsters the new view, posing a powerful challenge to conventional, heroic views of technology that characterize progress as a sequence of extraordinary contributions by "Great Men" (occasionally "Great Women") and their "Great Inventions." In contrast to this popular view, historians of technology have carefully delineated the incremental and cumulative way most technologies actually develop. In general, a specific field of knowledge builds up slowly through diverse contributions over time until—at a particular moment when enough has been established—the next so-called "breakthrough" becomes all but inevitable.

Often many people reach the same point at virtually the same time, for the simple reason that they all are working from the same developing information and research base. The next step commonly becomes obvious (or if not obvious, very likely to be taken within a few months or years). We tend to give credit to the person who gets there first—or rather, who gets the first public attention, since often the real originator is not as good at public relations as the one who jumps to the front of the line and claims credit. Thus, we remember Alexander Graham Bell as the inventor of the telephone even though, among others, Elisha Gray and Antonio Meucci got there at the same time or even before him. Newton and Leibniz hit upon the calculus at roughly the same time in the 1670s; Darwin and Alfred Russel Wallace produced essentially the same theory of evolution at roughly the same time in the late 1850s.

Less important than who gets the credit is the simple fact that most breakthroughs occur not so much thanks to one "genius," but because of the longer historical unfolding of knowledge. All of this knowledge—the overwhelming source of all modern wealth—comes to us today *through no effort of our own*. It is the generous and unearned gift of the past. In the words of Northwestern economist Joel Mokyr, it is a "free lunch."

Collective knowledge is often created by formal public efforts as well, a point progressives often stress. Many of the advances which propelled our high-tech economy in the early 1990s grew directly out of research programs and technical systems financed and often collaboratively developed by the federal government. The Internet, to take the most obvious example, began as a government defense project, the ARPANET, in the early 1960s. Up through the 1980s there was little private investment or interest in developing computer networks. Today's vast software industry also rests on a foundation of computer language and operating hardware developed in large part with public support. The Bill Gateses of the world—the heroes of the "New Economy"—might still be working with vacuum tubes and punch cards were it not for critical research and technology programs created or financed by the federal government after World War II. Other illustrations range from jet airplanes and radar to the basic life science research undergirding many pharmaceutical industry advances. Yet the truth is that the role of collectively inherited knowledge is far, far greater than just the contributions made by direct public support, important as they are.

A straightforward but rarely confronted question arises from these facts: If most of what we have today is attributable to advances we inherit in common, then why should this gift of our collective history not more generously benefit all members of society?

The top 1% of U.S. households now receives more income than the bottom 120 million Americans combined. The richest 1% of households owns nearly half of all investment assets (stocks and mutual funds, financial securities, business equity, trusts, non-home real estate). The bottom 90% of the population owns less than 15%; the bottom half—150 million Americans—owns less than 1%. If America's vast wealth is mainly a gift of our common past, what justifies such disparities?

Robert Dahl, one of America's leading political scientists—and one of the few to have confronted these facts—put it this way after reading economist Edward Denison's pioneering work on growth accounting: "It is immediately obvious that little growth in the American economy can be attributed to the actions of particular individuals." He concluded straightforwardly that, accordingly, "the control and ownership of the economy rightfully belongs to 'society.'"

Contrast Dahl's view with that of Joe the Plumber, who famously inserted himself into the 2008 presidential campaign with his repeated claim that he has "earned" everything he gets and so any attempt to tax his earnings is totally unjustified. Likewise, "we didn't rely on somebody else to build what we built," banking titan Sanford Weill tells us in a *New York Times* front-page story on the "New Gilded Age." "I think there are people," another executive tells the *Times*, "who because of their uniqueness warrant whatever the market will bear."

A direct confrontation with the role of knowledge—and especially inherited knowledge—goes to the root of a profound challenge to such arguments. One way to think about all this is by focusing on the concept of "earned" versus "unearned" income. Today this distinction can be found in conservative attacks on welfare "cheats" who refuse to work to earn their keep, as well as in calls even by some Republican senators to tax the windfall oil-company profits occasioned by the Iraq war and Hurricane Katrina.

The concept of unearned income first came into clear focus during the era of rapidly rising land values caused by grain shortages in early 19th-century England. Wealth derived *simply* from owning land whose price was escalating appeared illegitimate because no individual truly "earned" such wealth. Land values—and especially explosively high values—were largely the product of factors such as fertility, location, and population pressures. The huge profits (unearned "rents," in the technical language of economics) landowners reaped when there were food shortages were viewed as particularly egregious. David Ricardo's influential theory of "differential rent"—i.e., that land values are determined by differences in fertility and location between different plots of land—along with religious perspectives reaching back to the Book of Genesis played a central role in sharpening this critical moral distinction.

John Stuart Mill, among others, developed the distinction between "earned" and "unearned" in the middle decades of the 19th century and applied it to other forms of "external wealth," or what he called "wealth created by circumstances." Mill's approach fed into a growing sense of the importance of societal inputs which produce economic gains beyond what can be ascribed to one person working alone in nature without benefit of civilization's many contributions. Here a second element of what appears, historically, as a slowly evolving understanding also becomes clear: If contribution is important in determining rewards, then, Mill and others urged, since society at large makes major contributions to economic achievement, it too has "earned" and deserves a share of what has been created. Mill believed strongly in personal contribution and individual reward, but he held that in principle wealth "created by circumstances" should be reclaimed for social purposes. Karl Marx, of course, tapped the distinction between earned and unearned in his much broader attack on capitalism and its exploitation of workers' labor.

The American republican writer Thomas Paine was among the first to articulate a societal theory of wealth based directly on the earned\unearned distinction. Paine argued that everything "beyond what a man's own hands produce" was a gift which came to him simply by living in society, and hence "he owes on every principle of justice, of gratitude, and of civilization, a part of that accumulation back again to society from whence the whole came." A later American reformer, Henry George, focused on urban land rather than the agricultural land at the heart of Ricardo's concern. George challenged what he called "the unearned increment" which is created when population growth and other societal factors increase land values. In Britain, J. A. Hobson argued that the unearned value created by the industrial system in general was much larger than just the part which accrued to landowners, and that it should be treated in a similar (if not more radical and comprehensive) fashion. In a similar vein, Hobson's early 20th-century contemporary Leonard Trelawny Hobhouse declared that the "prosperous business man" should consider "what single step he could have taken" without the "sum of intelligence which civilization has placed at his disposal." More recently, the famed American social scientist Herbert Simon judged that if "we are very generous with ourselves, I suppose we might claim that we 'earned' as much as one fifth of [our income]."

The distinction between earned and unearned gains is central to most of these thinkers, as is the notion that societal contributions—including everything an industrial economy requires, from the creation of laws, police, and courts to the development of schools, trade restrictions, and patents—must be recognized and rewarded. The understanding that such societal contributions are both contemporary and have made a huge and cumulative contribution over all of history is also widely accepted. Much of the income they permit and confer now appears broadly analogous to the unearned rent a landlord claims. What is new and significant here is the further clarification that by far the most important element in all this is the accumulated *knowledge* which society contributes over time.

All of this, as sociologist Daniel Bell has suggested, requires a new "knowledge theory of value"—especially as we move deeper into the high-tech era through computerization, the Internet, cybernetics, and cutting-edge fields such as gene therapy and nanotechnology. One way to grasp what is at stake is the following: A person today working the same number of hours as a similar person in 1870—working just as hard but no harder—will produce perhaps 15 times as much economic output. It is clear that the contemporary person can hardly be said to have "earned" his much greater productivity.

Consider further that if we project forward the past century's rate of growth, a person working a century from now would be able to produce—and potentially receive as "income"—up to seven times today's average income. By far the greatest part of this gain will also come to this person as a free gift of the past—the gift of the new knowledge created, passed on, and inherited from our own time forward.

She and her descendents, in fact, will inevitably contribute less, relative to the huge and now expanded contribution of the past, than we do today. The obvious question, again, is simply this: to what degree is it meaningful to say that this person will have "earned" all that may come her way? These and other realities suggest that the quiet revolution in our understanding of how wealth is created has ramifications for a much more profound and far-reaching challenge to today's untenable distribution of income and wealth.

Article 7.4

CAUSE OF DEATH: INEQUALITY

BY ALEJANDRO REUSS
May/June 2001

Inequality kills.

You won't see inequality on a medical chart or a coroner's report under "cause of death." You won't see it listed among the top killers in the United States each year. All too often, however, it is social inequality that lurks behind a more immediate cause of death, be it heart disease or diabetes, accidental injury or homicide. Few of the top causes of death are "equal opportunity killers." Instead, they tend to strike poor people more than rich people, the less educated more than the highly educated, people lower on the occupational ladder more than those higher up, or people of color more than white people.

Statistics on mortality and life expectancy do not pro-vide a perfect map of social inequality. For example, the life expectancy for women in the United States is about six years longer than the life expectancy for men, despite the many ways in which women are subordinated to men. Take most indicators of socioeconomic status, however, and most causes of death, and it's a strong bet that you'll find illness and injury (or "morbidity") and mortality increasing as status decreases.

Men with less than 12 years of education are more than twice as likely to die of chronic diseases (e.g., heart disease), more than three times as likely to die as a result of injury, and nearly twice as likely to die of communicable diseases, compared to those with 13 or more years of education. Women with family incomes below $10,000 are more than three times as likely to die of heart disease and nearly three times as likely to die of diabetes, compared to those with family incomes above $25,000. African Americans are more likely than whites to die of heart disease; stroke; lung, colon, prostate, and breast cancer, as well as all cancers combined; liver disease; diabetes; AIDS; accidental injury; and homicide. In all, the lower you are in a social hierarchy, the worse your health and the shorter your life are likely to be.

The Worse off in the United States Are Not Well off by World Standards.

You often hear it said that even poor people in rich countries like the United States are rich compared to ordinary people in poor countries. While that may be true when it comes to consumer goods like televisions or telephones, which are widely available even to poor people in the United States, it's completely wrong when it comes to health.

In a 1996 study published in the *New England Journal of Medicine*, University of Michigan researchers found that African-American females living to age 15 in Harlem had a 65% chance of surviving to age 65, about the same as women in India. Meanwhile, Harlem's African-American males had only a 37% chance of surviving to age 65, about the same as men in Angola or the Democratic Republic of Congo. Among both African-American men and women, infectious diseases and diseases of the circulatory system were the prime causes of high mortality.

It takes more income to achieve a given life expectancy in a rich country like the United States than it does to achieve the same life expectancy in a less affluent country. So the higher money income of a low-income person in the United States, compared to a middle-income person in a poor country, does not necessarily translate into a longer life span. The average income per person in African-American families, for example, is more than five times the per capita income of El Salvador. The life expectancy for African-American men in the United States, however, is only about 67 years, the same as the average life expectancy for men in El Salvador.

Health Inequalities Are Not Just about Access to Health Care.

Nearly one-sixth of the U.S. population lacks health insurance, including about 44% of poor people. A poor adult with a health problem is only half as likely to see a doctor as a high-income adult. Adults living in low-income areas are more than twice as likely to be hospitalized for a health problem that could have been effectively treated with timely outpatient care, compared with adults living in high-income areas. Obviously, lack of access to health care is a major health problem.

But so are environmental and occupational hazards; communicable diseases; homicide and firearm-related injuries; and smoking, alcohol consumption, lack of exercise, and other risk factors. These dangers all tend to affect lower-income people more than higher-income, less-educated people more than more-educated, and people of color more than whites. African-American children are more than twice as likely as white children to be hospitalized for asthma, which is linked to air pollution. Poor men are nearly six times as likely as high-income men to have elevated blood-lead levels, which reflect both residential and workplace environmental hazards. African-American men are more than seven times as likely to fall victim to homicide as white men; African-American women, more than four times as likely as white women. The less education someone has, the more likely they are to smoke or to drink heavily. The lower someone's income, the less likely they are to get regular exercise.

Michael Marmot, a pioneer in the study of social inequality and health, notes that so-called diseases of affluence—disorders, like heart disease, associated with high-calorie and high-fat diets, lack of physical activity, etc.—are most prevalent among the *least affluent* people in rich societies. While recognizing the role of such "behavioral" risk factors as smoking in producing poor health, he argues, "It is not sufficient … to ask what contribution smoking makes to generating the social gradient in ill health, but we must ask, why is there a social gradient in smoking?" What appear to be individual "lifestyle" decisions often reflect a broader *social* epidemiology.

Greater Income Inequality Goes Hand in Hand with Poorer Health.

Numerous studies suggest that the more unequal the income distribution in a country, state, or city, the lower the life expectancies for people at all income levels. One study published in the *American Journal of Public Health*, for example, shows that U.S. metropolitan areas with low per capita incomes and low levels of income inequality have lower mortality rates than areas with high median incomes and high levels of income inequality. Meanwhile, for a given per capita income range, mortality rates always decline as inequality declines.

R.G. Wilkinson, perhaps the researcher most responsible for relating health outcomes to overall levels of inequality (rather than individual income levels), argues that greater income inequality causes worse health out-comes independent of its effects on poverty. Wilkinson and his associates suggest several explanations for this relationship. First, the bigger the income gap between rich and poor, the less inclined the well off are to pay taxes for public services they either do not use or use in low proportion to the taxes they pay. Lower spending on public hospitals, schools, and other basic services does not affect wealthy people's life expectancies very much, but it affects poor people's life expectancies a great deal. Second, the bigger the income gap, the lower the overall level of social cohesion. High levels of social cohesion are associated with good health outcomes for several reasons. For example, people in highly cohesive societies are more likely to be active in their communities, reducing social isolation, a known health risk factor.

Numerous researchers have criticized Wilkinson's conclusions, arguing that the real reason income inequality tends to be associated with worse health outcomes is that it is associated with higher rates of poverty. But even if they are right and income inequality causes worse health *simply by bringing about greater poverty*, that hardly makes for a defense of inequality. Poverty and inequality are like partners in crime. "[W]hether public policy focuses primarily on the elimination of poverty or on reduction in income disparity," argue Wilkinson critics Kevin Fiscella and Peter Franks, "neither goal is likely to be achieved in the absence of the other."

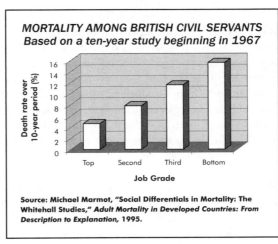

MORTALITY AMONG BRITISH CIVIL SERVANTS
Based on a ten-year study beginning in 1967

Death rate over 10-year period (%)

Job Grade: Top, Second, Third, Bottom

Source: Michael Marmot, "Social Differentials in Mortality: The Whitehall Studies," *Adult Mortality in Developed Countries: From Description to Explanation*, 1995.

Differences in Status May be Just as Important as Income Levels.

Even after accounting for differences in income, education, and other factors, the life expectancy for African Americans is less than that for whites. U.S. researchers are beginning to explore the relationship between high blood pressure among African Americans and the racism of the surrounding society. African Americans tend to suffer from high blood pressure, a risk factor for circulatory disease, more often than whites. Moreover, studies have found that, when confronted with racism, African Americans suffer larger and longer-lasting increases in blood pressure than when faced with other stressful situations. Broader surveys relating blood pressure in African Americans to perceived instances of racial discrimination have yielded complex results, depending on social class, gender, and other factors.

Stresses cascade down social hierarchies and accumulate among the least empowered. Even researchers focusing on social inequality and health, however, have been surprised by the large effects on mortality. Over 30 years ago, Michael Marmot and his associates undertook a landmark study, known as Whitehall I, of health among British civil servants. Since the civil servants shared many character-istics regardless of job classification—an office work environment, a high degree of job security, etc.—the researchers expected to find only modest health differences among them. To their surprise, the study revealed a sharp increase in mortality with each step down the job hierarchy—even from the highest grade to the second high-est. Over ten years, employees in the lowest grade were three times as likely to die as those in the highest grade. One factor was that people in lower grades showed a higher incidence of many "lifestyle" risk factors, like smoking, poor diet, and lack of exercise. Even when the researchers controlled for such factors, however, more than half the mortality gap remained.

Marmot noted that people in the lower job grades were less likely to describe themselves as having "control over their working lives" or being "satisfied with their work situation," compared to those higher up. While people in higher job grades were more likely to report "having to work at a fast pace," lower-level civil servants were more likely to report feelings of hostility, the main stress-related risk factor for heart disease. Marmot concluded that "psycho-social" factors—the psychological costs of being lower in the hierarchy—played an important role in the unexplained mortality gap. Many of us have probably said to ourselves, after a trying day on the job, "They're killing me." Turns out it's not just a figure of speech. Inequality kills—and it starts at the bottom.

Resources: Lisa Berkman, "Social Inequalities and Health: Five Key Points for Policy-Makers to Know," February 5, 2001, Kennedy School of Government, Harvard University; *Health, United States, 1998, with Socioeconomic Status and Health Chart-book*, National Center for Health Statistics <www.cdc.gov/nchs>; Ichiro Kawachi, Bruce P. Kennedy, and Richard G. Wilkinson, eds., *The Society and Population Health Reader, Volume I: Income Inequality and Health*, 1999; Michael Marmot, "Social Differences in Mortality: The Whitehall Studies," *Adult Mortality in Developed Countries: From Description to Explanation*, Alan D. Lopez, Graziella Caselli, and Tapani Valkonen, eds., 1995; Michael Marmot, "The Social Pattern of Health and Disease," *Health and Social Organization: Towards a Health Policy for the Twenty-First Centrury*, David Blane, Eric Brunner, and Richard Wilkinson, eds., 1996; Arline T. Geronimus, et al., "Excess Mortality Among Blacks and Whites in the United States," *The New England Journal of Medicine* 335 (21), November 21, 1996; Nancy Krieger, Ph.D., and Stephen Sidney, M.D., "Racial Discrimination and Blood Pressure: The CARDIA Study of Young Black and White Adults," *American Journal of Public Health* 86 (10), October 1996; *Human Development Report 2000*, UN Development Programme; *World Development Indicators 2000*, World Bank.

Article 7.5

SLICING UP AT THE LONG BARBEQUE
Who gorges, who serves, and who gets roasted?

BY JAMES M. CYPHER
January/February 2007

Economic inequality has been on the rise in the United States for 30-odd years. Not since the Gilded Age of the late 19th century—during what Mark Twain referred to as "the Great Barbeque"—has the country witnessed such a rapid shift in the distribution of economic resources.

Still, most mainstream economists do not pay too much attention to the distribution of income and wealth—that is, how the value of current production (income) and past accumulated assets (wealth) is divided up among U.S. households. Some economists focus their attention on theory for theory's sake and do not work much with empirical data of any kind. Others who *are* interested in these on-the-ground data simply assume that each individual or group gets what it deserves from a capitalist economy. In their view, if the share of income going to wage earners goes up, that must mean that wage earners are more productive and thus deserve a larger slice of the nation's total income—and vice versa if that share goes down.

Heterodox economists, however, frequently look upon the distribution of income and wealth as among the most important shorthand guides to the overall state of a society and its economy. Some are interested in economic justice; others may or may not be, but nonetheless are convinced that changes in income distribution signal underlying societal trends and perhaps important points of political tension. And the general public appears to be paying increasing attention to income and wealth inequality. Consider the strong support voters have given to recent ballot questions raising state minimum wages and the ex-tensive coverage of economic inequality that has suddenly begun to appear in mainstream news outlets like the *New York Times*, the *Los Angeles Times*, and the *Wall Street Journal*, all of which published lengthy article series on the topic in the past few years. Just last month, news outlets around the country spotlighted the extravagant bonuses paid out by investment firm Goldman Sachs, including a $53.4 million bonus to the firm's CEO.

By now, economists and others who do pay attention to the issue are aware that income and wealth inequality in the United States rose steadily during the last three decades of the 20th century. But now that we are several years into the 21st, what do we know about income and wealth distribution today? Has the trend toward inequality continued, or are there signs of a reversal? And what can an understanding of the entire post-World War II era tell us about how to move again toward greater economic equality?

The short answers are: (1) Income distribution is even more unequal that we thought; (2) The newest data suggest the trend toward greater inequality continues, with no signs of a reversal; (3) We all do better when we all do better. During the 30 or so years after World War II the economy boomed and every stratum of society did better—pretty much at the same rate. When the era of shared growth ended, so too did much of the growth: the U.S. economy slowed down and recessions were deeper, more frequent, and harder to overcome. Growth spurts that did occur left most people out: the bottom 60% of U.S. households earned only 95 cents in 2004 for every dollar they made in 1979. A quarter century of falling incomes for the vast majority, even though average household income rose by 27% in real terms. Whew!

The Classless Society?

Throughout the 1950s, 1960s, and 1970s, sociologists preached that the United States was an essentially "classless" society in which everyone belonged to the middle class. A new "mass market" society with an essentially affluent, economically homogeneous population, they claimed, had emerged. Exaggerated as these claims were in the 1950s, there was some reason for their popular acceptance. Union membership reached its peak share of the private-sector labor force in the early 1950s; unions were able to force corporations of the day to share the benefits of strong economic growth. The union wage created a target for non-union workers as well, pulling up all but the lowest of wages as workers sought to match the union wage and employers often granted it as a tactic for keeping unions out. Under these circumstances, millions of families entered the lower middle class and saw their standard of living rise markedly. All of this made the distribution of income more equal for decades until the late 1970s. Of course there were outliers—some millions of poor, disproportionately blacks, and the rich family here and there.

Something serious must have happened in the 1970s as the trend toward greater economic equality rapidly reversed. Here are the numbers. The share of income received by the bottom 90% of the population was a modest 67% in 1970, but by 2000 this had shrunk to a mere 52%, according to a detailed study of U.S. income distribution conducted by Thomas Piketty and Emmanuel Saez, published by the prestigious National Bureau of Economic Research in 2002. Put another way, the top 10% in-creased their overall share of the nation's total income by 15 percentage points from 1970 to 2000. This is a rather astonishing jump—the *gain* of the top 10% in these years was equivalent to more than the *total income received annually* by the bottom 40% of households.

To get on the bottom rung of the top 10% of households in 2000, it would have been necessary to have an adjusted gross income of $104,000 a year. The real money, though, starts on the 99th rung of the income ladder—the top 1% received an unbelievable 21.7% of all income in 2000. To get a handhold on the very bottom of this top rung took more than $384,000.

The Piketty-Saez study (and subsequent updates), which included in its measure of annual household income some data, such as income from capital gains, that generally are not factored in, verified a rising *trend* in income inequality which had been widely noted by others, and a *degree* of inequality which was far beyond most current estimates.

The Internal Revenue Service has essentially duplicated the Piketty-Saez study. They find that in 2003, the share of total income going to the "bottom" four-fifths of house-holds (that's 80% of the population!) was only slightly above 40%. (See Figure 1.) Both of these studies show much higher levels of inequality than were previously thought to exist based on widely referenced Census Bureau studies. The Census studies still attribute 50% of total income to the top fifth for 2003, but this number appears to understate what the top fifth now receives—nearly 60%, according to the IRS.

A Brave New (Globalized) World for Workers

Why the big change from 1970 to 2000? That is too long a story to tell here in full. But briefly, we can say that beginning in the early 1970s, U.S. corporations and the wealthy individuals who largely own them had the means, the motive, and the opportunity to garner a larger share of the nation's income—and they did so.

Let's start with the motive. The 1970s saw a significant slowdown in U.S. economic growth, which made corporations and stockholders anxious to stop sharing the benefits of growth to the degree they had in the im-mediate postwar era.

Opportunity appeared in the form of an accelerating globalization of economic activity. Beginning in the 1970s, more and more U.S.-based corporations began to set up production operations overseas. The trend has only accelerated since, in part because international communication and transportation costs have fallen dramatically. Until the 1970s, it was very difficult—essentially unprofitable—for giants like General Electric or General Motors to operate plants offshore and then import their foreign-made products into the United States. So from the 1940s to the 1970s, U.S. workers had a geographic lever, one they have now almost entirely lost. This erosion in workers' bargaining power has undermined the middle class and decimated the unions that once managed to assure the working class a generally comfortable economic existence. And today, of course, the tendency to send jobs offshore is affecting many highly trained professionals such as engineers. So this process of gutting the middle class has not run its course.

Given the opportunity presented by globalization, companies took a two-pronged approach to strengthening their hand vis-à-vis workers: (1) a frontal assault on unions, with decertification elections and get-tough tactics during unionization attempts, and (2) a debilitating war of nerves whereby corporations threatened to move offshore unless workers scaled back their demands or agreed to givebacks of prior gains in wage and benefit levels or working conditions.

A succession of U.S. governments that pursued conservative—or pro-corporate—economic policies provided the means. Since the 1970s, both Republican and Democratic administrations have tailored their eco-nomic policies to benefit corporations and shareholders over workers. The laundry list of such policies includes

- new trade agreements, such as NAFTA, that allow companies to cement favorable deals to move offshore to host nations such as Mexico;
- tax cuts for corporations and for the wealthiest house-holds, along with hikes in the payroll taxes that represent the largest share of the tax burden on the working and middle classes;
- lax enforcement of labor laws that are supposed to protect the right to organize unions and bargain collectively.

Exploding Millionairism

Given these shifts in the political economy of the United States, it is not surprising that economic inequality in 2000 was higher than in 1970. But at this point, careful readers may well ask whether it is misleading to use data for the year 2000, as the studies reported above do, to demonstrate rising inequality. After all, wasn't 2000 the year the NASDAQ peaked, the year the dot-com bubble reached its maximum volume? So if the wealthiest households received an especially large slice of the nation's total income that year, doesn't that just reflect a bubble about to burst rather than an underlying trend?

To begin to answer this question, we need to look at the trends in income and wealth distribution *since* 2000. And it turns out that after a slight pause in 2000-2001, inequality has continued to rise. Look at household income, for example. According to the standard indicators, the U.S. economy saw a brief recession in 2000-2001 and has been in a recovery ever since. But the median household income has failed to recover. In 2000 the median household had an annual income of $49,133; by 2005, after adjusting for inflation, the figure stood at $46,242. This 6% drop in median household income occurred while the inflation-adjusted Gross Domestic Product *expanded* by 14.4%.

When the Census Bureau released these data, it noted that median household income had gone up slightly between 2004 and 2005. This point was seized upon by Bush administration officials to bolster their claim that times are good for American

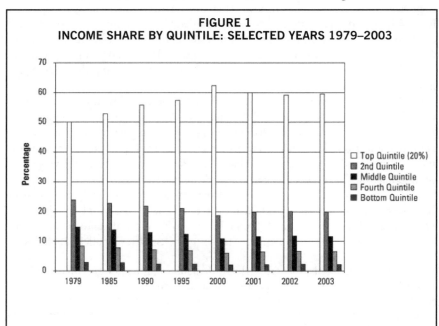

FIGURE 1
INCOME SHARE BY QUINTILE: SELECTED YEARS 1979–2003

Source: "Further Analysis Of The Distribution Of Income And Taxes, 1979–2002," Michael Strudler and Tom Petska, Statistics of Income Division, Internal Revenue Service, and Ryan Petska, Quantitative Economics and Statistics, Ernst and Young LLP. Accompanying Excel files include data to 2003. Available at www.irs.gov/taxstats/article/0,,id=131260,00.html.

workers. A closer look at the data, however, revealed a rather astounding fact: Only 23 million households moved ahead in 2005, most headed by someone aged 65 or above. In other words, subtracting out the cost-of-living increase in Social Security benefits and increases in investment income (such as profits, dividends, interest, capital gains, and rents) to the over-65 group, workers again suffered a *decline* in income in 2005.

Another bit of evidence is the number of millionaire households—those with net worth of $1 million or more excluding the value of a primary residence and any IRAs. In 1999, just before the bubbles burst, there were 7.1 million millionaire households in the United States. In 2005, there were 8.9 million, a record number. Ordinary workers may not have recovered from the 2000–2001 rough patch yet, but evidently the wealthiest households have!

Many economists pay scant attention to income distribution patterns on the assumption that those shifts merely reflect trends in the productivity of labor or the return to risk-taking. But worker productivity *rose* in the 2000-2005 period, by 27.1% (see Figure 2). At the same time, from 2003 to 2005 average hourly pay *fell* by 1.2%. (Total compensation, including all forms of benefits, rose by 7.2% between 2000 and 2005. Most of the higher compensation spending merely reflects rapid increases in the health insurance premiums that employers have to pay just to maintain the same levels of coverage. But even if benefits are counted as part of workers' pay—a common and questionable practice—productivity growth outpaced this elastic definition of "pay" by 50% between 1972 and 2005.)

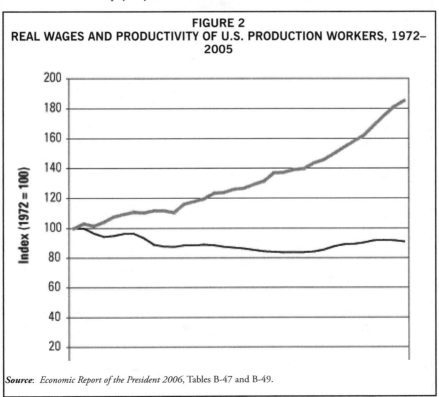

FIGURE 2
REAL WAGES AND PRODUCTIVITY OF U.S. PRODUCTION WORKERS, 1972–2005

Index (1972 = 100)

Source: *Economic Report of the President 2006*, Tables B-47 and B-49.

And at the macro level, recent data released by the Commerce Department demonstrate that the share of the country's GDP going to wages and salaries sank to its lowest postwar level, 45.4%, in the third quarter of 2006 (see Figure 3). And this figure actually overstates how well ordinary workers are doing. The "Wage & Salary" share includes *all* income of this type, not just production workers' pay. Corporate executives' increasingly munificent salaries are included as well. Workers got roughly 65% of total wage and salary income in 2005, according to survey data from the U.S. Department of Labor; the other 35% went to salaried professionals—medical doctors and technicians, managers, and lawyers—who comprised only 15.6% of the sample.

Moreover, the "Wage & Salary" share shown in the National Income and Product Accounts includes bonuses, overtime, and other forms of payment not included in the Labor Department survey. If this income were factored in, the share going to nonprofessional, nonmanagerial workers would be even smaller. Bonuses and other forms of income to top employees can be many times base pay in important areas such as law and banking. Goldman Sachs's notorious 2006 bonuses are a case in point; the typical managing director on Wall Street garnered a bonus ranging between $1 and $3 million.

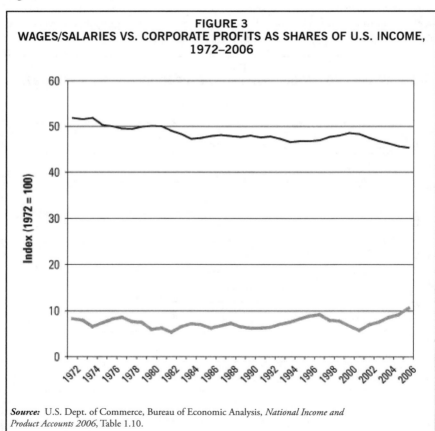

FIGURE 3
WAGES/SALARIES VS. CORPORATE PROFITS AS SHARES OF U.S. INCOME, 1972–2006

Source: U.S. Dept. of Commerce, Bureau of Economic Analysis, *National Income and Product Accounts 2006*, Table 1.10.

So, labor's share of the nation's income is falling, as Figure 3 shows, but it is actually falling much faster than these data suggest. Profits, meanwhile, are at their highest level as a share of GDP since the booming 1960s.

These numbers should come as no surprise to anyone who reads the paper: story after story illustrates how cor-porations are continuing to squeeze workers. For instance, workers at the giant auto parts manufacturer Delphi have been told to pre-pare for a drop in wages from $27.50 an hour in 2006 to $16.50 an hour in 2007. In order to keep some of Caterpillar's manufacturing work in the United States, the union was cornered into accepting a contract in 2006 that limits new workers to a maximum salary of $27,000 a year—no matter how long they work there—com-pared to the $38,000 or more that long-time Caterpillar workers make today. More generally, for young women with a high school diploma, average entry-level pay fell to only $9.08 an hour in 2005, down by 4.9% just since 2001. For male college graduates, starter-job pay fell by 7.3% over the same period.

Aiding and Abetting

And the federal government is continuing to play its part, facilitating the transfer of an ever-larger share of the nation's income to its wealthiest households. George W. Bush once joked that his constituency was "the haves and the have-mores"—this may have been one of the few instances in which he was actually leveling with his audience. Consider aspects of the four tax cuts for individuals that Bush has imple-mented since taking office. The first two cut the top *nominal* tax rate from 39.6% to 35%. Then, in 2003, the third cut benefited solely those who hold wealth, reduc-ing taxes on dividends from 39.6% to 15% and on capital gains from 20% to 15%. (Bush's fourth tax cut—in 2006—is expected to drop taxes by 4.8% percent for the top one tenth of one percent of all households, while the median household will luxuriate with an extra nickel per day.)

So, if you make your money by the sweat of your brow and you earned $200,000 in 2003, you paid an *effective* tax rate of 21%. If you earned a bit more, say another $60,500, you paid an effective tax rate of 35% on the additional income. But if, with a flick of the wrist on your laptop, you flipped some stock you had held for six months and cleared $60,500 on the transaction, you paid the IRS an effective tax rate of only 15%. What difference does it make? Well, in 2003 the 6,126 households with incomes over $10 million saw their taxes go down by an average of $521,905 from this one tax cut alone.

These tax cuts represent only one of the many Bush administration policies that have abetted the ongoing shift of income away from most households and toward the wealthiest ones. And what do these top-tier households do with all this new-found money? For one thing, they save. This is in sharp contrast to most households. While the top fifth of households by income has a savings rate of 23%, the bot-tom 80% as a group dissave—in other words, they go into debt, spending more than they earn. Households headed by a person under 35 currently show a negative savings rate of 16% of income. Today *overall* savings—the savings of the top fifth minus the dis-savings of the bottom four-fifths—are slightly negative, for the first time since the Great Depression.

Here we find the crucial link between income and wealth accumulation. Able to save nearly a quarter of their income, the rich search out financial assets (and sometimes real assets such as houses and businesses) to pour their vast funds into. In many instances, sometimes with inside information, they are able to generate considerable future income from their invested savings. Like a snowball rolling downhill, savings for the rich can have a turbo effect—more savings generates more income, which then accumulates as wealth.

Lifestyles of the Rich

Make the rich even richer and the creative forces of market capitalism will be unleashed, resulting in more savings and consequently more capital investment, raising productivity and creating abundance for all. At any rate, that's the supply-side/neoliberal theory. However—and reminiscent of the false boom that defined the Japanese economy in the late 1980s—the big money has not gone into pro-ductive investments in the United States. Stripping out the money pumped into the residential real estate bubble, inflation-adjusted investment in machinery, equipment, technology, and structures increased only 1.4% from 1999 through 2005—an average of 0.23% per year. Essentially, productive investment has stagnated since the close of the dot-com boom.

Instead, the money has poured into high-risk hedge funds. These are vast pools of unregulated funds that are now generating 40% to 50% of the trades in the New York Stock Exchange and account for very large portions of trad-ing in many U.S. and foreign credit and debt markets.

And where is the income from these investments going? Last fall media mogul David Geffen sold two paintings at record prices, a Jasper Johns ($80 million) and a Willem de Kooning ($63.5 million), to two of "today's crop of hedge-fund billionaires" whose cash is making the art market "red-hot," according to the *New York Times*.

Other forms of conspicuous consumption have their allure as well. Boeing and Lufthansa are expecting brisk business for the newly introduced 787 airplane. The commercial version of the new Boeing jet will seat 330, but the VIP version offered by Lufthansa Technik (for a mere $240 million) will have seating for 35 or fewer, leaving room for master bedrooms, a bar, and the transport of racehorses or Rolls Royces. And if you lose your auto assembly job? It should be easy to find work as a dog walker: High-end pet care services are booming, with sales more than doubling between 2000 and 2004. Opened in 2001, Just Dogs Gourmet expects to have 45 franchises in place by the end of 2006 selling hand-decorated doggie treats. And then there is Camp Bow Wow, which offers piped-in classical music for the dogs (oops, "guests") and a live Camper Cam for their owners. Started only three years ago, the company already has 140 franchises up and running.

According to David Butler, the manager of a premiere auto dealership outside of Detroit, sales of Bentleys, at $180,000 a pop, are brisk. But not many $300,000 Rolls Royces are selling. "It's not that they can't afford it," Butler told the *New York Times*, "it's because of the image it would give." Just what is the image problem in Detroit? Well, maybe it has something to do with those Delphi workers facing a 40% pay cut. Michigan's economy is one of the hardest-hit in the nation. GM, long a symbol of U.S. manufacturing prowess, is staggering, with rumors of possible bankruptcy rife. The best union in terms of delivering the goods for the U.S. working class, the United Auto Workers, is facing an implosion. Thousands of Michigan workers at Delphi, GM, and Ford will be out on the streets very soon. (The top three domestic car makers are determined to permanently lay off three-quar-ters of their U.S. assembly-line workers—nearly 200,000 hourly employees. If they do, then the number of auto-workers employed by the Big Three—Ford, Chrysler, and GM—will have shrunk by a staggering 900,000 since 1978.) So, this might not be the time to buy a Rolls. But a mere $180,000 Bentley—why not?

Had Enough of the "Haves"?

In the era Twain decried as the "great barbeque," the outrageous concentration of income and wealth eventually sparked a reaction and a vast reform movement. But it was not until the onset of the Great Depression, decades later, that massive labor/ social unrest and economic collapse forced the country's political elite to check the growing concentration of income and wealth.

Today, it does not appear that there are, as yet, any viable forces at work to put the brakes on the current runaway process of rising inequality. Nor does it appear that this era's power elite is ready to accept any new social compact. In a recent report on the "new king of Wall Street" (a co-founder of the hedge fund/ private-equity buyout corporation Blackstone Group) that seemed to typify elite perspectives on today's inequality, the *New York Times* gushed that "a crashing wave of capital is minting new billionaires each year." Naturally, the *Times* was too discreet to mention is that those same "crashing waves" have flattened the middle class. And their backwash has turned the working class every-which-way while pulling it down, down, down.

But perhaps those who decry the trend can find at least symbolic hope in the new boom in yet another luxury good. Private mausoleums, in vogue during that earlier Gilded Age, are back. For $650,000, one was recently constructed at Daytona Memorial Park in Florida—with matching $4,000 Medjool date palms for shade. Another, complete with granite patio, meditation room, and doors of hand cast bronze, went up in the same cemetery. Business is booming, apparently, with 2,000 private mausoleums sold in 2005, up from a single-year peak of 65 in the 1980s. Some cost "well into the millions," according to one the nation's largest makers of cemetery monuments. Who knows: maybe the mausoleum boom portends the ulti-mate (dead) end for the neo-Gilded Age.

Sources: Jenny Anderson, "As Lenders, Hedge Funds Draw Insider Scrutiny," *NY Times* 10/16/06; Steven Greenhouse, "Many Entry-Level Workers Feel Pinch of Rough Market," *NY Times* 9/4/06; Greenhouse and David Leonhardt, "Real Wages Fail to Match a Rise in Productivity," *NY Times* 8/28/06; Paul Krugman, "Feeling No Pain," *NY Times* 3/6/06; Krugman, "Graduates vs. Oligarchs," *NY Times* 2/27/06; David Cay Johnston, *Perfectly Legal* (Penguin Books, 2003); Johnston, "Big Gain for Rich Seen in Tax Cuts for Investments," *NY Times* 4/5/06; Johnston, "New Rise in Number of Millionaire Families," *NY Times* 3/28/06; Johnston, "'04 Income in US was Below 2000 Level," *NY Times* 11/28/06; Leonhardt, "The Economics of Henry Ford May Be

Passé," *NY Times* 4/5/06; Rick Lyman, "Census Reports Slight Increase in '05 Incomes," *NY Times* 8/30/06; Micheline Maynard and Nick Bunkley, "Ford is Offering 75,000 Employees Buyout Packages," *NY Times* 9/15/06; Jeremy W. Peters, "Delphi Is Said to Offer Union a One-Time Sweetener," *NY Times* 3/28/06; Joe Sharky, "For the Super-Rich, It's Time to Upgrade the Old Jumbo Jet," *NY Times* 10/17/06; Guy Trebay, "For a Price, Final Resting Place that Tut Would Find Pleasant" *NY Times* 4/17/06.

Article 7.6

THE "DOUBLE-TAXATION" OF CORPORATIONS

BY RAMAA VASUDEVAN
January/February 2007

Dear Dr. Dollar:
My congressman, John Mica (R-Fla.), sent me a letter claiming that "the high income tax rate of 40% for U.S. corporations, unlike most competitors, does not provide relief for the double taxation of corporate income." Like the double talk? He wants to reduce the incentives for companies to move offshore by lowering corporate income taxes. But what's the best response to this claim about "double-taxation"? I don't know much about economics, but I do know enough to know that this position is a con job.
                                              —*Sandra Holt, Casselberry, Fla.*

When corporations and their friends in Washington go on about "double taxation," what they're referring to is the notion that if corporations are taxed on their income and shareholders on their dividends, then the same income is getting taxed twice, with the implication that this is unfair or unduly burdensome. You're right to view this idea as a con job. Here's why:

First, the corporation as an entity is legally distinct from its shareholders. This distinction lies at the core of the notion of limited liability and protects individual share-holders from liability for damages caused by the corporation's pursuit of profits. The claim of "double-taxation" is bogus because the two taxes apply to different taxpayers—corporations versus individual shareholders.

Second, the double taxation claim is a bit of a red her-ring since many kinds of income are in effect double taxed. For instance, along with the income tax, workers also have to pay Medicare and Social Security taxes on their earnings.

In fact, investment income is currently treated more favorably by the tax code than wage income. Investment income is taxed at an average rate of 9.6%, compared to 23.4 % for wages. One reason for this disparity is that investment income is exempt from Medicare and Social Security taxes. But a second key reason is the reduced special tax rate for investment income approved by Congress during Bush's first term. This includes cutting the top tax rate on dividends from around 35% to 15%. As David Cay Johnston of The *New York Times* has observed, "the wealthiest Americans now pay much higher direct taxes on money they work for than on money that works for them."

Who benefits when the tax code rewards investment rather than wage earning? The wealthy, who garner most investment income: about 43% of total investment income goes to the top 1% of taxpayers.

Repealing the dividend tax would only exacerbate that disparity. According to Federal Reserve Board data, fewer than 20% of families hold stocks outside of retirement accounts. Individual stockholdings are concentrated among the richest families, who would be the real beneficiaries of a dividend tax break. Some 42% of benefits from repealing the dividend tax would go to the richest 1% of taxpayers, and about 75% would go to the richest 10% of taxpayers.

In contrast, the vast majority of those who own any stock at all hold their stocks in retirement accounts. They neither receive dividends on these shares directly nor pay a dividend tax—but they'll find themselves paying the normal income tax as soon as they begin drawing on their retirement accounts.

Do taxes impose a disproportionately heavy burden on U.S. corporations? The oft-quoted 40% tax rate applies only to a tiny proportion of corporate income. The official tax rate for most corporate profits is 35%; the very smallest corporations (those with income under $50,000 per year) are subject to a rate of only 15%. Moreover, the official tax rates are higher than the effective tax rates that corporations actually end up paying. A variety of tax breaks allow corporations to reap tremendous tax savings, estimated at $87 billion to $170 billion in 2002-2003 alone, according to a study by Citizens for Tax Justice. The double-taxation argument would have meaning only if the actual burden of corporate taxes were excessive. But it is not. In 2002–03, U.S. corporations paid an effective tax rate of only about 23%. Forty-six large corporations, including Pfizer, Boeing, and AT&T, actually received tax rebates (negative taxes)! Far from being a crushing burden, corporate income tax in the United States has fallen from an average of nearly 5% of GDP in the fifties to 2% in the nineties and about 1.5% (projected) in 2005-2009.

Is the U.S. corporate tax burden higher that that of its competitors? Comparisons of 29 developed countries reveal that only three—Iceland, Germany, and Poland—collected less corporate income tax as a share of GDP than the United States. This represents a reversal from the 1960s, when corporate income tax as a share of GDP in the United States was nearly double that of other developed countries.

The demand for cutting dividend taxes needs to be exposed for what it is: an attempt to create yet another windfall for upper income families who earn the bulk of their income from financial investments. It would not stimulate business investment. And it would exacerbate, rather than redress, the many real inequities in the tax code.

Resources: John Miller, "Double Taxation Double Speak: Why repealing the dividend tax is unfair," *Dollars & Sense*, March–April 2003; Dean Baker "The Dividend Taxbreak; Taxing Logic," Center for Economic and Policy Research, 2003; Joel Friedman, "The Decline of Corporate income tax revenues," Center on Budget and Policy Priorities, 2003; David Cay Johnston, *Perfectly Legal: The Covert Campaign to Rig our Tax System to Benefit the Super-Rich—and Cheat Everybody Else*, Portfolio, 2003.

Article 7.7

HAVE THE RICH WON?

Maybe not. A new approach to capping income at the top is starting to gain momentum.

BY SAM PIZZIGATI
November/December 2009

Back in 1974, the inaugural year for *Dollars & Sense*, young economic justice activists—like me—felt we had our hands full. I was working, at the time, in upstate New York, helping mobile home owners organize against trailer park landlord extortion. I had one friend active on a campaign to win bargaining rights for the local university's food service workers, another pushing for public housing, still another advocating for a badly needed primary health care clinic.

Everywhere we all looked, we saw people hurting, we saw unfairness, we saw economic injustice. Today, 35 years later, I've come to understand what we didn't see: the big picture.

Yes, back then in 1974, we certainly did face injustice at every turn. But we were living, thanks to years of struggle—and success—by our activist forebears, in a society where politics actually revolved around confronting those injustices and making change that could really help average working people.

And, even better, we had a realistic shot at achieving that change. The reason? Our activist forebears had sliced the single greatest obstacle to social progress—the rich and powerful—down to democratic size. In 1974 we were living in a society with an enfeebled wealthy, and we didn't know it.

Shame on us. By not understanding—and not appreciating—the equality our progressive predecessors had battled so hard to achieve, we failed to defend it. We let the wealthy come back. We let grand concentrations of private wealth reconstitute themselves across the American economic landscape. We let the super rich regain their power to dictate and distort America's political discourse.

How rich—and powerful—have today's rich become? Some numbers can help tell the story. In 1974, the most affluent 1% of Americans averaged, in today's dollars, $380,000 in income.

Now let's fast-forward. In 2007, the most recent year with stats, households in America's top 1% averaged $1.4 million, well over triple what top 1% households averaged back in 1974—and, remember, this tripling came *after* adjusting for inflation.

Americans in the bottom 90%, meanwhile, saw their average incomes increase a meager $47 a year between 1974 and 2007, not enough to foot the bill for a month's worth of cable TV.

The bottom line: top-1% households made 12 times more income than bottom-90% households in 1974, 42 times more in 2007.

The numbers become even more striking when we go back a bit further in time and focus not on the top 1%, but on the richest of the rich, the top 400, the living symbol of wealth and power in the United States ever since America's original Gilded Age in the late 19th century.

In 1955, our 400 highest incomes averaged $12.3 million, in today's dollars. But the top 400 in 1955 didn't get to enjoy all those millions. On average, after exploiting every tax loophole they could find, they actually paid over half their incomes, 51.2%, in federal income tax.

Today's super rich are doing better, fantastically better, both before *and* after taxes. In 2006, the top 400 averaged an astounding $263 million each in income. These 400 financially fortunate paid, after loopholes, just 17.2% of their incomes in federal tax.

After taxes, as a group, the top 400 of 2006 had $84 *billion* more in their pockets than 1955's top 400, $84 billion more they could put to work bankrolling politicians and right-wing think tanks and Swift Boat ad blitzes against progressive candidates and causes.

How could America's super rich have so little, relatively speaking, back in 1955 and so much today? What has changed between the mid 20th century and the first decade of the 21st? We have lost, simply put, the economic checks and balances that so significantly discouraged grand concentrations of private wealth in the years right after World War II.

Among the most important of these checks and balances: steeply graduated progressive tax rates. Over most of the quarter-century between the early 1940s and the mid 1960s, America's richest faced at least a 91% federal tax rate on "earned" income over $400,000. By 1974, that top rate had dropped, but only to a still steep 70%. The top rate today: 35%.

Tax rates on income from the sale of stocks, bonds, and other property—capital gains—have traveled the same trend line. In the postwar years, the wealthy paid a 25% tax on capital gains. The current rate: just 15%.

So what should today's activists for economic justice do about all this? Hit the repeat button and re-fight the struggles of our activist forbears?

That course certainly seems reasonable. Our forbears, after all, pulled off quite a stunner. They faced, a century ago, a super rich every bit as rich and powerful as the super rich we confront today. Over the course of the next half-century, they leveled that super rich.

By the 1950s, the incomes of America's richest had been "hacked to pieces," as bestselling author Frederick Lewis Allen would marvel in a 1952 book. The grand estates of the super rich, jubilant postwar progressives would add, had become housing tracts and college campuses for the first mass middle class nation the world had ever seen.

But this triumph would not stand the test of time. The 20th century would end as it began, with phenomenal wealth and power concentrated at America's economic summit. By century's end, the leveling institutions our progressive predecessors had fought so hard to win—progressive tax rates, a vital trade union presence, regulatory restrictions on corporate behavior—had all come unraveled.

Maybe we ought to ask why, before we rush to re-fight the struggles our forbears so nobly waged. Why, for instance, did the single most potent leveling instrument of the mid-20th century, the steeply graduated rates of the progressive income tax, prove unsustainable?

These steep rates, in their time, certainly did work wonders. In the mid-20th century, with these rates in effect, the U.S. economy essentially stopped generating colossal new concentrations of wealth and power. Of the 40 richest individuals in U.S. history, not one made the bulk of his fortune during the years of this progressive tax rate heyday.

The big fortunes that did amass in these years mostly belonged to oil magnates. They enjoyed what the rest of America's rich did not: a super loophole, the oil depletion allowance, that essentially shielded them from the stiff tax rates that applied to every other deep pocket.

But steeply graduated tax rates have an Achilles' heel: the rich hate them with an incredibly intense passion. That wouldn't matter, of course, if everyone else loved these rates with equal fervor. But they don't—because high tax rates on high incomes only impact the wealthy directly. The wealthy feel the "pain." They also see no benefits—because they don't need or use the public services high taxes on high incomes make possible.

Those who *do* benefit from these public services, on the other hand, don't automatically connect the availability of these services to progressive tax rates.

The end result of these political dynamics: Steeply graduated tax rates—as traditionally structured—have never been able to stand the test of time, anywhere. The rich attack these rates with far more single-minded zeal than the general public supports them.

High tax rates on high incomes typically only come into effect during periods of great social upheaval, during wars and severe economic downturns that knock the wealthy off their political stride. But after these upheavals, amid "normalcy," the wealthy's fervid and focused opposition to high rates eventually wears down the public political will to maintain these rates. The rates shrink, wealth re-concentrates.

Today's mainstream policy makers and politicos seem to have concluded, from this history, that any attempt to tax the rich significantly makes no sense.

The Obama White House, for instance, wants to up the top income tax rate on the wealthy, but just to the 39.6% rate in effect before the George W. Bush tax cuts. If the top U.S. tax rate does rise to 39.6%, America's rich would be paying taxes at less than half the rate they faced in the 1950s under President Dwight D. Eisenhower, a Republican.

Even worse: Merely repealing the Bush tax cuts, as current White House economist Lawrence Summers himself acknowledged in a 2007 Brookings Institution paper, would only wipe away one-sixth of the income inequality the nation has experienced since 1979.

Similar tax games are playing out in Britain, where the current government is upping the top tax rate on some high incomes from 40 to 50%. The new rate would still constitute a bargain, by historical standards, for the British rich, who, at one point last century, faced a 97% top rate.

Progressives in the UK, not surprisingly, are challenging their government's tax-the-rich timidity. But they're not stopping there. These progressives are also arguing that we need to go well beyond the traditional progressive tax remedies previous progressive generations put in place, beyond taxing the rich to actually capping their income.

And this capping, these British progressives believe, ought to be done in a manner that gives average working families a clear and powerful vested self-interest in keeping the caps in place. How do they propose to accomplish this goal? They're suggesting we link income ceilings at the top to income floors at the bottom. In effect, they seek a "maximum wage" tied to a minimum.

With a "maximum" set as a multiple of a minimum, society's richest and most powerful would only be able to increase their incomes if the incomes of society's poorest and least powerful increased first. These rich, to become richer, have historically sought to depress wages. A maximum coupled to the minimum would instantly create a counter-incentive: the higher the wage at the bottom, the better for the rich—and the better, of course, for the bottom, too.

In this new maximum wage environment, unions and other traditional advocates for higher wages at the bottom might suddenly find quite a few new—and distinctly wealthy—people in their corner.

Leading UK progressives have opened a campaign to inject these notions into Britain's mainstream political discourse. This past August, 100 British progressive luminaries—all-stars who included three dozen members of Parliament, veteran activists and economists, and the UK's most important labor leader, Trades Union Congress general secretary Brendan Barber—called on their government to establish a "High Pay Commission" and "launch a wide-ranging review of pay at the top."

This High Pay Commission, the progressive luminaries urged, "should consider proposals to restrict excessive remuneration such as maximum wage ratios."

Thousands of British grassroots activists have since signed on to the High Pay Commission call. And one party in the British parliament, based in Wales, has already made advocacy for a UK-wide "maximum wage" part of its official platform.

How exactly could a "maximum wage ratio" principle be implemented? Top-bottom ratios could be tied directly to the expenditure of tax dollars. A government could, for example, insist that all publicly owned enterprises limit the pay between their top executives and their workers.

Late in 2007, delegates to Ecuador's Constituent Assembly enacted legislation along this line. They created a *remuneración máxima*—a "maximum wage"—for all agencies and enterprises that take in over half their financing from tax dollars. The cap limits the pay of top executives in Ecuador's publicly subsidized sector to 25 times the Ecuadorian minimum wage.

Executives at Ecuador's Banco del Pacifico, a huge bank nationalized after a 1999 financial crisis, have been able to exploit and expand exceptions in the original legislation. But the principle still stands.

Governments could also apply that principle much more broadly, by mandating top-bottom pay ratios for any enterprises that seek government contracts or subsidies or tax breaks. The British government, as campaigners for a High Pay Commission note, could insist on "reasonable pay structures" within private enterprises that gain "public procurement contracts."

Under current law, in both Britain and the United States, private enterprises that win government contracts can pay their top executives as much as they please. The CEO at Lockheed Martin, a company that feeds almost exclusively off government contracts, last year took home $26.5 million. That's over 700 times the take-home of the average American worker.

Lockheed, of course, only represents the tip of the taxpayer-subsidized iceberg. Almost every major corporation and bank in the United States is currently raking in big-time taxpayer dollars, either through government contracts, economic development subsidies and tax breaks, or, most recently, outright billion-dollar bailouts.

These taxpayer dollars are making rich people richer. Since the beginning of 2008, the Institute for Policy Studies recently reported, the 20 U.S. banks that have received the most bailout dollars have laid off 160,000 workers. The 100 top executives at these 20 banks, in 2008 alone, collected a combined $791.5 million in personal compensation.

Our tax dollars, in short, are increasing economic inequality in the United States. They are growing the gap between our richest and everyone else. That need not be. If we leveraged the power of the public purse—as we already do in the struggle against gender and racial inequality—our tax dollars could be helping us narrow, not expand, the economic gaps that divide us.

Under existing U.S. law, companies that discriminate against women and minorities in their employment practices cannot gain government contracts. As a society, we've decided that we don't want our tax dollars subsidizing companies that increase gender or racial inequality. So why should we let our tax dollars subsidize companies that increase *economic* inequality—by compensating top executives at levels that dwarf the pay that goes to average workers?

Rep Jan Schakowsky, a progressive Democrat from Illinois, doesn't think we should. Schakowsky has introduced legislation, the Patriot Corporations Act, that would give tax breaks and a preference in the government contract bidding process to companies that pay their executives less than 100 times what they compensate their lowest-paid workers.

That standard, suitably expanded and strengthened, could become a progressive principle worth rallying around: No tax dollars, in any way, shape, or form, for any companies or banks that pay their executives at over 25 times what their workers receive.

Why 25 times? The President of the United States currently makes just under 25 times the annual pay of the lowest-paid federal worker. Why then should we let our tax dollars go to executives who demand—and get—hundreds of times more than their own workers?

Back in 1974, in a far more equal United States, we never needed to ponder questions like these. Now we do.

Sources: For more on progressive tax rates in the United States, see the April 2009 Institute for Policy Studies report, *Reversing the Great Tax Shift*, available at the website of the Institute for Policy Studies (www.ips-dc.org). Detail on the UK campaign for a High Pay Commission can be found at compassonline.org.uk. For other references, email the author at editor@toomuchonline.org.

Chapter 8

MARKET FAILURE, GOVERNMENT POLICY, AND CORPORATE GOVERNANCE

INTRODUCTION

Markets sometimes fail. Mainstream economists typically focus on failures in which existing markets fall short of facilitating exchanges that would make both parties better off. When a factory pollutes the air, people downwind suffer a cost, and might be willing to pay the polluter to curb emissions—but there is no market for clean air. In cases like this, the logical solution is for the government to step in with regulations that ban industries from imposing pollution costs on others. The same goes when private markets do not provide sufficient amounts of public goods—things like vaccines, which everyone benefits from whether they contribute to paying for them or not. Again, government must step in. But what percentage of pollution should industries be required to eliminate? How much should be spent on public health? To decide how *much* government should step in, economists propose cost-benefit analysis, suggesting that the government weigh benefits against costs like a firm deciding how many cars to produce.

Orthodox economists typically see market failures as fairly limited in scope. In fact, they do not consider many negative consequences of markets to be failures at all. When workers are paid wages too low to meet their basic needs, economists do not usually call their poverty and overwork "market failures," but "incentives" to get a higher-paying job. As we saw in the last chapter, mainstream economists are less concerned about how equally the pie is distributed than the overall size of the pie, although most would agree that governments should help those most in need. Still, when economists do recognize market failures, most argue that they are best solved by markets themselves—so pollution should be reduced by allowing firms to trade for the right to pollute, and failing schools should be improved by introducing competition with vouchers and charter schools. Finally, orthodox economists worry about *government* failure—the possibility that government responses to market failures may cause more problems than they solve. They conclude that the "invisible hand" of the market works pretty well, and that alternatives to it may be far worse.

The authors in this chapter see market failures as far more widespread and systemic. They place a high value on outcomes beyond "the size of the pie": environmental sustainability, equality, and economic democracy. And some of them step beyond the "market vs. government" dichotomy to propose other systems of economic governance. Chris Tilly launches the debate by explaining why the invisible hand does not work as well as mainstream theory suggests (Article 8.1). Peter Barnes follows up, challenging the way that conventional economics views issues of the environment and other goods that are shared by many people (Article 8.2). Joel Harrison explores the American healthcare system as a classic example of market failure that systemically misallocates resources, institutionalizes inefficiency, and generally fails to provide health care to the country (Article 8.3). Rachel Keeler describes how one particular global regulatory failure, the proliferation of offshore tax havens, helped cause the current recession (Article 8.7), while Lisa Heinzerling and Frank Ackerman point out key flaws in the use of cost-benefit analysis to guide government action (Article 8.4). Alejandro Reuss argues that our dependence on the car has become unsustainable, and that the solution must be a new transportation system based on alternatives to the auto (Article 8.5).

Frank Ackerman provides a seminal primer for framing the analysis of global warming. In conjunction with the essay on cost-benefit analysis (8.4) this piece provides much-needed context for the most pressing issue of our time (Article 8.6). Creative policy proposals like these contrast with the relatively narrow discussion of the government's role found in most standard texts.

Discussion Questions

1) (Article 8.1) Chris Tilly highlights several important exceptions to the principle that "markets work for the greater good of all." These are exceptions that standard textbooks acknowledge as well. The disagreement comes over how serious these shortcomings are. Given the flaws in the principle of the invisible hand, do you think it is still a useful principle in guiding economic policy? If your answer is no, why do you think it is so widely used?

2) (Article 8.2) Peter Barnes says that an enormous number of resources we take for granted—including the natural environment, but also the laws and institutions that make business possible. Is his point the same thing as saying that there are market failures, such as pollution externalities, that prevent markets from taking into account the full value of the environment? Explain how it is the same or different. In particular, what is the connection between equality/inequality and market failures?

3) (Article 8.3) Is the current system of health care in the United States "efficient"? Define this term and explain. Is health care a "public good" or a private "commodity"? Explore this issue.

4) (Article 8.4) Make a list of types of goods that are harder to put a price on than others. Why is it so hard to price these types of goods?

5) (Article 8.4) Lisa Heinzerling and Frank Ackerman point out a number of flaws in cost-benefit analysis. These weaknesses suggest that the cost-benefit approach will work better in some situations, worse in others. Describe when you would expect it to work better and worse, and explain.

6) (Articles 8.4 and 8.5) Alejandro Reuss lists the many costs of using cars for transportation. Take a devil's advocate position, and explain why the benefits outweigh the costs. Which point of view do you find more convincing? Why?

7) (Article 8.5) Conventional economics emphasizes individual choice. But Alejandro Reuss says that the reasons for over-dependence on cars are rooted in an auto-based transportation system. What is a transportation system? How might it limit individual choices? Does this idea of a system help understand markets other than transportation?

8) (Articles 8.2, 8.4, and 8.5) Standard theory offers support for "market-based" environmental reforms, such as systems that allow companies to buy and sell the right to pollute. Marc Breslow in Chapter 2 (Article 2.4) also sees advantages to this kind of reform. However, such reforms run counter to Peter Barnes's vision of regarding the environment as common property, and to Alejandro Reuss's notion that there has to be a concerted push to change whole technological systems. Outline the strengths and weaknesses of such market-based environmentalism, referring to the articles and your main textbook as appropriate.

9) (Article 8.6) Frank Ackerman provides "four easy pieces" to allow economics to better complement the science of climate change. Why are these four pieces necessary for economics as a discipline to "get it" about climate change? What doesn't neoclassical economics (in this case William Nordhaus) "get" about climate change?

10) (Article 8.7) What is a "tax haven" and how did tax havens contribute to the 2008 financial crash? Why is the regulation of tax havens especially difficult? Why does the author believe that the 2008 crash increased the likelihood of such regulation?

Article 8.1

SHAKING THE INVISIBLE HAND
The Uncertain Foundations of Free-Market Economics

BY CHRIS TILLY
November 1989

> "It is not from the benevolence of the butcher, the brewer or the baker that we expect our dinner, but from their regard to their own interest... [No individual] intends to promote the public interest... [rather, he is] led by an invisible hand to promote an end which was no part of his intention."
>
> —Adam Smith, *The Wealth of Nations*, 1776

Seen the Invisible Hand lately? It's all around us these days, propping up conservative arguments in favor of free trade, deregulation, and tax-cutting.

Today's advocates for "free," competitive markets echo Adam Smith's claim that unfettered markets translate the selfish pursuit of individual gain into the greatest benefit for all. They trumpet the superiority of capitalist free enterprise over socialist efforts to supplant the market with a planned economy, and even decry liberal attempts to moderate the market. Anything short of competitive markets, they proclaim, yields economic inefficiency, making society worse off.

But the economic principle underlying this fanfare is shaky indeed. Since the late 19th century, mainstream economists have struggled to prove that Smith was right—that the chaos of free markets leads to a blissful economic order. In the 1950s, U.S. economists Kenneth Arrow and Gerard Debreu finally came up with a theoretical proof, which many orthodox economists view as the centerpiece of modern economic theory.

Although this proof is the product of the best minds of mainstream economics, it ends up saying surprisingly little in defense of free markets. The modern theory of the Invisible Hand shows that given certain assumptions, free markets reduce the wasteful use of economic resources—but perpetuate unequal income distribution.

To prove free markets cut waste, economists must make a number of far-fetched assumptions: there are no concentrations of economic power; buyers and sellers know every detail about the present and future economy; and all costs of production are borne by producers while all benefits from consumption are paid for by consumers (see box for a complete list). Take away any one of these assumptions and markets can lead to stagnation, recession, and other forms of waste—as in fact they do.

In short, the economic theory invoked by conservatives to justify free markets instead starkly reveals their limitations.

The Fruits of Free Markets

The basic idea behind the Invisible Hand can be illustrated with a story. Suppose that I grow apples and you grow oranges. We both grow tired of eating the same fruit all the time and decide to trade. Perhaps we start by trading one apple for one orange. This exchange satisfies both of us, because in fact I would gladly give up more than one apple to get an orange, and you would readily pay more than one orange for an apple. And as long as swapping one more apple for one more orange makes us both better off, we will continue to trade.

Eventually, the trading will come to a stop. I begin to notice that the novelty of oranges wears old as I accumulate a larger pile of them and the apples I once had a surplus of become more precious to me as they grow scarcer. At some point, I draw the line: in order to obtain one more apple from me, you must give me more than one orange. But your remaining oranges have also become more valuable to you. Up to now, each successive trade has made both of us better off. Now there is no further exchange that benefits us both, so we agree to stop trading until the next crop comes in.

Note several features of this parable. Both you and I end up happier by trading freely. If the government stepped in and limited fruit trading, neither of us would be as well off. In fact, the government cannot do anything in the apple/orange market that will make both of us better off than does the free market.

Adding more economic actors, products, money, and costly production processes complicates the picture, but we reach the same conclusions. Most of us sell our labor time in the market rather than fruit; we sell it for money that we then use to buy apples, oranges, and whatever else we need. The theory of the Invisible Hand tells us a trip to the fruit stand improves the lot of both consumer and seller; likewise, the sale of labor time benefits both employer and employee. What's more, according to the theory, competition between apple farmers insures that consumers will get apples produced at the lowest possible cost. Government intervention still can only make things worse.

This fable provides a ready-made policy guide. Substitute "Japanese autos" and "U.S. agricultural products" for apples and oranges, and the fable tells you that import quotas or tariffs only make the people of both countries worse off. Change the industries to airlines or telephone services, and the fable calls for deregulation. Or re-tell the tale in the labor market: minimum wages and unions (which prevent workers from individually bargaining over their wages) hurt employers and workers.

Fruit Salad

Unfortunately for free-market boosters, two major short-comings make a fruit salad out of this story. First, even if free markets perform as advertised, they deliver only one benefit—the prevention of certain economically wasteful practices—while preserving inequality. According to the theory, competitive markets wipe out two kinds of waste: unrealized trades and inefficient production. Given the right assumptions, markets ensure that when two parties both stand to gain from a trade, they make that trade, as in the apples-and-oranges story. Competition compels producers to search for the most efficient, lowest-cost production methods—again, given the right preconditions.

Though eliminating waste is a worthy goal, it leaves economic inequality untouched. Returning once more to the orchard, if I start out with all of the apples and oranges and you start out with none, that situation is free of waste: no swap can make us both better off since you have nothing to trade! Orthodox economists acknowledge that even in the ideal competitive market, those who start out rich stay rich, while the poor remain poor. Many of them argue that attempts at redistributing income will most certainly create economic inefficiencies, justifying the preservation of current inequities.

But in real-life economics, competition does lead to waste. Companies wastefully duplicate each other's research and build excess productive capacity. Cost-cutting often leads to shoddy products, worker speedup, and unsafe working conditions. People and factories stand idle while houses go unbuilt and people go unfed. That's because of the second major problem: real economies don't match the assumptions of the Invisible Hand theory.

Of course, all economic theories build their arguments on a set of simplifying assumptions about the world. These assumptions often sacrifice some less important aspects of reality in order to focus on the economic mechanisms of interest. But in the case of the Invisible Hand, the theoretical preconditions contradict several central features of the economy.

Assumptions and Reality

The claim that free markets lead to efficiency and reduced waste rests on seven main assumptions. However, these assumptions differ sharply from economic reality. (Assumptions 1, 3, 4, and 5 are discussed in more detail in the article.)

ASSUMPTION ONE: No market power. No individual buyer or seller, nor any group of buyers or sellers, has the power to affect the market-wide level of prices, wages, or profits.

REALITY ONE: Our economy is dotted with centers of market power, from large corporations to unions. Furthermore, employers have an edge in bargaining with workers because of the threat of unemployment.

ASSUMPTION TWO: No economies of scale. Small plants can produce as cheaply as large ones.

REALITY TWO: In fields such as mass-production industry, transportation, communications, and agriculture, large producers enjoy a cost advantage, limiting competition.

ASSUMPTION THREE: Perfect information about the present. Buyers and sellers know everything there is to know about the goods being exchanged. Also, each is aware of the wishes of every other potential buyer and seller in the market.

REALITY THREE: The world is full of lemons—goods about which the

For one thing, markets are only guaranteed to prevent waste if the economy runs on "perfect competition": individual sellers compete by cutting prices, individual buyers compete by raising price offers, and nobody holds concentrated economic power. But today's giant corporations hardly match this description. Coke and Pepsi compete with advertising rather than price cuts. The oil companies keep prices high enough to register massive profits every year. Employers coordinate the pay and benefits they offer to avoid bidding up compensation. Workers, in turn, marshal their own forces via unionization—another departure from perfect competition.

Indeed, the jargon of "perfect competition" overlooks the fact that property ownership itself confers disproportionate economic power. "In the competitive model," orthodox economist Paul Samuelson commented, "it makes no difference whether capital hires labor or the other way around." He argued that given perfect competition among workers and among capitalists, wages and profits would remain the same regardless of who does the hiring. But unemployment—a persistent feature of market-driven economies—makes job loss very costly to workers. The sting my boss feels when I "fire" him by quitting my job hardly equals the setback I experience when he fires me.

---

buyer is inadequately informed. Also, people are not mind-readers, so sellers get stuck with surpluses and willing buyers are unable to find the products they want.

ASSUMPTION FOUR: Perfect information about the future. Contracts between buyers and sellers cover every possible future eventuality.

REALITY FOUR: Uncertainty clouds the future of any economy. Futures markets are limited.

ASSUMPTION FIVE: You only get what you pay for. Nobody can impose a cost on somebody else, nor obtain a benefit from them, without paying.

REALITY FIVE: In a free market, polluters can impose costs on the rest of us without paying. And when a public good like a park is built or roads are maintained, everyone benefits whether or not they helped to pay for it.

ASSUMPTION SIX: Self-interest. In economic matters, each person cares only about his or her own level of well-being.

REALITY SIX: Solidarity, jealousy, and even love for one's family violate this assumption.

ASSUMPTION SEVEN: No joint production. Each production process has only one product.

REALITY SEVEN: Even in an age of specialization, there are plenty of exceptions to this rule. For example, large service firms such as hospitals or universities produce a variety of different services using the same resources.

Perfect Information?

In addition, the grip of the Invisible Hand is only sure if all buyers and sellers have "perfect information" about the present and future state of markets. In the present, this implies consumers know exactly what they are buying—an assumption hard to swallow in these days of leaky breast implants and chicken à la Salmonella. Employers must know exactly what skills workers have and how hard they will work—suppositions any real-life manager would laugh at.

Perfect information also means sellers can always sniff out unsatisfied demands, and buyers can detect any excess supplies of goods. Orthodox economists rely on the metaphor of an omnipresent "auctioneer" who is always calling out prices so all buyers and sellers can find mutually agreeable prices and consummate every possible sale. But in the actual economy, the auctioneer is nowhere to be found, and markets are plagued by surpluses and shortages.

Perfect information about the future is even harder to come by. For example, a company decides whether or not to build a new plant based on whether it expects sales to rise. But predicting future demand is a tricky matter. One reason is that people may save money today in order to buy (demand) goods and services in the future. The problem comes in predicting when. As economist John Maynard Keynes observed in 1934, "An act of individual saving means—so to speak—a decision not to have dinner today. But it does not necessitate a decision to have dinner or to buy a pair of boots a week hence...or to consume any specified thing at any specified date. Thus it depresses the business of preparing today's dinner without stimulating the business of making ready for some future act of consumption." Keynes concluded that far from curtailing waste, free markets gave rise to the colossal waste of human and economic resources that was the Great Depression—in part because of this type of uncertainty about the future.

Free Lunch

The dexterity of the Invisible Hand also depends on the principle that "You only get what you pay for." This "no free lunch" principle seems at first glance a reasonable description of the economy. But major exceptions arise. One is what economists call "externalities"—economic transactions that take place outside the market. Consider a hospital that dumps syringes at sea. In effect, the hospital gets a free lunch by passing the costs of waste disposal on to the rest of us. Because no market exists where the right to dump is bought and sold, free markets do nothing to compel the hospital to bear the costs of dumping—which is why the government must step in.

Public goods such as sewer systems also violate the "no free lunch" rule. Once the sewer system is in place, everyone shares in the benefits of the waste disposal, regardless of whether or not they helped pay for it. Suppose sewer systems were sold in a free market, in which each person had the opportunity to buy an individual share. Then any sensible, self-interested consumer would hold back from buying his or her fair share—and wait for others to provide the service. This irrational situation would persist unless consumers could somehow collectively agree on how extensive a sewer system to produce—once more bringing government into the picture.

Most orthodox economists claim that the list of externalities and public goods in the economy is short and easily addressed. Liberals and radicals, on the other hand, offer a long list: for example, public goods include education, health care, and decent public transportation—all in short supply in our society.

Because real markets deviate from the ideal markets envisioned in the theory of the Invisible Hand, they give us both inequality and waste. But if the theory is so far off the mark, why do mainstream economists and policymakers place so much stock in it? They fundamentally believe the profit motive is the best guide for the economy. If you believe that "What's good for General Motors is good for the USA," the Invisible Hand theory can seem quite reasonable. Business interests, government, and the media constantly reinforce this belief, and reward those who can dress it up in theoretical terms. As long as capital remains the dominant force in society, the Invisible Hand will maintain its grip on the hearts and minds of us all.

Article 8.2

SHARING THE WEALTH OF THE COMMONS

BY PETER BARNES
November/December 2004

We're all familiar with private wealth, even if we don't have much. Economists and the media celebrate it every day. But there's another trove of wealth we barely notice: our common wealth.

Each of us is the beneficiary of a vast inheritance. This common wealth includes our air and water, habitats and ecosystems, languages and cultures, science and technologies, political and monetary systems, and quite a bit more. To say we share this inheritance doesn't mean we can call a broker and sell our shares tomorrow. It does mean we're responsible for the commons and entitled to any income it generates. Both the responsibility and the entitlement are ours by birth. They're part of the obligation each generation owes to the next, and each living human owes to other beings.

At present, however, our economic system scarcely recognizes the commons. This omission causes two major tragedies: ceaseless destruction of nature and widening inequality among humans. Nature gets destroyed because no one's unequivocally responsible for protecting it. Inequality widens because private wealth concentrates while common wealth shrinks.

The great challenges for the 21st century are, first of all, to make the commons visible; second, to give it proper reverence; and third, to translate that reverence into property rights and legal institutions that are on a par with those supporting private property. If we do this, we can avert the twin tragedies currently built into our market-driven system.

Defining the Commons

What exactly is the commons? Here is a workable definition: The commons includes all the assets we inherit together and are morally obligated to pass on, undiminished, to future generations.

This definition is a practical one. It designates a set of assets that have three specific characteristics: they're (1) inherited, (2) shared, and (3) worthy of long-term preservation. Usually it's obvious whether an asset has these characteristics or not.

At the same time, the definition is broad. It encompasses assets that are natural as well as social, intangible as well as tangible, small as well as large. It also introduces a moral factor that is absent from other economic definitions: it requires us to consider whether an asset is worthy of long-term preservation. At present, capitalism has no interest in this question. If an asset is likely to yield a competitive return to capital, it's kept alive; if not, it's destroyed or allowed to run down. Assets in the commons, by contrast, are meant to be preserved regardless of their return.

This definition sorts all economic assets into two baskets, the market and the commons. In the market basket are those assets we want to own privately and manage for profit. In the commons basket are the assets we want to hold in common and manage for long-term preservation. These baskets then are, or ought to be, the yin and yang of economic activity; each should enhance and contain the other. The role of the state should be to maintain a healthy balance between them.

The Value of the Commons

For most of human existence, the commons supplied everyone's food, water, fuel, and medicines. People hunted, fished, gathered fruits and herbs, collected firewood and building materials, and grazed their animals in common lands and waters. In other words, the commons was the source of basic sustenance. This is still true today in many parts of the world, and even in San Francisco, where I live, cash-poor people fish in the bay not for sport, but for food.

Though sustenance in the industrialized world now flows mostly through markets, the commons remains hugely valuable. It's the source of all natural resources and nature's many replenishing services. Water, air, DNA, seeds, topsoil, minerals, the protective ozone layer, the atmosphere's climate regulation, and much more, are gifts of nature to us all.

Just as crucially, the commons is our ultimate waste sink. It recycles water, oxygen, carbon, and everything else we excrete, exhale, or throw away. It's the place we store, or try to store, the residues of our industrial system.

The commons also holds humanity's vast accumulation of knowledge, art, and thought. As Isaac Newton said, "If I have seen further it is by standing on the shoulders of giants." So, too, the legal, political, and economic institutions we inherit—even the market itself—were built by the efforts of millions. Without these gifts we'd be hugely poorer than we are today.

To be sure, thinking of these natural and social inheritances primarily as economic assets is a limited way of viewing them. I deeply believe they are much more than that. But if treating portions of the commons as economic assets can help us conserve them, it's surely worth doing so.

How much might the commons be worth in monetary terms? It's relatively easy to put a dollar value on private assets. Accountants and appraisers do it every day, aided by the fact that private assets are regularly traded for money.

This isn't the case with most shared assets. How much is clean air, an intact wetlands,

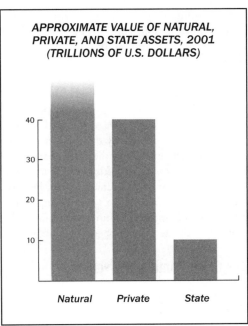

APPROXIMATE VALUE OF NATURAL, PRIVATE, AND STATE ASSETS, 2001 (TRILLIONS OF U.S. DOLLARS)

Natural   Private   State

or Darwin's theory of evolution worth in dollar terms? Clearly, many shared inheritances are simply priceless. Others are potentially quantifiable, but there's no current market for them. Fortunately, economists have developed methods to quantify the value of things that aren't traded, so it's possible to estimate the value of the "price-able" part of the commons within an order of magnitude. The surprising conclusion that emerges from numerous studies is that the wealth we share is worth more than the wealth we own privately.

This fact bears repeating. Even though much of the commons can't be valued in monetary terms, the parts that can be valued are worth more than all private assets combined.

It's worth noting that these estimates understate the gap between common and private assets because a significant portion of the value attributed to private wealth is in fact an appropriation of common wealth. If this mislabeled portion was subtracted from private wealth and added to common wealth, the gap between the two would widen further.

Two examples will make this point clear. Suppose you buy a house for $200,000 and, without improving it, sell it a few years later for $300,000. You pay off the mortgage and walk away with a pile of cash. But what caused the house to rise in value? It wasn't anything you did. Rather, it was the fact that your neighborhood became more popular, likely a result of the efforts of community members, improvements in public services, and similar factors.

Or consider another fount of private wealth, the social invention and public expansion of the stock market. Suppose you start a business that goes "public" through an offering of stock. Within a few years, you're able to sell your stock for a spectacular capital gain.

Much of this gain is a social creation, the result of centuries of monetary-system evolution, laws and regulations, and whole industries devoted to accounting, sharing information, and trading stocks. What's more, there's a direct correlation between the scale and quality of the stock market as an institution and the size of the private gain. You'll fetch a higher price if you sell into a market of millions than into a market of two. Similarly, you'll gain more if transaction costs are low and trust in public information is high. Thus, stock that's traded on a regulated exchange sells for a higher multiple of earnings than unlisted stock. This socially created premium can account for 30% of the stock's value. If you're the lucky seller, you'll reap that extra cash—in no way thanks to anything you did as an individual.

Real estate gains and the stock market's social premium are just two instances of common assets contributing to private gain. Still, most rich people would like us to think it's their extraordinary talent, hard work, and risk-taking that create their well-deserved wealth. That's like saying a flower's beauty is due solely to its own efforts, owing nothing to nutrients in the soil, energy from the sun, water from the aquifer, or the activity of bees.

The Great Commons Giveaway

That we inherit a trove of common wealth is the good news. The bad news, alas, is that our inheritance is being grossly mismanaged. As a recent report by the advocacy group Friends of the Commons concludes, "Maintenance of the commons is terrible, theft is rampant, and rents often aren't collected. To put it bluntly, our common wealth—and our children's—is being squandered. We are all poorer as a result."

Examples of commons mismanagement include the handout of broadcast spectrum to media conglomerates, the giveaway of pollution rights to polluters, the extension of copyrights to entertainment companies, the patenting of seeds and genes, the privatization of water, and the relentless destruction of habitat, wildlife, and ecosystems.

This mismanagement, though currently extreme, is not new. For over 200 years, the market has been devouring the commons in two ways. With one hand, the market takes valuable stuff from the commons and privatizes it. This is called "enclosure." With the other hand, the market dumps bad stuff into the commons and says, "It's your problem." This is called "externalizing." Much that is called economic growth today is actually a form of cannibalization in which the market diminishes the commons that ultimately sustains it.

Enclosure—the taking of good stuff from the commons—at first meant privatization of land by the gentry. Today it means privatization of many common assets by corporations. Either way, it means that what once belonged to everyone now belongs to a few.

Enclosure is usually justified in the name of efficiency. And sometimes, though not always, it does result in efficiency gains. But what also results from enclosure is the impoverishment of those who lose access to the commons, and the enrichment of those who take title to it. In other words, enclosure widens the gap between those with income-producing property and those without.

Externalizing—the dumping of bad stuff into the commons—is an automatic behavior pattern of profit-maximizing corporations: if they can avoid any out-of-pocket costs, they will. If workers, taxpayers, anyone downwind, future generations, or nature have to absorb added costs, so be it.

For decades, economists have agreed we'd be better served if businesses "internalized" their externalities—that is, paid in real time the costs they now shift to the commons. The reason this doesn't happen is that there's no one to set prices and collect them. Unlike private wealth, the commons lacks property rights and institutions to represent it in the marketplace.

The seeds of such institutions, however, are starting to emerge. Consider one of the environmental protection tools the U.S. currently uses, pollution trading. So-called cap-and-trade programs put a cap on total pollution, then grant portions of the total, via permits, to each polluting firm. Companies may buy other firms' permits if they want to pollute more than their allotment allows, or sell unused permits if they manage to pollute less. Such programs are generally supported by business because they allow polluters to find the cheapest ways to reduce pollution.

Public discussion of cap-and-trade programs has focused exclusively on their trading features. What's been overlooked is how they give away common wealth to polluters.

To date, all cap-and-trade programs have begun by giving pollution rights to existing polluters for free. This treats polluters as if they own our sky and rivers. It means that future polluters will have to pay old polluters for the scarce—hence valuable—right to dump wastes into nature. Imagine that: because a corporation polluted in the past, it gets free income forever! And, because ultimately we'll all pay for limited pollution via higher prices, this amounts to an enormous transfer of wealth—trillions of dollars—to shareholders of historically polluting corporations.

In theory, though, there is no reason that the initial pollution rights should not reside with the public. Clean air and the atmosphere's capacity to absorb pollutants are "wealth" that belongs to everyone. Hence, when polluters use up these parts of the commons, they should pay the public—not the other way around.

Taking the Commons Back

How can we correct the system omission that permits, and indeed promotes, destruction of nature and ever-widening inequality among humans? The answer lies in building a new sector of the economy whose clear legal mission is to preserve shared inheritances for everyone. Just as the market is populated by profit-maximizing corporations, so this new sector would be populated by asset-preserving trusts.

Here a brief description of trusts may be helpful. The trust is a private institution that's even older than the corporation. The essence of a trust is a fiduciary relationship. A trust holds and manages property for another person or for many other people. A simple example is a trust set up by a grandparent to pay for a grandchild's education. Other trusts include pension funds, charitable foundations, and university endowments. There are also hundreds of trusts in America, like the Nature Conservancy and the Trust for Public Land, that own land or conservation easements in perpetuity.

If we were to design an institution to protect pieces of the commons, we couldn't do much better than a trust. The goal of commons management, after all, is to preserve assets and deliver benefits to broad classes of beneficiaries. That's what trusts do, and it's not rocket science.

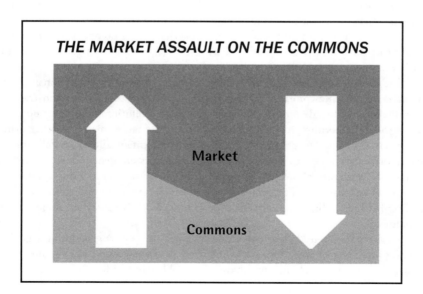

THE MARKET ASSAULT ON THE COMMONS

Market

Commons

Over centuries, several principles of trust management have evolved. These include:

- Trustees have a fiduciary responsibility to beneficiaries. If a trustee fails in this obligation, he or she can be removed and penalized.

- Trustees must preserve the original asset. It's okay to spend income, but don't invade the principal.

- Trustees must assure transparency. Information about money flows should be readily available to beneficiaries.

Trusts in the new commons sector would be endowed with rights comparable to those of corporations. Their trustees would take binding oaths of office and, like judges, serve long terms. Though protecting common assets would be their primary job, they would also distribute income from those assets to beneficiaries. These beneficiaries would include all citizens within a jurisdiction, large classes of citizens (children, the elderly), and/or agencies serving common purposes such as public transit or ecological restoration. When distributing income to individuals, the allocation formula would be one person, one share. The right to receive commons income would be a nontransferable birthright, not a property right that could be traded.

Fortuitously, a working model of such a trust already exists: the Alaska Permanent Fund. When oil drilling on the North Slope began in the 1970s, Gov. Jay Hammond, a Republican, proposed that 25% of the state's royalties be placed in a mutual fund to be invested on behalf of Alaska's citizens. Voters approved in a referendum. Since then, the Alaska Permanent Fund has grown to over $28 billion, and Alaskans have received roughly $22,000 apiece in dividends. In 2003 the per capita dividend was $1,107; a family of four received $4,428.

What Alaska did with its oil can be replicated for other gifts of nature. For example, we could create a nationwide Sky Trust to stabilize the climate for future generations. The trust would restrict emissions of heat-trapping gases and sell a declining number of emission permits to polluters. The income would be returned to U.S. residents in equal yearly dividends, thus reversing the wealth transfer built into current cap-and-trade programs. Instead of everyone paying historic polluters, polluters would pay all of us.

Just as a Sky Trust could represent our equity in the natural commons, a Public Stock Trust could embody our equity in the social commons. Such a trust would capture some of the socially created stock-market premium that currently flows only to shareholders and their investment bankers. As noted earlier, this premium is sizeable—roughly 30% of the value of publicly traded stock. A simple way to share it would be to create a giant mutual fund—call it the American Permanent Fund—that would hold, say, 10% of the shares of publicly traded companies. This mutual fund, in turn, would be owned by all Americans on a one share per person basis (perhaps linked to their Social Security accounts).

To build up the fund without precipitating a fall in share prices, companies would contribute shares at the rate of, say, 1% per year. The contributions would be the price companies pay for the benefits they derive from a commons asset, the large, trusted market for stock—a small price, indeed, for the hefty benefits. Over time, the mutual fund would assure that when the economy grows, everyone benefits. The top 5% would still own more than the bottom 90%, but at least every American would have some property income, and a slightly larger slice of our economic pie.

Sharing the Wealth

The perpetuation of inequality is built into the current design of capitalism. Because of the skewed distribution of private wealth, a small self-perpetuating minority receives a disproportionate share of America's nonlabor income.

Tom Paine had something to say about this. In his essay "Agrarian Justice," written in 1790, he argued that, because enclosure of the commons had separated so many people from their primary source of sustenance, it was necessary to create a functional equivalent of the commons in the form of a National Fund. Here is how he put it:

> There are two kinds of property. Firstly, natural property, or that which comes to us from the Creator of the universe—such as the earth, air, water. Secondly, artificial or acquired property—the invention of men. In the latter, equality is impossible; for to distribute it equally, it would be necessary that all should have contributed in the same proportion, which can never be the case .... Equality of natural property is different. Every individual in the world is born with legitimate claims on this property, or its equivalent.

Enclosure of the commons, he went on, was necessary to improve the efficiency of cultivation. But:

> The landed monopoly that began with [enclosure] has produced the greatest evil. It has dispossessed more than half the inhabitants of every nation of their natural inheritance, without providing for them, as ought to have been done, an indemnification for that loss, and has thereby created a species of poverty and wretchedness that did not exist before.

The appropriate compensation for loss of the commons, Paine said, was a national fund financed by rents paid by land owners. Out of this fund, every person reaching age 21 would get 15 pounds a year, and every person over 50 would receive an additional 10 pounds. (Think of Social Security, financed by commons rents instead of payroll taxes.)

A Progressive Offensive

Paine's vision, allowing for inflation and new forms of enclosure, could not be more timely today. Surely from our vast common inheritance—not just the land, but the atmosphere, the broadcast spectrum, our mineral resources, our threatened habitats and water supplies—enough rent can be collected to pay every American over age 21 a modest annual dividend, and every person reaching 21 a small start-up inheritance.

Such a proposal may seem utopian. In today's political climate, perhaps it is. But consider this. About 20 years ago, right-wing think tanks laid out a bold agenda. They called for lowering taxes on private wealth, privatizing much of government, and deregulating industry. Amazingly, this radical agenda has largely been achieved.

It's time for progressives to mount an equally bold offensive. The old shibboleths—let's gin up the economy, create jobs, and expand government programs—no longer excite. We need to talk about fixing the economy, not just growing it; about income for everyone, not just jobs; about nurturing ecosystems, cultures, and communities, not just our individual selves. More broadly, we need to celebrate the commons as an essential counterpoise to the market.

Unfortunately, many progressives have viewed the state as the only possible counterpoise to the market. The trouble is, the state has been captured by corporations. This capture isn't accidental or temporary; it's structural and long-term.

This doesn't mean progressives can't occasionally recapture the state. We've done so before and will do so again. It does mean that progressive control of the state is the exception, not the norm; in due course, corporate capture will resume. It follows that if we want lasting fixes to capitalism's tragic flaws, we must use our brief moments of political ascendancy to build institutions that endure.

Programs that rely on taxes, appropriations, or regulations are inherently transitory; they get weakened or repealed when political power shifts. By contrast, institutions that are self-perpetuating and have broad constituencies are likely to last. (It also helps if they mail out checks periodically.) This was the genius of Social Security, which has survived—indeed grown—through numerous Republican administrations.

If progressives are smart, we'll use our next New Deal to create common property trusts that include all Americans as beneficiaries. These trusts will then be to the 21st century what social insurance was to the 20th: sturdy pillars of shared responsibility and entitlement. Through them, the commons will be a source of sustenance for all, as it was before enclosure. Life-long income will be linked to generations-long ecological health. Isn't that a future most Americans would welcome?

Article 8.3

PAYING MORE, GETTING LESS

How much is the sick U.S. health care system costing you?

BY JOEL A. HARRISON

March/April 2008

By any measure, the United States spends an enormous amount of money on health care. Here are a few of those measures. Last year, U.S. health care spending exceeded 16% of the nation's GDP. To put U.S. spending into perspective: the United States spent 15.3% of GDP on health care in 2004, while Canada spent 9.9%, France 10.7%, Germany 10.9%, Sweden 9.1%, and the United Kingdom 8.7%. Or consider per capita spending: the United States spent $6,037 per person in 2004, compared to Canada at $3,161, France at $3,191, Germany at $3,169, and the U.K. at $2,560.

By now the high overall cost of health care in the United States is broadly recognized. And many Americans are acutely aware of how much they pay for their own care. Those without health insurance face sky-high doctor and hospital bills and ever more aggressive collection tactics—when they receive care at all. Those who are fortunate enough to have insurance experience steep annual premium hikes along with rising deductibles and co-pays, and, all too often, a well-founded fear of losing their coverage should they lose a job or have a serious illness in the family.

Still, Americans may well *underestimate* the degree to which they subsidize the current U.S. health care system out of their own pockets. And almost no one recognizes that even people without health insurance pay substantial sums into the system today. If more people understood the full size of the health care bill that they as individuals are already paying—and for a system that provides seriously inadequate care to millions of Americans—then the corporate opponents of a universal single-payer system might find it far more difficult to frighten the public about the costs of that system. In other words, to recognize the advantages of a single-payer system, we have to understand how the United States funds health care and health research and how much it actually costs us today.

Paying through the Taxman

The U.S. health care system is typically characterized as a largely private-sector system, so it may come as a surprise that more than 60% of the $2 trillion annual U.S. health care bill is paid through taxes, according to a 2002 analysis published in *Health Affairs* by Harvard Medical School associate professors Steffie Woolhandler and David Himmelstein. Tax dollars pay for Medicare and Medicaid, for the Veterans Administration and the Indian Health Service. Tax dollars pay for health coverage for federal, state, and municipal government employees and their families, as well as for many employees of private   companies working on government contracts. Less visible but no less important, the tax deduction for employer-paid health insurance, along with other health care-related tax deductions, also represents a form of government spending on health care. It makes little difference whether the government gives taxpayers (or their employers) a deduction for their health care spending, on the one hand, or collects their taxes then pays for their health care, either directly or via a voucher, on the other. Moreover, tax dollars also pay for critical elements of the health care system apart from direct care—Medicare funds much of the expensive equipment hospitals use, for instance, along with all medical residencies.

All told, then, tax dollars already pay for at least $1.2 trillion in annual U.S. health care expenses. Since federal, state, and local governments collect about $3.48 trillion annually in taxes of all kinds—income, sales, property, corporate—that means that *more than one third (34.4%)* of the aggregate tax revenues collected in the United States go to pay for health care.

Beyond their direct payments to health care providers and health insurance companies, then, Americans already make a sizeable annual payment into the health care system via taxes. How much does a typical household contribute to the country's health care system altogether? Of course, households pay varying amounts in taxes depending on income and many other factors. Moreover, some households have no health insurance coverage; others do have coverage for which they may pay some or all of the premium cost. What I aim to do here is to estimate the average size of the health care cost burden for households at different income levels, both those with job-based health coverage and those with no coverage.

Note that the estimates in the table (next page) *do not include* out-of-pocket expenses. For those with health insurance, these include co-pays, deductibles, and uncovered expenses (consider, for example, that even my high-end policy does not cover commonly used home medical equipment such as oxygen). For those without insurance, of course, out-of-pocket expenses include their full hospital, doctor, and pharmacy bills.

The first row ("Share and Amount of Income Going to Health Care via Taxes Alone") shows how much of the total tax burden on households at three income levels goes into the nation's health care system. In other words, a family with an annual income of $50,000 that has no health insurance nonetheless contributes nearly 10% of its income to health care merely by paying typical income, payroll, sales, excise, and other taxes. A person who earns about $25,000 a year and has no health coverage already contributes over $2,400 a year to the system—enough for a healthy young adult to purchase a year's worth of health insurance.

The next two rows add in, for individuals and for families, the cost of employer-based health insurance. So, a household at the $50,000 income level with family health insurance coverage is paying *over a quarter* of its income into the health care system.

How were these figures derived? The tax component of the figures represents 34.4% of the total tax burden (federal, state, and local) on households at the three income levels. Of course, estimating average combined federal, state, and local taxes paid by households at different income levels is not a simple matter. The most comprehensive of such estimates come from the Tax Foundation, a conservative think tank. Other analysts, however, including the liberal Center on Budget and Policy Priorities, view the Tax Foundation's figures as overestimating the total tax burden.

The center has published its own estimates, based on figures from the Congressional Budget Office and Congress's Joint Committee on Taxation. The figures in the table are based on the CBO's numbers, which fall in between the Tax Foundation's estimates and the JCT-based estimates. (Estimates based on the Tax Foundation and JCT figures, along with details of the analysis, can be found at www.dollarsand-sense.org.) It is worth noting that using the Tax Foundation's numbers, which show a larger share of income going to taxes at every income level, would have made the story even worse. For a family with health insurance earning $50,000 a year, for instance, the share of income going into health care would have been 28.7% rather than 26.4%.

For insurance premiums: in 2007, the average annual premiums for health insurance policies offered through employers were $4,479 for individuals and $12,106 for families, according to the Kaiser Family Foundation's annual survey of health benefits. Of course, some employers pay all or a large share of that premium while others pay half or less, leaving much of the premium cost to the worker. Either way, however, the full premium cost represents a bite taken out of the worker's total "wage packet"—the cost of wages plus benefits. This becomes evident when premiums go up: workers either see their own premium payments rise directly, or else face cuts or stagnation in their wages and non-health benefits. For that reason, economists typically view the entire premium as a cost imposed on the worker regardless of variations in employer contribution.

These figures are not meant to be exact, but do offer reasonable estimates of how much U.S. families are actually paying into the country's health care system today. Again, they do not include out-of-pocket expenses, which averaged 13.2% of

What Americans Pay into the U.S. Health Care System Today		Household Income Level		
		$25,000	$50,000	$75,000
Share and Amount of Income Going to Health Care via Taxes Alone		9.0% ($2,425)	9.8% ($5,300)	10.7% ($8,633)
Share and Amount of Total Wage Packet Going to Health Care for Households with Insurance	Individual	22.0% ($6,904)	16.8% ($9,779)	15.4% ($13,112)
	Family	37.2% ($14,531)	26.4% ($17,406)	22.3% ($20,749)

Note: The share of total wage packet going to health care was calculated as follows:

$$\frac{\text{(amount of total tax burden going to health + annual health insurance premium)}}{\text{(annual salary + payroll tax [FICA and Medicare] + annual health insurance premium)}}$$

Further details of the calculations are available at www.dollarsandsense.org/harrison.

all health care expenditures in 2005. Moreover, they do not include the risk of bankruptcy that health care costs impose: 50% of consumer bankruptcies in the United States stem from medical bills, including a surprising number among households that do have some kind of health coverage. Nor do they include the approximately 20% of auto insurance premiums or the 40% of workers' compensation premiums that pay for medical expenses.

Where Does All the Money Go?

After you've finished gasping in surprise at the share of your income that is already going into health care, you may wonder where all that money goes. One answer is that the United States has the most bureaucratic health care system in the world, including over 1,500 different companies, each offering multiple plans, each with its own marketing program and enrollment procedures, its own paperwork and policies, its CEO salaries, sales commissions, and other non-clinical costs—and, of course, if it is a for-profit company, its profits. Compared to the overhead costs of the single-payer approach, this fragmented system takes almost 25 cents more out of every health care dollar for expenses other than actually providing care.

Of the additional overhead in the current U.S. system, approximately half is borne by doctors' offices and hospitals, which are forced to maintain large billing and negotiating staffs to deal with all the plans. By contrast, under Canada's single-payer system (which is run by the provinces, not by the federal government), each medical specialty organization negotiates once a year with the nonprofit payer for each province to set fees, and doctors and hospitals need only bill that one payer.

Of course, the United States already has a universal, single-payer health care program: Medicare. Medicare, which serves the elderly and people with disabilities, operates with overhead costs equal to just 3% of total expenditures, compared to 15% to 25% overhead in private health programs. Since Medicare collects its revenue through the IRS, there is no need to collect from individuals, groups, or businesses. Some complexity remains—after all, Medicare must exist in the fragmented world that is American health care—but no matter how creative the opponents of single-payer get, there is no way they can show convincingly how the administrative costs of a single-payer system could come close to the current level.

Some opponents use current U.S. government expenditures for Medicare and Medicaid to arrive at frightening cost estimates for a universal single-payer health care system. They may use Medicare's $8,568 per person, or $34,272 for a family of four (2006). But they fail to mention that Medicare covers a very atypical, high-cost slice of the U.S. population: senior citizens, regardless of pre-existing conditions, and people with disabilities, including diagnoses such as AIDS and end-stage renal disease. Or they use Medicaid costs—forgetting to mention that half of Medicaid dollars pay for nursing homes, while the other half of Medicaid provides basic health care coverage, primarily to children in low-income households, at a cost of only about $1,500 a year per child.

Getting What We've Already Paid For

Americans spend more than anyone else in the world on health care. Each health insurer adds its bureaucracy, profits, high corporate salaries, advertising, and sales commissions to the actual cost of providing care. Not only is this money lost to health care, but it pays for a system that often makes it more difficult and complicated to receive the care we've already paid for. Shareholders are the primary clients of for-profit insurance companies, not patients.

Moreover, households' actual costs as a percentage of their incomes are far higher today than most imagine. Even families with no health insurance contribute substantially to our health care system through taxes. Recognizing the hidden costs that U.S. households pay for health care today makes it far easier to see how a universal single-payer system—with all of its obvious advantages—can cost most Americans less than the one we have today.

Sources: Center on Budget and Policy Priorities, "The Debate Over Tax Levels: How Much Does a Typical Family Pay?" March 11, 1998; Center on Budget and Policy Priorities, "Tax Foundation Figures Do Not Represent Middle-Income Tax Burdens: Figures May Mislead Policymakers, Journalists, and the Public," April 13, 2006; Center on Budget and Policy Priorities, "Clearing Up Confusion on the Cost of Covering Uninsured Children Eligible for Medicaid or SCHIP," March 13, 2007; Gary Claxton et al., "Health Benefits in 2007: Premium Increases Fall to an Eight-Year Low, While Offer Rates and Enrollment Remain Stable," *Health Affairs* 26(5), 2007 [based on "Employer Health Benefits 2007 Annual Survey" by the Kaiser Family Foundation]; Congressional Research Service, "U.S. Health Care Spending: Comparison with Other OECD Countries," September 17, 2007; Andrés de Francisco and Stephen Matlin, eds., *Monitoring Financial Flows for Health Research 2006* (Global Forum for Health Research, 2006); Tax Foundation, "Who Pays America's Tax Burden, and Who Gets the Most Government Spending?" March 2007; Public Citizen Congress Watch, "Rx R&D Myths: The Case Against the Drug Industry's R&D 'Scare Card'," July 2001; Steffie Woolhandler et al., "Health Care Administration in the United States and Canada: Micromanagement, Macro Costs," *Int'l Journal of Health Services* 34(1), 2004; Steffie Woolhandler and David Himmelstein, "Paying for National Health Insurance—And Not Getting It," *Health Affairs* 21(4), July/August 2002.

Article 8.4

PRICING THE PRICELESS
Inside the Strange World of Cost-Benefit Analysis

BY LIZ HEINZERLING AND FRANK ACKERMAN
March/April 2003

How strictly should we regulate arsenic in drinking water? Or carbon dioxide in the atmosphere? Or pesticides in our food? Or oil drilling in scenic places? The list of environmental harms and potential regulatory remedies often appears to be endless. In evaluating a proposed new initiative, how do we know if it is worth doing or not? Is there an objective way to decide how to proceed? Cost-benefit analysis promises to provide the solution—to add up the benefits of a public policy and compare them to the costs.

The costs of protecting health and the environment through pollution control devices and other approaches are, by their very nature, measured in dollars. The other side of the balance, calculating the benefits of life, health, and nature in dollars and cents, is far more problematic. Since there are no natural prices for a healthy environment, cost-benefit analysis creates artificial ones. Researchers, for example, may ask a cross-section of the affected population how much they would pay to preserve or protect something that can't be bought in a store. The average American household is supposedly willing to pay $257 to prevent the extinction of bald eagles, $208 to protect humpback whales, and $80 to protect gray wolves.

Costs and benefits of a policy, however, frequently fall at different times. When the analysis spans a number of years, future costs and benefits are *discounted,* or treated as equivalent to smaller amounts of money in today's dollars. The case for discounting begins with the observation that money received today is worth a little more than money received in the future. (For example, if the interest rate is 3%, you only need to deposit about $97 today to get $100 next year. Economists would say that, at a *3% discount rate,* $100 next year has a *present value* of $97.) For longer periods of time, or higher discount rates, the effect is magnified. The important issue for environmental policy is whether this logic also applies to outcomes far in the future, and to opportunities—like long life and good health—that are not naturally stated in dollar terms.

Why Cost-Benefit Analysis Doesn't Work

The case for cost-benefit analysis of environmental protection is, at best, wildly optimistic and, at worst, demonstrably wrong. The method simply does not offer the policy-making panacea its adherents promise. In practice, cost-benefit analysis frequently produces false and misleading results. Moreover, there is no quick fix, because these failures are intrinsic to the methodology, appearing whenever it is applied to any complex environmental problem.

It puts dollar figures on values that are not commodities, and have no price.
Artificial prices have been estimated for many benefits of environmental regulation. Preventing retardation due to childhood lead poisoning comes in at about $9,000 per lost IQ point. Saving a life is ostensibly worth $6.3 million. But what can it mean to say that one life is worth $6.3 million? You cannot buy the right to kill someone for $6.3 million, nor for any other price. If analysts calculated the value of life itself by asking people what it is worth to them (the most common method of valuation of other environmental benefits), the answer would be infinite. The standard response is that a value like $6.3 million is not actually a price on an individual's life or death. Rather, it is a way of expressing the value of small risks of death. If people are willing to pay $6.30 to avoid a one in a million increase in the risk of death, then the "value of a statistical life" is $6.3 million.

It ignores the collective choice presented to society by most public health and environmental problems.
Under the cost-benefit approach, valuation of environmental benefits is based on individuals' private decisions as consumers or workers, not on their public values as citizens. However, policies that protect the environment are often public goods, and are not available for purchase in individual portions. In a classic example of this distinction, the philosopher Mark Sagoff found that his students, in their role as citizens, opposed commercial ski development in a nearby wilderness area, but, in their role as consumers, would plan to go skiing there if the development was built. There is no contradiction between these two views: as individual consumers, the students would have no way to express their collective preference for wilderness preservation. Their individual willingness to pay for skiing would send a misleading signal about their views as citizens.

It is often impossible to arrive at a meaningful social valuation by adding up the willingness to pay expressed by individuals. What could it mean to ask how much you personally are willing to pay to clean up a major oil spill? If no one else contributes, the clean-up won't happen regardless of your decision. As the Nobel Prize-winning economist Amartya Sen has pointed out, if your willingness to pay for a large-scale public initiative is independent of what others are paying, then you probably have not understood the nature of the problem.

It systematically downgrades the importance of the future.
One of the great triumphs of environmental law is that it seeks to avert harms to people and to natural resources in the future, and not only within this generation, but in future generations as well. Indeed, one of the primary objectives of the National Environmental Policy Act, which has been called our basic charter of environmental protection, is to nudge the nation into "fulfill[ing] the responsibilities of each generation as trustee of the environment for succeeding generations."

The time periods involved in protecting the environment are often enormous—even many centuries, in such cases as climate change, radioactive waste, etc. With time spans this long, any discounting will make even global catastrophes seem trivial. At a discount rate of 5%, for example, the deaths of a billion people 500 years from now become less serious than the death of one person today. Seen in this way, discounting looks like a fancy justification for foisting our problems off onto the people who come after us.

It ignores considerations of distribution and fairness.
Cost-benefit analysis adds up all the costs of a policy, adds up all the benefits, and compares the totals. Implicit in this innocuous-sounding procedure is the assumption that it doesn't matter who gets the benefits and who pays the costs. Yet isn't there is an important difference between spending state tax revenues, say, to improve the parks in rich communities, and spending the same revenues to clean up pollution in poor communities?

The problem of equity runs even deeper. Benefits are typically measured by willingness to pay for environmental improvement, and the rich are able and willing to pay for more than the poor. Imagine a cost-benefit analysis of locating an undesirable facility, such as a landfill or incinerator. Wealthy communities are willing to pay more for the benefit of not having the facility in their backyards; thus, under the logic of cost-benefit analysis, the net benefits to society will be maximized by putting the facility in a low-income area. In reality, pollution is typically dumped on the poor without waiting for formal analysis. Still, cost-benefit analysis rationalizes and reinforces the problem, allowing environmental burdens to flow downhill along the income slopes of an unequal society.

Conclusion

There is nothing objective about the basic premises of cost-benefit analysis. Treating individuals solely as consumers, rather than as citizens with a sense of moral responsibility, represents a distinct and highly questionable worldview. Likewise, discounting reflects judgments about the nature of environmental risks and citizens' responsibilities toward future generations.

These assumptions beg fundamental questions about ethics and equity, and one cannot decide whether to embrace them without thinking through the whole range of moral issues they raise. Yet once one has thought through these issues, there is no need then to collapse the complex moral inquiry into a series of numbers. Pricing the priceless just translates our inquiry into a different language, one with a painfully impoverished vocabulary.

This article is a condensed version of the report Pricing the Priceless, *published by the Georgetown Environmental Law and Policy Institute at Georgetown University Law Center. The full report is available on-line at www. ase.tufts.edu/gdae. See also Ackerman and Heinzerling's book on these and related issues,* Priceless: Human Health, the Environment, and the Limits of the Market, *The New Press, January 2004.*

Article 8.5

CAR TROUBLE
The automobile as an environmental and health disaster

BY ALEJANDRO REUSS
March/April 2003

(Scene: Los Angeles, the 1940s)

Eddie Valiant: A freeway? What the hell's a freeway?

Judge Doom: Eight lanes of shimmering cement running from here to Pasadena. Smooth, straight, fast. Traffic jams will be a thing of the past.... I see a place where people get off and on the freeway. On and off. Off and on. All day, all night. Soon where Toontown once stood will be a string of gas stations. Inexpensive motels. Restaurants that serve rapidly prepared food. Tire salons. Automobile dealerships. And wonderful, wonderful billboards reaching as far as the eye can see.... My god, it'll be beautiful.

Eddie Valiant: Come on. Nobody's gonna drive this lousy freeway when they can take the Red Car [trolley] for a nickel.

Judge Doom: Oh, they'll drive. They'll have to. You see, I bought the Red Car so I could dismantle it.

—Who Framed Roger Rabbit? (1988)

At the end of *Roger Rabbit*, a speeding train saves the day, destroying the solvent-spraying juggernaut that is set to level the fictitious Toontown for the freeway. In other words, the movie is a fairy tale about how the modern American city did *not* come into existence. In reality, Los Angeles came to represent the awful extreme of U.S. car culture. Auto companies *did* buy up the city's Red Car trolley and dismantle it. The landscape became just the cluttered wasteland of highways, fast-food joints, filling stations, and billboards dreamed by the villainous Judge Doom.

The federal government rolled out an asphalt carpet for the automobile: It built the interstate highways that fueled "white flight" to the new suburban sprawl, and carried the new "middle class" on its summer vacations. Soon, freeways criss-crossed American cities, slicing through low-income neighborhoods and consigning commuters to the twice-daily ordeal of gridlock. Roads and highways (along with the military, for which the interstates were originally intended) were politically acceptable objects of public spending even in the postwar United States. And why not? They represented an enormous subsidy to the private industries at the heart of U.S. capitalism—oil, steel, and cars.

The car effectively privatized a wide swath of the public arena. In place of the city square, it created the four-way intersection. Instead of walking or riding a trolley, the motorists sealed themselves inside their individual steel cocoons. Cars offered convenience—for grocery shopping, trips to the mall, chauffeuring the kids to school and practice, etc.—to those who got them. Their real triumph, however, was to manufacture inconvenience for those who didn't. People who could not afford cars had such unenviable choices as navigating the brave new world of speeding traffic on foot or waiting for the bus. A genuine political commitment to public transportation might have lessened the class and race divide. Most public transportation funding, however, has gone to road and highway construction geared to the motorist, and much of what remains for mass transit has been devoted to commuter trains serving the suburban middle class. Low-income city residents have largely been abandoned to an infrequent and polluting diesel bus.

As it turned out, life inside the car was not all it was cracked up to be either—especially when traffic on the freeway slowed to a crawl. In gridlock, you can practically see the steam coming out of drivers' ears. As odious as much of the time spent in cars might be, however, Americans have learned, or been convinced, to "love the car." It has become a fetish object—a symbol of freedom and individualism, power and sex appeal. The commercials always seem to show a carefree motorist speeding through the countryside or climbing a secluded mountain to gaze on the landscape below. Fortunately, not too many SUV owners actually spend their time tearing up the wilderness. Unfortunately, they spend much of it spewing exhaust into the city air.

The SUV certainly ranks among the more absurd expressions of American over-consumption (General Motors' Yukon XL Denali, to cite an extreme example, is over 18 feet long and weighs about three tons). But it is too easy to condemn this overgrown behemoth and then hop self-satisfied back into a midsize sedan. Most of what is wrong with the SUV—the resources it swallows, the dangers it poses, and the blight it creates—is wrong with the automobile system as a whole. Automobiles pollute the oceans and the air, overheat cities and the earth, devour land and time, produce waste and noise, and cause injury and illness.

Here, in more detail, is an indictment of the car as an environmental and public-health menace:

The Bill of Particulars

Oil Pollution

Transportation accounts for over two-thirds of U.S. oil consumption, according to the Department of Energy. The problem of oil pollution, therefore, lands squarely at the doorstep of a transportation system based on internal combustion. Oil tanker spills are the most visible scourge of the world's oceans. According to the National Research Council study Oil in the Sea, tankers spew 400 million tons of oil into the world's oceans each year. Technologies to prevent or contain oil spills, however, cannot solve the problem of marine oil pollution, since the main cause is not spills, but the consumption of oil. Urban consumption, including runoff from roads and used motor oil just poured down the drain, accounts for more than half of the ocean pollution, over one billion tons of oil annually. That does not count, of course, oil that does not make it to the seas, that stains roadways, contaminates the land, or spoils fresh water supplies.

Air Pollution

Automotive emissions are a major source of ozone and carbon monoxide pollution. "[I]n numerous cities across the country," according to the Environmental Protection Agency (EPA), "the personal automobile is the single greatest polluter." Ozone, a major component of urban smog, is formed by unburned fuel reacting with other compounds in the atmosphere. It causes irritation of the eyes and lungs, aggravates respiratory problems, and can damage lung tissue. Researchers at the Centers for Disease Control in Atlanta took advantage of temporary traffic reduction during the 1996 Olympic Games to observe the effects of automotive emissions on asthma attacks. Their study, published in the *Journal of the American Medical Association*, showed a 28% reduction of peak ozone levels and an 11–44% drop in the number of children requiring acute asthma care (depending on the sample). Carbon monoxide, formed by incomplete burning of fuel, impairs the oxygen-carrying ability of the blood. According to the EPA, "In urban areas, the motor vehicle contribution to carbon monoxide pollution can exceed 90 percent." A 2002 study published in the journal *Circulation* showed a link between automotive exhaust and heart attacks, and Harvard Medical School researchers called exhaust an "insidious contributor to heart disease."

Climate Change

Automotive exhaust also contains carbon dioxide, a "greenhouse gas" and the principal culprit in climate change (or "global warming"). It is produced, in the words of the EPA, by the "perfect combustion" of hydrocarbons. Internal combustion engines generate this greenhouse gas no matter how efficient or well-tuned they may be. In the United States, the country with the world's highest per capita carbon dioxide emissions, transportation accounts for over 30% of total emissions, according to a 1998 report of the United Nations Framework Convention on Climate Change. More than half that amount, reports the EPA, is due to personal transportation. As average fuel efficiency gets worse (it declined by nearly 7% between 1987 and 1997) and U.S. motorists rack up more vehicle miles (they increased by a third over the same period), the automobile contributes more and more to global warming.

Heat Islands

The temperature in a major city on a summer day can be as much as 8°F higher than that of surrounding rural areas, according to the Berkeley National Laboratory's Heat Island Group. The automobile contributes to "heat islands" mainly through increased demand for roads and parking. The asphalt and concrete used for these surfaces are among the most heat-absorbent materials in the urban environment. Paving also contributes to the loss of trees, which provide shade and dissipate heat. In the 1930s, when orchards dotted Los Angeles, summer temperatures peaked at 97°F, according to the Heat Island Group. Since then L.A. has become one of the country's worst heat islands, with summer temperatures reaching over 105°F. This does not just make the city less pleasant in the summertime. Heat islands cause increased energy use for cooling and increased ozone formation. Researchers estimate a 2% increase in Los Angeles's total power use and a 3% increase in smog for every 1°F increase in the city's daily high temperature.

Land Use

Cars occupy a huge amount of space. Paved roads occupy over 13,000 square miles of land area across the United States—nearly 750 square meters per U.S. motor vehicle—and parking occupies another 3,000 square miles, according to a report by Todd Litman of the Victoria Transport Policy Institute. In urban areas, roads and parking take up 20-30% of the total surface area; in commercial districts, 50-60%. When moving, vehicles require a "buffer zone" that varies with size and speed. Litman calculates, for example, that a pedestrian walking at 3 miles per hour (m.p.h.) requires 20 square feet of space. A cyclist riding at 10 m.p.h. needs 50 square feet. At full occupancy, a bus traveling at 30 m.p.h. requires 75 square feet per passenger. Meanwhile, a car traveling at 30 m.p.h. demands 1,500 square feet. In short, much of the road space is not required by on-road transportation as such, but by the private car. The same goes for parking space. A parked car requires twenty times the space as a parked bicycle, and eighty times the space as a person.

Materials

In the words of the EPA, "Vehicles require a lot of energy and materials to make, consume a lot of energy when used, and present unique waste disposal challenges at end-of-life." The auto industry uses nearly two thirds of the rubber, over one third of the iron, and over one fourth of the aluminum produced in the United States. Over ten million cars, moreover, are junked in the United States each year. About three fourths of the average car's weight—including the vast majority of the steel—is recycled. The rest crowds garbage dumps and contributes to toxic pollution. About 270 million tires (about 3.4 million tons) are scrapped in the United States annually. While nearly half are burned for energy, about 500 million tires now swell U.S. junk piles, where they "act as breeding grounds for rats and mosquitoes," according to the EPA, and periodically erupt into toxic tire fires. The U.S. cars scrapped each year also contain upwards of 8 tons of mercury. Meanwhile, polyvinyl chloride from scrap cars produces dioxins and other toxic pollutants. The study *End-of-Life Vehicles: A Threat to the Environment* concludes that the cars scrapped in Europe each year (75-85% as many as in the United States) produce 2 million tons of hazardous waste, about one tenth of the EU's total hazardous waste production.

Time

Car travel swallows more and more time as commutes grow longer and congestion more severe. The 2002 Urban Mobility Report from the Texas Transportation Institute calculated, on the basis of data from 75 U.S. cities, that the average motorist wasted 62 hours per year sitting in rush-hour traffic. (That's just the difference between rush-hour travel time and the normal time required to make the same trip.) In Los Angeles, the figure reached 136 hours. All told, over one third of the average rush-hour trip in the very large cities surveyed was wasted on traffic congestion. How is that an environmental or health issue? According to report Transport, Environment, and Health, issued by the World Health Organization (WHO) Regional Office for Europe, studies have connected traffic congestion with increased stress and blood pressure, as well as "aggressive behavior and increased likelihood of involvement in a crash."

Activity

Lack of exercise contributes to coronary heart disease, hypertension, some cancers, osteoporosis, poor coordination and stamina, and low self-esteem. The WHO Regional Office for Europe argues that "walking and cycling as part of daily activities should become a major pillar" of public-health strategy, and that daily travel offers the most promise to "integrate physical activities into daily schedules." Car dependence, instead, extends the sedentary lifestyle even to mobility. Half of all car trips in Europe, according to the WHO Regional Office, are under 5 km, distances most people can cover by bicycle in less than 20 minutes and on foot in well under one hour. High levels of automotive traffic, moreover, may deter people from walking or cycling—due to the unpleasantness of auto exhaust, the fear of crossing fast-moving traffic, or the dangers of riding a bicycle surrounded by cars. Some people may substitute car trips, but those without access to cars (especially children and elderly people) may simply venture outside less frequently, contributing to social isolation (another health risk factor).

Noise

Noise pollution is no mere nuisance. Researchers are beginning to document the damage that noise, even at relatively low levels, can do to human health. A 2001 study by Gary Evans of Cornell University, for example, has shown that children chronically exposed to low-level traffic noise suffer elevated blood pressure, increased changes in heart rate when stressed, and higher overall levels of stress-related hormones. In a separate study, on children exposed to low-level noise from aircraft flight patterns, Evans also documented negative effects of noise pollution on children's attention spans and learning abilities.

Collisions

Finally, the car crash ranks among the leading causes of death and injury in the United States. The statistics for 2001, compiled by the National Highway Traffic Safety Administration, were typical: over 42,000 people killed, over 360,000 people suffering incapacitating injuries, and over 3 million people injured overall. Over the last 25 years, the number of people killed per vehicle mile has declined by over 50%—undoubtedly thanks to such factors as increased availability and use of safety belts and airbags, improved vehicle design, and improved trauma care. The absolute number of deaths, however, has decreased by less than 20% (using the benchmark of 51,000 in 1980), as total vehicle miles traveled have more than doubled. Overall, the U.S. death toll from car crashes over the last quarter century is over one million people. During just the last decade, the total number of people injured in U.S. car crashes has topped 32 million.

The Path of Redemption

The environmental and public-health problems associated with the automobile have often inspired well-meaning exhortations to car-pool, drive less, or drive smaller cars, as well as dreams of "cars of the future" requiring less material or burning cleaner fuels. On the whole, however, the problems are neither individual nor technological—but social. So no individual nor technological solution will do. A comprehensive solution requires turning the "machine space" built for and dominated by the car back into human space: In the place of sprawl, compact development with work, school, stores, and recreation nearby and reachable without a car. In the place of the private car, reliable, clean, and accessible public transportation (along with small, efficient, nonpolluting vehicles for those who need them). In the place of internal combustion, the cyclist and the pedestrian—no longer marginalized and endangered, but respected as integral parts of a new, sustainable transportation system.

Cuba and China are the world's leading countries in bicycle use. Even in the rich capitalist counties, however, there are islands of sanity where public and human-powered transportation exist at least on a par with the automobile. Groningen, the Netherlands' sixth-largest city, suggests the possibilities: low speed limits reduce the dangers of urban traffic to cyclists and pedestrians; cars are not permitted on some streets, while bicycles can travel on any public way (including bike-only lanes and paths); parking for cars is restricted to garages, while secure bicycle parking facilities are plentiful (especially near train stations); cars are excluded from all squares in the city center, while careful city planning ensures that places of work and commerce are accessible to public transportation, cyclists, and pedestrians. As a result, Groningen residents now make nearly half of all in-city trips by bicycle; less than one third by car. The Dutch city of Delft, and the German cities of Freiburg and Muenster, are similar harbingers of a possible sustainable future.

The sustainable-transportation movement has shown encouraging worldwide growth in recent years. Transportation activists in the United Kingdom have carried out direct-action "street takings," closing off roads and highways and prompting spontaneous street fairs, to show what a car-free future might look like. The "Critical Mass" movement, starting in San Francisco in 1992 but quickly spreading to other cities, has brought together cyclists for rolling protest "marches" against auto hegemony. Activists have promoted worldwide car-free days, in which residents of hundreds of cities have participated. Bogotá, Colombia, a city of 7 million, held its first annual car-free day in 2000, complete with fines for any motorists caught within the city limits. Its popularity among city residents has bolstered long-term plans to exclude cars from the city, on a permanent basis, during peak morning and afternoon travel hours. In 2002, Seattle became the first U.S. city to officially host a car-free day.

With greater struggle, a more thorough-going transportation reform might be possible even within the confines of capitalism. This would require, however, a colossal economic shift—away the production of private automobiles, gasoline, and roads, and toward the reconstruction of public transportation and public space in general. It's highly unlikely, considering the ruin of former auto production centers like Detroit and Flint, that the "free market" could manage such a shift without imposing a wrenching dislocation on individuals and communities dependent on auto production. Moreover, it's virtually unimaginable, considering the trends toward privatization and commodification rampant in contemporary capitalism, that it would carry out such a transformation spontaneously.

Article 8.6

CLIMATE ECONOMICS IN FOUR EASY PIECES

Conventional cost-benefit models cannot inform our decisions about how to address the threat of climate change.

FRANK ACKERMAN
November/December 2008

Once upon a time, debates about climate policy were primarily about the science. An inordinate amount of attention was focused on the handful of "climate skeptics" who challenged the scientific understanding of climate change. The influence of the skeptics, however, is rapidly fading; few people were swayed by their arguments, and doubt about the major results of climate science is no longer important in shaping public policy.

As the climate *science* debate is reaching closure, the climate *economics* debate is heating up. The controversial issue now is the fear that overly ambitious climate initiatives could hurt the economy. Mainstream economists emphasizing that fear have, in effect, replaced the climate skeptics as the intellectual enablers of inaction.

For example, William Nordhaus, the U.S. economist best known for his work on climate change, pays lip service to scientists' calls for decisive action. He finds, however, that the "optimal" policy is a very small carbon tax that would reduce greenhouse gas emissions only 25% below "business-as-usual" levels by 2050—that would, in other words, allow emissions to rise well above current levels by mid-century. Richard Tol, a European economist who has written widely on climate change, favors an even smaller carbon tax of just $2 per ton of carbon dioxide. That would amount to all of $0.02 per gallon of gasoline, a microscopic "incentive" for change that consumers would never notice.

There are other voices in the climate economics debate; in particular, the British government's Stern Review offers a different perspective. Economist Nicholas Stern's analysis is much less wrong than the traditional Nordhaus-Tol approach, but even Stern has not challenged the conventional view enough.

What will it take to build a better economics of climate change, one that is consistent with the urgency expressed by the latest climate science? The issues that matter are big, non-technical principles, capable of being expressed in bumper-sticker format. Here are the four bumper stickers for a better climate economics:

- Our grandchildren's lives are important.

- We need to buy insurance for the planet.

- Climate damages are too valuable to have prices.

- Some costs are better than others.

1. Our grandchildren's lives are important.

The most widely debated challenge of climate economics is the valuation of the very long run. For ordinary loans and investments, both the costs today and the resulting future benefits typically occur within a single lifetime. In such cases, it makes sense to think in terms of the same person experiencing and comparing the costs and the benefits.

In the case of climate change, the time spans involved are well beyond those encountered in most areas of economics. The most important consequences of today's choices will be felt by generations to come, long after all of us making those choices have passed away. As a result, the costs of reducing emissions today and the benefits in the far future will not be experienced by the same people. The economics of climate change is centrally concerned with our relationship to our descendants whom we will never meet. As a bridge to that unknowable future, consider our grandchildren—the last generation most of us will ever know.

Suppose that you want your grandchildren to receive $100 (in today's dollars, corrected for inflation), 60 years from now. How much would you have to put in a bank account today, to ensure that the $100 will be there 60 years from now? The answer is $55 at 1% interest, or just over $5 at 5%.

In parallel fashion, economists routinely deal with future costs and benefits by "discounting" them, or converting them to "present values"—a process that is simply compound interest in reverse. In the standard jargon, the *present value* of $100, to be received 60 years from now, is $55 at a 1% *discount rate*, or about $5 at a 5% discount rate. As this example shows, a higher discount rate implies a smaller present value.

The central problem of climate economics, in a cost-benefit framework, is deciding how much to spend today on preventing future harms. What should we spend to prevent $100 of climate damages 60 years from now? The standard answer is, no more than the present value of that future loss: $55 at a discount rate of 1%, or $5 at 5%. The higher the discount rate, the less it is "worth" spending today on protecting our grandchildren.

The effect of a change in the discount rate becomes much more pronounced as the time period lengthens. Damages of $1 million occurring 200 years from now have a present value of only about $60 at a 5% discount rate, versus more than $130,000 at a 1% discount rate. The choice of the discount rate is all-important to our stance toward the far future: should we spend as much as $130,000, or as little as $60, to avoid one million dollars of climate damages in the early twenty-third century?

For financial transactions within a single lifetime, it makes sense to use market interest rates as the discount rate. Climate change, however, involves public policy decisions with impacts spanning centuries; there is no market in which public resources are traded from one century to the next. The choice of an intergenerational discount rate is a matter of ethics and policy, not a market-determined result.

Economists commonly identify two separate aspects of long-term discounting, each contributing to the discount rate.

One component of the discount rate is based on the assumption of an upward trend in income and wealth. If future generations will be richer than we are, they will need less help from us, and they will get less benefit from an additional dollar of income than we do. So we can discount benefits that will flow to our wealthier descendants, at a rate based on the expected growth of per capita incomes. Among economists, the income-related motive for discounting may be the least controversial part of the picture.

Setting aside changes in per capita income from one generation to the next, there may still be a reason to discount a sum many years in the future. This component of the discount rate, known as "pure time preference," is the subject of longstanding ethical, philosophical, and economic debate. On the one hand, there are reasons to think that pure time preference is greater than zero: both psychological experiments and common sense suggest that people are impatient, and prefer money now to money later. On the other hand, a pure time preference of zero expresses the equal worth of people of all generations, and the equal importance of reducing climate impacts and other burdens on them (assuming that all generations have equal incomes).

The Stern Review provides an excellent discussion of the debate, explaining Stern's assumption of pure time preference close to zero and an overall discount rate of 1.4%. This discount rate alone is sufficient to explain Stern's support for a substantial program of climate protection: at the higher discount rates used in more traditional analyses, the Stern program would look "inefficient," since the costs would outweigh the present value of the benefits.

2. We need to buy insurance for the planet.

Does climate science predict that things are certain to get worse? Or does it tell us that we are uncertain about what will happen next? Unfortunately, the answer seems to be yes to both questions. For example, the most likely level of sea level rise in this century, according to the latest Intergovernmental Panel on Climate Change reports, is no more than one meter or so—a real threat to low-lying coastal areas and islands that will face increasing storm damages, but survivable, with some adaptation efforts, for most of the world. On the other hand, there is a worst-case risk of an abrupt loss of the Greenland ice sheet, or perhaps of a large portion of the West Antarctic ice sheet. Either one could cause an eventual seven-meter rise in sea level—a catastrophic impact on coastal communities, economic activity, and infrastructure everywhere, and well beyond the range of plausible adaptation efforts in most places.

The evaluation of climate damages thus depends on whether we focus on the most likely outcomes or the credible worst-case risks; the latter, of course, are much larger.

Cost-benefit analysis conventionally rests on average or expected outcomes. But this is not the only way that people make decisions. When faced with uncertain, potentially large risks, people do not normally act on the basis of average outcomes; instead, they typically focus on protection against worst-case scenarios. When you go to the airport, do you leave just enough time for the average traffic delay (so that you would catch your plane, on average, half of the time)? Or do you allow time for some estimate of worst-case traffic jams? Once you get there, of course, you will experience additional delays due to security, which is all about worst cases: your *average* fellow passenger is not a threat to anyone's safety.

The very existence of the insurance industry is evidence of the desire to avoid or control worst-case scenarios. It is impossible for an insurance company to pay out in claims as much as its customers pay in premiums; if it did, there would be no money left to pay the costs of running the company, or the profits received by its owners. People who buy insurance are therefore guaranteed to get back less than they, on average, have paid; they (we) are paying for the security that insurance provides in case the worst should happen. This way of thinking does not apply to every decision: in casino games, people make bets based on averages and probabilities, and no one has any insurance against losing the next round. But life is not a casino, and public policy should not be a gamble.

Should climate policy be based on the most likely outcomes, or on the worst-case risks? Should we be investing in climate protection as if we expect sea level rise of one meter, or as if we are buying insurance to be sure of preventing a seven-meters rise?

In fact, the worst-case climate risks are even more unknown than the individual risks of fire and death that motivate insurance purchases. You do not know whether or not you will have a fire next year or die before the year is over, but you have very good information about the likelihood of these tragic events. So does the insurance industry, which is why they are willing to insure you. In contrast, there is no body of statistical information about the probability of Greenland-sized ice sheets collapsing at various temperatures; it's not an experiment that anyone can perform over and over again.

A recent analysis by Martin Weitzman argues that the probabilities of the worst outcomes are inescapably unknowable—and this deep uncertainty is more important than anything we do know in motivating concern about climate change. There is a technical sense in which the expected value of future climate damages can be infinite because we know so little about the probability of the worst, most damaging possibilities. The practical implication of infinite expected damages is that the most likely outcome is irrelevant; what matters is buying insurance for the planet, i.e., doing our best to understand and prevent the worst-case risks.

3. Climate damages are too valuable to have prices.

To decide whether climate protection is worthwhile, in cost-benefit terms, we would need to know the monetary value of everything important that is being protected. Even if we could price everything affected by climate change, the prices would conceal a critical form of international inequity. The emissions that cause climate change have come predominantly from rich countries, while the damages will be felt first and worst in some of the world's poorest, tropical countries (although no one will be immune from harm for long). There are, however, no meaningful prices for many of the benefits of health and environmental protection. What is the dollar value of a human life saved? How much is it worth to save an endangered species from extinction, or to preserve a unique location or ecosystem? Economists have made up price tags for such priceless values, but the results do not always pass the laugh test.

Is a human life worth $6.1 million, as estimated by the Clinton administration, based on small differences in the wages paid for more and less risky jobs? Or is it worth $3.7 million, as the (second) Bush administration concluded on the basis of questionnaires about people's willingness to pay for reducing small, hypothetical risks? Are lives of people in rich countries worth much more than those in poor countries, as some economists infamously argued in the IPCC's 1995 report? Can the value of an endangered species be determined by survey research on how much people would pay to protect it? If, as one study found, the U.S. population as a whole would pay $18 billion to protect the existence of humpback whales, would it be acceptable for someone to pay $36 billion for the right to hunt and kill the entire species?

The only sensible response to such nonsensical questions is that there are many crucially important values that do not have meaningful prices. This is not a new idea: as the eighteenth-century philosopher Immanuel Kant put it, some things have a price, or relative worth, while other things have a dignity, or inner worth. No price tag does justice to the dignity of human life or the natural world.

Since some of the most important benefits of climate protection are priceless, any monetary value for total benefits will necessarily be incomplete. The corollary is that preventive action may be justified even in the absence of a complete monetary measure of the benefits of doing so.

4. Some costs are better than others.

The language of cost-benefit analysis embodies a clear normative slant: benefits are good, costs are bad. The goal is always to have larger benefits and smaller costs. In some respects, measurement and monetary valuation are easier for costs than for benefits: implementing pollution control measures typically involves changes in such areas as manufacturing, construction, and fuel use, all of which have well-defined prices. Yet conventional economic theory distorts the interpretation of costs in ways that exaggerate the burdens of environmental protection and hide the positive features of some of the "costs."

Average Risks or Worst-Case Scenarios?

You don't have to look far to find situations in which the sensible policy is to address worst-case outcomes rather than average outcomes. The annual number of residential fires in the United States is about 0.4% of the number of housing units. This means that a fire occurs, on average, about once every 250 years in each home—not even close to once per lifetime. By far the most likely number of fires a homeowner will experience next year, or even in a lifetime, is zero. Why don't these statistics inspire you to cancel your fire insurance? Unless you are extremely wealthy, the loss of your home in a fire would be a devastating financial blow; despite the low probability, you cannot afford to take any chances on it.

What are the chances of the ultimate loss? The probability that you will die next year is under 0.1% if you are in your twenties, under 0.2% in your thirties, under 0.4% in your forties. It is not until age 61 that you have as much as a 1% chance of death within the coming year. Yet most U.S. families with dependent children buy life insurance. Without it, the risk to children of losing their parents' income would be too great—even though the parents are, on average, extraordinarily likely to survive.

For instance, empirical studies of energy use and carbon emissions repeatedly find significant opportunities for emissions reduction at zero or negative net cost—the so-called "no regrets" options.

According to a longstanding tradition in economic theory, however, cost-free energy savings are impossible. The textbook theory of competitive markets assumes that every resource is productively employed in its most valuable use—in other words, that every no-regrets option must already have been taken. As the saying goes, there are no free lunches; there cannot be any $20 bills on the sidewalk because someone would have picked them up already. Any new emissions reduction measures, then, must have positive costs. This leads to greater estimates of climate policy costs than the bottom-up studies that reveal extensive opportunities for costless savings.

In the medium term, we will need to move beyond the no-regrets options; how much will it cost to finish the job of climate protection? Again, there are rival interpretations of the costs based on rival assumptions about the economy. The same economic theory that proclaimed the absence of $20 bills on the sidewalk is responsible for the idea that all costs are bad. Since the free market lets everyone spend their money in whatever way they choose, any new cost must represent a loss: it leaves people with less to spend on whatever purchases they had previously selected to maximize their satisfaction in life. Climate damages are one source of loss, and spending on climate protection is another; both reduce the resources available for the desirable things in life.

But are the two kinds of costs really comparable? Is it really a matter of indifference whether we spend $1 billion on bigger and better levees or lose $1 billion to storm damages? In the real-world economy, money spent on building levees creates jobs and incomes. The construction workers buy groceries, clothing, and so on, indirectly creating other jobs. With more people working, tax revenues increase while unemployment compensation payments decrease.

None of this happens if the levees are not built and the storm damages are allowed to occur. The costs of prevention are good costs, with numerous indirect benefits; the costs of climate damages are bad costs, representing pure physical destruction. One worthwhile goal is to keep total costs as low as possible; another is to have as much as possible of good costs rather than bad costs. Think of it as the cholesterol theory of climate costs.

In the long run, the deep reductions in carbon emissions needed for climate stabilization will require new technologies that have not yet been invented, or at best exist only in small, expensive prototypes. How much will it cost to invent, develop, and implement the low-carbon technologies of the future?

Lacking a rigorous theory of innovation, economists modeling climate change have often assumed that new technologies simply appear, making the economy inexorably more efficient over time. A more realistic view observes that the costs of producing a new product typically decline as industry gains more experience with it, in a pattern called "learning by doing" or the "learning curve" effect. Public investment is often necessary to support the innovation process in its early, expensive stages. Wind power is now relatively cheap and competitive, in suitable locations; this is a direct result of decades of public investment in the United States and Europe, starting when wind turbines were still quite expensive. The costs of climate policy, in the long run, will include doing the same for other promising new technologies, investing public resources in jump-starting a set of slightly different industries than we might have chosen in the absence of climate change. If this is a cost, many communities would be better off with more of it.

A widely publicized, conventional economic analysis recommends inaction on climate change, claiming that the costs currently outweigh the benefits for anything more than the smallest steps toward reducing carbon emissions. Put our "four easy pieces" together, and we have the outline of an economics that complements the science of climate change and endorses active, large-scale climate protection.

How realistic is it to expect that the world will shake off its inertia and act boldly and rapidly enough to make a difference? This may be the last generation that will have a real chance at protecting the earth's climate. Projections from the latest IPCC reports, the Stern Review, and other sources suggest that it is still possible to save the planet—if we start at once.

Sources: Frank Ackerman, *Can We Afford the Future? Economics for a Warming World*, Zed Books, 2008; Frank Ackerman, *Poisoned for Pennies: The Economics of Toxics and Precaution*, Island Press, 2008; Frank Ackerman and Lisa Heinzerling, *Priceless: On Knowing the Price of Everything and the Value of Nothing*, The New Press, 2004; J. Creyts, A. Derkach, S. Nyquist, K. Ostrowski and J. Stephenson, *Reducing U.S. Greenhouse Gas Emissions: How Much at What Cost?*, McKinsey & Co., 2007; P.-A. Enkvist, T. Naucler and J. Rosander, "A Cost Curve for Greenhouse Gas Reduction," *The McKinsey Quarterly*, 2007; Immanuel Kant, *Groundwork for the Metaphysics of Morals*, translated by Thomas K. Abbot, with revisions by Lara Denis, Broadview Press, 2005 [1785]; B. Lomborg, *Cool It: The Skeptical Environmentalist's Guide to Global Warming*, Alfred A. Knopf, 2007; W.D. Nordhaus, *A Question of Balance: Economic Modeling of Global Warming*, Yale University Press, 2008; F.P. Ramsey, "A mathematical theory of saving," *The Economic Journal* 138(152): 543-59, 1928; Nicholas Stern *et al.*, *The Stern Review: The Economics of Climate Change*, HM Treasury, 2006; U.S. Census Bureau, "Statistical Abstract of the United States." 127th edition. 2008; M.L. Weitzman, "On Modeling and Interpreting the Economics of Catastrophic Climate Change," December 5, 2007 version, www.economics.harvard.edu/faculty/weitzman/files/modeling.pdf.

Article 8.7

TAX HAVENS AND THE FINANCIAL CRISIS

From offshore havens to financial centers, banking secrecy faces scrutiny.

BY RACHEL KEELER
May/June 2009

When an entire global financial system collapses, it is reasonable to expect some bickering over the ultimate fixing of things. Rumors of dissention and talk of stimulus-paved roads to hell made everyone squeamish going into the April summit of the G20 group of large and industrialized nations in London. French President Nicolas Sarkozy even threatened to walk out on the whole thing if he didn't get his way.

The French were perhaps right to be nervous: they were taking a somewhat socialist stand, declaring that unregulated shadow banking and offshore tax havens were at the heart of the financial crisis and had to be either controlled or eradicated. They were doing it in a city at the center of the shadow system, and at a summit chaired by British Prime Minister Gordon Brown, a man recently described by the *Financial Times* as "one of the principal cheerleaders for the competitive international deregulation of international financial markets."

But Gordon Brown had already announced his intention to lead the global crackdown on tax havens as a first step toward global financial recovery. German Chancellor Angela Merkel had long backed France in calling for regulation of hedge funds, the poster boys of shadow banking charged with fostering the crisis. And, to Sarkozy's delight, everyone kept their promises at the G20.

"Major failures in the financial sector and in financial regulation and supervision were fundamental causes of the crisis," read the summit's reassuringly clear communiqué. World leaders agreed to regulate all systemically important financial institutions, including hedge funds and those located in tax havens, under threat of sanctions for noncompliance. "The era of banking secrecy is over," they concluded, as close to united as anyone could have dreamed.

But unity that looks good on paper is always more difficult to achieve in reality. The lingering questions post-summit are the same ones Sarkozy may have pondered on his way to London: will leaders from countries made rich from offshore banking follow through to shut it down? What is at stake, and what will the globally coordinated regulation everyone agrees is necessary actually look like? Not surprisingly, there are no easy answers.

Nature of the Beast

Over the years, trillions of dollars in both corporate profits and personal wealth have migrated "offshore" in search of rock bottom tax rates and the comfort of no questions asked. Tax havens and other financial centers promoting low tax rates, light regulation, and financial secrecy include a long list of tropical nations like the Cayman Islands as well as whole mainland economies from Switzerland to Singapore.

Tax Justice Network, an international non-profit advocating tax haven reform, estimates one-third of global assets are held offshore. The offshore world harbors $11.5 trillion in individual wealth alone, representing $250 billion in lost annual tax revenue. Treasury figures show tax havens sucking $100 billion a year out of U.S. coffers. And these numbers have all been growing steadily over the past decade. A *Tax Notes* study found that between 1999 and 2002, the amount of profits U.S. companies reported in tax havens grew from $88 billion to $149 billion.

With little patience left for fat-cat tax scams, the public is finally cheering for reform. Tax havens, it seems, have become the perfect embodiment of suddenly unfashionable capitalist greed. Unemployed workers and unhappy investors grow hot with anger as they imagine exotic hideouts where businessmen go to sip poolside martinis and laugh off their national tax burden.

Reformers have tried and failed in the past to shut down these locales. But analysts say 2008, the year the global financial system finally collapsed under its own liberalized weight, made all the difference. Not only are governments now desperate for tax revenue to help fund bailouts, but a recognition of the role offshore financial centers played in the system's implosion is dawning.

Along with the G20 fanfare, economists and policymakers including Treasury Secretary Timothy Geithner have pointed to the shadow banking system as a root cause of the global crisis. They're talking about the raft of highly-leveraged, virtually unregulated investment vehicles developed over the last 20 years: hedge funds, private equity, conduits, structured investment vehicles (SIVs), collateralized debt obligations (CDOs), and other wildly arcane investment banker toys.

While most of these innovations were born of Wall Street imaginations, few found their home in New York. Seventy-five percent of the world's hedge funds are based in four Caribbean tax havens: the Cayman Islands, Bermuda, the British Virgin Islands, and the Bahamas. The two subprime mortgage-backed Bear Stearns funds that collapsed in 2007, precipitating the credit crisis, were incorporated in the Caymans. Jersey and Guernsey, offshore financial centers in the Channel Islands, specialize in private equity. Many SIVs were created offshore, far from regulatory eyes.

We now know that hedge funds made their record profits from offshore bases by taking long-term gambles with short-term loans. The risky funds were often backed by onshore banks but kept off those institutions' books as they were repackaged and sold around the world. Regulators never took much notice: one, because lobbyists told them not to; two, because the funds were so complex that George Soros barely understood them; and three, because many of the deals were happening offshore.

Beneath regulatory radar, shadow bankers were able to scrap capital cushions, conceal illiquidity, and muddle debt accountability while depending on constant refinancing to survive. When the bubble burst and investors made a run for their money, panicked fund managers found it impossible to honor their debts, or even figure out how to price them as the markets crumbled.

William Cohan writes in his new book on the Bear Stearns collapse (*House of Cards: A Tale of Hubris and Wretched Excess on Wall Street*) that it took the brokerage three weeks working day and night to value illiquid securities when two of its Cayman-based hedge funds fell apart in 2007. In the end, the firm realized it was off by $1 billion from its original guesstimate, on just $1.5 billion in funds.

Mortgage-backed securities that once flourished in offshore tax havens are now the toxic assets that U.S. taxpayers are being asked to salvage through the trillion-dollar TARP and TALF programs.

Last Laughs

This convoluted network of offshore escapades is what world leaders have vowed to bring under global regulatory watch in order to restore worldwide financial stability. To their credit, the crackdown on banking secrecy has already begun in a big way.

In February, secret Swiss bank accounts were blown open to permit an unprecedented Internal Revenue Service probe. Europe's UBS bank has admitted to helping wealthy Americans evade what prosecutors believe to be $300 million a year in taxes.

Switzerland, the world's biggest tax haven where at least $2 trillion in offshore money is stashed, has long refused to recognize tax evasion as a crime. Every nation has the sovereign right to set its own tax code, which is why regulators have had such a hard time challenging offshore banking in the past. The dirty secret of tax havens, as President Obama once noted, is that they're mostly legal.

Under U.S. law, tax avoidance (legal) only becomes tax evasion (illegal) in the absence of other, more credible perks. In other words, a company is free to establish foreign subsidiaries in search of financial expertise, global reach, convenience, etc., just so long as tax dodging does not appear to be the sole reason for relocation.

The IRS will tax individual American income wherever it's found, but finding it is often the key. To access account information in Switzerland, authorities had to have proof not merely of tax evasion but of fraud, which is what much white-knuckled investigation finally produced on UBS. In the wake of this success, and under threat of landing on the OECD's new list of "uncooperative" tax havens, all of Europe's secrecy jurisdictions—Liechtenstein, Andorra, Austria, Luxembourg, and Switzerland—have signed information-sharing agreements.

Following the blood trail, congressional investigators descended on the Cayman Islands in March to tour the infamous Ugland House: one building supposedly home to 12,748 U.S. companies. The trip was an attempt to verify some of the implicit accusations made by a Government Accountability Office report in January which found that 83 of the United States' top 100 companies operate subsidiaries in tax havens.

Many of those, including Citigroup (which holds 90 subsidiaries in the Cayman Islands alone), Bank of America, and AIG, have received billions in taxpayer-funded bailouts. But the report failed to establish whether the subsidiaries were set up for the sole purpose of tax evasion.

Offshore Arguments

Politicians are already patting themselves on the back for their success in tackling tax crime. Everyone is making a big deal of the new tax information-exchange standard that all but three nations (Costa Rica, Malaysia, and the Philippines—the OECD's freshly minted blacklist) have agreed to implement in the wake of the G20 meeting. What leaders aren't saying is that before it became a G20 talking point, tax information exchange was actually tax haven *fans'* favored reform measure.

The first thing most offshore officials claim when confronted with criticism is that their countries are not, indeed, tax havens. Since the OECD launched a tax policy campaign in 1996, many of the offshore centers have been working to clean up their acts. A hoard of information-exchange agreements with onshore economies were signed even before Switzerland took the plunge. Geoff Cook, head of Jersey Finance, says Jersey's agreements with the United States, Germany, Sweden, and others have long outpaced what banks in Switzerland and Singapore traditionally maintained. "Our only fear in this is that people wouldn't look into the subject deep enough to draw those distinctions," Cook said.

But analysts say the agreements lack teeth. To request information from offshore, authorities must already have some evidence of misconduct. And the information-exchange standard still only covers illegal tax evasion, not legal tax avoidance. More importantly, what is already evident is that these agreements don't change much about the way offshore financial centers function. Offshore centers that agree to open up their books still have the luxury of setting their own regulatory standards and will continue to attract business based on their shadow banking credentials.

The G20 decided that shadow banking must be subjected to the same regulation as onshore commercial activity, which will also see more diligent oversight. Financial activity everywhere will be required to maintain better capital buffers, they said, monitored by a new Financial Stability Board; and excessive risk-taking will be rebuked. But the push for harmonized regulation across all financial centers revokes a degree of local liberty. Big ideas about state sovereignty and economic growth are at stake, which is probably what made Sarkozy so nervous about taking his regulatory demands global.

"People come here for expertise and knowledge," argues head of Guernsey Finance Peter Niven, and he may have a point. Many in finance think it's wrong to put all the blame on private funds and offshore centers for a crisis of such complex origins. Havens say stripping away their financial freedoms is hypocritical and shortsighted. "It's really not about the Cayman Islands, it's about the U.S. tax gap—and we're the collateral damage," said one frustrated Cayman Island official, adding: "Everybody needs liquidity and everyone needs money. That's what we do."

Predictably, reform critics warn that responding to the global crisis with "too much" regulation will stifle economic growth, something they know world leaders are quite conscious of. "International Financial Centres such as Jersey play an important role as conduits in the flow of international capital around the world by providing liquidity in neighbouring (often onshore) financial centres, the very lubrication which markets now need," wrote Cook in a recent statement.

Overall, attempting to move beyond paltry information exchange to implementing real regulation of shadow banking across national jurisdictions promises to be extremely difficult.

Real Reform

Part of the solution starts at home. Offshore enthusiasts might be the first to point out that the Securities and Exchange Commission never had the remit to regulate *onshore* hedge funds because Congress didn't give it to them. Wall Street deregulation is often cited in Europe as the base rot in the system.

But demanding more regulation onshore won't do any good if you can't regulate in the same way offshore. A serious aspect of the tax haven problem is a kind of global regulatory arbitrage: widespread onshore deregulation over the last 20 years came alongside an affinity for doing business offshore where even less regulation was possible, which in turn encouraged tax haven-style policies in countries like Britain, the United States, Singapore, and Ireland, all fighting to draw finance back into their economies.

President Obama has long been a champion of both domestic and offshore financial reform, and a critic of the deregulation popular during the Bush years. But for global action to happen, Obama needs Europe's help (not to mention cooperation from Asia and the Middle East) and no one knows how deep Gordon Brown's commitment runs. It is only very recently that Brown transformed himself from deregulation cheerleader as chancellor of the exchequer under Tony Blair to global regulatory savior as Britain's new prime minister.

In an interview late last year, Tax Justice Network's John Christensen predicted Britain could become a barrier to reform. "Britain, I think, will become increasingly isolated, particularly in Europe where the City of London is regarded as a tax haven," he said. Even if Gordon Brown is on board, Britain's finance sector hates to see itself sink. Moreover, some say the UK's lax financial regulatory system has saved the wider economy from decay. When British manufacturing declined, the City of London became the nation's new breadwinner. It grew into the powerhouse it is today largely by luring business away from other centers with the promise of adventurous profit-making and mild public oversight.

The City now funnels much of its business through British overseas territories that make up a big faction in the world's offshore banking club. Many offshore officials have accused Britain of making a show of tax haven reform to deflect attention from its own dirty dealings onshore.

Other obstacles to reform could come from Belgium and Luxembourg, which each hold important votes at the Basel Committee on Banking Supervision (a leading international regulatory voice) and the EU. Neither country has shown much enthusiasm for Europe's reform agenda. And no one will soon forget that China nearly neutered the G20 communiqué when it refused to "endorse" an OECD tax haven blacklist that would allow Europe to chastise financial activities in Hong Kong and Macau.

Still, the regulatory tide is strong and rising; even global financial heavyweights may find it unwise or simply impossible to swim against it. For perhaps the first time since the end of World War II, the world appears open to the kind of global cooperation necessary to facilitate global integration in a socially responsible way.

But the tiny nations that have built empires around unfettered financial services will surely continue to fight for their place in the sun. Some may go the way of Darwinian selection. Declining tourism is already crippling economies across the Caribbean. But many more are optimistic about their ability to hang on. Guernsey is pursuing Chinese markets. Jersey claims business in private equity remains strong. Bermuda still has insurance and hopes to dabble in gambling. Many offshore say they welcome the coming reforms.

"We look forward to those challenges," said Michael Dunkley, leader of the United Bermuda Party, noting that Bermuda, a tiny island with a population of just 66,000 people, is not encumbered by big bureaucracy when it comes to getting things done. Whatever new regulations come up, he said: "Bermuda would be at the cutting edge of making sure it worked."

Accusations of capitalist evil aside, one can't help but admire their spirit.

Sources: Willem Buiter, "Making monetary policy in the UK has become simpler, in no small part thanks to Gordon Brown," *Financial Times*, October 26, 2008; G20 Final Communiqué, "The Global Plan for Recovery and Reform," April 2, 2009; Tax Justice Network, taxjustice.net; Martin Sullivan, Data Shows Dramatic Shift of Profits to Tax Havens, *Tax Notes*, September 13, 2004; William Cohan, *House of Cards: A Tale of Hubris and Wretched Excess on Wall Street*, March 2009; U.S. Government Accountability Office, "International Taxation: Large US corporations and federal contractors in jurisdictions listed as tax havens or financial privacy jurisdictions," December 2008; Organisation for Economic Co-operation and Development. "A Progress Report on the Jurisdictions Surveyed by the OECD Global Forum in Implementing the Internationally Agreed Tax Standard," April 2, 2009; Geoff Cook, Response to *Financial Times* Comment, mail. jerseyfinance.je; March 5, 2009; William Brittain-Catlin, "How offshore capitalism ate our economies—and itself," *The Guardian*, Feb. 5, 2009.

Chapter 9

POLICY SPOTLIGHT:
GLOBALIZATION AND ECONOMIC DEVELOPMENT

INTRODUCTION

Given the economic turmoil of the last two years in the developed world, it is ironic, if unsurprising, that the developing world has been urged for several decades now to adopt free markets and increased privatization as the keys to catching up with the West. These "neoliberal" policy prescriptions were applied across the developing world as a one-size-fits-all solution to problems as wide-ranging as poverty, malnutrition, and political conflict. While 10% unemployment in the United States has led to trillion-dollar increases in government spending, developing countries with double-digit unemployment were routinely assured that macroeconomic crises could only be dealt with by "tightening their belts." And while the West, having experienced a financial crisis, now calls for increased financial regulation, similar calls for more regulation from developing countries that suffered such crises multiple times were dismissed as misguided.

The contributors to this section take on different aspects of the neoliberal policy mix, raising questions that recur through this entire volume. Where do the limits of the market lie? At what point do we decide that markets cease to serve the citizens whose well-being economists claim to advocate for? And to what extent should communities, via politically representative bodies of all kinds, be able to regulate and control markets?

The first article of the neoliberal faith is the belief that openness to international trade, i.e. economic globalization, is the key to growth and development. Ramaa Vasudevan therefore starts off the section with a critique of the concept of comparative advantage that is so central to the argument about free trade (Article 9.1).

Ellen Frank points out that contrary to the claims of globalization advocates, the historical record in fact suggests that protectionism may be a better strategy for economic development (Article 9.2).

Mark Engler (Article 9.3) challenges Thomas Friedman's famous claim that globalization has leveled the playing field across countries. He points out the extent to which Friedman's view of the benefits of globalization requires internalizing the views of global corporate elites, completely ignoring the ways in which workers across the world have been "flattened" in the last two decades.

In response to several articles in the *New York Times* praising "sweatshops" by Nicholas Kristof, John Miller provides "Nike to the Rescue?" (Article 9.4). Miller addresses the issue of sweatshops within the context of the causal link between globalization and growth and finds that here, too, mainstream economists are on shaky ground.

In his role as the intrepid Dr. Dollar, Arthur MacEwan responds to an inquiry as to the relative merits of international labor standards (Article 9.5) and whether or not labor and progressive groups should support such standards in trade agreements. In response to critics of labor standards, MacEwan argues that while claiming to be advocates for workers in developing countries, such critics regularly deny those same workers' demands for better working conditions within their own countries. Ultimately, he argues, we should take our cues from these workers themselves, which is only possible if we make it easier for them to organize and unionize.

Robert Pollin (Article 9.6) summarizes the set of policies that constitute neoliberalism and describes their destructive impact upon the developing world. He then identifies three fundamental problems with neoliberal policy: the Marx, Keynes, and Polanyi problems.

Our first case study of development in this "spotlight" chapter is of Brazil and land reform under President Luiz Inácio "Lula" da Silva's regime. Article 9.7 follows this central issue of Brazil's development and explores the interconnected issues of land reform and poverty.

In a particularly timely piece, Smriti Rao (Article 9.8) has shown how the developing countries that most aggressively followed a neoliberal regime of economic development were the ones most adversely affected by the spillover of the economic crisis from the United States to the rest of the world.

Driving this irony home is John Miller (Article 9.9), who notes that the Heritage Foundation's annual Index of Economic Freedom has found that the most "free" economies on the planet are also the ones that took the biggest dive from the recent financial crisis.

Our last essay (Article 9.10) is a short piece on Haiti that reminds us that the crippling poverty which contributed to such a large death toll from the recent earthquake has at its root the dependent relationship that Haiti has endured with the United States. If Haiti is a case study of what not to do in economics development, it is also a case study of the consequences of ignoring real development.

Discussion Questions

1) (Article 9.1) Under what conditions might the mainstream argument about the advantages of specialization based on comparative advantage break down?

2) (Article 9.2) What is the basic argument in favor of free trade? Ellen Frank argues that free trade can prevent poorer countries from developing, rather than helping them do so. (The same argument applies to poorer regions within the United States.) What is her reasoning? How do you think a pro-free-trade economist would respond?

3) (Article 9.4) According to Nicolas Kristof, the "anti-sweatshop movement hurts the very workers it intends to benefit." Why does John Miller believe Kristof is wrong? Who do you find more convincing and why?

4) (Article 9.5) What is MacEwan's argument for supporting International labor Standards in trade agreements?

5) (Article 9.6) According to Robert Pollin, neoliberalism as a policy regime suffers from three primary problems. What are the "Marx Problem," the "Keynes Problem," and the "Polanyi Problem"?

6) (Article 9.7) Is Lula making a "Faustian bargain" by choosing short-term economic growth over long-term land reform?

7) (Article 9.7) Can substantive land reform take place without an active and militant political constituency driving the issue?

8) (Article 9.8) Smriti Rao has identified a particularly "cruel irony" as to the global effect of the current economic crisis which originated in the United States. What has been the effect of the current crisis on the countries that most enthusiastically embraced the neoliberal regime? What is the relationship between "risk" and "economic efficiency" based on the theory of comparative advantage?

9) (Article 9.9) John Miller has identified an even more remarkable "irony" between the economic assumptions and recent economic performance of the Heritage Foundation's Index of Economic Freedom. What claim does the Heritage Foundation make as to a correlation between economic growth and "freedom?" Empirically speaking, how has this claim worked out over the last two years for developing countries around the world that have followed this prescribed neoliberal "free market" path? What is the relationship between "risk" and "economic efficiency" based on the theory of comparative advantage?

10) (Article 9.10) "Poor Mexico, So far from God, So close to the United States." Those oft-quoted words of the late Mexican dictator Porfirio Díaz come to mind when reading Marie Kennedy and Chris Tilly's brief article on Haiti. How might the dictator's words be applied to the tragic situation in Haiti? Can a country truly be "too close to the United States"?

Article 9.1

COMPARATIVE ADVANTAGE

BY RAMAA VASUDEVAN
July/August 2007

Dear Dr. Dollar:
When economists argue that the outsourcing of jobs might be a plus for the U.S. economy, they often mention the idea of comparative advantage. So free trade would allow the United States to specialize in higher-end service-sector businesses, creating higher-paying jobs than the ones that would be outsourced. But is it really true that free trade leads to universal benefits?
—*David Goodman, Boston, Mass.*

You're right: The purveyors of the free trade gospel do invoke the doctrine of comparative advantage to dismiss widespread concerns about the export of jobs. Attributed to 19th-century British political-economist David Ricardo, the doctrine says that a nation always stands to gain if it exports the goods it produces *relatively* more cheaply in exchange for goods that it can get *comparatively* more cheaply from abroad. Free trade would lead to each country specializing in the products it can produce at *relatively* lower costs. Such specialization allows both trading partners to gain from trade, the theory goes, even if in one of the countries production of *both* goods costs more in absolute terms.

For instance, suppose that in the United States the cost to produce one car equals the cost to produce 10 bags of cotton, while in the Philippines the cost to produce one car equals the cost to produce 100 bags of cotton. The Philippines would then have a comparative advantage in the production of cotton, producing one bag at a cost equal to the production cost of 1/100 of a car, versus 1/10 of a car in the United States; likewise, the United States would hold a comparative advantage in the production of cars. Whatever the prices of cars and cotton in the global market, the theory goes, the Philippines would be better off producing only cotton and importing all its cars from the United States, and the United States would be better off producing only cars and importing all of its cotton from the Philippines. If the international terms of trade—the relative price—is one car for 50 bags, then the United States will take in 50 bags of cotton for each car it exports, 40 more than the 10 bags it forgoes by putting its productive resources into making the car rather than growing cotton. The Philippines is also better off: it can import a car in exchange for the export of 50 bags of cotton, whereas it would have had to forgo the production of 100 bags of cotton in order to produce that car domestically. If the price of cars goes up in the global marketplace, the Philippines will lose out in relative terms—but will still be better off than if it tried to produce its own cars.

The real world, unfortunately, does not always conform to the assumptions underlying comparative-advantage theory. One assumption is that trade is balanced. But many countries are running persistent deficits, notably the United States, whose trade deficit is now at nearly 7% of its GDP. A second premise, that there is full employment within the trading nations, is also patently unrealistic. As global trade intensifies, jobs created in the export sector do not necessarily compensate for the jobs lost in the sectors wiped out by foreign competition.

The comparative advantage story faces more direct empirical challenges as well. Nearly 70% of U.S. trade is trade in similar goods, known as *intra-industry trade*: for example, exporting Fords and importing BMWs. And about one third of U.S. trade as of the late 1990s was trade between branches of a single corporation located in different countries (*intra-firm trade*). Comparative advantage cannot explain these patterns.

Comparative advantage is a static concept that identifies immediate gains from trade but is a poor guide to economic development, a process of structural change over time which is by definition dynamic. Thus the comparative advantage tale is particularly pernicious when preached to developing countries, consigning many to "specialize" in agricultural goods or be forced into a race to the bottom where cheap sweatshop labor is their sole source of competitiveness.

The irony, of course, is that none of the rich countries got that way by following the maxim that they now preach. These countries historically relied on tariff walls and other forms of protectionism to build their industrial base. And even now, they continue to protect sectors like agriculture with subsidies. The countries now touted as new models of the benefits of free trade—South Korea and the other "Asian tigers," for instance—actually flouted this economic wisdom, nurturing their technological capabilities in specific manufacturing sectors and taking advantage of their lower wage costs to *gradually* become effective competitors of the United States and Europe in manufacturing.

The fundamental point is this: contrary to the comparative-advantage claim that trade is universally beneficial, nations as a whole do not prosper from free trade. Free trade creates winners and losers, both within and between countries. In today's context it is the global corporate giants that are propelling and profiting from "free trade": not only outsourcing white-collar jobs, but creating global commodity chains linking sweatshop labor in the developing countries of Latin America and Asia (Africa being largely left out of the game aside from the export of natural resources such as oil) with ever-more insecure consumers in the developed world. Promoting "free trade" as a political cause enables this process to continue.

It is a process with real human costs in terms of both wages and work. People in developing countries across the globe continue to face these costs as trade liberalization measures are enforced; and the working class in the United States is also being forced to bear the brunt of the relentless logic of competition.

Sources: Arthur MacEwan, "The Gospel of Free Trade: The New Evangelists," *Dollars & Sense,* July/August 2002; Ha-Joon Chang, *Kicking away the Ladder: The Real History of Fair Trade,* Foreign Policy in Focus, 2003; Anwar Shaikh, "Globalization and the Myths of Free Trade," in *Globalization and the Myths of Free Trade: History, Theory, and Empirical Evidence,* ed. Anwar Shaikh, Routledge 2007.

Article 9.2

SHOULD DEVELOPING COUNTRIES EMBRACE PROTECTIONISM?

BY ELLEN FRANK
July 2004

> Dear Dr. Dollar:
> Supposedly, countries should produce what they are best at. If the United States makes computers and China produces rice, then the theory of free trade says China should trade its rice for computers. But if China puts tariffs on U.S.-made computers and builds up its own computer industry, then it will become best at making them and can buy rice from Vietnam. Isn't it advantageous for poor countries to practice protectionism and become industrial powers themselves, rather than simply producing mono-crop commodities? I'm asking because local alternative currencies like Ithaca Hours benefit local businesses, though they restrict consumers to local goods that may be more expensive than goods from further away.
> —*Matt Cary, Hollywood, Fla.*

The modern theory of free trade argues that countries are "endowed" with certain quantities of labor, capital, and natural resources. A country with lots of labor but little capital should specialize in the production of labor-intensive goods, like hand-woven rugs, hand-sewn garments, or hand-picked fruit. By ramping up produc-tion of these goods, a developing country can trade on world markets, earning the foreign exchange to purchase capital-intensive products like computers and cars. Free trade thus permits poor countries (or, to be more precise, their most well-off citizens) to *consume* high-tech goods that they lack the ability to *produce* and so obtain higher living standards. "Capital-rich" countries like the United States benefit from relatively cheap fruit and garments, freeing up their workforce to focus on high-tech goods. Free trade, according to this story, is a win-win game for everyone.

The flaw in this tale, which you have hit upon exactly, is that being "capital-rich" or "capital-poor" is not a natural phenomenon like having lots of oil. Capital is created—typically with plenty of government assistance and protection.

Developing countries can create industrial capacity and train their citizens to manufacture high-tech goods. But doing so takes time. Building up the capacity to manufacture computers, for example, at prices that are competitive with firms in developed countries may take several years. To buy this time, a government needs to keep foreign-made computers from flooding its market and undercutting less-established local producers. It also needs to limit inflows of foreign capital. Studies show that when foreign firms set up production facilities in developing countries, they are unlikely to share their latest techniques, so such foreign investment does not typically build local expertise or benefit local entrepreneurs.

The United States and other rich countries employed these protectionist strategies. In the 1800s, American entrepreneurs traveled to England and France to learn the latest manufacturing techniques and freely appropriated designs for cutting-edge industrial equipment. The U.S. government protected its nascent industries with high tariff walls until they could compete with European manufacturers.

After World War II, Japan effectively froze out foreign goods while building up world-class auto, computer, and electronics industries. Korea later followed Japan's strategy; in recent years, so has China. There, "infant industries" are heavily protected by tariffs, quotas, and other trade barriers. Foreign producers are welcome only if they establish high-tech facilities in which Chinese engineers and production workers can garner the most modern skills.

Development economists like Alice Amsden and Dani Rodrik are increasingly reaching the conclusion that carefully designed industrial policies, combined with protections for infant industries, are most effective in promoting internal development in poor countries. "Free-trade" policies, on the other hand, seem to lock poor countries into producing low-tech goods like garments and agricultural commodities, whose prices tend to decline on world markets due to intense competition with other poor countries.

In the contemporary global economy, however, there are three difficulties with implementing a local development strategy. First, some countries have bargained away their right to protect local firms by entering into free-trade agreements. Second, protectionism means that local consumers are denied the benefits of cheap manufactured goods from abroad, at least in the short run.

Finally, in many parts of the world the floodgates of foreign-made goods have already been opened and, with the middle and upper classes enjoying their computers and cell phones, it may be impossible to build the political consensus to close them. This last concern bears on the prospects for local alternative currencies. Since it is impos-sible to "close off" the local economy, the success of local currencies in bolstering hometown businesses depends on the willingness of local residents to deny themselves the benefits of cheaper nonlocal goods. Like national protectionist polices, local currencies restrict consumer choice.

Ultimately, the success or failure of such ventures rests on the degree of public support for local business. With local currencies, participation is voluntary and attitudes toward local producers often favorable. National protectionist polices, however, entail coerced public participation and generally fail when governments are corrupt and unable to command public support.

Article 9.3

THE WORLD IS NOT FLAT

How Thomas Friedman gets it wrong about globalization.

BY MARK ENGLER

May 2008

Turn on the TV and flip to a C-SPAN or CNN discussion of the global economy and you are likely to spot the square head and mustachioed face of *New York Times* columnist Thomas Friedman, who will probably be expressing enthusiasm for the business world's newest high-tech innovations. With his best-selling book *The Lexus and the Olive Tree*, Friedman stepped forward in the late 1990s as a leading cheerleader of neoliberal globalization. Then, in the wake of 9/11, he made common cause with White House militarists. He became a high-profile "liberal hawk" and supported the war in Iraq—only to distance himself later in the Bush era and return to championing corporate expansion with a second widely read book on globalization, *The World Is Flat*. For better or for worse, his punditry provides an indispensable guide to how mainstream commentators have tried to defend neoliberalism in the face of challenges from worldwide social movements. Moreover, Friedman's renewed emphasis on corporate globalization in the wake of the botched war in Iraq may also be a significant bellwether for how the Democratic Party—especially the more conservative "New Democrat" wing of the party—crafts a vision for international relations after Bush.

You Can't Stop the Dawn

In Friedman's view, the end of the Cold War left the world with a single, unassailable ideology. "Globalization," he wrote in *The Lexus and the Olive Tree*, "means the spread of free market capitalism to every country in the world." He saw this as an unmitigated good: "[T]he more you open your economy to free trade and competition, the more efficient and flourishing your economy will be." He marveled that "computerization, miniaturization, digitization, satellite communications, fiber optics, and the Internet" were bringing about untold wonders.

Friedman's conversion into the church of corporate expansion took place over many years. His academic training is not in economics, but in Middle Eastern studies. During the 1980s, Friedman was a respected *New York Times* correspondent in Israel and Lebanon, winning two Pulitzer Prizes for his reporting from the region. In 1994, just at the beginning of the Internet boom, he switched to a beat covering the intersection of politics and economics, and his excitement for globalization began to mount in earnest. By the time he became the *Times'* foreign affairs columnist the following year, he was perfectly positioned to evangelize about how unregulated markets and new technology were reshaping global affairs.

Aware that many people saw him as a modern-day Pangloss extolling the best of all possible worlds, Friedman contended in *The Lexus and the Olive Tree* that he was "not a salesman for globalization." But this is precisely what he was. More than any other public personality, he was responsible for portraying neoliberalism as an inevitable and laudable march of progress. "I feel about globalization a lot like I feel about the dawn," he wrote. "[E]ven if I didn't care much for the dawn there isn't much I could do about it. I didn't start globalization, I can't stop it—except at a huge cost to human development." By defining "globalization" as a broad, sweeping phenomenon—political, economic, technological, and cultural—he saw resistance as ridiculous. So when massive protests erupted at the World Trade Organization meetings in Seattle in late 1999, he disgustedly derided the demonstrators as "a Noah's ark of flat-earth advocates, protectionist trade unions and yuppies looking for their 1960s fix."

You might think that the deflating of the dot-com bubble that began in March 2000 would have quelled Friedman's fervor, but you would be wrong. In Friedman's view, the end of the 1990s boom only led to more advancement. "[T]he dot-com bust," he later wrote, "actually drove globalization into hypermode by forcing companies to outsource and offshore more and more functions in order to save on scarce capital." Friedman's cheerleading, too, would go into "hypermode," but not before the columnist took a detour to become one of the country's most prominent liberal hawks in the wake of 9/11. When Friedman did return to the subject of economic globalization with his 2005 book, *The World Is Flat*, he was once again wowed. Over the course of just a few years, he concluded, "we entered a whole new era: Globalization 3.0."

Fueled now by wireless technology and ever-smaller microchips, this wave of capitalism was "shrinking the world from a size small to a size tiny and flattening the playing field at the same time." Hospitals in the United States were sending CT scans to India for analysis; other corporations opened bustling call centers there to handle customer service calls, training their new South Asian employees to speak in American accents; globetrotting columnists could file their stories from the middle of a golf course in China by using their Blackberries. The march of progress was back on.

Friedman is known for conveying complicated ideas through the use of colorful metaphors. Yet his metaphors consistently get so mixed and muddled as to require delicate linguistic untangling. In the course of his two books on globalization, Friedman goes from seeing the world in 3-D to, remarkably enough, seeing it in at least six dimensions. Technological advance, he tells us, has now accelerated so much that we have gone through Globalization versions 1.0 and 2.0 and entered version 3.0. Friedman presents ten "flatteners," four "steroids," and a "triple convergence," plus at least seven releases of "DOScapital." Various steroids and flatteners are meant to have multiplied globalization's effects exponentially. Journalist Matt Taibbi, who has written the most cutting analysis of Friedman's peculiar language, notes, "Friedman's book is the first I have encountered, anywhere, in which the reader needs a calculator to figure the value of the author's metaphors."

If ever Orwell's warnings that "the slovenliness of our language makes it easier for us to have foolish thoughts" and that the world's "present political chaos is connected with the decay of language" apply to anyone, they apply to Friedman. The connection between Friedman's hazy writing and his suspect conclusions about the global economy shows up in the very premise of his second book on globalization. During a meeting between Friedman and Nandan Nilekani in Bangalore, the

Infosys CEO offers that "the playing field is being leveled." For Friedman, the tired cliché is a revelation. He mulls it over for hours and then, suddenly, decides: "My God, he's telling me the world is flat!"

Now, it is quite a stretch to take a routine sports metaphor and superimpose it on the globe; there could be few worse metaphors for talking about a global system that is more integrated and networked than ever before. "Friedman is a person who not only speaks in malapropisms, he also hears malapropisms," Taibbi argues. Nilekani off-handedly mentions a level field and Friedman attributes to him the radical idea of a flat world. "This is the intellectual version of Far Out Space Nuts, when NASA repairman Bob Denver sets a whole sitcom in motion by pressing 'launch' instead of 'lunch' in a space capsule. And once he hits that button, the rocket takes off."

It would all be funny if it didn't mask a deeper political problem: For the world's poor, the playing field is far from level. Our world is not flat.

Putting on Reagan's Jacket

With the ideology of neoliberalism steadily losing ground in international discussion, it is important to see how a leading apologist mounts a defense. In Friedman's case, he does so by holding on to dogmatic assumptions, training his sights on high technology, conducting his interviews largely within the insular world of jet-setting corporate elites, and ignoring a world of evidence that would contradict his selective viewpoint.

Some reviewers have applauded Friedman for acknowledging negative aspects of globalization in his books. But for Friedman, this does not mean looking at the realities of exploitation or environmental destruction that have resulted from corporate expansion. Instead, his caveats boil down to two points: that terrorists, too, can use the Internet, and that many countries, especially in "unflat" Africa, are too backward to read the signs that would put them on the high tech, "free trade" superhighway to prosperity. With regard to the latter, it's not that anything is wrong really, only that the process has not gone far enough and fast enough for everyone to benefit yet.

Needless to say, Friedman's is hardly a biting exposé. In fact, it is virtually impossible to find any evidence that might make him skeptical about the fundamental greatness of corporate globalization. In 1999, even *BusinessWeek* argued "The Asian financial crisis of 1997–99 shows that unfettered liberalization of capital markets without proper regulation can lead the world to the brink of disaster." But for Friedman this crisis, too, was all for the best. He writes, "I believe globalization did us all a favor by melting down the economies of Thailand, Korea, Malaysia, Indonesia, Mexico, Russia and Brazil in the 1990s, because it laid bare a lot of the rotten practices and institutions in countries that had prematurely globalized." He slams the countries for corruption and cronyism, suggesting that they deserved their fates. But by "prematurely globalized" he does not mean that these countries should have been more cautious about linking their fates to speculative international markets. Rather, he believes that they had not done enough to "reduce the role of government" and "let markets more freely allocate resources." Friedman's solution to the dangers of unregulated markets is more deregulation, the remedy for the excesses of unfettered capitalism is even more excess. The argument is airtight.

Missing from this account, of course, is any sense of the social impact of the Asian crisis. In the end, wealthy foreign investors were bailed out by the International Monetary Fund and lost little. The real losers were an untold number of middle-class families in places like Thailand and Korea whose savings were wiped out overnight, as well as the poor in places like Indonesia who went hungry when the government cut food subsidies. It takes a very twisted viewpoint to say that the Asian financial crisis did these people a favor.

Friedman holds that the Internet age has created a "flat" world with opportunity for all. Yet he freely admits that the system he describes is founded on the Reagan-Thatcher model of extreme, "trickle down" neoliberalism—one of the most unequal methods of distributing social goods ever devised. Friedman writes: "Thatcher and Reagan combined to strip huge chunks of economic decision-making power from the state, from the advocates of the Great Society and from traditional Keynesian economics, and hand them over to the free market." Countries now have one choice for economic policy: neoliberalism. They must radically deregulate and privatize their economies. Friedman calls this the "Golden Straitjacket." It's "golden" because the model supposedly creates widespread affluence. But it's a "straitjacket" because it radically constricts democracy. Sounding a lot like Ralph Nader, Friedman writes:

Once your country puts [the Golden Straitjacket] on, its political choices get reduced to Pepsi or Coke—to slight nuances of taste, slight nuances of policy, slight alterations in design ... but never any major deviation from the core golden rules. Governments—be they led by Democrats or Republicans, Conservatives or Labourites, Gaullists or Socialists, Christian Democrats or Social Democrats—that deviate too far away from the core rules will see their investors stampede away, interest rates rise, and stock market valuations fall.

The difference between Friedman and Nader is that the *New York Times* columnist approves of this situation. He does not condemn it as an assault on democracy; he says it's just the way things are. Of the Democrats, he writes, "Mr. Clinton effectively kidnapped the Democratic Party ... moved it into the Republican economic agenda—including free trade, NAFTA and the WTO for China—while holding onto much of the Democrats' social agenda." Any Democrat who would try to move it back meets Friedman's wrath. In the new global age, all those to the left of Ronald Reagan on economic policy are simply out of luck.

Sitting On Top Of The World

Friedman's contention that everyone benefits when countries bind themselves into market fundamentalism is based less on a careful review of the evidence than on blind faith. In July of 2006, he made a startling admission during a CNBC interview with Tim Russert. He said:

We got this free market, and I admit, I was speaking out in Minnesota—my hometown, in fact, and a guy stood up in the audience, said, "Mr. Friedman, is there any free trade agreement you'd oppose?" I said, "No, absolutely not." I said,

> "You know what, sir? I wrote a column supporting the CAFTA, the Caribbean
> Free Trade initiative. I didn't even know what was in it. I just knew two words:
> free trade."

That a nationally prominent columnist would gloat about such ignorance is a sad statement about the health of our political debate. "Free trade" is an incredibly politicized phrase, with little concrete meaning. For instance, CAFTA (which actually stands for the *Central American* Free Trade Agreement) includes provisions designed to protect the monopoly rights of giant pharmaceutical companies rather than to create "free" commerce.

But the larger point is that neoliberal globalization does not make winners of everyone. Its global track record for producing GDP growth is dismal. In fact, its main accomplishment may be to produce inequality. And Friedman's own position amid this global divide is telling. He regularly represents himself as just an average guy from Minnesota trying to make sense of the world. The real picture is far from average. In July 2006, *Washingtonian* magazine reported that in the 1970s Friedman married into one of the 100 richest families in the United States—the Bucksbaums—who have amassed a fortune worth some $2.7 billion, with origins in real estate development. The magazine noted that he lives in "a palatial 11,400-square-foot house, now valued at $9.3 million, on a 7.5-acre parcel just blocks from I-495 and the Bethesda Country Club." Given that the über-rich, those with huge stock portfolios and investments in multinational corporations, have benefited tremendously from corporate globalization, commentators like David Sirota have suggested that Friedman's vast wealth represents an undisclosed conflict of interest in his journalism. It is as if multimillionaire Richard Mellon Scaife were to write about the repeal of the estate tax without disclosing that he stands to profit handsomely from such a policy change.

Whether or not that is the case, Friedman's position at the very pinnacle of global prosperity is certainly reflected in his view of the world. In a telling admission, he relates in *The Lexus and the Olive Tree* that his "best intellectual sources" about globalization are hedge fund managers. Hedge funds are elite, largely unregulated investment pools that handle money for individuals of extremely high net worth. Their managers are among the highest paid individuals in the United States. In 2006, the top 25 hedge fund managers in the country made in excess of $240 million each. This means they each pulled in $27,000 per hour, 24 hours per day, whether waking or sleeping, whether at the office or teeing off on the ninth hole. Corporate CEOs and hedge fund managers may indeed be well informed about certain aspects of the global economy. But if that is where you get your information, you end up with a very partial view of the world. You get the winner's view.

In an eloquent critique of *The World Is Flat*, Indian eco-feminist Vandana Shiva writes:

> Friedman has reduced the world to the friends he visits, the CEOs he knows,
> and the golf courses he plays at. From this microcosm of privilege, exclusion,
> blindness, he shuts out both the beauty of diversity and the brutality of
> exploitation and inequality ...

That is why he talks of 550 million Indian youth overtaking Americans in a flat world, when the entire information technology/outsourcing sector in India employs only a million out of 1.2 billion people. Food and farming, textiles and clothing, health and education are nowhere in Friedman's monoculture of mind locked into IT. Friedman presents a 0.1% picture and hides 99.9%. ... In the eclipsed 99.9% are the 25 million women who disappeared in high growth areas of India because a commodified world has rendered women a dispensable sex. In the hidden 99.9% ... are thousands of tribal children in Orissa, Maharashtra, Rajasthan who died of hunger because the public distribution system for food has been dismantled to create markets for agribusiness.

A Race to the Top?

The corporate globalization that Friedman champions has alarming changes in store not just for the poor of the global South, but also for working people in the United States and Europe. One of the things that Friedman particularly lauds about Reagan and Thatcher is their success in breaking unions. He writes: "it may turn out that one of the key turning points in American history, going into the millennium, was Ronald Reagan's decision to fire all the striking air traffic controllers in 1981." "No single event," he notes with satisfaction, "did more to alter the balance of power between management and workers." Everyone wins from this, he argues, since "[t]he easier it is to fire workers, the more incentive employers have to hire them." Because America busted its unions and Western European countries did not, he contends, the United States developed a more dynamic economy.

What Friedman fails to note is that real wages for working people in the United States have been largely stagnant since the early 1970s, while working hours have sky-rocketed. When compared with workers in Western Europe, the average American works 350 hours more per year, the equivalent of nine extra weeks. A study by the International Labor Organization reported that in 2000 the average U.S. worker put in 199 more hours than in 1973. Dramatizing such realities, a group of union and nonprofit activists now observe "Take Back Your Time Day" every October 24. On that day, if the U.S. workload were on par with the rest of the industrialized world, Americans would have the rest of the year off.

Friedman utters not a word of protest about the trend toward more work; in fact, he celebrates it. He argues that European social democracies are obsolete, even though they are successful capitalist countries. These nations are running on the wrong version of "DOScapital," Friedman contends, and need to shift to U.S. standards. Never mind that economies like Sweden's have performed very well over the past decade, all while maintaining a much higher quality of life for their citizens.

He has a special hatred for the French, who, he writes, "are trying to preserve a 35-hour work week in a world where Indian engineers are ready to work a 35-hour day." In what he calls a "race to the top," Friedman predicts a turbulent decade for Western Europe, as aging, inflexible economies—which have grown used to six-week vacations and unemployment insurance that is almost as good as having a job—become more intimately integrated with Eastern Europe, India and China in a flattening world. ... The dirty little secret is that India is taking work from Europe or America not simply because of low wages. It is also because Indians are ready to work harder and can do anything from answering your phone to designing your next airplane or car. They are not racing us to the bottom. They are racing us to the top. ... Yes, this is a bad time for France and friends to lose their appetite for hard work—just when India, China and Poland are rediscovering theirs.

It is unclear what Friedman sees as getting to the "top" if paid vacations, unemployment insurance, and retirement—benefits traditionally regarded as signs of a civilized economy—must be sacrificed. But, Friedman tells us, that is the new reality.

Ultimately, the "race to the top" is another of Friedman's botched metaphors. In the long-standing progressive argument that corporate globalization creates a "race to the bottom," it is not Indian or Chinese workers who are doing the racing at all. It's capital. Deregulation allows corporations to wander the globe in search of ever lower wages and laxer environmental standards. The moment workers stand up for their rights, refusing to tolerate a "35-hour day," a company can pick up and move elsewhere. The governments that might curb such abuses are in straitjackets. The unions that workers might have organized themselves into have been busted. All Friedman can offer is this cryptic and seemingly masochistic advice: "When the world goes flat—and you are feeling flattened—reach for a shovel and dig into yourself. Don't try to build walls."

Globalization from Below

An interesting aspect of Friedman's renewed focus on corporate globalization at the end of the Bush era is that governments and international financial institutions have faded from his picture of the integrating world. Even corporations are becoming less relevant. In his view, the new era of "Globalization 3.0" is all about *individuals*. Today, it is up to all people to pull themselves up by their bootstraps. He writes, "every person now must, and can, ask: Where do *I* as an individual fit into the global competition and opportunities of the day, and how can *I*, on my own, collaborate with others globally?"

Conveniently enough, accepting this idea makes it impossible to oppose neoliberalism. In a world of extreme individualism, no one in particular is responsible for setting the rules of the world order. It is pointless to protest governments or international financial institutions. Globalization is unstoppable because people want it.

These arguments are not new. With scant evidence, Friedman has long claimed that there is a "groundswell" of people throughout the developing world demanding corporate globalization. Of course, the massive protests of the past decade would seem to contradict his assertion. But he does not see this as a problem. He dismisses global justice activism by arguing, "from its origins, the movement that emerged in Seattle was primarily a Western-driven phenomenon." The backlash that does exist in poorer countries, he argues, is not rational politics but simple lawlessness: "what we have been seeing in many countries, instead of popular mass opposition to globalization, is wave after wave of crime—people just grabbing what they need, weaving their own social safety nets and not worrying about the theory or the ideology." In the end, Friedman seems ideologically incapable of accepting that people in the global South could organize their own movements or articulate a coherent politics of resistance.

Today, with much of the world in open rebellion against neoliberalism, this fiction is getting harder and harder to maintain. That Friedman has perpetually failed to spot the vibrant network of grassroots organizations that has built a worldwide campaign against the Washington Consensus is not a sign of widespread support for corporate globalization. It is an indictment of his reporting. Well before Seattle, there had been protests of millions of people throughout the global South against the "Golden Straitjacket."

These have continued into the new millennium. In their book *Globalization from Below*, Jeremy Brecher, Tim Costello, and Brendan Smith note that in just a two-month period, in May and June of 2000, there were six general strikes against the impact of neoliberalism. In India, as many as 20 million farmers and workers struck, protesting their government's involvement with the WTO and the IMF. Twelve million Argentineans went on strike in response to fiscal austerity policies imposed by the IMF. Nigeria was paralyzed by strikes against neoliberal price hikes on fuel. South Koreans demanded a shorter workweek and the full protection of part-time and temporary employees by the country's labor laws. Finally, general strikes in South Africa and Uruguay protested increasing unemployment rates, which resulted from IMF austerity policies. All of these escaped Friedman's notice.

In truth, they are only suggestions of wider resistance. The people of Latin America have certainly not joined the groundswell of support for neoliberal ideology. In country after country they have ousted conservative governments since 2000 and elected more progressive leaders, redrawing the region's political map. The columnist has yet to comment.

There is a way in which Friedman perfectly matches the politics of our times. "Like George Bush, he's in the reality-making business," Matt Taibbi argues. "You no longer have to worry about actually convincing anyone; the process ends when you make the case. Things are true because you say they are. The only thing that matters is how sure you sound when you say it."

As much as he might resemble Bush in this respect, however, Friedman also tells us something important about the post-Bush moment. As a new administration takes over, an increasing number of politicians will seek to move the United States away from the aggressive militarism of imperial globalization and back toward a softer approach to ruling the world. Following Friedman, many will look to revitalize corporate globalization as a model for international affairs. These "New Democrats" will promise a fresh approach to foreign affairs. But really, they will return to something old: a Clintonian model of corporate globalization. Like Friedman, many will proclaim it as the best of all possible worlds, a global order both exciting and unavoidable. It will be up to the world's citizens to demand something better.

Sources: By Thomas Friedman: *The Lexus and the Olive Tree: Understanding Globalization* (Anchor Books, 2000); *The World Is Flat* (Farrar, Straus & Giroux, 2005); "Senseless in Seattle," *New York Times*, December 1, 1999; "Senseless in Seattle II," *New York Times*, December 8, 1999; "A Race To The Top," *New York Times*, June 3, 2005. Other sources: Matt Taibbi, "Flathead: The peculiar genius of Thomas L. Friedman," *New York Press*, April 27, 2005; "The Lessons of Seattle," *BusinessWeek*, December 13, 1999; Robin Broad and John Cavanagh, "The Hijacking of the Development Debate: How Friedman and Sachs Got It Wrong," *World Policy Journal*, Summer 2006; David Sirota, "Caught on Tape: Tom Friedman's Truly Shocking Admission,"

SirotaBlog, July 24, 2006; Garrett M. Graff, "Thomas Friedman is On Top of the World," *The Washingtonian*, July 2006; David Sirota, "Billionaire Scion Tom Friedman," DailyKos, July 31, 2006; Roger Lowenstein, "The Inequality Conundrum," *New York Times Magazine*, June 10, 2007; Vandana Shiva, "The Polarised World Of Globalisation," ZNet, May 27, 2005; Jeremy Brecher et al., *Globalization from Below* (South End Press, 2000).

Article 9.4

NIKE TO THE RESCUE?

Africa needs better jobs, not sweatshops.

BY JOHN MILLER
September/October 2006

"In Praise of the Maligned Sweatshop"

WINDHOEK, Namibia—Africa desperately needs Western help in the form of schools, clinics and sweatshops.

On a street here in the capital of Namibia, in the southwestern corner of Africa, I spoke to a group of young men who were trying to get hired as day laborers on construction sites.

"I come here every day," said Naftal Shaanika, a 20-year-old. "I actually find work only about once a week."

Mr. Shaanika and the other young men noted that the construction jobs were dangerous and arduous, and that they would vastly prefer steady jobs in, yes, sweatshops. Sure, sweatshop work is tedious, grueling and sometimes dangerous. But over all, sewing clothes is considerably less dangerous or arduous—or sweaty—than most alternatives in poor countries.

Well-meaning American university students regularly campaign against sweatshops. But instead, anyone who cares about fighting poverty should campaign in favor of sweatshops, demanding that companies set up factories in Africa.

The problem is that it's still costly to manufacture in Africa. The headaches across much of the continent include red tape, corruption, political instability, unreliable electricity and ports, and an inexperienced labor force that leads to low productivity and quality. The anti-sweatshop movement isn't a prime obstacle, but it's one more reason not to manufacture in Africa.

Imagine that a Nike vice president proposed manufacturing cheap T-shirts in Ethiopia. The boss would reply: "You're crazy! We'd be boycotted on every campus in the country."

Some of those who campaign against sweatshops respond to my arguments by noting that they aren't against factories in Africa, but only demand a "living wage" in them. After all, if labor costs amount to only $1 per shirt, then doubling wages would barely make a difference in the final cost.

One problem ... is that it already isn't profitable to pay respectable salaries, and so any pressure to raise them becomes one more reason to avoid Africa altogether.

One of the best U.S. initiatives in Africa has been the African Growth and Opportunity Act, which allows duty-free imports from Africa—and thus has stimulated manufacturing there.

—Op-ed by Nicholas Kristof, *New York Times*, June 6, 2006

Nicholas Kristof has been beating the pro-sweatshop drum for quite a while. Shortly after the East Asian financial crisis of the late 1990s, Kristof, the Pulitzer Prize-winning journalist and now columnist for the *New York Times*, reported the story of an Indonesian recycler who, picking through the metal scraps of a garbage dump, dreamed that her son would grow up to be a sweatshop worker. Then, in 2000, Kristof and his wife, *Times* reporter Sheryl WuDunn, published "Two Cheers for Sweatshops" in the *Times Magazine*. In 2002, Kristof's column advised G-8 leaders to "start an international campaign to promote imports from sweatshops, perhaps with bold labels depicting an unrecognizable flag and the words 'Proudly Made in a Third World Sweatshop.'"

Now Kristof laments that too few poor, young African men have the opportunity to enter the satanic mill of sweatshop employment. Like his earlier efforts, Kristof's latest pro-sweatshop ditty synthesizes plenty of half-truths. Let's take a closer look and see why there is still no reason to give it up for sweatshops.

A Better Alternative?

It is hardly surprising that young men on the streets of Namibia's capital might find sweatshop jobs more appealing than irregular work as day laborers on construction sites.

The alternative jobs available to sweatshop workers are often worse and, as Kristof loves to point out, usually involve more sweating than those in world export factories. Most poor people in the developing world eke out their livelihoods from subsistence agriculture or by plying petty trades. Others on the edge of urban centers work as street-hawkers or hold other jobs in the informal sector. As economist Arthur MacEwan wrote a few years back in *Dollars & Sense*, in a poor country like Indonesia, where women working in manufacturing earn five times as much as those in agriculture, sweatshops have no trouble finding workers.

But let's be clear about a few things. First, export factory jobs, especially in labor-intensive industries, often are just "a ticket to slightly less impoverishment," as even economist and sweatshop defender Jagdish Bhagwati allows.

Beyond that, these jobs seldom go to those without work or to the poorest of the poor. One study by sociologist Kurt Ver Beek showed that 60% of first-time Honduran *maquila* workers were previously employed. Typically they were not destitute, and they were better educated than most Hondurans.

Sweatshops don't just fail to rescue people from poverty. Setting up export factories where workers have few job alternatives has actually been a recipe for serious worker abuse. In *Beyond Sweatshops*, a book arguing for the benefits of direct foreign investment in the developing world, Brookings Institution economist Theodore Moran recounts the disastrous decision of the Philippine government to build the Bataan Export Processing Zone in an isolated mountainous area to lure foreign investors with the prospect of cheap labor. With few alternatives, Filipinos took jobs in the garment factories that sprung up in the zone. The manufacturers typically paid less than the minimum wage and forced employees to work overtime in factories filled with dust and fumes. Fed up, the workers eventually mounted a series of crippling strikes. Many factories shut down and occupancy rates in the zone plummeted, as did the value of exports, which declined by more than half between 1980 and 1986.

Kristof's argument is no excuse for sweatshop abuse: that conditions are worse elsewhere does nothing to alleviate the suffering of workers in export factories. They are often denied the right to organize, subjected to unsafe working conditions and to verbal, physical, and sexual abuse, forced to work overtime, coerced into pregnancy tests and even abortions, and paid less than a living wage. It remains useful and important to combat these conditions even if alternative jobs are worse yet.

The fact that young men in Namibia find sweatshop jobs appealing testifies to how harsh conditions are for workers in Africa, not the desirability of export factory employment.

Oddly, Kristof's desire to introduce new sweatshops to sub-Saharan Africa finds no support in the African Growth and Opportunity Act (AGOA) that he praises. The Act grants sub-Saharan apparel manufacturers preferential access to U.S. markets. But shortly after its passage, U.S. Trade Representative Robert Zoellick assured the press that the AGOA would not create sweatshops in Africa because it requires protective standards for workers consistent with those set by the International Labor Organization.

Antisweatshop Activism and Jobs

Kristof is convinced that the antisweatshop movement hurts the very workers it intends to help. His position has a certain seductive logic to it. As anyone who has suffered through introductory economics will tell you, holding everything else the same, a labor standard that forces multinational corporations and their subcontractors to boost wages should result in their hiring fewer workers.

But in practice does it? The only evidence Kristof produces is an imaginary conversation in which a boss incredulously refuses a Nike vice president's proposal to open a factory in Ethiopia paying wages of 25 cents a hour: "You're crazy! We'd be boycotted on every campus in the country."

While Kristof has an active imagination, there are some things wrong with this conversation.

First off, the antisweatshop movement seldom initiates boycotts. An organizer with United Students Against Sweatshops (USAS) responded on Kristof's blog: "We never call for apparel boycotts unless we are explicitly asked to by workers at a particular factory. This is, of course, exceedingly rare, because, as you so persuasively argued, people generally want to be employed." The National Labor Committee, the largest antisweatshop organization in the United States, takes the same position.

Moreover, when economists Ann Harrison and Jason Scorse conducted a systematic study of the effects of the antisweatshop movement on factory employment, they found no negative employment effect. Harrison and Scorse looked at Indonesia, where Nike was one of the targets of an energetic campaign calling for better wages and working conditions among the country's subcontractors. Their statistical analysis found that the antisweatshop campaign was responsible for 20% of the increase in the real wages of unskilled workers in factories exporting textiles, footwear, and apparel from 1991 to 1996. Harrison and Scorse also found that "antisweatshop activism did not have significant adverse effects on employment" in these sectors.

Campaigns for higher wages are unlikely to destroy jobs because, for multinationals and their subcontractors, wages make up a small portion of their overall costs. Even Kristof accepts this point, well documented by economists opposed to sweatshop labor. In Mexico's apparel industry, for instance, economists Robert Pollin, James Heintz, and Justine Burns from the Political Economy Research Institute found that doubling the pay of nonsupervisory workers would add just $1.80 to the production cost of a $100 men's sports jacket. A recent survey by the National Bureau of Economic Research found that U.S. consumers would be willing to pay $115 for the same jacket if they knew that it had not been made under sweatshop conditions.

Globalization in Sub-Saharan Africa

Kristof is right that Africa, especially sub-Saharan Africa, has lost out in the globalization process. Sub-Saharan Africa suffers from slower growth, less direct foreign investment, lower education levels, and higher poverty rates than most every other part of the world. A stunning 37 of the region's 47 countries are classified as "low-income" by the World Bank, each with a gross national income less than $825 per person. Many countries in the region bear the burdens of high external debt and a crippling HIV crisis that Kristof has made heroic efforts to bring to the world's attention.

But have multinational corporations avoided investing in sub-Saharan Africa because labor costs are too high? While labor costs in South Africa and Mauritius are high, those in the other countries of the region are modest by international standards, and quite low in some cases. Take Lesotho, the largest exporter of apparel from sub-Saharan Africa to the United States. In the country's factories that subcontract with Wal-Mart, the predominantly female workforce earns an average of just $54 a month. That's below the United Nations poverty line of $2 per day, and it includes regular forced overtime. In Madagascar, the region's third largest exporter of clothes to the United States, wages in the apparel industry are just 33 cents per hour, lower than those in China and among the lowest in the world. And at Ramatex Textile, the large Malaysian-owned textile factory in Namibia, workers only earn about $100 per month according to the Labour Resource and Research Institute in Windhoek. Most workers share their limited incomes with extended families and children, and they walk long distances to work because they can't afford better transportation.

On the other hand, recent experience shows that sub-Saharan countries with decent labor standards *can* develop strong manufacturing export sectors. In the late 1990s, Francis Teal of Oxford's Centre for the Study of African Economies compared Mauritius's successful export industries with Ghana's unsuccessful ones. Teal found that workers in Mauritius earned ten times as much as those in Ghana— $384 a month in Mauritius as opposed to $36 in Ghana. Mauritius's textile and garment industry remained competitive because its workforce was better educated and far more productive than Ghana's. Despite paying poverty wages, the Ghanaian factories floundered.

Kristof knows full well the real reason garment factories in the region are shutting down: the expiration of the Multifiber Agreement last January. The agreement, which set national export quotas for clothing and textiles, protected the garment industries in smaller countries around the world from direct competition with

China. Now China and, to a lesser degree, India, are increasingly displacing other garment producers. In this new context, lower wages alone are unlikely to sustain the sub-Saharan garment industry. Industry sources report that sub-Saharan Africa suffers from several other drawbacks as an apparel producer, including relatively high utility and transportation costs and long shipping times to the United States. The region also has lower productivity and less skilled labor than Asia, and it has fewer sources of cotton yarn and higher-priced fabrics than China and India.

If Kristof is hell-bent on expanding the sub-Saharan apparel industry, he would do better to call for sub-Saharan economies to gain unrestricted access to the Quad markets—the United States, Canada, Japan, and Europe. Economists Stephen N. Karingi, Romain Perez, and Hakim Ben Hammouda estimate that the welfare gains associated with unrestricted market access could amount to $1.2 billion in sub-Saharan Africa, favoring primarily unskilled workers.

But why insist on apparel production in the first place? Namibia has sources of wealth besides a cheap labor pool for Nike's sewing machines. The *Economist* reports that Namibia is a world-class producer of two mineral products: diamonds (the country ranks seventh by value) and uranium (it ranks fifth by volume). The mining industry is the heart of Namibia's export economy and accounts for about 20% of the country's GDP. But turning the mining sector into a vehicle for national economic development would mean confronting the foreign corporations that control the diamond industry, such as the South African De Beers Corporation. That is a tougher assignment than scapegoating antisweatshop activists.

More and Better African Jobs

So why have multinational corporations avoided investing in sub-Saharan Africa? The answer, according to international trade economist Dani Rodrik, is "entirely due to the slow growth" of the sub-Saharan economies. Rodrik estimates that the region participates in international trade as much as can be expected given its economies' income levels, country size, and geography.

Rodrik's analysis suggests that the best thing to do for poor workers in Africa would be to lift the debt burdens on their governments and support their efforts to build functional economies. That means investing in human resources and physical infrastructure, and implementing credible macroeconomic policies that put job creation first. But these investments, as Rodrik points out, take time.

In the meantime, international policies establishing a floor for wages and safeguards for workers across the globe would do more for the young men on Windhoek's street corners than subjecting them to sweatshop abuse, because grinding poverty leaves people willing to enter into any number of desperate exchanges. And if Namibia is closing its garment factories because Chinese imports are cheaper, isn't that an argument for trying to improve labor standards in China, not lower them in sub-Saharan Africa? Abusive labor practices are rife in China's export factories, as the National Labor Committee and *BusinessWeek* have documented. Workers put in 13- to 16-hour days, seven days a week. They enjoy little to no health and safety enforcement, and their take-home pay falls below the minimum wage after the fines and deductions their employers sometimes withhold.

Spreading these abuses in sub-Saharan Africa will not empower workers there. Instead it will take advantage of the fact that they are among the most marginalized workers in the world. Debt relief, international labor standards, and public investments in education and infrastructure are surely better ways to fight African poverty than Kristof's sweatshop proposal.

Sources: Arthur MacEwan, "Ask Dr. Dollar," *Dollars & Sense*, Sept–Oct 1998; John Miller, "Why Economists Are Wrong About Sweatshops and the Antisweatshop Movement," *Challenge*, Jan–Feb 2003; R. Pollin, J. Burns, and J. Heintz, "Global Apparel Production and Sweatshop Labor: Can Raising Retail Prices Finance Living Wages?" Political Economy Research Institute, Working Paper 19, DATE; N. Kristof, "In Praise of the Maligned Sweatshop,"*New York Times*, June 6, 2006; N. Kristof, "Let Them Sweat," *NYT*, June 25, 2002; N. Kristof, "Two Cheers for Sweatshops," *NYT*, Sept 24, 2000; N. Kristof, "Asia'[s Crisis Upsets Rising Effort to Confront Blight of Sweatshops," *NYT*, June 15, 1998; A. Harrison and J. Scorse, "Improving the Conditions of Workers? Minimum Wage Legislation and Anti-Sweatshop Activism," *Calif. Management Review*, Oct 2005; Herbert Jauch, "Africa's Clothing and Textile Industry: The Case of Ramatex in Namibia," in *The Future of the Textile and Clothing Industry in Sub-Saharan Africa*, ed. H. Jauch and R. Traub-Merz (Friedrich-Ebert-Stiftung, 2006); Kurt Alan Ver Beek, "Maquiladoras: Exploitation or Emancipation? An Overview of the Situation of Maquiladora Workers in Honduras," *World Development*, 29(9), 2001; Theodore Moran, *Beyond Sweatshops: Foreign Direct Investment and Globalization in Developing Countries* (Brookings Institution Press, 2002); "Comparative Assessment of the Competitiveness of the Textile and Apparel Sector in Selected Countries," in *Textiles and Apparel: Assessment of the Competitiveness of Certain Foreign Suppliers to the United States Market*, Vol. 1, U.S. International Trade Commission, Jan 2004; S. N. Karingi, R. Perez, and H. Ben Hammouda, "Could Extended Preferences Reward Sub-Saharan Africa's Participation in the Doha Round Negotiations?," *World Economy*, 2006; Francis Teal, "Why Can Mauritius Export Manufactures and Ghana Can Not?," *The World Economy*, 22 (7), 1999; Dani Rodrik, "Trade Policy and Economic Performance in Sub-Saharan Africa," Paper prepared for the Swedish Ministry for Foreign Affairs, Nov 1997.

Article 9.5

INTERNATIONAL LABOR STANDARDS

BY ARTHUR MacEWAN

September/October 2008

Dear Dr. Dollar:

U.S. activists have pushed to get foreign trade agreements to include higher labor standards. But then you hear that developing countries don't want that because cheaper labor without a lot of rules and regulations is what's helping them to bring industries in and build their economies. Is there a way to reconcile these views? Or are the activists just blind to the real needs of the countries they supposedly want to help?

—*Philip Bereaud, Swampscott, Mass.*

In 1971, General Emilio Medici, the then-military dictator of Brazil, commented on economic conditions in his country with the infamous line: "The economy is doing fine, but the people aren't."

Like General Medici, the government officials of many low-income countries today see the well-being of their economies in terms of overall output and the profits of firms—those profits that keep bringing in new investment, new industries that "build their economies." It is these officials who typically get to speak for their countries. When someone says that these countries "want" this or that—or "don't want" this or that—it is usually because the countries' officials have expressed this position.

Do we know what the people in these countries want? The people who work in the new, rapidly growing industries, in the mines and fields, and in the small shops and market stalls of low-income countries? Certainly they want better conditions—more to eat, better housing, security for their children, improved health and safety. The officials claim that to obtain these better conditions, they must "build their economies." But just because "the economy is doing fine" does not mean that the people are doing fine.

In fact, in many low-income countries, economic expansion comes along with severe inequality. The people who do the work are not getting a reasonable share of the rising national income (and are sometimes worse off even in absolute terms). Brazil in the early 1970s was a prime example and, in spite of major political change, remains a highly unequal country. Today, in both India and China, as in several other countries, economic growth is coming with increasingly severe inequality.

Workers in these countries struggle to improve their positions. They form—or try to form—independent unions. They demand higher wages and better working conditions. They struggle for political rights. It seems obvious that we should support those struggles, just as we support parallel struggles of workers in our own country. The first principle in supporting workers' struggles, here or anywhere else, is supporting their right to struggle—the right, in particular, to form independent unions without fear of reprisal. Indeed, in the ongoing controversy over the U.S.-

Colombia Free Trade Agreement, the assassination of trade union leaders has rightly been a major issue.

Just how we offer our support—in particular, how we incorporate that support into trade agreements—is a complicated question. Pressure from abroad can help, but applying it is a complex process. A ban on goods produced with child labor, for example, could harm the most impoverished families that depend on children's earnings, or could force some children into worse forms of work (e.g., prostitution). On the other hand, using trade agreements to pressure governments to allow unhindered union organizing efforts by workers seems perfectly legitimate. When workers are denied the right to organize, their work is just one step up from slavery. Trade agreements can also be used to support a set of basic health and safety rights for workers. (Indeed, it might be useful if a few countries refused to enter into trade agreements with the United States until we improve workers' basic organizing rights and health and safety conditions in our own country!)

There is no doubt that the pressures that come through trade sanctions (restricting or banning commerce with another country) or simply from denying free access to the U.S. market can do immediate harm to workers and the general populace of low-income countries. Any struggle for change can generate short-run costs, but the long-run gains—even the hope of those gains—can make those costs acceptable. Consider, for example, the Apartheid-era trade sanctions against South Africa. To the extent that those sanctions were effective, some South African workers were deprived of employment. Nonetheless, the sanctions were widely supported by mass organizations in South Africa. Or note that when workers in this country strike or advocate a boycott of their company in an effort to obtain better conditions, they both lose income and run the risk that their employer will close up shop.

Efforts by people in this country to use trade agreements to raise labor standards in other countries should, whenever possible, take their lead from workers in those countries. It is up to them to decide what costs are acceptable. There are times, however, when popular forces are denied even basic rights to struggle. The best thing we can do, then, is to push for those rights—particularly the right to organize independent unions—that help create the opportunity for workers in poor countries to choose what to fight for.

Article 9.6

WHAT'S WRONG WITH NEOLIBERALISM?
The Marx, Keynes, and Polanyi Problems

BY ROBERT POLLIN
May/June 2004

During the years of the Clinton administration, the term "Washington Consensus" began circulating to designate the common policy positions of the U.S. administration along with the International Monetary Fund (IMF) and World Bank. These positions, implemented in the United States and abroad, included free trade, a smaller government share of the economy, and the deregulation of financial markets. This policy approach has also become widely known as *neoliberalism*, a term which draws upon the classical meaning of the word *liberalism*.

Classical liberalism is the political philosophy that embraces the virtues of free-market capitalism and the corresponding minimal role for government interventions, especially as regards measures to promote economic equality within capitalist societies. Thus, a classical liberal would favor minimal levels of government spending and taxation, and minimal levels of government regulation over the economy, including financial and labor markets. According to the classical liberal view, businesses should be free to operate as they wish, and to succeed or fail as such in a competitive marketplace. Meanwhile, consumers rather than government should be responsible for deciding which businesses produce goods and services that are of sufficient quality as well as reasonably priced. Businesses that provide overexpensive or low-quality products will then be out-competed in the marketplace regardless of the regulatory standards established by governments. Similarly, if businesses offer workers a wage below what the worker is worth, then a competitor firm will offer this worker a higher wage. The firm unwilling to offer fair wages would not survive over time in the competitive marketplace.

This same reasoning also carries over to the international level. Classical liberals favor free trade between countries rather than countries operating with tariffs or other barriers to the free flow of goods and services between countries. They argue that restrictions on the free movement of products and money between countries only protects uncompetitive firms from market competition, and thus holds back the economic development of countries that choose to erect such barriers.

Neoliberalism and the Washington Consensus are contemporary variants of this longstanding political and economic philosophy. The major difference between classical liberalism as a philosophy and contemporary neoliberalism as a set of policy measures is with implementation. Washington Consensus policy makers are committed to free-market policies when they support the interests of big business, as, for example, with lowering regulations at the workplace. But these same policy makers become far less insistent on free-market principles when invoking such principles might damage big business interests. Federal Reserve and IMF interventions to bail out wealthy asset holders during the frequent global financial crises in the 1990s are obvious violations of free-market precepts.

Broadly speaking, the effects of neoliberalism in the less developed countries over the 1990s reflected the experience of the Clinton years in the United States. A high proportion of less developed countries were successful, just in the manner of the United States under Clinton, in reducing inflation and government budget deficits, and creating a more welcoming climate for foreign trade, multinational corporations, and financial market investors. At the same time, most of Latin America, Africa, and Asia—with China being the one major exception—experienced deepening problems of poverty and inequality in the 1990s, along with slower growth and frequent financial market crises, which in turn produced still more poverty and inequality.

If free-market capitalism is a powerful mechanism for creating wealth, why does a neoliberal policy approach, whether pursued by Clinton, Bush, or the IMF, produce severe difficulties in terms of inequality and financial instability, which in turn diminish the market mechanism's ability to even promote economic growth? It will be helpful to consider this in terms of three fundamental problems that result from a free-market system, which I term "the Marx Problem," "the Keynes problem," and "the Polanyi problem." Let us take these up in turn.

The Marx Problem

Does someone in your family have a job and, if so, how much does it pay? For the majority of the world's population, how one answers these two questions determines, more than anything else, what one's standard of living will be. But how is it decided whether a person has a job and what their pay will be? Getting down to the most immediate level of decision-making, this occurs through various types of bargaining in labor markets between workers and employers. Karl Marx argued that, in a free-market economy generally, workers have less power than employers in this bargaining process because workers cannot fall back on other means of staying alive if they fail to get hired into a job. Capitalists gain higher profits through having this relatively stronger bargaining position. But Marx also stressed that workers' bargaining power diminishes further when unemployment and underemployment are high, since that means that employed workers can be more readily replaced by what Marx called "the reserve army" of the unemployed outside the office, mine, or factory gates.

Neoliberalism has brought increasing integration of the world's labor markets through reducing barriers to international trade and investment by multinationals. For workers in high-wage countries such as the United States, this effectively means that the reserve army of workers willing to accept jobs at lower pay than U.S. workers expands to include workers in less developed countries. It isn't the case that businesses will always move to less developed countries or that domestically produced goods will necessarily be supplanted by imports from low-wage countries. The point is that U.S. workers face an increased *credible* threat that they can be supplanted. If everything else were to remain the same in the U.S. labor market, this would then mean that global integration would erode the bargaining power of U.S. workers and thus tend to bring lower wages.

But even if this is true for workers in the United States and other rich countries, shouldn't it also mean that workers in poor countries have greater job opportunities and better bargaining positions? In fact, there are areas where workers in poor countries are gaining enhanced job opportunities through international trade and multinational investments. But these gains are generally quite limited. This is because a long-term transition out of agriculture in poor countries continues to expand the reserve army of unemployed and underemployed workers in these countries as well. Moreover, when neoliberal governments in poor countries reduce their support for agriculture—through cuts in both tariffs on imported food products and subsidies for domestic farmers—this makes it more difficult for poor farmers to compete with multinational agribusiness firms. This is especially so when the rich countries maintain or increase their own agricultural supports, as has been done in the United States under Bush. In addition, much of the growth in the recently developed export-oriented manufacturing sectors of poor countries has failed to significantly increase jobs even in this sector. This is because the new export-oriented production sites frequently do not represent net additions to the country's total supply of manufacturing firms. They rather replace older firms that were focused on supplying goods to domestic markets. The net result is that the number of people looking for jobs in the developing countries grows faster than the employers seeking new workers. Here again, workers' bargaining power diminishes.

This does not mean that global integration of labor markets must necessarily bring weakened bargaining power and lower wages for workers. But it does mean that unless some non-market forces in the economy, such as government regulations or effective labor unions, are able to counteract these market processes, workers will indeed continue to experience weakened bargaining strength and eroding living standards.

The Keynes Problem

In a free-market economy, investment spending by busi-nesses is the main driving force that produces economic growth, innovation, and jobs. But as John Maynard Keynes stressed, private investment decisions are also unavoidably risky ventures. Businesses have to put up money without knowing whether they will produce any profits in the future. As such, investment spending by business is likely to fluctuate far more than, say, decisions by households as to how much they will spend per week on groceries.

But investment fluctuations will also affect overall spending in the economy, including that of households. When investment spending declines, this means that businesses will hire fewer workers. Unemployment rises as a result, and this in turn will lead to cuts in household spending. Declines in business investment spending can therefore set off a vicious cycle: the investment decline leads to employment declines, then to cuts in household spending and corresponding increases in household financial problems, which then brings still more cuts in business investment and financial difficulties for the business sector. This is how capitalist economies produce mass unemployment, financial crises, and recessions.

Keynes also described a second major source of instability associated with private investment activity. Precisely because private investments are highly risky propositions, financial markets have evolved to make this risk more manageable for any given investor. Through financial markets, investors can sell off their investments if they need or want to, converting their office buildings, factories, and stock of machinery into cash much more readily than they could if they always had to find buyers on their own. But Keynes warned that when financial markets convert long-term assets into short-term commitments for investors, this also fosters a speculative mentality in the markets. What becomes central for investors is not whether a company's products will produce profits over a long term, but rather whether the short-term financial market investors *think* a company's fortunes will be strong enough in the present and immediate future to drive the stock price up. Or, to be more precise, what really matters for a speculative investor is not what they think about a given company's prospects per se, but rather what they think *other investors are thinking*, since that will be what determines where the stock price goes in the short term.

Because of this, the financial markets are highly susceptible to rumors, fads, and all sorts of deceptive accounting practices, since all of these can help drive the stock price up in the present, regardless of what they accomplish in the longer term. Thus, if U.S. stock traders are convinced that Alan Greenspan is a *maestro*, and if there is news that he is about to intervene with some kind of policy shift, then the rumor of Greenspan's policy shift can itself drive prices up, as the more nimble speculators try to keep one step ahead of the herd of Greenspan-philes.

Still, as with the Marx problem, it does not follow that the inherent instability of private investment and speculation in financial markets are uncontrollable, leading inevitably to persistent problems of mass unemployment and recession. But these social pathologies will become increasingly common through a neoliberal policy approach committed to minimizing government interventions to stabilize investment.

The Polanyi Problem

Karl Polanyi wrote his classic book *The Great Transformation* in the context of the 1930s depression, World War II, and the developing worldwide competition with Communist governments. He was also reflecting on the 1920s, dominated, as with our current epoch, by a free-market ethos. Polanyi wrote of the 1920s that "economic liberalism made a supreme bid to restore the self-regulation of the system by eliminating all interventionist policies which interfered with the freedom of markets."

Considering all of these experiences, Polanyi argued that for market economies to function with some modicum of fairness, they must be embedded in social norms and institutions that effectively promote broadly accepted notions of the common good. Otherwise, acquisitiveness and competition—the two driving forces of market economies—achieve overwhelming dominance as cultural forces, rendering life under capitalism a Hobbesian "war of all against all." This same idea is also central for Adam Smith. Smith showed how the invisible hand of self-interest and competition will yield higher levels of individual effort that increases the wealth of nations, but that it will also produce the corruption of our moral sentiments unless the market is itself governed at a fundamental level by norms of solidarity.

In the post-World War II period, various social democratic movements within the advanced capitalist economies adapted the Polanyi perspective. They argued in favor of government interventions to achieve three basic ends: stabilizing overall demand in the economy at a level that will provide for full employment; creating a financial market environment that is stable and conducive to the effective allocation of investment funds; and distributing equitably the rewards from high employment and a stable investment process. There were two basic means of achieving equitable distribution: relatively rapid wage growth, promoted by labor laws that were supportive of unions, minimum wage standards, and similar interventions in labor markets; and welfare state policies, including progressive taxation and redistributive programs such as Social Security. The political ascendancy of these ideas was the basis for a dramatic increase in the role of government in the post-World War II capitalist economies. As one indicator of this, total government expenditures in the United States rose from 8% of GDP in 1913, to 21% in 1950, then to 38% by 1992. The International Monetary Fund and World Bank were also formed in the mid-1940s to advance such policy ideas throughout the world—that is, to implement policies virtually the opposite of those they presently favor. John Maynard Keynes himself was a leading intellectual force contributing to the initial design of the International Monetary Fund and World Bank.

From Social Democracy to Neoliberalism

But the implementation of a social democratic capitalism, guided by a commitment to full employment and the welfare state, did also face serious and persistent difficulties, and we need to recognize them as part of a consideration of the Marx, Keynes, and Polanyi problems. In particular, many sectors of business opposed efforts to sustain full employment because, following the logic of the Marx problem, full employment provides greater bargaining power for workers in labor markets, even if it also increases the economy's total production of goods and services. Greater worker bargaining power can also create inflationary pressures because businesses will try to absorb their higher wage costs by raising prices. In addition, market-inhibiting financial regulations limit the capacity of financial market players to diversify their risk and speculate.

Corporations in the United States and Western Europe were experiencing some combination of these problems associated with social democratic capitalism. In particular, they were faced with rising labor costs associated with low unemployment rates, which then led to either inflation, when corporations had the ability to pass on their higher labor costs to consumers, or to a squeeze on profits, when competitive pressures prevented corporations from raising their prices in response to the rising labor costs. These pressures were compounded by the two oil price "shocks" initiated by the Oil Producing Exporting Countries (OPEC)—an initial fourfold increase in the world price of oil in 1973, then a second four-fold price spike in 1979.

These were the conditions that by the end of the 1970s led to the decline of social democratic approaches to policymaking and the ascendancy of neoliberalism. The two leading signposts of this historic transition were the election in 1979 of Margaret Thatcher as Prime Minister of the United Kingdom and in 1980 of Ronald Reagan as the President of the United States. Indeed, it was at this point that Mrs. Thatcher made her famous pronouncement that "there is no alternative" to neoliberalism.

This brings us to the contemporary era of smaller government, fiscal stringency and deregulation, i.e., to neoliberalism under Clinton, Bush, and throughout the less-developed world. The issue is not a simple juxtaposition between either regulating or deregulating markets. Rather it is that markets have become deregulated to support the interests of business and financial markets, even as these same groups still benefit greatly from many forms of government support, including investment subsidies, tax concessions, and rescue operations when financial crises get out of hand. At the same time, the deregulation of markets that favors business and finance is correspondingly the most powerful regulatory mechanism limiting the demands of workers, in that deregulation has been congruent with the worldwide expansion of the reserve army of labor and the declining capacity of national governments to implement full-employment and macroeconomic policies. In other words, deregulation has exacerbated both the Marx and Keynes problems.

Given the ways in which neoliberalism worsens the Marx, Keynes, and Polanyi problems, we should not be surprised by the wreckage that it has wrought since the late 1970s, when it became the ascendant policy model. Over the past generation, with neoliberals in the saddle almost everywhere in the world, the results have been straightforward: worsening inequality and poverty, along with slower economic growth and far more unstable financial markets. While Margaret Thatcher famously declared that "there is no alternative" to neoliberalism, there are in fact alternatives. The experience over the past generation demonstrates how important it is to develop them in the most workable and coherent ways possible.

Article 9.7

LAND REFORM UNDER LULA: ONE STEP FORWARD, ONE STEP BACK

BY CHRIS TILLY, MARIE KENNEDY, AND TARSO LUÍS RAMOS
August 2009

The Landless Workers' Movement (MST) of Brazil, which has mobilized more than a million Brazilians to occupy and farm large landholdings, was cautiously optimistic when Luiz Inácio "Lula" da Silva of the Workers Party won the presidency in 2002. "We campaign for Lula," remarked MST organizer Jonas da Silva (no relation) during the campaign, "even though we are critical of him for shaping his discourse for the middle class." In the country with perhaps the most unequal land distribution in the world, electing a pro-worker, pro-poor president marked a potential turning point.

But as Lula finishes up his second term (new presidential elections take place in October 2010), the MST's assessment is grim. Land redistribution has stagnated, the government continues to bet on agribusiness as a development strategy and, most threateningly, powerful regional politicians are moving to criminalize the land seizure movement as "terrorist." The MST is doing its best to fight back, but controversial recent MST strategies and antagonistic mass media have diminished the popularity of a movement that once enjoyed widespread national support.

Land Reform, "Não!" Agribusiness, "Sim!"

Lula followed on the two presidential terms of Fernando Henrique Cardoso, who had implemented an unapologetic neoliberal program of free trade, privatization, and containing the demands of workers and the urban and rural poor. There was good reason for hope, since the Workers Party had formed close alliances with the MST and a variety of other social movements. The post-dictatorship constitution of 1988 affirms that land is for socially productive uses, a requirement past governments have at times invoked under pressure to confiscate and redistribute property. But to the dismay of landless families hoping for a plot to cultivate, land redistribution actually moved slightly more *slowly* in Lula's first term than under Cardoso. As the end of his second term approaches, it seems unlikely that Lula will manage to settle more families through agrarian reform than his neoliberal predecessor. What's more, three-quarters of the land redistributed by Lula has been in the remote (and in many cases ecologically fragile) Amazonia region, far from the concentrations of people petitioning for land, such as in the impoverished Northeast. Nearly half of Cardoso's land grants were in Amazonia.

Despite the slow pace of land reform, there are some signs of progress. João Paulo Rodrigues, a MST National Directorate member based in São Paulo, noted, "Lula has provided better supports for small farmers in the form of credit, technical assistance, education, electrification, and roads"—though still not enough. He added that the Lula administration has dropped the Cardoso government's campaign to criminalize the MST (though, as we will explain further below, various state governments have revived that effort). While the number of killings of landless activists surged the first year Lula was in power as the movement shifted land occupations into high gear, violence has now abated to a lower level than under Cardoso. "There is a change in the form of persecution," explained Maria Luisa Mendonça of Social Network for Justice and Human Rights (*Rede Social*), a human rights group that works closely with the MST. "Instead of killing activists, now they [state governments, which are chiefly responsible for law enforcement] arrest them. It's better than killing them, but it doesn't mean that the persecution has ended."

Lula's government has also undertaken other progressive reforms, most notably the "Bolsa Familia" (literally, family pocketbook) program that provides a basic income to the very poorest families. Though the aid does not confront the structural causes of poverty, it provides a crucial margin of survival and offers incentives for families to keep their children in school. Responding to criticism that Bolsa Familia is a form of clientelism, the MST's Rodrigues reasoned, "Yes, it's clientelism. But given the extreme poverty in Brazil and the large numbers of people going hungry, these clientelist policies are necessary." He quickly added, "Necessary, but insufficient." The MST's support (if grudging) is notable, because arguably the stipend reduces the incentive for families to take the risk of occupying land, potentially weakening the landless movement's social base.

The MST's biggest disappointment with Lula has been the former militant union leader's enthusiastic embrace of agribusiness. The Brazilian economy rode high on the commodities boom of the 2000s, with huge expansions in soy, sugar cane, and eucalyptus plantations (the last primarily for paper production). Factory farming is expanding at a ferocious clip: according to MST leader Rodrigues, in three years in the southern state of Rio Grande do Sul alone, 300,000 new hectares of eucalyptus have been planted (a hectare is about 2.5 acres), dwarfing the 100,000 hectares the MST has put into cultivation in its entire 25 years of activity. The environmental consequences have been predictably negative: monocropping, heavy use of chemical inputs and genetically modified strains, voracious water consumption (eucalyptus plantations have been dubbed "green deserts"), toxic by-products, and expansion into wetlands in the Amazon and other areas—especially in the case of sugar cane. Ironically, much of the sugar cane goes into Brazil's massive "eco-friendly" ethanol fuel industry. Unlike the U.S.'s corn-based ethanol industry, Brazil's cane-based system makes money without subsidies—but this accounting overlooks the unmeasured costs of environmental devastation and labor exploitation (or the fossil fuel used in its production and, in the case of export, transportation). The Brazilian government was to announce regional zoning barring sugar cane from Amazonia in February 2009, but that declaration has not yet materialized and human rights advocate Mendonça states flatly, "I don't think it's going to happen."

But if the environmental consequences of agribusiness have been dire, the social consequences are at least as ominous. Far from displacing Brazil's traditional landed oligarchy, the agribusiness boom has forged a new alliance between giant landowners, chemical-agricultural transnationals such as Monsanto and Syngenta, and the national government. The plantations generate exports, but few jobs: the MST estimates that eucalyptus monocropping creates one job per 185 hectares, as compared to one job per hectare for small-scale farming. Those jobs created are often poor, sometimes to the point of being subhuman. Social Network found that in 2007-8, half the reported cases of slave labor in Brazil (3,000 of 6,000 cases) were found in the sugar cane industry. Despite such concerns, the scale of government support has been nothing short of astounding. According to American University political scientist Miguel Carter, "from 2003 to 2007, state support for the rural elite was seven times larger than that offered to the nation's family farmers, even though the latter represent 87 percent of Brazil's rural labor force and produce the bulk of food consumed by its inhabitants." The reason for this asymmetry is not just economic pragmatism, but also political arithmetic: despite a nominally democratic system, the tiny minority of large landowners controls the majority of seats in Congress. As the MST's Rodrigues wryly observed, "Lula has a majority in the House of Representatives and only falls a little short in the Senate. But he gets that majority by proposing policies that serve agribusiness."

From Escalation to Criminalization

Sizing up the agribusiness menace and the opportunity posed by Lula's victory, the MST made two fateful decisions in 2003. One was to accelerate land occupations to force the land question with Lula's government. The second move was to depart from its historic policy of only taking lands that were fallow or where major violations of labor rights were taking place, and adding to its targets productive agribusiness plantations, which the movement sees as the principal threat to the survival and expansion of small farms in Brazil. In some cases, activists have adopted disruption, as when close to 2,000 women affiliated with the Peasant Women's Movement (MMC)—which, like the MST, is a member of the global peasant coalition La Vía Campesina—entered a facility of the Aracruz Cellulose corporation and speedily destroyed greenhouses and nearly eight million eucalyptus saplings on International Women's Day in April 2006. The protest was particularly embarrassing to Lula's government, taking place as it did just outside the city of Porto Alegre where the president was busy hosting the United Nations' International Conference on Agrarian Reform and Development (ICARRD) and positioning his government and Brazil as a world leader on land reform. The major Brazilian media, as tightly tied to the big landowners as is Brazil's Congress and always quick to find fault with the MST, cried foul. They were joined by a number of prominent intellectuals, such as José de Souza Martins, the country's best-known rural sociologist, who, even before the action, had branded the MST as Luddites.

Tactical escalation combined with media condemnation turned Brazilian public opinion, quite favorable in the late 1990s, against the MST. This even extends to likely supporters: in a mid-2009 interview, a youth organizer in a São Paulo *favela* (slum), whose philosophy and organizing approach mesh closely with the MST's, decried the organization's alleged violence and confrontational attitude; he conceded that his source for the information was the same media he didn't trust as a source on urban issues. A Social Network review of 300 articles about the MST in Brazil's four largest-circulation dailies found only eight that were neutral or partly positive.

Complicating matters, being the largest and best-known agrarian reform movement in Brazil, the MST is saddled with the negative press coverage given to other radical groups working for land redistribution. Even as public opinion turned against the Landless Workers' Movement, former close MST allies such as the left-leaning Unified Federation of Workers (CUT) union closed ranks with the Lula administration against threats from the right, distancing themselves from the MST.

The worst was yet to come. In 2006, conservative Yeda Crusius won the governorship in Rio Grande do Sul, a state with strong MST organization and a high pitch of militant land struggles (including the Aracruz action). Crusius set out to target the MST. She attempted to eliminate the so-called "itinerant schools" that provide funding for teachers to travel to rural areas—a keystone of the infrastructure of the temporary encampments where MST families live while fighting to obtain land. The MST has developed its own curriculum and teacher training (based on Freirean pedagogy), oriented to the realities of rural life and a participatory vision of citizenship, and closing the itinerant schools would have wiped out this curriculum and compelled children to travel to the cities for their education. Crusius' administration spoke of "saving children from aggressive indoctrination." The governor finally backed off in mid-2009 as international criticism mounted, and the mayors of the state made it clear that they did not want farm children flooding their schools.

But even more significantly, once she was elected, Crusius swiftly mobilized the Office of the Federal Prosecutor to criminalize the MST, dusting off the dictatorship-era National Security Law to charge eight movement leaders with belonging to an organization that uses violent means to undermine democracy (charges were later dropped against two of the eight). The case includes far-fetched allegations, for example that the MST is allied with Colombia's rebel Revolutionary Armed Forces (FARC), but the prosecutions are bolstered by what lawyer/advocate Aton Fon Filho of Social Network calls "the most conservative judiciary in the country." Fon, who is defending the MST activists, said, "We think we'll win the case. But meanwhile, it has a huge propaganda impact—all those headlines saying 'MST leaders charged with terrorism!'"

The MST is not the only land rights organization suffering from a government crackdown. "There is more organized persecution of social movements in general," said Fon, though other prosecutions involve individual charges rather than an attempt to criminalize an entire organization. For example, in the state of Tocantins in the north, the government has arrested 16 activists of the Movement of Dam Affected Peoples (MAB). And the killings of land reform leaders have not ended. Two activists from the Pastoral Land Commissions (the Catholic Church-based organizations that spawned the MST) in Mato Grosso do Sul were killed in June 2009. And in the Amazon state of Pará, trials are continuing of the accused in the 2005 murder of American nun Sister Dorothy Stang, who challenged deforestation and supported redistribution of lands the military dictatorship had awarded to local elites. According to Fon, "The person convicted of ordering the murder is free pending a fourth trial in the case while the rancher suspected of actually orchestrating the plot has yet to be tried."

A Cloudy Future

One could criticize the MST for ramping up its tactics at a delicate moment, but that would be missing the point: through its entire history, the MST has only been able to chip away at the disproportionate power of the landholding minority via high-profile tactics of civil disobedience and disruption. Others might argue that the MST is holding Lula's feet to the fire in terms of accountability and promises made on agrarian reform. But that said, what are the prospects for near-term success? "Agrarian reform depends on two things," the MST's Rodrigues explained. "The organization of the people, and a progressive government willing to work with us. In 25 years of work, we have made much progress in organizing, but we have not encountered a people's government truly committed to agrarian reform."

The 2010 presidential elections do not hold out much hope in this regard. The two likely leading candidates are Lula's chief of staff, Dilma Rousseff of the Workers' Party, and José Serra of the Brazilian Social Democratic Party (the party of Cardoso and Crusius). "Both are to the right of Lula," commented Rodrigues. Given the political context, the MST is doing its best to fend off legal challenges, build new alliances, and continue organizing. International support can be tremendously important, as in the case of the itinerant schools in Rio Grande do Sul. And the underlying social issues are not going away. At bottom, as long as the distribution of land in Brazil remains so lopsided, there will be a mission and a social base for organizing the landless.

Article 9.8

PUTTING THE "GLOBAL" IN THE GLOBAL ECONOMIC CRISIS

BY SMRITI RAO

November/December 2009

There is no question that the current economic crisis originated in the developed world, and primarily in the United States. Much of the analysis of the crisis has thus focused on institutional failures within the United States and there is, rightly, tremendous concern here about high rates of domestic unemployment and under-employment. But after three decades of globalization, what happens in the United States does not stay in the United States; the actions of traders in New York City will mean hunger for children in Nairobi. We now know what crisis looks like in the age of globalization and it is not pretty.

This crisis is uniquely a child of the neoliberal global order. For developing countries the key elements of neoliberalism have consisted of trade liberalization and an emphasis on exports; reductions in government social welfare spending; a greater reliance on the market for determining the price of everything from the currency exchange rate to water from the tap; and, last but not least, economy-wide privatization and deregulation. In each case, the aim was also to promote cross-border flows of goods, services, and capital—and, to a far lesser degree, of people.

Despite Thomas Friedman's assertions of a "flat" world, this age of globalization did not in fact eliminate global inequality. Indeed if we exclude China and India, inequality between countries actually increased during this period. The globalization of the last 30 years was predicated upon the extraction by the developed world of the natural resources, cheap labor, and, in particular, capital of the developing world, the latter via financial markets that siphoned the world's savings to pay for U.S. middle-class consumption. What could be more ironic than the billions of dollars in capital flowing every year from developing countries with unfunded domestic needs to developed countries, which then failed to meet even their minimum obligations with respect to foreign aid? Africa, for example, has actually been a net creditor to the United States for some time, suggesting that the underlying dynamic of the world economy today is not that different from the colonialism of past centuries.

These "reverse flows" are partly the result of attempts by developing countries to ward off balance-of-payment crises by holding large foreign exchange reserves. Within the United States, this capital helped sustain massive borrowing by households, corporations, and governments, exacerbating the debt bubble of the last eight years. Meanwhile, the global "race to the bottom" among developing-county exporters ensured that the prices of most manufactured goods and services remained low, taking the threat of inflation off the table and enabling the U.S. Federal Reserve to keep interest rates low and facilitate the housing bubble.

Now that this debt bubble has finally burst, it is no surprise that the crisis has been transmitted back to the global South at record speed.

Measuring the Impact

A country-by-country comparison of the growth in real (i.e., inflation-adjusted) GDP from 2007 to 2008 against the average annual growth of the preceding three years (2005-2007) gives us a picture of the differential impact of the economic crisis—at least in its early stages—on various countries. Consistent data are available for 178 developed and developing countries.

Overall, GDP growth for these 178 countries was down by 1.3 percentage points in 2008 compared to the average for 2005-2007. Of course, the financial crisis only hit in full force in September 2008, so the 2009 data will give us a more complete picture of the impact of the crisis. The International Monetary Fund (IMF) estimates that global GDP will decline in 2009 for the first time since World War II. Currently, the IMF is expecting a 1.4% contraction this year. According to the International Labor Organization, global unemployment increased by 10.7 million in 2008, with a further increase of 19 million expected in 2009 by relatively conservative estimates. As a result, the number of people living in poverty will increase by an estimated 46 million this year according to the World Bank.

The initial impact in 2008 was greatest in Eastern Europe and Central Asia: six of the ten countries with the steepest declines in real GDP growth were from the Eastern Europe/Central Asia region (see Table 1, p. 307). Joined by Ireland, this is a list of global high-fliers—countries with very high rates of growth (before 2008, that is) that had globalized rapidly and enthusiastically in the last decade and a half. Singapore of course was an early adopter of globalization, touted by the IMF as a model for other small countries, while Seychelles has depended heavily on international tourism. Myanmar would seem to be the exception to this pattern of intensive globalization, given its political isolation. From an economic perspective, however, this was a country whose economic growth depended heavily on the rising prices of its commodity exports (natural gas and gems).

Indeed, if we rank these 178 countries by the share of their GDP represented by exports before the crisis, we find a correlation between dependence on exports and steeper declines in GDP growth. The 50 most export-dependent countries actually saw larger declines in GDP in 2008 than those less dependent on exports (see Table 2, p. 308). Likewise with certain other key markers of neoliberal globalization.

That globalizers appear to be most affected by the crisis is no accident. It turns out that each of the three primary channels through which the crisis has been transmitted from the United States to other countries is a direct outcome of the policy choices that developing countries were urged and sometimes coerced into making— with assurances that this particular form of globalization was the best way to build a healthy and prosperous economy (see Figure 1 for a summary).

Transmission Channels of the Crisis

Lowered exports and remittances. The recession in the United States and Europe has hit exports from the developing world hard. Globally, trade in goods and services did rise by 3% in 2008, but that was compared to 10% and 7% in the previous two years. Trade is expected to decline by a sharp 12% in 2009. The United States, the world's most important importer, has seen imports drop by an unprecedented 30% since July 2008. For countries ranging from Pakistan to Cameroon, this has meant lower foreign exchange earnings, slower economic growth, and higher unemployment.

Meanwhile, for many developing countries, the emphasis on export promotion meant the increasing export not of goods and services but of people, who sought work in richer countries and sent part of their earnings back home. Remittance flows from temporary and permanent migrants accounted for 25% of net inflows of private capital to the global South in 2007. These flows are also affected by the crisis, although they have proved more resilient than other sources of private capital.

Migrant workers in construction, in particular, find that they are no longer able to find work and send money back home, and countries in Latin America have seen

---

FIGURE 1: THE CURRENT CRISIS AND IMF POLICIES: MAKING THE LINKS

Lowered exports, remittances ("openness")
+
Outflows of portfolio capital ("openness" + no capital controls)
=
Depreciating currencies (floating exchange rates)
=>
Worsening current account balances/debt burdens
X
Falling flows of FDI and development aid
X
"Inflation targeting" and "fiscal restraint"

---

sharp declines in remittance inflows. However, as Indian economist Jayati Ghosh points out, women migrants working as maids, nurses, and nannies in the West have not been as hard hit by the recession. This has meant that remittance flows to countries with primarily female migrants, such as Sri Lanka and the Philippines, are not as badly affected. The Middle Eastern countries that are important host countries for many Asian migrants have also been relatively shielded from the crisis. As a result, for the developing world as a whole, remittances actually rose in 2008. Because other private capital flows declined sharply post-crisis, remittances accounted for 46% of net private capital inflows to the developing world in 2008.

Outflows of portfolio capital. In the boom years up to 2007, developing countries were encouraged to liberalize their financial sectors. This meant removing regulatory barriers to the inflow (and outflow) of foreign investors and their money. While some foreign investors did buy factories and other actual physical assets in the developing world, a substantial portion of foreign capital came in the form of portfolio capital—short-term investments in stock and real estate markets. Portfolio capital is called "hot money" for a reason: it tends to be incredibly mobile, and its mobility has been enhanced by the systematic dismantling of various government restrictions ("capital controls") that formerly prevented this money from entering or leaving countries at the volume and speed it can today.

Around the time of the collapse of Bear Stearns in the United States in early 2008, various global financial powerhouses began pulling their money out of developing-country markets. The pace of the pullout only accelerated after the crash that September. One consequence for developing countries was a fall in their stock market indices, which in turn depressed growth. Another was that as foreign investors converted their krona, rupees, or rubles into dollars in order to leave, the value of the local currency got pushed down.

The IMF has long touted the virtues of allowing freely floating exchange rates, where market forces determine the value of each currency. In the aftermath of the financial crisis, this meant a sharp depreciation in the value of many local currencies relative to the dollar. This in turn meant that every gallon of oil priced in dollars would cost that many more, say, rupees. Similarly, any dollar-denominated debt a country held became harder to repay. The dollar cost of imports and debt servicing went up, just as exports and remittances—the ability to earn those dollars—were falling. Predictably, countries with floating (i.e., market-determined) exchange rates were harder hit in 2008 (see Table 3, p. 308).

Falling flows of FDI and development aid. Meanwhile, one other source of foreign exchange, foreign investment in actual physical assets such as factories (known as foreign direct investment, or FDI), is stagnant and likely to fall as companies across the world shelve expansion plans. The signs of vulnerability are evident in the fact that countries most dependent upon FDI inflows (as a percentage of GDP) between 2005 and 2007 suffered greater relative GDP declines in 2008 (see Table 2, p. 308).

Developed countries are also cutting back on foreign aid budgets, citing the cost of domestic stimulus programs and reduced tax revenues. Such cuts particularly affect the

TABLE 1: STEEPEST DECLINES IN ECONOMIC GROWTH		
Top ten countries by decline in 2008 real GDP growth vs. 2005-07 annual average.		
	Country	Change in 2008 real GDP growth compared to 2005-07 average(in percentage points)
1	Latvia	−15.56
2	Azerbaijan	−14.44
3	Estonia	−12.26
4	Georgia	−8.42
5	Myanmar	−8.32
6	Ireland	−8.30
7	Seychelles	−7.62
8	Armenia	−6.85
9	Singapore	−6.66
10	Kazakhstan	−6.57

Source: Author's calculations based on data from World Development Indicators online, World Bank, June 2009.

poorest countries. With the economic slowdown their governments are losing domestic tax and other revenues, so falling aid flows are likely to hurt even more. The importance of continued aid flows can be seen in the fact that higher levels of aid per capita from 2005 to 2007 were actually associated with more mild drops in GDP growth in 2008 (see Table 2). This may be partly due to the fact that these countries already had low or negative rates of GDP growth so that 2008 declines appear smaller relative to that baseline. Nevertheless, aid flows appear to have protected the most vulnerable countries from even greater economic disaster. In fact the so-called HIPC group (highly indebted poor countries) actually saw an increase of one percentage point in GDP growth rates when compared to the 2005-2007 average.

Both FDI and aid work their way into and out of economies more slowly, so we may have to wait for 2009 data to estimate the full impact of the crisis via this channel.

TABLE 2: EXPORTS AND FOREIGN INVESTMENT

Change in 2008 real GDP growth compared to 2005-07 average (in percentage points) for countries ranked by:

	Export share of GDP	FDI share of GDP
Average for top 50 countries	−2.25	−1.85
Average for countries ranked 51-100	−1.50	−1.70
Average for the remaining countries	−0.88	−1.07
Total number of countries	167	171

TABLE 3: EXCHANGE RATE AND FISCAL POLICY

Average change in 2008 real GDP growth compared to 2005-07 average (in percentage points) for country groupings:

Exchange Rate Policy		Fiscal Policy	
Countries with fixed exchange rate	−1.19	Countries with no inflation targeting	−1.18
Countries with managed float or other mixed policy	−1.19	Countries with inflation targeting	−2.35
Countries with freely floating exchange rate	−2.04		
Total number of countries	178		171

Sources: Author's calculations based on data from World Development Indicators online, World Bank, June 2009 and De Facto Classification of Exchange Rate Regimes and Monetary Policy Frameworks as of April 31, 2008, IMF.

The simultaneous transmission of the crisis through these three channels has left developing countries reeling. What makes the situation even worse is that unlike developed countries, developing countries are unlikely to be able to afford generous stimulus packages (China is an important exception). Meanwhile, the IMF and its allies, rather than supporting developing-country governments in their quest to stimulate domestic demand and investment, are hindering the process by insisting on the same old policy mix of deficit reductions and interest rate hikes. In an illustration of how ruinous this policy mix can be, countries that had followed IMF advice and adopted "inflation targeting" before the crisis suffered greater relative GDP declines once the crisis hit (see Table 3).

The tragedy of course is that while the remnants of the welfare state still protect citizens of the developed world from the very worst effects of the crisis, developing countries have been urged for two decades to abandon the food and fuel subsidies and public sector provision of essential services that are the only things that come close to resembling a floor for living standards. They were told they didn't need that safety net, that it only got in the way; now, of course, they are free to fall.

For those unwilling to let this tragedy unfold, this is the time to apply pressure on developed-country governments to maintain aid flows. Even more importantly, this is the time to apply pressure on the IMF and the other multilateral development banks, and on their supporters in the halls of power, so that they offer developing countries a genuine chance to survive this crisis and begin to rebuild for the future.

It is worth recalling that the end of the previous "age of globalization," signaled by the Great Depression, led to a renewed role for the public sector the world over and an attempt to achieve growth alongside self-reliance. In the years after World War II, led by Latin America, newly independent developing countries attempted to prioritize building a domestic producer and consumer base. In the long run, perhaps this crisis will result in a similar rethinking of the currently dominant model of development. In the short run, however, the world seems ready to stand by and watch while the poor and vulnerable in developing countries, truly innocent bystanders, suffer.

Sources: Dilip Ratha, Sanket Mohapatra, and Ani Silwal, "Migration and Development Brief 10," Migration and Remittances Team, Development Prospects Group, World Bank, July 13, 2009; Atish R. Ghosh et al. 2009, "Coping with the Crisis: Policy Options for Emerging Market Countries," IMF Staff Position Note, SPN/09/08, April 23, 2009; World Bank, "Swimming Against the Tide: How Developing Countries Are Coping with the Global Crisis," Background Paper prepared by World Bank Staff for the G20 Finance Ministers and Central Bank Governors Meeting, Horsham, United Kingdom on March 13-14, 2009; Jayati Ghosh, "Current Global Financial Crisis: Curse or Blessing in Disguise for Developing Countries?" Presentation prepared for the IWG-GEM Workshop, Levy Economics Institute, New York, June 29-July 10, 2009.

Article 9.9

(ECONOMIC) FREEDOM'S JUST ANOTHER WORD FOR...CRISIS-PRONE

BY JOHN MILLER
September/October 2009

In "Capitalism in Crisis," his May op-ed in the *Wall Street Journal*, U.S. Court of Appeals judge and archconservative legal scholar Richard Posner argued that "a capitalist economy, while immensely dynamic and productive, is not inherently stable." Posner, the long-time cheerleader for deregulation added, quite sensibly, "we may need more regulation of banking to reduce its inherent riskiness."

That may seem like a no-brainer to you and me, right there in the middle of the road with yellow-lines and dead armadillos, as Jim Hightower is fond of saying. But *Journal* readers were having none of it. They wrote in to set Judge Posner straight. "It is not free markets that fail, but government-controlled ones," protested one reader.

And why wouldn't they protest? The *Journal* has repeatedly told readers that "economic freedom" is "the real key to development." And each January for 15 years now the *Journal* tries to elevate that claim to a scientific truth by publishing a summary of the Heritage Foundation Index of Economic Freedom, which they assure readers proves the veracity of the claim. But in the hands of the editors of the *Wall Street Journal* and the researchers from the Heritage Foundation, Washington's foremost right-wing think tank, the Index of Economic Freedom is a barometer of corporate and entrepreneurial freedom from accountability rather than a guide to which countries are giving people more control over their economic lives and over the institutions that govern them.

This January was no different. "The 2009 Index provides strong evidence that the countries that maintain the freest economies do the best job promoting prosperity for all citizens," proclaimed this year's editorial, "Freedom is Still the Winning Formula." But with economies across the globe in recession, the virtues of free markets are a harder sell this year. That is not lost on *Wall Street Journal* editor Paul Gigot, who wrote the foreword to this year's report. Gigot allows that, "ostensibly free-market policymakers in the U.S. lost their monetary policy discipline, and we are now paying a terrible price." Still Gigot maintains that, "the *Index of Economic Freedom* exists to chronicle how steep that price will be and to point the way back to policy wisdom."

What the Heritage report fails to mention is this: while the global economy is in recession, many of the star performers in the Economic Freedom Index are tanking. Fully one half of the ten hardest-hit economies in the world are among the 30 "free" and "mostly free" economies at the top of the Economic Freedom Index rankings of 179 countries.

Here's the damage, according to the IMF. Singapore, the Southeast Asian trading center and perennial number two in the Index, will suffer a 10.0% drop in output this year. Slotting in at number 4, Ireland, the so-called Celtic tiger, has seen its rapid export-led growth give way to an 8.0% drop in output. Number 13 and number 30, the foreign-direct-investment-favored Baltic states, Estonia and Lithuania, will each endure a 10.0% loss of output this year. Finally, the economy of Iceland, the loosely regulated European banking center that sits at number 14 on the Index, will contract 10.6% in 2009.

As a group, the Index's 30 most "free" economies will contract 4.1% in 2009. All of the other groups in the Index ("moderately free," "mostly unfree," and "repressed" economies) will muddle through 2009 with a much smaller loss of output or with moderate growth. The 67 "mostly unfree" countries in the Index will post the fastest growth rate for the year, 2.3%.

So it seems that if the Index of Economic Freedom can be trusted, then Judge Posner was not so far off the mark when he described capitalism as dynamic but "not inherently stable." That wouldn't be so bad, one *Journal* reader pointed out in a letter: "Economic recessions are the cost we pay for our economic freedom and economic prosperity is the benefit. We've had many more years of the latter than the former."

Not to Be Trusted

But the Index of Economic Freedom cannot and should not be trusted. How free or unfree an economy is according to the Index seems to have little do with how quickly it grows. For instance, economist Jeffery Sachs found "no correlation" between a country's ranking in the Index and its per capita growth rates from 1995 to 2003. Also, in this year's report North America is the "freest" of its six regions of the world, but logged the slowest average rate over the last five years, 2.7% per annum. The Asia-Pacific region, which is "less free" than every other region except Sub-Saharan Africa according to the Index, posted the fastest average growth over the last five years, 7.8% per annum. That region includes several of fastest growing of the world's economies, India, China, and Vietnam, which ranked 123, 132, and 145 respectively in the Index and were classified as "mostly unfree." And there are plenty of relatively slow growers among the countries high up in the Index, including Switzerland (which ranks ninth).

The Heritage Foundation folks who edited the Index objected to Sachs' criticisms, pointing out that they claimed "a close relationship" between *changes* in

ECONOMIC FREEDOM AND ECONOMIC GROWTH IN 2009	
Degree of Economic Freedom	IMF Projected Growth Rate for 2009
"Free" (7 Countries)	-4.54%
"Mostly Free" (23 Counties)	-3.99%
"Moderately Free" (53 Countries)	-0.92%
"Mostly Unfree" (67 Countries)	+2.31%
"Repressed" (69 Counties)	+1.65%
Sources: International Monetary Fund, *World Economic Outlook,: Crisis and Recovery*, April 2009, Tables A1, A2, A3; Terry Miller and Kim R. Holmes, eds., *2009 Index of Economic Freedom*, heritage.org/Index/, Executive Summary.	

economic freedom, not the *level* of economic freedom, and growth. But even that claim is fraught with problems. Statistically it doesn't hold up. Economic journalist Doug Henwood found that improvements in the index and GDP growth from 1997 to 2003 could explain no more than 10% of GDP growth. In addition, even a tight correlation would not resolve the problem that many of the fastest growing economies are "mostly unfree" according to the Index.

But even more fundamental flaws with the Index render any claim about the relationship between prosperity and economic freedom, as measured by the Heritage Foundation, questionable. Consider just two of the ten components the Economic Freedom Index uses to rank countries: fiscal freedom and government size.

Fiscal freedom (what we might call the "hell-if-I'm-going-to-pay-for-government" index) relies on the top income tax and corporate income tax brackets as two of its three measures of the tax burden. These are decidedly flawed measures even if all that concerned you was the tax burden of the rich and owners of corporations (or the super-rich). Besides ignoring the burden of other taxes, singling out these two top tax rates don't get at effective corporate and income tax rates, or how much of a taxpayer's total income goes to paying these taxes. For example, on paper U.S. corporate tax rates are higher than those in Europe. But nearly one half of U.S. corporate profits go untaxed. The effective rate of taxation on U.S. corporate profits currently stands at 15%, far below the top corporate tax rate of 35%. And relative to GDP, U.S. corporate income taxes are no more than half those of other OECD countries.

Even their third measure of fiscal freedom, government tax revenues relative to GDP, bears little relationship to economic growth. After an exhaustive review, economist Joel Selmrod, former member of the Reagan Treasury Department, concludes that the literature reveals "no consensus" about the relationship between the level of taxation and economic growth.

The Index's treatment of government size, which relies exclusively on the level of government spending relative to GDP, is just as flawed as the fiscal freedom index. First, "richer countries do not tax and spend less" than poorer countries, reports economist Peter Lindhert. Beyond that, this measure does not take into account how the government uses its money. Social spending programs—public education, child-care and parental support, and public health programs—can make people more productive and promote economic growth. That lesson is not lost on Hong Kong and Singapore, number one and number two in the index. They both provide universal access to health care, despite the small size of their governments.

The size-of-government index also misses the mark because it fails to account for industrial policy. This is a serious mistake, because it overestimates the degree to which some of the fastest growing economies of the last few decades, such as Taiwan and South Korea, relied on the market and underestimates the positive role that government played in directing economic development in those countries by guiding investment and protecting infant industries.

This flaw is thrown into sharp relief by the recent report of the World Bank's Commission on Growth and Development. That group studied 13 economies that grew at least 7% a year for at least 25 years since 1950. Three of the Index's "free" and "mostly free" countries made the list (Singapore, Hong Kong, and Japan) but so did three of the index's "mostly unfree" countries (China, Brazil, and Indonesia). While these rapid growers were all export-oriented, their governments "were not free-market purists," according the Commission's report. "They tried a variety of policies to help diversify exports or sustain competitiveness. These included industrial policies to promote new investments."

Still More

Beyond all that, the Index says nothing about political freedom. Consider once again the two city-states, Hong Kong and Singapore, which top their list of free countries. Both are only "partially free" according to Freedom House, which the editors have called "the Michelin Guide to democracy's development." Hong Kong is still without direct elections for it legislatures or its chief executive and a proposed internal security laws threaten press and academic freedom as well as political dissent. In Singapore, freedom of the press and rights to demonstrate are limited, films, TV and the like are censored, and preventive detention is legal.

So it seems that the Index of Economic Freedom in practice tells us little about the cost of abandoning free market policies and offers little proof that government intervention into the economy would either retard economic growth or contract political freedom. In actuality, this rather objective-looking index is a slip-shod measure that would seem to have no other purpose than to sell the neoliberal policies that brought on the current crisis, and to stand in the way of policies that might correct the crisis.

Sources: "Capitalism in Crisis," by Richard A Posner, *Wall Street Journal*, 5/07/09; "Letters: Recessions are the Price We Pay for Economic Freedom," *Wall Street Journal*, 5/19/09/; "Freedom is Still the Winning Formula," by Terry Miller, *Wall Street Journal*, 1/13/09 ; "The Real Key to Development," by Mary Anastasia O'Grady, *Wall Street Journal*, 1/15/08; Terry Miller and Kim R. Holmes, eds., *2009 Index of Economic Freedom*, heritage.org/Index/; Freedom House, "Freedom in the World 2009 Survey," freedomhouse.org; Joel Selmrod and Jon Bakija, *Taxing Ourselves: A Citizen's Guide to the Debate over Taxes*, MIT Press, 2008; International Monetary Fund, *World Economic Outlook,: Crisis and Recovery*, April 2009; Peter H. Lindert, *Growing Public*, Cambridge University Press, 2004; Doug Henwood, "*Laissez-faire* Olympics: An LBO Special Report," leftbusinessobserver.com, March 26, 2005; Jeffrey Sachs, *The End of Poverty: Economic Possibilities for Our Time*, Penguin, 2005.

Article 9.10

HAITI'S FAULT LINES: MADE IN THE U.S.A.

BY MARIE KENNEDY AND CHRIS TILLY
March/April 2010

The mainstream media got half the story right about Haiti. Reporters observed that Haiti's stark poverty intensified the devastation caused by the recent earthquake. True: hillside shantytowns, widespread concrete construction without rebar reinforcement, a grossly inadequate road network, and a health-care system mainly designed to cater to the small elite all contributed mightily to death and destruction.

But what caused that poverty? U.S. readers and viewers might be forgiven for concluding that some inexplicable curse has handed Haiti corrupt and unstable governments, unproductive agriculture, and widespread illiteracy. Televangelist Pat Robertson simply took this line of "explanation" to its nutty, racist conclusion when he opined that Haitians were paying for a pact with the devil.

But the devil had little to do with Haiti's underdevelopment. Instead, the fingerprints of more mundane actors—France and later the United States—are all over the crime scene. After the slave rebellion of 1791, France wrought massive destruction in attempting to recapture its former colony, then extracted 150 million francs of reparations, only fully paid off in 1947. France's most poisonous legacy may have been the skin-color hierarchy that sparked fratricidal violence and still divides Haiti.

While France accepted Haiti once the government started paying up, the United States, alarmed by the example of a slave republic, refused to recognize Haiti until 1862. That late-arriving recognition kicked off a continuing series of military and political interventions. The U.S. Marines occupied Haiti outright 1915-34, modernizing the infrastructure but also revising laws to allow foreign ownership, turning over the country's Treasury to a New York bank, saddling Haiti with a $40 million debt to the United States, and reinforcing the status gap between mulattos and blacks. American governments backed the brutal, kleptocratic two-generation Duvalier dictatorship from 1957-86. When populist priest Jean-Bertrand Aristide was elected president in 1990, the Bush I administration winked at the coup that ousted him a year later. Bill Clinton reversed course, ordering an invasion to restore Aristide, but used that intervention to impose the same free-trade "structural adjustment" Bush had sought. Bush II closed the circle by backing rebels who re-overthrew the re-elected Aristide in 2004. No wonder many Haitians are suspicious of the U.S. troops who poured in after the earthquake.

Though coups and invasions grab headlines, U.S. economic interventions have had equally far-reaching effects. U.S. goals for the last thirty years have been to open Haiti to American products, push Haiti's self-sufficient peasants off the land, and redirect the Haitian economy to plantation-grown luxury crops and export assembly, both underpinned by cheap labor. Though Haiti has yet to boost its export capacity, the first two goals have succeeded, shattering Haiti's former productive capacity. In the early 1980s, the U.S. Agency for International Development exterminated Haiti's hardy Creole pigs in the name of preventing a swine flu epidemic, then helpfully offered U.S. pigs that require expensive U.S.-produced feeds and medicines. Cheap American rice imports crippled the country's breadbasket, the Artibonite, so that Haiti, a rice exporter in the 1980s, now imports massive amounts. Former peasants flooded into Port-au-Prince, doubling the population over the last quarter century, building makeshift housing, and setting the stage for the current catastrophe.

In the wake of the disaster, U.S. aid continues to have two-edged effects. Each aid shipment that flies in American rice and flour instead of buying and distributing local rice or cassava continues to undermine agriculture and deepen dependency. Precious trucks and airstrips are used to marshal U.S. troops against overblown "security threats," crowding out humanitarian assistance. The United States and other international donors show signs of once more using aid to leverage a free-trade agenda. If we seek to end Haiti's curse, the first step is to realize that one of the curse's main sources is...us.

CONTRIBUTORS

Frank Ackerman an economist with the Stockholm Environment Institute, and a founder of *Dollars & Sense*. His latest book is *Can We Afford the Future? Economics for a Warming World* (Zed Books, 2009).

Gar Alperovitz is a professor of political economy at the University of Maryland and co-author, with Lew Daly, of *Unjust Deserts: How the Rich Are Taking Our Common Inheritance and Why We Should Take It Back* (New Press, 2009).

Dean Baker is co-director of the Center for Economic and Policy Research.

Peter Barnes, co-founder of Working Assets, is a senior fellow at the Tomales Bay Institute.

Heather Boushey is a senior economist at the Center for American Progress.

Marc Breslow is co-chair of the Massachusetts Climate Action Network and a former *Dollars & Sense* collective member.

Roger Bybee is the former editor of the union weekly *Racine Labor* and is now a consultant and freelance writer.

Ben Collins is a member of the *Dollars & Sense* collective and a research analyst at a sustainable investment research company.

Paul Cummings is a software engineer with a long-standing interest in environmental and social issues.

James Cypher is professor-investigador, Programa de Doctorado en Estudios del Desarrollo, Universidad Autonoma de Zacatecas, Mexico and a *Dollars & Sense* Associate.

Lew Daly is a senior fellow at Demos and co-author, with Gar Alperovitz, of *Unjust Deserts: How the Rich Are Taking Our Common Inheritance and Why We Should Take It Back* (New Press, 2009).

Alan Durning founded Sightline Institute (formerly Northwest Environment Watch) and is a former senior researcher at the Worldwatch Institute.

Mark Engler is an analyst with Foreign Policy In Focus and author of *How to Rule the World: The Coming Battle Over the Global Economy* (Nation Books, 2008).

Ellen Frank teaches economics at the University of Massachusetts-Boston and is a *Dollars & Sense* Associate.

Amy Gluckman is co-editor of *Dollars & Sense*.

Joel A. Harrison, PhD, MPH, lives in San Diego, where he does consulting in epidemiology and research design. He has worked in the areas of preventive medicine, infectious diseases, medical outcomes research, and evidence-based clinical practice guidelines.

Lisa Heinzerling is a professor of law at Georgetown University Law School, specializing in environmental law.

Edward S. Herman is an economist and co-author of *The Global Media: The New Missionaries of Corporate Capitalism* (Continuum, 1997).

Marianne Hill is an economist who has published articles in the *Journal of Human Development*, *Feminist Economics*, and other economics journals. She also writes for the American Forum and the Mississippi Forum.

Rachel Keeler holds an MSc in Global Politics from the London School of Economics and is a freelance international business journalist.

Marie Kennedy is professor emerita of Community Planning at the University of Massachusetts-Boston and visiting professor in Urban Planning at UCLA. She is a member of the board of directors of Grassroots International.

Robert Larson is assistant professor of economics at Ivy Tech Community College in Bloomington, Indiana.

Jabulani Leffall is Associate Editor of FactSet Research Systems' News and Media group and a former editor for both the London *Financial Times* and *Variety*.

Arthur MacEwan, a *Dollars & Sense* Associate, is professor emeritus of economics at the University of Massachusetts-Boston.

Mark Maier teaches economics at Glendale Community College in Glendale, CA. He is co-author, with Julie Nelson, of *Introducing Economics: A Critical Guide for Teaching* (M.E. Sharpe, 2007).

Nina Martin is a researcher at the Center for Urban Economic Development (CUED).

Siobhán McGrath is a Policy Research Associate with the Economic Justice Project at the Brennan Center for Justice.

John Miller, a *Dollars & Sense* collective member, teaches economics at Wheaton College.

Julie Nelson is a senior research associate with the Global Development and Environment Institute at Tufts University. She is co-author, with Mark Maier, of *Introducing Economics: A Critical Guide for Teaching* (M.E. Sharpe, 2007).

Immanuel Ness is professor of political science at Brooklyn College, City University of New York.

Thomas Palley is an economist who has held positions at the AFL-CIO, Open Society Institute, and the U.S./China Economic and Security Review Commission.

Michael Perelman is a professor of economics at California State University, Chico.

Sam Pizzigati is a labor journalist and an associate fellow at the Institute for Policy Studies, in Washington, D.C. He edits Too Much (www.toomuchonline.org), an online weekly on excess and inequality.

Robert Pollin is professor of economics and co-director of the Political Economy Research Institute at the University of Massachusetts, Amherst.

Smriti Rao (co-editor of this volume) is a member of the *Dollars & Sense* collective and teaches economics at Assumption College in Worcester, Mass.

Alejandro Reuss teaches economics at Bunker Hill Community College and is a member of the *Dollars & Sense* collective.

Helen Scharber is a staff economist for the Center for Popular Economics in Amherst, Massachusetts.

Bryan Snyder (co-editor of this volume) is a senior lecturer in economics at Bentley University.

Chris Sturr (co-editor of this volume) is co-editor of *Dollars & Sense*.

Anna Sussman is a freelance print and radio reporter.

Chris Tilly is a *Dollars & Sense* Associate and director of UCLA's Institute for Research on Labor and Employment and professor in the Urban Planning Department.

Ramaa Vasudevan teaches economics at Colorado State University and is a *Dollars & Sense* Associate.

Stacy Warner Maddern is a Ph.D. candidate in political science at the University of Connecticut.

Jeannette Wicks-Lim is an economist and research fellow at the Political Economy Research Institute at the University of Massachusetts-Amherst.

Thad Williamson, a *Dollars & Sense* Associate, is assistant professor of leadership studies at the University of Richmond. He is the author of four books, including *Sprawl, Justice, and Citizenship: The Civic Costs of the American Way of Life* (Oxford, 2010).

Marty Wolfson is a professor of economics at the University of Notre Dame and a former economist with the Federal Reserve Board in Washington, D.C.